PALGRAVE *Studies in Oral History*

Series Editors: David P. Cline and Natalie Fousekis
Founding Series Editors: Linda Shopes and Bruce M. Stave

The Order Has Been Carried Out: History, Memory, and Meaning of a Nazi Massacre in Rome, by Alessandro Portelli (2003)

Sticking to the Union: An Oral History of the Life and Times of Julia Ruuttila, by Sandy Polishuk (2003)

To Wear the Dust of War: From Bialystok to Shanghai to the Promised Land, an Oral History, by Samuel Iwry, edited by L. J. H. Kelley (2004)

Education as My Agenda: Gertrude Williams, Race, and the Baltimore Public Schools, by Jo Ann Robinson (2005)

Remembering: Oral History Performance, edited by Della Pollock (2005)

Postmemories of Terror: A New Generation Copes with the Legacy of the "Dirty War," by Susana Kaiser (2005)

Growing Up in The People's Republic: Conversations between Two Daughters of China's Revolution, by Ye Weili and Ma Xiaodong (2005)

Life and Death in the Delta: African American Narratives of Violence, Resilience, and Social Change, by Kim Lacy Rogers (2006)

Creating Choice: A Community Responds to the Need for Abortion and Birth Control, 1961–1973, by David P. Cline (2006)

Voices from This Long Brown Land: Oral Recollections of Owens Valley Lives and Manzanar Pasts, by Jane Wehrey (2006)

Radicals, Rhetoric, and the War: The University of Nevada in the Wake of Kent State, by Brad E. Lucas (2006)

The Unquiet Nisei: An Oral History of the Life of Sue Kunitomi Embrey, by Diana Meyers Bahr (2007)

Sisters in the Brotherhoods: Working Women Organizing for Equality in New York City, by Jane LaTour (2008)

Iraq's Last Jews: Stories of Daily Life, Upheaval, and Escape from Modern Babylon, edited by Tamar Morad, Dennis Shasha, and Robert Shasha (2008)

Soldiers and Citizens: An Oral History of Operation Iraqi Freedom from the Battlefield to the Pentagon, by Carl Mirra (2008)

Overcoming Katrina: African American Voices from the Crescent City and Beyond, by D'Ann R. Penner and Keith C. Ferdinand (2009)

Bringing Desegregation Home: Memories of the Struggle toward School Integration in Rural North Carolina, by Kate Willink (2009)

I Saw It Coming: Worker Narratives of Plant Closings and Job Loss, by Tracy E. K'Meyer and Joy L. Hart (2010)

Speaking History: Oral Histories of the American Past, 1865-Present, by Sue Armitage and Laurie Mercier (2010)

Surviving Bhopal: Dancing Bodies, Written Texts, and Oral Testimonials of Women in the Wake of an Industrial Disaster, by Suroopa Mukherjee (2010)

Living with Jim Crow: African American Women and Memories of the Segregated South, by Anne Valk and Leslie Brown (2010)

Gulag Voices: Oral Histories of Soviet Incarceration and Exile, by Jehanne M. Gheith and Katherine R. Jolluck (2011)

Detained without Cause: Muslims' Stories of Detention and Deportation in America after 9/11, by Irum Shiekh (2011)

Soviet Communal Living: An Oral History of the Kommunalka, by Paola Messana (2011)

No Room of Her Own: Women's Stories of Homelessness, Life, Death, and Resistance, by Desiree Hellegers (2011)

Oral History and Photography, edited by Alexander Freund and Alistair Thomson (2011)

Place, Writing, and Voice in Oral History, edited by Shelley Trower (2011)

Oral History, Community, and Displacement: Imagining Memories in Post-Apartheid South Africa, by Sean Field (2012)

Second Wind: Oral Histories of Lung Transplant Survivors, by Mary Jo Festle (2012)

Black Leaders on Leadership

Conversations with Julian Bond

Phyllis Leffler

with interviews and foreword by Julian Bond

palgrave
macmillan

30741 7970

First published in 2014 by
PALGRAVE MACMILLAN®
in the United States—a division of St. Martin's Press LLC,
175 Fifth Avenue, New York, NY 10010.

Where this book is distributed in the UK, Europe and the rest of the world,
this is by Palgrave Macmillan, a division of Macmillan Publishers Limited,
registered in England, company number 785998, of Houndmills,
Basingstoke, Hampshire RG21 6XS.

Palgrave Macmillan is the global academic imprint of the above companies
and has companies and representatives throughout the world.

Palgrave® and Macmillan® are registered trademarks in the United States,
the United Kingdom, Europe and other countries.

ISBN: 978–1–137–34249–2 (hc)
ISBN: 978–1–137–34250–8 (Pbk)

Library of Congress Cataloging-in-Publication Data is available from the
Library of Congress.

A catalogue record of the book is available from the British Library.

Design by Newgen Knowledge Works (P) Ltd., Chennai, India.

First edition: November 2014

10 9 8 7 6 5 4 3 2 1

For Melvyn Paul Leffler

Contents

.

Figures

Foreword

The civil rights movement shaped my life. My values—then and now—are defined by it. I saw how individuals stepped up. I witnessed how leaders emerged—often surprising themselves. I happened to be one of them. My eyes opened to the collective power we share to create the America we want.

In the 1960s I ran for public office. When the Georgia legislature refused three times to seat me—despite winning the popular vote—I took my case all the way to the US Supreme Court, and I won. I learned that leaders don't give up. We need to know their stories. They keep fighting. And when one door closes, another opens.

In 1990, the University of Virginia hired me to teach the history of the civil rights movement. From 1990 to 2012, thousands of students have taken my courses. I had a chance to share the stories of the movement with them, personalizing it through my own experiences and those of people who have become lifelong companions and collaborators. As technology became more available, I included newsreels, music, and film. Students get most excited about history when it becomes personal and when they can see its relationship to their lives. I am proud that I have had a role in grooming another generation of potential leaders who will feel the power of the 1960s.

The stories of those who shaped the movement can best be told by the individuals themselves. I brought some of them to the University of Virginia, capturing their self-understandings for posterity. In collaboration with my colleague, Phyllis Leffler, we developed the project that became the subject of this book. Leaders from diverse fields sat down for substantive discussion. Phyllis, as a public historian, understood how to formulate the core questions and how to make these materials accessible to a wide audience. You can find the interviews online at http://www.blackleadership. virginia.edu where you can hear the individuals tell their own stories and reflect on broader issues of leadership. Our project includes those who were shaped by the movement of the 1960s. But it also includes those much younger who were touched by the stories they heard, and who forged their own trajectories.

The interviews document the experiences and life stories of influential African American artists, legislators, lawyers, business leaders, educators, clergy, public servants, and cultural pioneers. People like Dorothy Height, Vernon Jordan, Earl Graves, Johnnetta Cole, Bill T. Jones, Calvin Butts, Geoffrey Canada, Freeman Hrabowski, William Raspberry, Clarence Thomas, Amiri Baraka, Eleanor Holmes Norton, John Lewis, Nikki Giovanni, and Angela Davis reflect on their experiences, aspirations, and styles of leadership. Younger leaders like Bakari Sellers, Benjamin Jealous, and Katori Hall define the challenges they see for a new generation that can build upon the successes of the civil rights movement. All discuss their vision of how leadership can be cultivated in today's world.

This book foregrounds stories of *identity*. These are stories about the self, stories about the group, and stories about value and meaning.[1] They demonstrate how leadership emerges from historical struggle rooted in the promise of a brighter future. They show us how memory shapes possibility, and how the capacity to channel memories toward positive ends inculcates leaders.

The portfolio of stories highlights people whose voices are too often marginalized in our public discourse. By using their own words as much as possible, we share with our readers their passion, their pain, and their power. The personal stories in this volume are a reminder that *we can overcome,* and that we must find the collective will to address the intractable disparities of race in America.

Black leaders' stories are narratives of hardship, determination, and success situated in local communities and national culture. They link the private and the public—the personal and the professional. The memories of black leaders exist in historical time, underscoring the reality that the past and present are inextricably linked. The lessons shared in this book acknowledge the burdens of race but also celebrate the ability of individuals to overcome adversity. This is ultimately an exploration of African American leadership in America through the eyes and words of the leaders themselves.

Black leaders now hold the highest offices in America. At the same time, incarceration rates and the achievement gap reveal mounting disparities by race.

We must find ways to inspire the next generation toward achievement. We must help them to see their own leadership potential. We must provide them with role models who imagined brighter futures despite the adversity they suffered. And we must challenge others of all colors to help build the communities for a stronger America.

The stories of the individuals we interviewed inspire me. I am not so naïve to believe that stories are enough to overcome the crushing deprivations of poverty. They are not the answer alone. But they are one means to reach out across generations with stories and advice that are timeless. Those who have achieved—both young and old—have wisdoms to impart to those who follow them. Their capacity to challenge the status quo and to thrive, their capacity to say "yes" rather than "no," and their capacity to fight against restraint are based on their sense of the self.

This book shows that the identities people construct and the values they have learned enable them to lead. Remarkably, there are common values that emerge across time, class, gender, region, and even political affiliation. This composite biography, using the life histories and experiences of more than half of our larger interview sample, illustrates what these common values are. I urge you to read it in conjunction with the fuller archive of complete interviews, where you can hear firsthand the voices of those I had the privilege to interview. I entreat you to think about the policy implications of these stories to continue our struggle for an America that embraces its highest ideals.

Each time I return to these interviews and think about their meaning, I am moved by their power. You will be too.

JULIAN BOND
December 2014

Black Leaders' Short Bios

More than 50 African-American leaders were interviewed in the *Explorations in Black Leadership* series. Detailed biographies can be found at www.blackleadership.virginia .edu.

Collectively, the following people inform this book:

Amiri Baraka—playright and poet; founder of Black Arts Movement; Poet Laureate of New Jersey

Mary Francis Berry—lawyer, civil rights activist, professor, author; Geraldine R. Segal Professor of American Social Thought and History, University of Pennsylvania; Provost, University of Maryland; chancellor, University of Colorado at Boulder; chair of US Commission on Civil Rights; Assistant Secretary for Education in HEW

Sanford Bishop, Jr.—public servant; US congressman from Georgia

Julian Bond—civil rights activist, public servant, professor; founding member of SNCC; national chair, National Association for Advancement of Colored People (NAACP); professor, University of Virginia and American University

Carol Moseley Braun—lawyer, public servant, business consultant; first African American US senator; US ambassador to New Zealand

Calvin Butts—religious leader, education administrator; pastor of Abyssinian Baptist Church and president of College at Old Westbury, New York

Geoffrey Canada—educator; president and CEO of Harlem Children's Zone

Julius Chambers—civil rights activist, lawyer; director-counsel of NAACP Legal Defense Fund; chancellor of North Carolina Central University; director of Center for Civil Rights at NCCU; partner at Ferguson, Chambers, and Sumter

James Clyburn—public servant; US congressman from South Carolina; House majority whip; assistant Democratic leader

Johnnetta Cole—anthropologist, professor, author, executive administrator; president of Spelman and Bennett College; presidential distinguished professor at Emory University; director of National Museum of African American Art

John Conyers, Jr.—public servant: US congressman from Michigan; longest serving African American in Congress

Angela Davis—feminist, activist, philosopher, author; professor at University of Santa Cruz, California

Rita Dove—poet, professor, University of Virginia; poet laureate of United States; poet laureate of Virginia; Pulitzer Prize in Poetry; National Medal of Arts

Floyd Flake—theologian, public servant, executive administrator; senior pastor of Allen A. M.E. Church, Queens, New York; former president of Wilberforce University; former US congressman

Robert Franklin—theologian, scholar, author, education administrator; president of Interdenominational Theological Center; president of Morehouse College; religion director at Chatauqua Institution

Mary Futrell—educator and academic executive administrator; president of VEA and NEA; dean of George Washington Graduate School of Education and Human Development

Nikki Giovanni—activist, educator, poet; University Distinguished Professor at Virginia Tech

Earl Graves—entrepreneur; CEO and chairman of Pepsi-Cola, Washington, D.C.; founder and publisher of *Black Enterprise* magazine

William H. Gray III—theologian, public servant, civil rights activist, administrator; president of United Negro College Fund; US congressman from Philadelphia; US Congress majority whip; pastor of Bright Hope Baptist Church.

Dick Gregory—entertainer, civil rights activist; internationally acclaimed comedian

Katori Hall—playwright; Ron Brown scholar; winner of England's Olivier Award

Dorothy Height—early civil rights activist, executive administrator; president of National Council of Negro Women; winner of Presidential Medal of Freedom

Oliver Hill—civil rights lawyer on major desegregation cases; winner of Presidential Medal of Freedom

Benjamin Hooks—civil rights activist, theologian; executive director of NAACP; Baptist minister; winner of Presidential Medal of Freedom

Freeman Hrabowski—mathematician; academic executive administrator; president of University of Maryland Baltimore County

Gwen Ifill—author and journalist; managing editor of *Washington Week*; senior correspondent for CBS News Hour

Benjamin Jealous—civil rights activist; executive administrator; CEO of NAACP

Bill T. Jones—choreographer, artistic director, dancer; founder of Bill T. Jones/ Arne Zane Dance Company; inducted into American Academy of Arts and Sciences

Elaine Jones—civil rights attorney and activist; president and director-counsel of NAACP Legal Defense Fund

Vernon Jordan—lawyer, civil rights activist, business executive; executive director of United Negro College Fund; president of National Urban League; senior partner at Akin Gump Strauss Hauer & Feld

Barbara Lee—civil rights and antiwar activist; US congresswoman from California

John Lewis—civil rights activist; author; chairman of SNCC; Freedom Rider; US congressman from Georgia; winner of Presidential Medal of Freedom.

Henry Marsh—civil rights lawyer; mayor of Richmond; senator from Commonwealth of Virginia

Gwendolyn Moore—civil rights activist and public servant; US congresswoman from Wisconsin

Robert Moses—civil rights activist; primary organizer of Freedom Summer; founder of Algebra Project; winner of McArthur grant

Eleanor Holmes Norton—civil rights activist and lawyer; US congresswoman from District of Columbia; professor of law at Georgetown University; chair of EEOC; SNCC organizer

Charles Ogletree, Jr.—lawyer, author, and civil rights activist; Jesse Climenko professor at Harvard Law School; founder of Charles Hamilton Houston Institute for Race and Justice

Vivian Pinn—doctor; director of Office of Research on Women's Health at NIH; president of National Medical Association; fellow of the American Academy of Arts and Sciences

Charles Rangel—lawyer; US congressman from New York serving Harlem; chair of Committee on Ways and Means

William Raspberry—Pulitzer Prize–winning syndicated columnist for *Washington Post*; founder of Baby Steps in Okolona, Mississippi

Bobby Lee Rush—civil rights activist and public servant; US congressman from Illinois; defense minister of Black Panther Illinois chapter

Yvonne Scruggs-Leftwich—author, public scholar, policy analyst; executive director and COO of Black Leadership Forum; deputy mayor of Philadelphia; New York Housing commissioner; professor at National Labor College

Bakari Sellers—lawyer and public servant; South Carolina House of Representatives

Lucius Theus—military; Tuskeegee Airman; major general in US Air Force; director of Accounting and Finance, US Air Force

Clarence Thomas—lawyer and public servant; associate justice in US Supreme Court; chair of EEOC; judge of the US Circuit Court of Appeals

Diane Watson—teacher and public servant; US congresswoman from California; US ambassador to Micronesia

L. Douglas Wilder—public servant; first African American governor of Virginia since Reconstruction; mayor of Richmond

Roger Wilkins—civil rights activist, lawyer, educator, author; Robinson Professor of History and Culture at George Mason University; journalist and Pulitzer Prize winner at *Washington Post*; US assistant attorney general; publisher of NAACP *The Crisis.*

Aaron S. Williams—public servant, executive administrator; director of US Peace Corps; senior official USAID; vice-president for international development at FTI International

Anthony A. Williams—two-term mayor of Washington, D.C.; chief financial officer for D.C.

Armstrong Williams—conservative journalist, political commentator, entrepreneur, author; host of *The Right Side*; presidential appointee to US Department of Agriculture; CEO of Graham Williams Group

A Note about the Web and Use of QR Codes

In this book, you will not only be able to read the words spoken by a group of remarkable African American leaders as they reflect on their own lives and careers. You will also be able to hear them speak the words directly. And you can explore their thoughts more fully by engaging with the website on which the videotaped oral histories can be found.

You can be witness to the rich conversations between Julian Bond and a group of both older and younger leaders. They tell us how they were shaped. They tell us what inspired them. They recall important people in their lives and significant experiences. They also reflect on our evolving world.

We urge you to use the QR codes and links embedded in the book to listen and to take your own journey beyond that which is written on the page. To activate the codes, download a free QR barcode reader/scanner to your camera-equipped mobile device and hold it over the QR code.

The website is fully searchable and will allow you to compare and contrast leaders' views on particular subjects. The website provides an archive of video-tapes that can be used as its own primary source. You will also find there useful educational resources, and a Glossary of terms used in the book. Through the use of QR codes, the website and book allow the reader an interactive, rich exploration into African American history, culture, and leadership in the twentieth and twenty-first centuries.

Acknowledgments

This book began with the effort to document the life journeys of African American leaders, whose personal and professional stories all too often are untold. Julian Bond, my friend and colleague at The University of Virginia, and I intended to create a digital archive for future research, and in the process, to collect important histories of twentieth-century black men and women in America. The information we collected was sufficiently compelling and the harmonies among interviewees so resonant to warrant this collective biography. The digital materials offer an uncommon opportunity to create an interactive composite biography, allowing the reader to move back and forth between the website and the analytical substance of the book.

Such a project could not have occurred without a team effort. First and foremost, I thank Julian Bond. Without his fortitude, commitment, and connections, this project could not have taken hold. It was his name that resonated with so many of the people we contacted. Because of the respect and even veneration that interviewees had for him, they agreed to come to the University of Virginia or for us to come to them to sit down in conversation. Despite the intense schedule that Julian was keeping during those years when he was also national chair of the NAACP, he found time to participate in the project and to stay the course. We began in the year 2000 and carried out the last interview in 2014. Julian was the consistent interviewer, because the power of the conversation often came from the interaction between two black leaders. I can't thank him strongly enough for his unswerving dedication to the project.

Others at The University of Virginia believed in this project and helped with financial, technical, and administrative support. The late Raymond Nelson, dean of the College of Arts and Sciences at the University of Virginia and Peter Onuf, then chair of history, created the opportunity to form the Institute for Public History, of which this was a major project. Initial seed money from the college allowed the project to get underway and small subsequent grants provided additional sustenance. Edward (Ted) Snyder, as dean of the Darden School of Business, formed a partnership with us in the early years of the project. He allowed us to the use the Darden recording studio to videotape the interviews and provided substantial funds to support the ongoing needs of the project. He understood the value of collecting leadership perspectives of diverse African Americans at the height of their professions, and for his interest and vision, I am extremely grateful.

As the project moved forward, and as the Darden studio and videographers were available on a less predictable basis, new allies emerged. I turned more regularly to the Strategic Communications Audio-Visual group at the University of Virginia, and they never disappointed. In particular Sheri Winston, director of University Communications, and Rob Smith, senior producer, have been steadfast supporters. They have generously given their time to find appropriate space to film the interviews, to arrange for the sometimes complicated logistics, and to produce the final videos. I am even more grateful for their personal encouragement and ongoing belief in the importance of the project.

At the onset of the project, I had no web-based skills. Although I have picked up some knowledge along the way, the major work of conceptualizing and building the website needed the support of experts. For that, I turned to the Digital Media Lab at the University of Virginia. Originally, Michael Tuite, and then later Jama Coartney both educated me and worked with me to lay out the very usable *Explorations in Black Leadership* site that serves as both a research and teaching tool. Jama, especially, continues to prod me to constantly think about ways to enhance the site. She has been unflappable as we have worked through numerous glitches. Her untiring work enormously enriches the book. She brought in two very talented students at a critical stage—Calisha Myers and Mark Laurent—who developed the technical structure for the site. A very talented undergraduate student, Michelle Delgado, went through all the interviews on the website, correcting the written transcripts with attention to nuance and diction. I am also grateful to Zachary Wheat and Lana Elam at the University of Virginia who generously gave their time to assist in the redesign of the website. At a critical juncture in thinking through the book and the website, my good friend, Jackie Lichtman, alerted me to the possibility of QR codes. That inspiration allows the book to break new ground in using digital technologies to both preserve and enhance the historical record.

The work of transcription is tedious and often frustrating. Donna Packard, the transcriber of the vast majority of interviews, has been a joy to work with. She, too, has been enthusiastic about the content and meaning of the interviews, and I appreciate her engagement in the process.

Graduate students frequently worked as interns in the Institute for Public History. In addition to preparing the background materials for the interviews, they often culled materials for me to use in writing, or even drafted substantive analyses that have formed some of my thinking for the individual chapters. Back in 2006, Jane Greenway Carr, then a graduate student in the English Department at the University of Virginia, helped me to think about the possible structure of a book centered around the videotaped materials. That formulation has changed some, but she deserves the credit and my thanks for facilitating the basic architecture that remains. Another graduate student in English, Camilla Amirratti, spent a summer culling through the interviews to think more deeply about the connections between oral history, African American traditions, and storytelling. Some of her insights inform chapter 1. Hephzibah Strimic-Pawl, a graduate student in sociology, helped with the research on families and networks, combing through a lot of secondary materials. An early formulation of the chapter on families benefits from her conceptualization of how to think about the black family. A joint article on this subject was published in *Ethnicities* in 2011. Jeanne Siler, first a graduate student in anthropology and now on the staff of the Virginia Foundation for the Humanities, offered assistance in a variety of ways. She helped prepare many of the transcripts by creating topical categories and uploading them to the website. A writer of considerable talent, she assisted with an early conference paper about the project. In the final stages, she read some of the early chapters and offered useful feedback. These people have supported the project and the book with their own intellectual capital, and I know the work is stronger as a result.

To prepare for all the interviews that transpired, numerous students prepared briefing books that Julian Bond and I could then use. Among those students who supported the project during its beginning stages, I especially want to thank Stephanie Taylor, Beth Anne Olson, and Brandi Hughes. They spent an entire summer reading extant literature on leadership and black leadership and helped to formulate the core questions for the interviews. In addition, they prepared early notebooks for interviews. Other research assistants on the project include Andy Morris, Liam Buckley, Carol Ann Friedmann, Mark Meier, and John Kiess. Whitney Naman, a graduate student in education, prepared the "Learning Modules" currently found in Education Resources on the website. Special thanks goes as well to Emily Senefeld and Scott Matthews, both graduate students in history, who have spent time both during the summer and academic year preparing notebooks on short notice as we learned of new people we might interview. Emily also helped carry out research on the civil rights movement, which has found its way into that chapter. Finally, Hannah Bondurrant and Kate Travis, both undergraduate students, devoted many hours of time to the Glossary and further website corrections. Kate has also worked ardently on the reconfiguration of the website and has assisted in many final details too innumerable to mention.

The writing of the book occurred largely in Washington, D.C. The Library of Congress provided a semiprivate office in the Adams Building, where I was able to order books and work in comparative isolation. Being in America's greatest library, surrounded by the resources so essential to the project, was a constant source of inspiration.

I am grateful to people who carefully read some or all of the chapters, offered suggestions for revision, and helped compile the index. Brian Balogh, a colleague and friend in the History Department, provided detailed feedback, as did Mical Schneider, a friend of 40 years standing. Victoria Baker, a professional indexer, demonstrated extraordinary commitment and became invested in ways

I could never have imagined. My husband, Mel, went over every page of the manuscript with a fine-tooth comb. As his own graduate students will attest, that kind of detailed reading can seem overwhelming, but is almost always incredibly helpful.

Of course, to him I owe far more than a careful reading of the book. His constancy, his unfailing love and support, his intellectual curiosity, and his own tireless work ethic provide the model for how to live richly in the world. His belief in me—as an historian and as a human being—mean far more than I can convey in words. He, together with our adult children, Sarah and Elliot, along with their partners, are a constant reminder that life is lived most fully when it is embraced with a strong love of family, ethical values, and purposefulness. I believe that this book and the people in it have been so important to me because I am reminded constantly of the values I care about most.

Black Leadership: A Collective Biography

Black leaders regularly contend with the historical and lingering effects of racism in American society. No matter the degree of success or accomplishment, or no matter the comfort level that blacks achieve within American society, there is always a persistent "otherness"—a need to prove oneself as well as to battle the negative assumptions of the larger society. Dorothy Height, who devoted her life to organizations that supported women and families and that built interracial understandings, contended that individuals do not need to be racist for racism to persist. "It's in the system in which we live," she said. "It operates whether you know it or not. The banking system, the housing system, the employment system. It affects me as it affects you. It affects you as it affects me."[1]

Through 51 oral history interviews, examined and synthesized, this book explores how a group of black men and women leaders navigated what were unquestionably rough waters. Their life stories illustrate how they were able to struggle against racial stereotypes, slights, and outright discrimination in order to become leaders. Gwendolyn Moore, congresswoman from Wisconsin, remembers her personal effort to resist being stereotyped: "Well, you know, I can tell you that I'm black and I'm a female and I remember making a vow that I would not be stereotyped as a black female and I got to Madison and about a week later I was a black female because I am who I am...."[2]

"Blackness" and "whiteness" are often set against one another, making it more difficult for persons of color to rise to leadership positions. Leaders imply followers, and followers often like to see themselves reflected in their leaders.[3] Since we do not yet live in a color-blind society, race consciousness remains central to issues of identity and identification.[4] What becomes clear, then, is that African Americans, in order to *become* leaders, must first psychologically negotiate their minority status vis-à-vis white societal expectations. They are "atypical leaders" who regularly confront obstacles of legitimacy and resistance.[5]

This remains true even while the dawn of the twenty-first century has seen black Americans at the very highest levels of leadership and responsibility in American society. In 2008, Americans elected Barack Obama as the 44th president of the United States. Before him, two other African Americans—Colin Powell and Condoleezza Rice—served as secretary of state in the administration of President George W. Bush. Blacks now climb the ladders of corporate America, sit on boards of the most important businesses and civic organizations, hold positions at the top echelons of the most prestigious universities, run multimillion dollar businesses, and influence state and national politics through mayoralties, the US Congress and the Senate. On some levels, then, race would not seem to be as significant a factor limiting opportunity in America as it once did.

Yet, history is never fully "past" and the present is infused—subtly or overtly—with inequalities that emanate from historical values of a society that tolerated slavery and then legally mandated racial segregation. The civil rights movement of the 1950s and 1960s, culminating in *Brown v. Board of Education of Topeka, Kansas* and the Civil Rights Acts of 1964 and 1965, may have changed the laws of America. But changing laws does not necessarily change underlying attitudes. In the early years of the twenty-first century, African Americans continue to suffer in the marketplace, in the courts, and in myriad contexts where stereotypes and discrimination prevail.

Blacks continue to live far less well than their white counterparts, fall economically somewhat below those of Hispanic origin and dramatically below Asian Americans. In 2011, the US Census reported median income for blacks at $32,366, compared with $38,624 for Hispanics, $55,412 for non-Hispanic whites, and $64,995 for Asians.[6] The official poverty rate in the United States in 2011 was 15 percent; for blacks that rate was 27.6 percent, constituting close to 11 million people.[7] Although African American children represent 14 percent of all children in America in 2009, they comprised 31 percent of all children living in single-mother households and 34 percent of all children living in poverty.[8] One in every three black children, then, continues to suffer from the consequences of socioeconomic disparity.

Census data also reveal that African Americans lag behind whites in terms of educational attainment. While 80 percent of blacks aged 25 or older graduated from high school in 2009, only 17 percent (compared to 30 percent of non-Hispanic whites) obtained a bachelor's degree.[9] It is well known that educational achievement correlates positively with income potential. Yet, the census data reveals that Hispanic Americans, despite attaining lower levels of college graduation, have a higher median income than do blacks.

Black males are imprisoned at six times the rate of white males. Among prisoners aged 18 to 19, the years when most young people would be in college, black males were imprisoned at nine times the rate of white males.[10] The proliferation of guns and illegal drugs, massive unemployment, failures of the educational system, industrial decline, and the continuing effects of poverty provide huge challenges for American blacks.[11]

As Cornel West so clearly stated, race matters.[12]

Why, some might ask, do we need yet another book on leadership or on black leaders? It is precisely because race continues to matter that a book on black leadership, created from the personal memories of the leaders themselves, is important. We need such a book because young blacks in America rarely get to hear the stories of those who succeeded despite the odds. They especially don't know the history of the 1960s, and therefore lack the basic "software" to manage their environments.[13] We need such a book because all "involuntary" minorities live with stigmas that too often translate into disillusionment and hopelessness.[14] And we need such a book in order to better understand how personal lives intersect with historical circumstances and regional experiences to produce black leaders.

An Historical and Humanist Approach to Leadership

This collective biography of 51 black leaders is based on oral interviews conducted between 2000 and 2014. The interviewees teach us about being black in America, overcoming adverse circumstances, and fighting for political, social and economic justice.

We come to understand the forces in play—both private and public—that propelled them to become leaders in their respective fields.

Understanding people—their personal backgrounds, life experiences, and ideas—is fundamental to a study of black leadership. It is impossible to divorce the person from the place, the times, or the issues. People are products of their cultures, heritage, and environments. The social fabrics of peoples' lives matter profoundly. This book explores the context of peoples' lives in order to explore what produced their capacity for leadership. It is their perspectives—the vantage point of their memories and their self-appraisal—that inform this analysis.

Embedded within peoples' life stories are principles and values. Both explicit and implicit, they are often expressed in terms of lessons handed down from generation to generation. For black leaders, some of the guiding values and principles are Afrocentric, moving people from the personal to the communal to the spiritually transcendent in order to bring about empowerment and ultimate liberation.[15] Each individual is a representative of the whole and each carries a sense of collective responsibility. This extended definition of self—focusing on the "we" rather than the "I"—has profound implications for leadership within and beyond black communities.[16]

It is also important that we hear about black leaders' lives and listen to their reflections on leadership in their own voices. The oral transmission of culture—the passing of histories and values multigenerationally—was a part of African tribal life that was carried into antebellum and postbellum black America. Leaders used oral communication strategies to persuade and engage groups for collective action. The interviewees highlighted in this book are especially gifted with the power of speech, and implicit in these interviews are styles of communication that have been highly effective.

The leaders exemplified in this book come in many varieties. They represent different disciplines; they have distinctive styles of communication; they can endorse diverse political and social visions. Some are quiet; others more boisterous. Some speak with oratorical flair; others use quiet persuasion. They may be direct or indirect leaders, either heading up organizations or leading through the power of their ideas. Some come from backgrounds of economic deprivation; others come from places of financial comfort. Access to educational opportunity was a struggle for some; expectation of educational achievement existed for those of the black elite. There is no "one size fits all."

This sample includes artists, journalists, elected officials, businessmen, clergy, educators, lawyers, physicians, military officers, public policy makers, and leaders of voluntary organizations. It includes men and women. People selected come from all regions of the country. Some lived with segregation; others were born after the *de jure* end to such racist policies. The breadth of this work extends beyond political ideologies, studies of particular types of leaders, analyses of gender, region, and an historical reconstruction of the civil rights movement. We[17] are interested in the larger question of how the experiences of individuals help shape leaders across the leadership spectrum. While we don't pretend to offer a scientifically based sample, we do claim that we have found a diverse group of people who speak powerfully about broader issues of black leadership in America. Their voices help us to assess the current state of African American leadership. Their reflections provide guidance for nurturing the next generation of leaders in the twenty-first century.

Oliver Hill, who died at the age of 100 in 2007, was one of the first people interviewed. As an NAACP lawyer who represented Virginia in the *Brown v. Board of Education* case that legally ended segregation in America's schools, his courageous leadership set the standard for many who came after him. His gentle and persistent leadership directly inspired people like Henry Marsh, a lawyer, member of the Virginia legislature, and the first black mayor of Richmond. This sample taps many lawyers—including Charles Ogletree, Elaine Jones, and Vernon Jordan among them. The law was a tool that allowed them to branch out in many directions—including elected office, leadership of nonprofit organizations, and academia. Within black America, the law has been an important instrument for combating the worst abuses of racism. It is not surprising that so many black leaders pursued legal training.

Likewise, education has always been regarded in the black community as the indispensable stepping stone to overcome poverty. Fighting for educational equity in schools is and always was a priority, since separate was by no means equal. Many in this sample built their careers as educators. Johnnetta Cole, president of two different black colleges and anthropologist, was an early visionary for the creation of African American studies as a field of inquiry. Geoffrey Canada, the director of the Harlem Children's Zone, created an educational model that expands to include all necessary supportive services within a disadvantaged neighborhood. The passion to pass on knowledge as a form of uplift has motivated many others to spend at least part of their productive lives in educational settings. They include Mary Futrell, Freeman Hrabowski, Mary Frances Berry, and the project's codirector Julian Bond, among others. All are teachers and administrators in the academy and often teachers outside as well. Many others have roles as educators, but have led in multiple capacities.

Long before African Americans could be lawyers or were even allowed to be educated, they could lead their own flocks through the ministry. The historical record of black religious leaders begins with Richard Allen, who founded the AME Church in 1787 in Philadelphia. In time, some were specifically trained for the ministry; others felt the calling and stepped up to the religious leadership plate. Dr. Martin Luther King, Jr., became the visionary leader who in the twentieth century moved so many people by embracing the concept of the "beloved community." John Lewis trained for the ministry specifically because of the influence of Dr. King. Within this sample, there are many who either combine the ministry with other professional callings or who build their careers through religious leadership. The late Benjamin Hooks and Bill Gray were ministers, lawyers, and public servants. Floyd Flake continues as the senior pastor of the Greater Allen AME Cathedral of Queens, New York, while previously also serving for 11 years in the US Congress and subsequently taking on the role of president at Wilberforce University in Ohio. Rev. Calvin Butts continues to serve both as pastor of the historical Abyssinian Baptist Church of New York and president of the College at Old Westbury. Their perspectives on leadership lie within.

In the late twentieth century, largely because of the Civil Rights Acts of the 1960s, many more black Americans have been elected to public office. To change the political fabric of America, they rely on the support of constituents; their leadership requires more followers than their competitors. How they lead in a still racially divided America, how they effectively negotiate among sometimes conflicting needs, and how they set agendas but know when to compromise is a compelling part of the black leadership story. James Clyburn knows well how critical it is to maintain the support of constituents, and he recognizes the importance of developing a leadership style: "if people don't like your style, you'll never get a chance to show them what substance there may be to you." Gwen Moore speaks about the central importance of consistency in message. Others, like Anthony Williams, emphasize the pragmatic aspects of effective leadership. Collectively, they and other political leaders represented open a window onto effective ways to exercise political leadership as black Americans.[18] How they explain the genesis for their leadership philosophy is an equally important part of this narrative.

We also spoke with those who lead without measurable followers. People influence, persuade, inspire—and therefore lead—with ideas that resonate throughout society. The late Amiri Baraka, a founder of the Black Arts movement in the 1960s and more recently poet laureate of New Jersey was one such leader of the arts; his message is one of resistance and defiance. Rita Dove, former poet laureate of the United States, poet laureate of the Commonwealth of Virginia, and recipient of a National Medal for the Arts, wants her poetry to engage all humanity. "I think that for me to have someone, a perfect stranger say, that they have felt the same way, too, and this perfect stranger may be a white man from rural Texas. That's an incredible victory for the human race and for civil rights and all of that to acknowledge, to realize that different skin colors, different classes, we're all human beings. This is where civil liberties and mutual respect begin."[19] Bill T. Jones, choreographer, uses dance as a means to embrace larger sociological issues. Dick Gregory early in his career discovered the power of comedy as a means of social commentary, while journalists, like the late William Raspberry, lead through the power of written persuasion. Younger playwrights like Katori Hall build upon these models. All reveal the diversity of indirect black leaders.

Finally, some in this sample affected significant change through distinctive roles in organizations and business. Dorothy Height is the *grande dame* of the civil rights movement and an early advocate for women, family, and children. The late Major General Lucius Theus' 36-year US Air Force career was dedicated to upgrading military administrative operations, improving human and race relations in the Armed Forces, and encouraging young people to pursue careers in aviation. Yvonne Scruggs-Leftwich was for many years the COO of the nonprofit Black Leadership Forum, Inc., a confederation of the top national civil rights and service organization. Vivian Pinn, director of the Office of Research on Women's Health at the National Institutes for Health, has quietly shaped changing health priorities. Julian Bond was chairman of the national NAACP Board from 1998 to 2010. Each, in his or her own voice, speaks powerfully about personal paths to leadership and the challenges of black leadership in America.

In short, this study on leadership portrays the multidimensional ways African Americans are engaged across America in effecting meaningful change. Their personal lives intersect with the history of the twentieth and now twenty-first centuries and must be understood in the context of race realities in America. Hearing their views expressed in their own words personalizes and humanizes our understanding of black leadership.

Methodology and Structure

These autobiographical recollections, told by individuals with different life experiences, constitute shared triumphs, shared tragedies, and shared strategies. As important as the individual details are the ways of telling and the meanings ascribed by the teller. Autobiographical stories are a way to better understand the thinking of individuals within a cultural paradigm. Through these living histories, we can develop a more authentic history of black people in America while also better understanding how leaders are made.[20]

We understand the selective nature of these reflections, and the ways in which memory differs from history. This book is not primarily a social or cultural history of African Americans, although it does draw upon that history for context. This book does not seek to rewrite the history of the civil rights movement or of black family, community, and educational experiences, although it does at times refer to particular aspects of that history. Nor does the book seek to interrogate the truth of every piece of information shared with us. We take the reflections of black leaders at face value, recognizing in them the deeply felt personal choices that people make in remembering their pasts.

The core questions that formed the basis for the original interviews are both personal and philosophical (see Appendix A). The questions were developed from an extensive study of leadership literature. We asked people to reflect on what aided them in their development and who supported them along the way. We also asked people to reflect on the skills needed for leadership and the challenges in particular faced by black leaders. The commonalities in responses create the structure for this analysis.

The videotaped interviews were carried out at The University of Virginia, the Congressional Recording Studio, and selective other places. On camera were Julian Bond and the interviewee. The interviewees knew the material would be available for others to see, and therefore there had to be a public aspect to what was otherwise an intimate conversation. We understand that there is a constructed, performative, and selective character to these interviews. Yet, we also believe that black leaders shared true and heartfelt memories of people, places, and events important to them. Through those memories, we come to better understand how prominent public figures use stories of identity to positive advantage.

The ways people choose to remember are as important as the realities of their lives. Individuals construct a narrative built retrospectively, with some issues repressed or deleted, and others highlighted. We learn very little about the mistakes and setbacks or their leadership stumbles and failures. In many ways, one can consider these interviews a reflection of the personal armour created as sustenance for hard times. In their own words, we learn what impelled them forward, what they are passionate about, and what they believe in their souls.

Fortunately, in addition to the full transcripts available on the Black Leadership website (www.blackleadership. virginia.edu), one can hear and see the conversation. The transcripts make every attempt to be true to the diction, grammar, and style of the speaker. But to fully appreciate the passion, emphasis, tone, gesture, and even silences, these interviews must be heard. This book is an analytic summary of what we can learn from these interviews. To fully appreciate each individual, we encourage readers to engage the website. For that reason, QR codes or links are incorporated into the text itself that will allow the words on the page to become audible and visual. By following the links, the reader will be able to hear the specific leader in a fuller context, and those words will be embedded within additional thoughts. This is a rare opportunity to enter the conversation about leadership more fully. Because the book uses the words of interviewees to engage contemporary issues about how best to create future leaders and because so many of our interviewees are still active leaders, I use the present tense to refer to the interviewees' ideas. Many of them are no longer alive, but their words still resonate and can be heard in the voice of the speaker.

There is no single path to leadership. Just as a pebble dropped in water sends out ripples, this book is structured around ever-widening concentric circles. Each circle broadens out from the previous, exploring what black leaders tell us about what shaped and inspired them. After focusing on the value of the oral tradition for learning about African American lives, each subsequent chapter concentrates on a few individuals who share characteristic perspectives of the leaders interviewed. A final chapter broadens out to explore leadership lessons gleaned from the collective whole. Together, the seven chapters create a composite biography.

In African and African American culture, the oral tradition is highly regarded as a means for personal remembrance and building community. Oral histories and oral memories illuminate shared histories that include marginalization, struggle, and ways of overcoming. If we lose these memories, we engage in "historical amnesia" and "historicidal" culture. Chapter 1, "Defining Self," focuses on the methodology of the interviews and uses the reflections of leaders themselves on the meaning of oral memory. Examining the dialogic process that emerges from the interviews reveals how identity is created for what Henry Louis Gates calls the "shaping of a black self."[21]

Chapter 2, "Families," begins with the most intimate and smallest circle of influence. Four leaders who represent very different leadership styles, political values, and career paths reveal how their families' structures and values helped them overcome what otherwise would have been profound hardships limiting their potential for success. Amiri Baraka, Clarence Thomas, Yvonne Scruggs-Leftwich, and Carol Moseley Braun reflect on ways in which their families provided the grounding for their success. They discuss the importance of fictive and extended kin relations, and they reflect on how racial socialization and diligence messages provided the confidence and direction to rise above societal constraints. Although these four individuals had vastly different early life experiences, their families supported them through similar networks and values.

Chapter 3 broadens the circle of influence to explore the centrality of education in the lives of six leaders who went on to become educators and educational reformers. They share with us the specific educational values that were transmitted in their classrooms—both segregated and integrated. William Raspberry, Johnnetta Cole, Mary Futrell, Freeman Hrabowski, Geoffrey Canada, and Rita Dove ultimately demonstrate how some of their own educational experiences prepared the way for their leadership and their understanding of America's educational challenges. Through their reflections, we can see the ways that educational institutions either supported or failed black youth in America.

For a generation of African Americans, networks and connections within communities shaped the construction of healthy individual and group identities. These leaders' stories are so important because they remind us of the vital connections between identity forming institutions, strong individuals, and energetic citizen participation. Collectively, their personal histories illustrate the power of individuals and organizations beyond the family and beyond educational institutions to train and cultivate future leaders. In Chapter 4, Dorothy Height, Elaine Jones, Vernon Jordan, Robert Franklin, and Bobby Rush emphasize the importance of individual mentors, community role models, and institutions. They speak about engagement as a means to instill self-confidence and personal discipline among young people. They recognize the ways in which opportunities emerge from group experiences. Some participated in cheerleading or scouting; others joined churches, fraternal, and political organizations, and the military.

As concentric circles broaden, one can see how national successes and triumphs catalyze leadership opportunities and aspirations. Early civil rights lawyers and social activists served as crucial models for later activists, lawyers, artists, and public figures. Black leaders reveal over and over again how national events captured their attention, creating the determination to become active participants in the struggle for social and economic justice. Using the stories of Oliver Hill, Henry Marsh, Charles Ogletree, Benjamin Jealous, and Bakari Sellers, Chapter 5 explores how the law empowered people to imagine change. The *Brown v. Board of Education* decision holds unique power for shaping black leadership in twentieth-century America. In some cases, a second generation of leaders watched the ways in which the *Brown* decision established the possibility for a race-neutral country. In other cases, the disappointments of *Brown* and the limitations of the law impelled younger black leaders to use the law as a jumping off point for careers in social justice. In all cases, understanding the connection between law and social change triggered active leadership.

As white supremacist tactics escalated to prevent the implementation of integration of schools, the limitations of the law became obvious. New grassroots strategies emerged, catalyzing the civil rights movement and widening the circles to include millions of Americans who could envision leadership roles for themselves. Chapter 6 focuses on three leaders who embraced different leadership philosophies during the foundational years of the 1960s and early 1970s movement. John Lewis, Julian Bond, and Angela Davis espoused prophetic, consensual, and militant leadership philosophies, awakening others who joined with them and younger blacks to imagine progress in new social and economic contexts. The civil rights movement created a mythos of African American leadership, thereby transforming black leadership possibilities.

Finally, Chapter 7 summarizes the lessons that can be learned from this composite examination of black leaders. Most black leaders interviewed feel a responsibility to be change agents and to work toward a more fair and equitable society. They also understand the enduring nature of their commitment and the sacrifices involved. As a group, they share an ability to work with adversaries, an inner core of patience and resolve, and vigilance to their values-driven compass. Most recall the injunction they heard growing up: "remember to lift others as you climb." Armed with a race consciousness either implicitly imposed or explicitly embraced, they are very comfortable exploring the connections between black leadership and American leadership. They understand the ways in which race defines them, but they refuse to be constrained by racial stereotypes. Their lessons resonate for all Americans who aspire to leadership.

Leadership Literature

In Western societies, leadership is a saleable commodity. Publications abound; leadership schools on both the undergraduate and graduate levels proliferate; self-help manuals and online learning opportunities exist. Aaron S. Williams, the former head of the US Peace Corps, commented that "in America, most people think they should be leaders. It is part of our society, our culture, our ethos."[22]

While we often talk about leaders and leadership as critical for societal progress, we rarely find agreement on essential traits and attributes of leaders or on the ways in which leaders are formed. Inspirational works and leadership programs pursue a variety of approaches. They focus on character, values, skills, traits, and outcomes. Some talk in terms of vision and transformation. Some speak of techniques and transactions. They write of charisma and personality, ethics, courage, persuasion, communication, authenticity, and realism. For almost all who promote the subject, leadership is (or can be) a learned trait. Stephen Covey and Sheryl Sandberg are among the authors whose books have sold millions of copies, telling us how to develop our potential and how to empower organizations.[23]

Much of the didactic literature on leadership emanates from the perspective of business and management. In *Managing the Dream*, Warren Bennis—a prominent voice in corporate leadership studies—distinguishes between leaders and managers. Leaders innovate, challenge systems, focus on people, remain attuned to societal obligations, and "manage the dream" while managers administer, work within the status quo, and focus on systems. Dreams and visions are central to the leadership paradigm.[24] Dreams, of course, must be communicated for leaders to have followers. Without followers, the leader's vision falls on deaf ears and cannot be implemented. Ultimately, leaders must "put words to the formless longing and deeply felt needs of others. They create communities out of words."[25]

The emphasis on a leader's power to persuade through language is developed much more fully by psychologist Howard Gardner. His cognitive approach to leadership centers on the personality of leaders and the stories they share. He contends that the most effective leaders use stories of identity to positive advantage, articulating narratives that help others reflect on the evolution of their lives.[26] Powerful leaders share through compelling narratives that convince others to believe in them—either because of their personal credibility (stories about self), or because their stories speak to the needs of a group, or because their stories are about value and meaning.[27] Leaders are largely motivated by the desire to effect change, but to do so they must find the cognitive approaches that persuade others of their authenticity and their vision.[28]

Literature on black leadership engages many of the issues discussed above, but also pushes us to think beyond them.[29]

To be black and to be a leader in America ultimately raises fundamental questions about one's place in American society. Historically, black agency developed specifically around resistance to the dominant white paradigm, as African Americans built foundations of self-help and solidarity. Progress would come only from internal resources. If that were the case, W. E. B. Du Bois queried, how could one be both black and American? Would success in America require giving up one's race identity?

> It is a peculiar sensation, this double-consciousness. . . . One ever feels his two-ness—An American, a Negro; two souls, two thoughts, two unreconciled strivings, two warring ideals in one dark body, whose dogged strength alone keeps it from being torn asunder.[30]

The "twoness" issue—that of two warring souls in one body—is still central to discussion of leadership, because African Americans still struggle against assumptions of social and political inferiority.[31] Black scholar Henry Louis Gates Jr. contends that narratives of ascent for black leaders are also narratives of alienation and loss.[32] The loss refers to that which was left behind and the need to move into new and unfamiliar worlds. For many, it requires a cultural and psychological shift from a position of resistance and "otherness" to a place of integration into the American mainstream. Success often requires a degree of assimilation and the abandonment of ethnic identities.

Writers on black leadership grapple with questions of definition and integration. Is a black leader someone who is black and has a leadership position? Or must the definition be tied to larger aspirations for black empowerment and social change? Has the potential to be a black leader been eroded by the achievements of the civil rights movement and the growth of a black middle class? Have the enormous gains in black political strength meant that blacks are now part of the status quo and therefore unable or unwilling to goad America's conscience? Has effective black leadership been lost in the transformation from protest to politics?[33] Have such elected officials become "transracial" leaders—that is, African American leaders whose constituencies and institutions are largely non–African American?[34] Must an African American leader be perceived as such by a majority of American blacks, or is it sufficient to have a prominent position with significant institutional or national responsibilities? Put simply, are Barack Obama, Clarence Thomas, and Kenneth Chenault, black leaders or leading blacks—and should we be concerned about the difference?[35]

Black leadership studies also focus on the deep history of African American struggles for justice and equality. At each stage of American history, black leaders appropriate for their own time emerged. They planned slave rebellions; they participated in the Underground Railroad; they became abolitionists; they established independent presses; they created organizations in the form of schools, mutual aid societies, churches, historical associations, musical groups, and literary societies. Examples include the AME Church, the Free African Societies, the New York African Free School, the *Freedom's Journal*, the American Negro Historical Society, the Association for the Study of African American Life and History, the Fisk Jubilee Singers, and the *New Negro*. These created the intellectual and ideological foundations for race pride and self-empowerment. Later, from the early twentieth century, the social movements followed that lay the foundations for the civil rights movement of the 1950s and 1960s. Organizations include the Niagara Movement, the NAACP, the National Urban League, the Brotherhood of Sleeping Car Porters, the Universal Negro Improvement Association, the Nation of Islam, the Congress of Racial Equality, and the Fellowship of Reconciliation. During the civil rights movement, there were yet other organizations, appropriate for the time—the Southern Christian Leadership Conference, Student Nonviolent Coordinating Committee, Black Panthers, Women's Political Council, and Wednesdays in Mississippi.

For each stage of the journey, there were leaders who provided the models for future ideological and strategic initiatives. Frederick Douglass used his powerful oratory and writing to help lead the abolitionist movement. A. Philip Randolph created the first predominantly black labor movement by organizing and leading the Brotherhood of Sleeping Car Porters. Sojourner Truth advocated for women's rights as well as abolition. Frederick D. Patterson founded the United Negro College Fund and became president of Tuskegee. Multiple others like Walter White, Thurgood Marshall, Charles Hamilton Houston, Alain Locke, Langston Hughes, Ida B. Wells-Barnett, Marcus Garvey, James Weldon Johnson, W. E. B. Du Bois, Booker T. Washington, Carter G. Woodson, John Hope, Whitney Young, Jr., Fannie Lou Hamer, and Elijah Muhammad became established leaders with varying messages and approaches. The historical literature that revolves around these individuals reminds us that black leadership comes in many forms, and that black leaders were not born with the civil rights movement.[36] They were agents of change throughout American history.

Yet, black leadership studies also remain conscious of the larger place of blacks in the American society. Leadership implies power and authority; blacks historically have been subordinate to whites. Thus, issues of race dominance are central to discussions of black leadership.[37]

Scholars of black leadership place less significance on individual traits and attributes.[38] Instead, they are most interested in analyzing strategies, agendas and outcomes. Gunnar Myrdal, in his seminal book, *An American Dilemma: The Negro Problem and Modern Democracy*, wrote in 1944 that that one needed to think of black leaders in terms of protest or accommodation.[39] From the 1960s on, many scholars have further developed this paradigm. They distinguish leaders in terms of traditional political labels—conservatives, liberals, moderates, radicals. Or as Uncle Toms, race men, liberals, and race diplomats. Some write in terms of conservatives, militants, and moderates. Others distinguish between separatist, accommodationist, and integrationist leaders. More recently, some writers even suggest that elected African American leaders are now less able to work for racial justice because they are unwilling to challenge the system of which they are a part.[40] In all these studies, the paramount issue is that of the relationship of blacks to whites, and the willingness to challenge the dominant class structure. Individuals may be highlighted, but it is the place of the individual in the system that matters.

It is not surprising that many studies on black leadership were produced in the 1960s.

The civil rights movement, beginning in the aftermath of World War II, altered American society radically. Black leaders played a central role in the struggle. Much has been written on the leadership of those times—focusing on particular leaders, organizations, and movements that made a difference. The generation of leaders born out of the civil rights movement were central to America's dismantling of segregation. They acted selflessly, because the times demanded it. The civil rights movement, Lea Williams writes, spawned "a style of African American leadership that was vocal, charismatic, visionary, and deeply committed to social change and political empowerment."[41] These were leaders who engaged in direct action to challenge the normative assumptions of caste within American society. They were willing to become "agents of disorder" on a large scale, and they forced national change upon America.[42] Many of them are in our interview pool.

These orientations within black leadership literature are both deeply embedded in black cultural traditions and reflections of contemporary realities. Some leadership/management scholars emphasize how the African concept of vital forces should be used to enrich organizational theory. The idea emerges out of African humanistic philosophy; it is a concept that emphasizes the power of relationships and is now being associated with great leadership.[43] Only recently have scholars begun to understand the incongruence between European and African-based cultural structures that affect organizational behaviors. The "communal and collectivist ethos" that inheres in African American culture is contrasted to the individualistic, self-reliant, and competitive European-American model of social culture and corporate design.[44] Clearly, there is much we can learn from African American leaders about ways of being in the world.

Black leaders have always had to find ways to use their collective resources to address the structural inequities that limited the expansion of American democracy.[45] Leadership, then, in the black community, has always been defined in terms of creating a more just and more equal America. Focusing on race is central to black leadership, interviewee Mary Frances Berry explains:

> talking about race is not something that people who are visible minorities...want to do. It is because we are the people who were ascribed and defined and confined and so we talk about our own condition and how we are the negative other in America....so we talk about it not because we decided to talk about it. We talk about it because it's the condition we were put in that we try to overcome and so American freedom has never existed in any pure form going back to the days of slavery until now and what it all is about is perfecting American freedom...and so to talk about race doesn't mean you're denying American freedom. It means you're trying to make it better.[46]

The leadership literature described above provided important background preparation as we defined the basic questions posed to interviewees. This voluminous literature uses the disciplines of sociology, psychology, political science, and management to propose paths to successful leadership. Much of the literature on African Americans in this period, understandably, concentrates on barriers faced and on the social, economic, and legal struggles of millions to remove them. Alternatively, black leadership studies focus on heroic lives of select leaders, notably Martin Luther King, Malcolm X, and most recently, Barack Obama.

This book adds to leadership literature by applying the perspective of historians using the techniques of oral history. As historians, we look for evidence of both continuity and change and we seek to understand the causal factors for each. We explore both systemic societal structures and human agency in the quest to derive a collective portrait of black leaders and black leadership. Using the interviews from the Black Leadership project, we distill the characteristics shared by a majority of black leaders over three generations. Compared to white leaders, African Americans stepped up to leadership positions with the deck stacked against them. These African American leaders relied upon a common set of resources – a profound belief in the power of education despite limited access to it, enduring networks that started at home but extended to fictive kin, mentors, and institutions, and powerful historic breakthroughs that signaled to successive generations that progress could be made legally, politically, and economically.

In America today, as this book makes clear, there is no dearth of leadership and no black leadership crisis. On the contrary, as our small sample demonstrates, African Americans leaders can be found in virtually every career path and have risen to the top echelons of positions that once would have been impossible and unthinkable.

This optimistic assessment about the state of black leadership should not be seen as a claim that race discrimination is behind us as a society. Continued vigilance and struggle are needed to achieve the highest ideals on which this country was founded. But there is also much to celebrate.

Black leaders have much to teach Americans about how to foster leadership and how to be effective leaders. They teach us the importance of negotiating societal expectations and pushing against the boundaries that constrain. They collectively represent a group of individuals who have the capacity to dream and to persuade others of their dream through stories of identity and empowerment. They model a communal and collectivist ethos. They allow us to think more broadly – to shift our gaze from leadership traits and attributes to the social and civic outcomes we might envision for a more just and equal America. That is why their stories and insights matter.

We are all part of the same circle: the living, the dead, and the yet unborn.[47]
—Johnnetta Cole.

CHAPTER 1

Defining Self: Oral History, Storytelling, and Leadership

Se wo were fi na wosankofa a yenkyi—
It is not wrong to go back for that which you have forgotten
[Akan proverb on the search for self and communal
knowledge—on how the past illuminates the present]

When Robert Franklin was a young teenager, his beloved Bishop Ford at
St. Paul's Church gave him an unusual role. He asked him to take over as the
Sunday school teacher for 13 unruly boys who had been disrupting their classes.
Ford rounded up the boys, took them to an isolated part of the church, and put
Franklin in charge. It was there that he discovered the power of stories:

> "All right, Brother Franklin, you're now in charge of these young men
> and you will have your own class, and I don't want to hear any more
> about problems and disruptions from you guys." So there I was, no cur-
> riculum, no experience, and sort of with what they all regarded as the
> most problematic and at-risk kids in the church. So we started slowly
> and I'm not quite sure where it occurred to me to allow these guys to tell
> their stories. So part of it was an introduction ritual. And it went on for
> so long we couldn't get to all the guys that first hour, hour and fifteen
> minutes, whatever we had, so the next Sunday we came back and we
> continued. "All right, you tell us your story. What school do you go to?
> Neighborhood you live in?"
>
> And one of the things that struck me as we were doing this, these
> guys had never had that opportunity to even for just sort of five-minute
> platforms to say, "This is who I am, this is where I'm from," etc. And
> so later in life I discover the importance of narrative and storytelling

for people to feel part of an organization. So we continued and then we expanded that, because each week we'd come back and, you know, we'd read the Biblical passage that the rest of the Sunday School were discussing, and I'd say a few words about it. But then we'd quickly go to their stories, "How has the week been for you?"

These young guys, these guys are twelve, thirteen years old, are sharing stories about being roughed up by police, about being recruited to gangs, about seeing their mothers brutalized by boyfriends. I thought, "Gee whiz, this is way over my head." But I realized it was important to allow these guys to talk through some of this stuff. And what I began to see was these guys who were kind of the "bad boys" in the church and in the neighborhood would listen to each other and were anxious to sort of get in and to have their time. And they were really very candid about some of the things that they were struggling with.[1]

Robert Franklin
http://blackleadership.virginia.edu/01

Franklin understands the power of storytelling to build community, heal lingering wounds, and understand individuals better. He also chooses a particular story to share about how he began to build his own leadership skills. In the telling of his chosen story, he demonstrates his capacity for empathy, awareness of black youth challenges, commitment to church-based interventions, and evolving leadership strategies. This single story about stories imparts multilayered meanings.

The stories people choose to tell about themselves are constructed on multiple levels. They are first and foremost stories of individual memories and meanings. We are products of intergenerational cultures that have geographic, ethnic, racial, linguistic, and ancestral roots. We also live in specific moments in time, regularly forging connections between the present, past, and future. And we inhabit particular spaces, either voluntarily or involuntarily, which form our reality of possibilities.[2] The stories we remember and the stories we choose to tell shape our personal consciousness. They also influence how others see us. Our stories impact our leadership potential.

Personal stories, then, have larger meanings. They can be especially helpful in placing grand narratives and national mythologies in context. For those who have been left out of the historical record, they can put more voices in play, illustrating the complex mosaic of how societies function. Telling one's personal story can also be therapeutic for those who feel marginalized and overlooked. Autobiographical reflections are historiographical acts, and help to create a collective consciousness and purpose.[3]

Narratives also function as moral tales. It is through such tales that people place themselves as moral beings within communities. Often memories are faulty, and details of specific historical occurrences can be flawed. But the stories that people tell about themselves and others in the present are the bases for the social construction of virtue. This is how people create moral communities and place themselves as moral beings within.[4]

For African Americans, the oral tradition is deeply embedded in culture.

When no other forms of resistance were possible and when enslaved African Americans were forbidden to learn how to write, they passed on their personal stories to the next generations verbally. In so doing, they were following venerable African traditions of oral autobiography.[5] Slavery unknowingly kept this communication system alive. Many language mechanisms evolved to express and conceal ideas at the same time, rich with irony and nuance.[6]

In West Africa, the *griot* was the person charged with narrating both his own and his community's autobiographies, thereby serving as "the memory of mankind."[7] Often, his oral chronicles stretched back hundreds or thousands of years, keeping alive cultural knowledge and tribal identity. For traditional African societies, this was often the only means to record survival struggles. In narrating both individual and communal stories for future generations, the *griot* served as a witness to history. Some scholars even argue that African and African American autobiographers build upon this *griot* tradition specifically establishing connections between themselves and their communities, rather than focusing on their individual story.[8] Joanne Braxton sees this as especially prevalent with black women autobiographers, writing that "like the blues singer, the autobiographer incorporates communal values into the performance of the autobiographical act, sometimes rising to function as the 'point of consciousness' of her people."[9]

In antebellum and postbellum America, oral transmission of culture and values remained a powerful means to create continuity between generations and resist the master narrative.[10] Rhetoric and public speaking, whether in churches or communal organizations, was a form of public dialogue. Through such dialogue, African Americans yearned for freedom and equality; they exposed the failure to adhere to American and Judeo-Christian ideals. Through such dialogue, they exhorted others to live up to their own highest ideals. In the process, they instilled black pride.[11]

The black leaders in this study participate in a rich oral autobiographical tradition. In narrating their personal stories, they too serve as witnesses to history. We learn about their neighborhoods, communities, and regions. They speak for themselves; they speak for their communities of origin; they speak about racial realities in America today; and they speak about future possibilities. Narratives become linked to future goals as part of a wider human discourse about culture and values. They operate both as arsenals and as battlegrounds for building authentic and vibrant communities.[12] Hearing their voices—incorporating at times passion, anger, reflection, sadness, and hope—not only connects these individuals to the oratorical traditions of black America, but also deepens our understanding of their individual and shared experiences.

Many interviewees have also written their life stories, available as published autobiographies. When accessible, these too are part of this larger study of black leadership. Sharing in the tradition of Maya Angelou, Malcolm X, and Zora Neale Hurston—among many others—their autobiographies hold a mirror to the experience of being black in America.

The "will to write" and by extension the will to speak out was often the will to challenge the supremacist power structure. The "shaping of a black self in words" has a long history in America as a means to bear witness to a collective race history.[13] Through their writings, black leaders link themselves to a rich African American intellectual tradition that often challenges America's perception of itself.[14] Through their insights into their interior lives—both its ordinariness and its extraordinariness—we come to appreciate shared cultural challenges and sensibilities. The autobiographical methodology, either oral or written, addresses both what is unique about "blackness" in America and what is shared in common with whites.

For African Americans, coming to terms with one's own personal history is often a way to counter the historical degradation of racism.[15] Talking or writing about one's self inevitably constructs a "dialectic between what you wish to become and what society has determined you are."[16] Within African American culture, such storytelling has also been the means to break down the barriers between the "I" and the "you." The "self" is always part of the "people."[17]

There are pitfalls of oral history—its potential for partial truths, the dangers of recast stories, the need to compensate for trauma or pain too great to share, and/or the possibility of self-aggrandizement.[18] Living histories are not always accurate accounts. Individuals remember events selectively. We hold on to specific moments, forget others, and process incidents and experiences in ways unique to our personalities and needs. Some remember names and dates in exquisite detail; others recall conversations with mentors or adversaries. How the interviewer asks the questions invariably influences the nature of the responses. The relationship between interviewer and interviewee is also a factor.

Nonetheless, memory is a highly significant component of self-identity. Much can be learned from what people choose to reveal, by what they remember, and by how they reconstruct the narratives of their lives. These stories are critically important for understanding how leaders emerge and how people build successful lives. They are also fundamental for comprehending the black experience in America.

The Stories Revealed

Through the voices of black leaders we receive the unique and powerful gift of personal narrative. Their individual stories intersect with some of the biggest and most difficult questions facing the African American community and

American society as a whole today. Their personal stories allow us to learn not just what is important to them, but provide insight into how they think about these moments in their lives. Understanding why and how is often more valuable than learning about who and when. Through the former, we develop insight into attitudes, cultural assumptions, social values, and personal opinions that account for why things happen as they do.[19] These stories bear witness to the collective experiences of black Americans. They establish a link between language, memory, history, and the self.[20]

Listening to individuals talk about their remembered pasts creates an intimate and vibrant opening into their lives. You can hear Carol Moseley Braun's laugh, observe Robert Franklin's calming demeanor, catch the dry tone of Earl Graves's wit, listen to the enthusiasm of Elaine Jones, take note of Amiri Baraka's anger, and reflect on the silences and inflections as the interview subjects relate the ups and downs of their paths to leadership. To listen directly to these powerful people is to share their life experiences, and perhaps also to begin to internalize the lessons offered. The analyses within this chapter and the chapters that follow have been informed by an ability to listen for intensity, intonation, passion, and reflection, as well as sadness, hope, and joy divulged through this conversational mode.

Taken as a whole, the interviews are more than individual stories about how leaders emerge and continue to hold on to leadership despite setbacks. These collective interviews reveal larger truths about the transmission of a cultural history and cultural memory. Through their conversational oral testimonies, three related patterns emerge that help us to see the value of the oral approach.

First, interviewees demonstrate how the personal, cultural, and national are intertwined. Public and personal space become integrated. In this process, they reveal themselves in very human terms. They transition from public representatives of a particular office or position to accessible individuals whose personal stories inspire us. We learn about their career challenges, but we also hear their commentary on what mattered most in the private sphere. We learn both about the nature of their upbringing and about their leadership philosophies, and we are able often to connect the two.

Second, interviewees are grounded in history and use that knowledge of the past to define the present and future, particularly with regard to the African American experience in the United States and with regard to the tradition of African American leadership. By sharing their life experiences, frequently tied to significant national moments in American history, they illustrate the reality that we are all products of our times and our environments. They illuminate how the past defines them and motivates them. They modulate between the past and the future.

Third, their personal stories reveal the fluid relationship between continuity and change. Being grounded in revered traditions that offer stability, yet knowing when to challenge the status quo in the interest of provoking change is a constant struggle for those who take up the mantle of leadership. Exploring how tradition and change have been negotiated by a group of thoughtful and self-reflective leaders within the African American community invigorates both twentieth-century black history and black leadership studies. Like all complex stories, the three themes are intertwined in the telling.

Public and Private Selves

At their best, conversations are intimate exchanges. In these interviews, black leaders become personal in ways that illuminate their character, values, and leadership training. They link their private experiences to their public leadership positions, illustrating how they overcame personal frailties, who they looked to for support and inspiration, and what memories they rely on to fortify themselves.[21]

Consider, for example, the public and private sides of Mary Futrell. Raised in a single-parent household by a mother who worked as a domestic and factory worker, Futrell went on to earn a degree from Virginia State University, and became a teacher in the turbulent years of the 1960s and 1970s. During those years when she helped integrate the teaching staff at George Washington High School, she also earned a master's degree in secondary education from George Washington University. Then, in the 1980s, she became the first African American woman to serve as president of the National Education Association, holding the position for three terms. In the 1990s, after earning an Ed.D, she was appointed dean of the Graduate School of Education and Human Development of George Washington University. Her public credentials and her career path might well seem unattainable, especially to those unable to see a way out of a culture of poverty. But then consider the Mary Futrell who discusses some of her high-school experiences:

> Well, when I was growing up, Julian, and don't fall off your chair laughing at this, but, my name was Bony Morony, my nickname was Skinny Minnie, my nickname was Seemo—"Seemo holes than you do clothes"—and so my friends made fun of me....so, I tended to be shy from the perspective of the material kinds of things that I did not have and my friends did have. And so I would not come forth. But once I got in the group, I was okay. And, for example...when I tried out for the cheering squad, I didn't make it. The first time, I didn't make it. But you know what I did? I stayed every day and when they practiced, I practiced. And finally throughout the year I had observed that kids would drop off. And so I was put on because I stayed there and I practiced, I made the team.[22]

Mary Futrell was a poor black child in an all-black school and she learned to negotiate insidious class-based distinctions. This was definitive in her rise to self-confident leadership.[23] She shares her self-understanding about personal striving. But she also offers a vignette into the history of southern black education and how that formed her sense of possibility.

Futrell tells a story that allows us to enter her private world. She is discussing her development as a leader and the lessons she learned along the way. Meanwhile, though, she tells the sort of story one might tell at a kitchen table. She talks about her personal, private memories, and she does so in a relatively informal way. Whatever personal stories she might tell, however, are revealed in the same sitting in which she discusses her public and political activities. She becomes more accessible to those who only know her current position. She allows us to see beyond her public face and in that process, provides some insight into *how* she developed. The dynamics of private and public identity come together in these moments, and it is through her storytelling that this mediation takes place.

These interviews are full of such revelations. Mary Futrell speaks of formative activities that helped her discover who she was and that gave her confidence in what she could become.

Vernon Jordan offers insight into his leadership training by sharing a story about one of his early jobs. In the 1960s, Jordan accepted a position as Georgia's field director for the National Association for the Advancement of Colored People (NAACP). He quickly moved from there to the Southern Regional Council and the Voter Education Project before being appointed the executive director of the United Negro College Fund and CEO and president of the National Urban League in the 1970s. A close friend of former president Bill Clinton, he became an important Washington power broker while he also served as the senior managing director at Lazard Frères and Co. But it was in the 1960s, in the Georgia field director's position, that he learned about leadership:

> in my second job as state director of the NAACP, I had the opportunity to pick up Roy Wilkins at the Atlanta Airport and drive him to Macon. And so, two years out of law school you have Roy Wilkins hostage, actually, to your questions and to your inquiries. Two hours to Macon and two hours back. And you see him working on his speech and you ask him about things. Same thing with Clarence Mitchell or Gloster Current or Ruby Hurley. I mean, that, in and of itself, was a huge, informal training ground. It was like getting a graduate degree in black politics and in institutional politics and in personal relationships. I learned a lot that way.[24]

What Vernon Jordan reveals is a strategy for becoming a leader. To succeed, one must be open to opportunities that some might consider beneath them. At the point when the story is told, Jordan was already a lawyer. He could have concluded that serving as a driver was a waste of his legal expertise. But he tells us, through the sharing of this private perspective, that he viewed it as a privilege to learn from—and to network with—people so fundamental to the civil rights movement. In fact, he couches the story in the larger context of networking, explaining that only after he finished law school and became a part of the community did he really understand "the value of the network, the value of talking to people." Commenting on influential people in black Atlanta like Rufus Clement, the longest-serving president of Atlanta University, and Benjamin Mays, president of Morehouse College, he reflects: "And so they were just examples of what I could be if I was prepared to make the kind of sacrifices that my parents told me I had to make to do that."[25] Vernon Jordan developed confidence in his dream by having others around him he could emulate. We learn, then, both about how he built his career and something about why he was able to succeed. Without his personal perception, we would see only the public Vernon Jordan, and we would be far less knowledgeable about pathways to leadership that worked for African Americans. We learn about the parallel world of the black network that was so fundamental to lifting up leaders.

While Mary Futrell tells a story of personal struggle and Vernon Jordan speaks about the value of networking, Nikki Giovanni offers a very different assessment of her life trajectory. We see her interior self. The author of some 30 books, recipient of some 25 honorary degrees, she has spent a major part of her career as a professor of English at Virginia Tech University. Writing in a voice of indignation about racial hatred and oppression, she has always used her poetry to raise social awareness. She has become a leader through her poetic voice—a voice that urgently insists on the need for blacks to develop strong self-identity. Only strong individuals will have the power to make a difference in the lives of others.

Nikki Giovanni takes pride in being a storyteller. "I could tell you eighty million stories," she says. She has a tremendous stock of stories, recollections both of her personal experience and her life as a public figure. Yet, the story she repeatedly tells about herself is about being "on the edge:"

> —there's an edge someplace.... So I'm always pushing for the edge... I don't want to repeat myself and I don't want to get comfortable where I am. I want to go and see—and push it, and if I fall, I fall and if I don't, I've got a new idea. That's what makes me happy.[26]

She insists that she dances to her own drummer. Writing poetry is about mixing oil and water. It is a form of storytelling. People from Appalachia, she explains, tell stories through song and folklore.[27] Mentors are not as important, she insists, as the capacity to develop self-confidence. She argues that she must be true to herself by carving an independent and interior identity that is both reflective and creative. She must be willing to be unconventional, take risks, and even fail. Only in that way can you make change, achieve new things, and do well in a society that often seems rigged against you. Artists lead by standing apart from society, she contends.

Giovanni's self-portrait is all about independence—independent thinker, independent identity. She tells a story about her given name, Yolanda, and the name she preferred—Nikki.

Ms. Peersaw, her third-grade teacher, insisted on scratching out the name "Nikki" on her papers and replacing it with "Yolanda." But, Giovanni would not allow "what was written on a piece of paper [to] become who you are."[28] She continued that fight with her teacher. She would be herself. This struggle for identity—for self-integrity—seems partially inborn, driven by a deeply felt need to be the person she saw herself to be. That struggle for identity is evident in her poetry as well.

But her ability to take that stand is also facilitated by those around her. She acclaims the strong women in her midst who encouraged her to take risks, even if those risks meant failure. More important than failure was the courage to think outside the box. What was not acceptable was to let others silence you. What was not acceptable was to be intimidated.[29]

One of the strongest women was her grandmother. Nikki Giovanni tells us that she moved in with her grandparents in order to be able to attend an all-black school in Knoxville, Tennessee, rather than the semi-integrated schools of Ohio. She credits that move with the opportunity to really know her grandmother, whose lessons translated into lifelong values. One story she chooses to tell clearly demonstrates how a private detail becomes a public action, rife with political import. The story centers on her grandmother's church-going activities. On that fateful day in September 1963 when four young girls were killed in a massive explosion at the 16th Street Baptist Church in Birmingham, Alabama, Nikki's grandmother went to a meeting at church. Those present proposed a march in Knoxville to protest the bombing. Her grandmother, deciding she was too old to march, volunteered her granddaughter. And Nikki knew she had to come up with the courage to participate, because her grandmother was more "formidable" than the action she was about to take.[30]

This particular story connects the individual and the community, the personal and the political, the past and the present, the present and the future. Giovanni's story is about relationships with elders. She came from a generation in which one did not say "no" to one's grandparents. That is one part of her teaching—the need for intergenerational respect. Through that relationship with a very strong woman, she was forced to take a personal stand, which taught her about standing up to oppression. She shows us how the personal becomes political. She also teaches us through this story about taking chances and being willing to fail. Progress cannot be made in society without that willingness to falter. Her story is part of a larger discourse on leadership and political action and change, tying the past to the present and future. Through this personal action of telling a story, we can see how narrative itself becomes political.

Mary Futrell, Vernon Jordan, and Nikki Giovanni construct a type of history that does not extract the personal from the public. In the telling of their stories, they allow us *inside* as they share their personal motivations and something of their psychic makeup. Neither a counterhistory nor a folk/myth history, they offer us a way to expand the historical record in ways that privilege the individual voice. Through their narratives, we see how they fashioned their self-identity and their leadership potential. These leaders provide rich vignettes on what it means to be black in America. In this way, they integrate the public and the private.

Grounded in History

History shapes identity in myriad ways. Recollections and memories of past time have enormous consequences for the future. When those historical memories relate to society's triumphs and traumas, as they often did in America's black communities, a particular event can become a defining moment. The decades of the 1950s and 1960s were rife with such moments. As Dr. Martin Luther King, Jr. said at the time of his arrest in Montgomery in 1955, "there comes a time when time itself is ready for change." He was making the claim that he was merely a vessel for historical change, and that the times created the movement.[31] Many interviewees for this project lived in just such times and were affected to their core.

For black Americans, the *Brown v. Board of Education* Supreme Court ruling and the events it unleashed hold iconic significance. Even if an individual was not yet alive or was too young to remember, she heard about the *Brown* decision in the course of familial or community conversation. Within the context of black history, historical events like the *Brown* decision become interrelated with the values of overcoming disrespect, isolation, invisibility, and ignorance. They are about creating positive self-identity against the odds. But they also reveal some of the very affirmative structures and historical memories within the black community that propelled people toward constructive and successful lives.

Henry Marsh, for example—the first black mayor of Richmond and a long-term member of the Virginia State Senate—was a college student when the decision was announced. As a child in Virginia, he walked five miles each way to a one-room school for black children, where a single teacher instructed 70 students, while whites travelled by bus to a large, modern school. He lived the effects of segregation, and saw firsthand the impact of unequal treatment. That inequality persisted in the job he had as a college student working in an ice-cream shop. White high school students scooped ice cream and chatted directly with customers, while Marsh washed dishes in a hot back room. "As I brought the glasses out they looked at me sort of funny and I said, 'What's wrong?' They didn't say anything." Marsh returned to the back room and turned on his radio. The US Supreme Court had reached its decision in the *Brown v. Board of Education* case. "'From now on race segregation in public education is illegal'. I knew why the young men were looking at me funny...when I heard that the decision was announced I knew that that was a change, and that in a little while [black] college students wouldn't be sweating over dishwashing machines while [white] high school students [were] making twice as much...scooping ice cream"[32] For Henry Marsh, the historical moment when the *Brown* decision was announced is forever linked in his mind with where he was, who else was present, the ways in which his opportunities were constrained, and the racism of segregation. But *Brown* also offered hope and opportunity. It meant that laws and values could change. For him, that past moment is linked to future possibilities, and his story demonstrates the connection.

For William H. Gray, Democratic congressman from Philadelphia, president and CEO of the United Negro College Fund, Baptist minister and lobbyist, the *Brown* decision was rendered when he was a 13-year-old boy. There had been much talk of the *Brown* decision as the case proceeded in his household. After all, he came from a multigenerational family of educators, and his parents knew all about educational opportunity, having served as presidents and deans of black colleges. So he understood that this was a momentous occasion. He articulates its meaning in prophetic terms:

> I remember being jubilant. I remember, you know, the feeling that, "Hey, a great thing has happened," you know, "we're on the way to the Promised Land; inevitably, things are moving in the right direction." There was a strong feeling that everything was possible now. There were just new possibilities for folk of color in this country, and for black folk.... I picked that up at thirteen, even though I didn't know what they were talking about sometimes. But the feeling definitely in Philadelphia was that "Hey, there are new possibilities, the horizon is unlimited, the Promised Land is just around the corner."[33]

From Philadelphia to Virginia, from family backgrounds of economic comfort to financial struggle, from those who were young schoolchildren to those already in college, the *Brown* decision is remembered as a transformative moment in the American moral saga for equality and justice. History and its possibilities were branded onto personal experience on that day and impacted the future in very concrete terms.

Participation in the civil rights movement created opportunities for future leaders to be part of a titanic historic struggle imbued with a sense of purpose that profoundly defined their self-identity.

Carol Moseley Braun, the country's first African American female in the US Senate (from Illinois) relates the power of marching with Dr. Martin Luther King, Jr. when she was a girl of 15:

> I remember it just as vividly as if it was yesterday because it was just that kind of a turning point and we marched and the rocks and the bottles started flying and the guy with whom I was marching was hit by a rock or a piece of glass or something and blood started coming down his face and, of course, I'm just horrified at this point, like, "Oh, my God." He just took his handkerchief out and put it up there and stopped it and then the catcalls were coming from the sides and I remember, you know, having, again, grown up in a...more or less Catholic family, the nuns who were marching in front of me were being called all kinds of horrible names and "When was the last time you slept with that black whatever, Sister?," you know, and so I was horrified....So we marched and got into the park itself and the violence was so horrible. I don't recollect gunshots, but I know it was rocks and bottles and bricks and glass. And so what they did was they put the women and children in the middle of the circle and then the activists around that, and then the hardcore activists were the outside perimeter. It got so bad, Dr. King was moved to the middle of the circle, and so he was as close to me as just right over there. I mean, literally touching distance almost and I remember, because you were supposed to cover your head up like this and we're down on the ground and covering up and he was standing there, and looking just as calm and sanguine in the face of all this and I remember, literally it was an epiphany for me because I was frankly ready to throw something back. I mean, that was my first reaction was "Okay, the next rock falls near me is going right back out there," but...what I came to understand to be the real message and the real power of non-violence which was that by standing there and by his example of peaceful resistance, by his example of claiming the moral high ground by his response, he had the victory, and that had he stooped, he would've been on the same level as the people against whom he was fighting. And so it was in that experience that I became committed really to non-violence and to his movement.[34]

Carol Moseley Braun
http://blackleadership.virginia.edu/02

Ultimately, there is profound power in Carol Moseley Braun's recollection. She sees herself as being permanently affected by her participation in the Chicago march. Instead of running in the other direction, her frightening and painful experience unleashed a lifetime commitment to a philosophy and to a set of behavioral principles. The Chicago march created for her a before and an after—and serves as an example of how the past defines her future.

Embedded in her story about marching with Dr. Martin Luther King, Jr., are many other aspects that relate to specific values that undergird Braun's life and help us to know her better. Her choice of these details tells us about her personal values. The disrespect shown to Catholic nuns marching for justice was etched into her consciousness that day. She would advocate for respect for all religious and all racial groups. The ability of King to show physical courage in the face of violence was so impressive that it inspired her commitment to nonviolence. Those details of a moment in time have stayed with her and continue to kindle her leadership.

For John Lewis, the critical historical markers that defined his life journey came from putting himself in harm's way during the 1960s—particularly with the Freedom Rides and the march from Selma to Montgomery. "The '60s," he says, "changed my life forever and gave me a sense of direction, a sense of purpose, gave me something to hold onto, something to believe in." Those historical moments defined his life commitment to nonviolence and the support of Beloved Community.[35]

There were also times where loss and tragedy created historical markers. Elaine Jones, for example, who served first as director-counsel and later president of the NAACP Legal Defense Fund, reflects on the potent silence of her fellow students, the largely white male population of the University of Virginia Law School, when King was assassinated:

> I came to school that day—no one said a word. Not a student, not a professor, no one said one word. Nothing! And at the end of the day I went to Jimmy, who was the other black person in my class, and I said, "Jimmy...," I said, "Do they know? Do they know?"...Of course, they knew. Of course they knew. But in many of their minds, King was a rabble rouser. And they didn't say it, but their thinking was, you know, he asked for it.[36]

Jones was rendered invisible that day, and one can hear in her recounting the pain of "otherness" of a young law student who had bravely been the first African American woman to integrate the class. Clearly, it was a reaction she would never forget, and a set of realities in the American race paradigm she would work to overcome.

Interviewees retain strong memories of working hand in hand with powerful black and white individuals committed to racial justice. Their lives have been defined by the history they share. Bobby Rush, now US congressman from Illinois, personally visited the scene of Fred Hampton's assassination in December of 1969—an event he says is "etched in my spirit and in my mind."[37] Earl Graves talks about working with Robert Kennedy, casually mentions conversations they had, and relates details about the aura of almost superhuman productivity that surrounded Kennedy. Amiri Baraka conjures up a powerful and lost moment in time when he took courses with Sterling Brown, remembering when the man himself invited Baraka and his classmates to his home to play Bessie Smith and Duke Ellington records and introduce them to their musical heritage. Through such moments, when interviewees place themselves in historic time and talk about the intersection of their lives with other well-known principal actors, they reveal the sources of their personal inspiration. But because these individuals are known within a more public history, they also establish a direct link between the past and the future.

The oral autobiographical tradition continues to be an important means for exhorting people to action and service and for inculcating a new generation of actors. Many leaders want to tell their stories because they understand the need to educate the next generation. Charles Ogletree refers to the fact that the tremendous sacrifices of many African Americans have yet to be documented in any serious way.[38] For him, hearing the stories about his grandparents' lives—many of them painful—created a context for his own life. He insists that "the painful history is an oral history that we need to appreciate so that I know that my grandparents and parents sacrificed so that I could be here. It makes clearer my responsibility to make considerably even more sacrifices for the next generation of children and grandchildren who will follow."[39] In these comments, he confirms how important the oral tradition is for creating values and identities for future generations that focus on constructive action.[40] He reminds us of the central role of personal ancestors in the African American tradition to establish cultural markers through the sharing of both personal and community stories. Past, present, and future are directly related to one another.

Black leaders often comment on the necessity of staying grounded in history, not just for the sake of education, but for the purpose of preserving its lessons and using them to inspire future generations of leaders to action. In all of these cases, the interviewees actively seek to mediate between the past and the future, not only describing what they feel to be the importance of the historical tradition but embodying the continuum by telling their stories for future audiences. As Carol Moseley Braun puts it, without role models "none of my story would be possible."[41] It is that much more significant, then, that she tell her story, continuing the tradition in hopes of making new stories of new leaders possible in the future.

Tradition and Change

Leadership requires risk-taking and vision. Sometimes leaders choose to maintain the status quo and work within existing structures. Sometimes they must be willing to consider alternatives—to create new organizations, implement change, and challenge the system. Knowing when to hold on to trusted traditions and when to change is fundamental to success.

These interviewees reflect often on the relationship between tradition and change. Many of them have a deep understanding of the necessity for moving beyond the systems that worked for parents and grandparents. They understand that their worlds have changed—for the better—and that it is essential to find ways to honor and revere the traditions that sustained family and community while looking ahead. The societal barriers enforced upon their ancestors mandated race separation. Within that restricted system, black Americans were often able to create personal and communal stability, and to look out for one another across class boundaries. Although many of them felt nurtured in this segregated setting, advocating its continuance in any form would be a prescription for returning to societal darkness. For many African Americans, having lived in both worlds, there is a deeply emotional and personal response to the tradition/change continuum.

Many recognize the importance of intellectual traditions that prepared them to think critically. Through these educational foundations, people learn to position themselves within Western and non-Western discourses, and to draw from both. They look to leadership figures who represented specific values and extract meaning from both black and white models. Bobby Rush, for example, talks about how Huey Newton encouraged him to read Kant, Kierkegaard, Nietzsche, Stalin, and Mao. He also describes his own focus, as a child, on figures such as Kit Carson and Abraham Lincoln. He articulates his early sense of wanting to make something of himself in reference to these figures. Abraham Lincoln inspired him, both because he was a reader and because he fought for black people: "I remember the statue out there in the park, Lincoln Park there, of Abraham Lincoln and I used to sit there and wonder. But it was, you know, my curiosity, I really wanted to learn more about things and I wanted to be a part of something. I wanted my life to be a significant life, not an insignificant life."[42] Baraka, too, calls up figures both near and far when he discusses his grounding in a mix of Western European authors, American and African American authors, and others.[43] Robert Franklin traces his own intellectual grounding from Martin Luther King and Malcolm X back through Plato.[44]

Intellectual moorings can come from multiple sources. They provide the philosophical foundations for thinking about social and political structures and values.

In addition to the intellectual forebears, there are "ancestors." The connection has a much stronger emotional claim. Ancestors can pull you far into the distant past. They speak to us in an evocative, metaphysical way. They tear at our soul. They motivate us to hold on to a heritage while also demanding that society be responsive to it. They make us revere tradition while being passionate for change.

Benjamin Jealous, the youngest person ever to be executive director of the NAACP, refers to those ancestors when explaining why he chose his career path. His white father, alienated from his own family by virtue of his marriage to a black woman, regularly told his son stories about the American Revolution, the women's suffrage movement, and both the founding and burnings of the Unitarian Church—all issues in which family members had been directly involved. His maternal grandmother also shared stories—stories about slavery, Reconstruction, Jim Crow, and present-day realities. He grew up believing in the nobility of working to "help finish the American experiment and really create a pluralistic democracy that worked for everybody." It was stories of ancestors, however, that catapulted him forward:

> There was also, and especially in my grandmother's stories and my mom's kind of spirituality and some of the conversations with Bill Starr, a notion that we were surrounded at any given moment by our ancestors, that there was a indebtedness that wasn't simply whatever you chose, however you chose to perceive it, but that that were actually real spirits that were judging you. And that sense—sort of metaphysical sense—of sort of responsibility and possibility, that on the one hand you had to continue the work that generations had started and on the other hand, that great changes were possible, led me to a place where I really have considered no other path.[45]

Nikki Giovanni also "answer[s] to an ancestor."[46] She does so in a discussion about African American hip-hop music. "When I look at rap...or that hop-hop nation, I see a train, Julian, and the train goes all the way back to 1619 to those first people that stepped off that ship in Jamestown being traded for food and water from a Dutch man-of-war to the British."[47] In this moment, she creates a kind of ancestry of the arts that integrates the history of music with the history of the African American experience.[48] She ensures that her identity as a leader in the arts locates her in a historical and cultural tradition that makes it impossible to separate current popularity and influence from an idea of ancestry and tradition. In addition to the blood relatives that one is born with, both Giovanni and Jealous remind us that there is a cultural ancestry that shapes a person's current identity and role. By recognizing specific antecedents, one can enrich one's own sense of purpose and identity. They suggest that the understanding of ancestry is important to any leader.

People, too, can establish traditions for their own times, which in turn influence future leaders. Perhaps no figure is more important in this regard for the African American community than Dr. Martin Luther King, Jr. For so many, of course, Dr. King became the exemplar of the public leader, establishing the parameters on which future black leaders would be judged. His was a leadership tradition nurtured through the Church, using religious rhetoric to exhort people to action. He spoke in terms of salvation for a nation through a concept of "beloved community," which both blacks and whites needed to create together. He spoke of dreams for what America could become. He used language to inspire and to create expectations for a new era.

Black leaders recall the power of Martin Luther King, Jr. on their lives. Vernon Jordan reflects on his determination and pride in giving the Emancipation Day Speech in Atlanta that King gave in 1955 at the Big Bethel AME Church. He remembers the earlier conversation he had with his father: "I said to my father, to his great disbelief—I mean, he just looked at me like I was crazy. I said, 'Daddy, you know what? I'm going to make that speech one day.' And in 1965, I was fortunate enough to be true to my promise to my father." For Jordan, the opportunity to give that speech was an important marker on his path to leadership—"a kind of affirmation, a confirmation process for me that I was on the leadership track," as he put it.[49] Dr. King used the language of scripture to inspire moral action and to create a more humane society, and he was especially gifted in his power of speech. Jordan understood that King was the exemplar against which he would be measured. Reaching for that standard was a test of future leadership potential.

Traditions are cultivated. Traditions are taught. They are nurtured privately at home. They are promoted through public discourse. Those traditional values often provided the anchors for black leaders.

Commitment to service is a persistent value that pulsates through African American society. It sustains communal life, nurtures kinship, and builds group identities. The teaching about service that is passed on by ancestors links the generations to a common tradition. Nikki Giovanni credits her grandmother, Emma Lou Watson, with instilling the value of giving back to the community:

> right after church you came home, changed your good clothes. Then you delivered dinners to the sick and shut-in. And that's what you do....I mean we were not going to be hungry, right? So there was no reason in Grandmother's mind since we weren't going to starve, there's no reason to be hungry, right? So before you sit down to eat you go and do your jobs. So even right now...I know that's Grandmother.

Service to others, she recalls, was just what you did on Sunday, after church, before you sat down to your own meal.[50]

While black leaders revere tradition and honor service, they embrace change. They came of age knowing they had to push beyond their comfort zones. Their times demanded it. As Elaine Jones declared, "Don't do it because it has been done that way. Find a different way to do it."[51] Johnnetta Cole similarly knew she had to break away from stifling intellectual traditions.[52] Passing on the specific history of "tradition and challenge" from generation to generation, Cole asserted, is the responsibility of black leaders.[53] Robert Franklin exhorts people to continue "crossing boundaries and negotiating difference and otherness."[54] Even as he does so, however, he grounds himself in the historical tradition by suggesting that the commitment to ongoing engagement with change comes out of the legacy of Martin Luther King, Jr.

This framework for viewing tradition and change underscores that both elements of the process are vital. One must "be critical of the larger structure in which you live and break out of it," says Eleanor Holmes Norton.[55] The responsibility for continuing the struggle never ends, she cautions: "you have to keep re-thinking. If you think of yourself as I think people in my generation thought of themselves as change-makers, then you can't just stop making change because you made some change when you were twenty-two. If you're a change-maker, you've got to be self-critical of the change you made."[56] To be a leader means you must assess, act, and adapt to the needs of the times.

Norton insists that leaders are not born to their roles but must find their way to become change makers.[57] Leaders must continually unearth new paradigms. Elaine Jones provocatively reminds us that we can't rely on old prototypes for leadership models:

> Martin is gone. We've seen Martin's characteristics. Martin's characteristics do not define leadership. Martin's characteristics define Martin's strengths and what Martin brought to the leadership table. But just like Martin brought his characteristics, you know, Jane Doe out there can bring her characteristics, and so we have to define them for ourselves and your characteristics depend on the time that you're in.[58]

Elaine Jones

http://blackleadership.virginia.edu/03

Jones invokes African American history here but does so only to insist on the acceptability, indeed the necessity, of looking outside the basic paradigm to open up the possibilities for the future. Furthermore, she frames her comments in terms of the African American tradition not only in naming one of its greatest icons but in using an oral pattern of repetition that draws on the tradition of

African American oratory. She does all of this, however, only to insist on the importance of being open to change and facilitating that change when possible.

*   *   *

Black leaders must forge strong identities in order to position themselves for leadership. Through the selective stories black leaders tell, we can see how they formed a positive sense of selfhood. We see how personal values emerge from formative moments, as interviewees with public stature share their private memories. We see how they regularly filter their memories through historical and social frames.[59] In so doing, they break down the hierarchies between documentary and oral evidence, deepening our knowledge of history in the twentieth and twenty-first centuries.[60] And, finally, we see how they negotiate the importance of maintaining tradition while advocating change.

Some will understandably ask: Where do these abilities come from? How are people who have suffered the indignities of segregation, who have been subject to discrimination by the larger society, and who often experienced economic hardship able to approach life with such an affirmative attitude? What formative experiences do individuals recall that allow them to develop such strong senses of self? What values do these eminent individuals—as a collective group—share? What prepared them for leadership? How do these black Americans speak *both* to their internal communities and to American society as a whole? What meaning can we derive for the cultivation of future leaders? The common elements across time and space that have been fundamental to a century of leaders are explored in the chapters that follow.

> *autobiography becomes a reflection of the realities of the lives of millions of African Americans: the realities of their oppression; the realities of their journey toward liberation and self-determination.*[61]—Johnnetta Cole

CHAPTER 2

Families: Extended and Fictive Kin, Racial Socialization, Diligence

When I see what has happened to children today, the importance of family to the survival of black people over the centuries and decades becomes more—becomes clearer to me than ever. When you consider that African Americans had nothing but their family and their church—the government not only didn't care about them but was working against them—and you see what's happened to so many black children today, then you have special appreciation for your own family.[1] —Eleanor Holmes Norton

Eleanor Holmes Norton, in talking about her family, remembers that the back door and backyards of her grandmother and her aunt faced the backyard of her parents' home, allowing her to run back and forth all the time. She was able to know her grandmother and her cousins intimately, living in an extended network of family members. She credits her grandmother, especially, with setting a standard—and doing so in a way that reflected wisdom. Returning from the errand that sent her to a local store to buy lamb chops when she was a mere seven years old, her grandmother said:

> "Eleanor, tell me about how you got him to give you these chops." This was when the Safeway had an actual butcher behind the counter. And I said, "Well, he asked me which did I want, and I said, 'I don't want that one, I want this one and this one.'"... In the summer and spring after school I would often sit with my grandmother on the front porch and there were some orange and green chairs, rocking chairs, and we'd rock and everybody goes by, [she] knows everybody, and you pass the news of the day. And the news of the day for days running was, "Let me tell you what this child did today. Well, I sent her to the Safeway and the man—she'd never been before—this was her first time. And when it came to

choosing lamb chops and you know how difficult that is to do," she would say, "This is what the child said—" Now, here I am sitting there rocking with grandmother, looking at her, listening to her brag on me that way. . . . She told other people about it. And somehow that said to me, "Well, my goodness, that's a standard." I think it said to me that is a standard I must try to meet more often.[2]

Eleanor Holmes Norton
http://blackleadership.virginia.edu/04

Holmes's story tells us a lot about black families and the strategies they developed for nurturing children. In this chapter, four leaders who come from very different kinds of family structures credit their families or specific family members for their own successes. As they reach back to their own memories of growing up, they remember the values they were taught and the support they received. They recognize the personal strengths that evolved from family relationships. They talk about support systems and the powerful internalized messages delivered by family members and others that helped them endure the implications of racism in America in the late twentieth century. Their memories and their stories are invaluable for fully understanding the African American experience in both sociological and historical terms. Their experiences corroborate some of the existing literature on ways in which ethnic subsocieties develop adaptive measures to both survive and excel.[3]

In many ways, their stories are inconsistent with the bulk of sociological, psychological, and historical research that focuses on the decline and failures of the black family in America.[4] In fact, some of the personal stories shared reveal family patterns that today would be considered dysfunctional. What was it, then, that these individuals point to as being so critical to their upbringing? What was so different within their own experiences from the vast literature today that suggests that black families are in deep trouble?

The family experiences of Amiri Baraka, Carol Moseley Braun, Yvonne Scruggs Leftwich, and Clarence Thomas form the centerpiece for this analysis of black family life. The reflections of numerous others supplement those of these central figures.[5] On the surface, the four primary figures could not be more different in terms of careers chosen, family structures, economic comfort, regional limitations, and sociopolitical values. Yet that is precisely the point for selecting them. For beneath the apparent differences, they remark on aspects of their family teachings that may well be more important.

All credit their families first and foremost for providing the ground beneath their feet. They recognize the ways they benefitted from a combination of love, support, discipline, toughness, understanding, and high expectations. These are the values that all healthy families support. But focusing on such aspects of family life would not highlight the most salient lessons that emerged from a collective analysis of stories shared.

These leaders' recollections reveal specific structures and values transmitted by black families; they point to the central importance of extended and fictive kin, racial socialization, and diligence. Understanding these structures and messages helps combat the racial paradigms that black families live with and reveals that characteristics often viewed as aberrant do, in fact, buttress sound and effective child-rearing practices. They implicitly contest the claims that a nuclear family structure is critical, strong women ruin strong men, black families are unsupportive of upward mobility, and black families are a racially essential "other."

The stories gathered here do *not* suggest that black families are broken; rather, they reveal how certain black family traits can be employed as exemplars for all families. They teach all of us important lessons.

The Leaders

The four leaders chosen as the primary focus of this chapter mirror the diversity that exists among African Americans.

The late Amiri Baraka (nee LeRoi Jones) was a prize-winning author, founder of the Black Arts movement during the 1960s, and poet laureate of New Jersey during 2002–2003. His writings include poetry, drama, music criticism, and fictional and nonfictional essays, all of which address black liberation and white racism. He embraced black nationalism, and then Marxism, convinced that the class struggle still reinforced white oppression. He received the PEN Open Book Award for *Tales of the Out and Gone* and an Obie award for *The Dutchman* and was inducted into the American Academy of Arts and Letters. He taught at Yale, George Washington University, the State University of New York at Buffalo, and the State University of New York at Stony Brook, from which he retired as an emeritus professor.

Clarence Thomas's career path is in public service and law. Positions as assistant attorney general of Missouri preceded his appointment by President Ronald Reagan as assistant secretary for education in the Office of Civil Rights, and then chairman of the Equal Employment Opportunity Commission. In 1991, President George H. W. Bush nominated him to the United States Supreme Court. At the time of his swearing in, he was the youngest person to be named to the Supreme Court and the second African American, following Thurgood Marshall. He has been a critic of affirmative action and all racial preferences, and is a strong conservative.

Carol Moseley Braun was a prosecutor in the US Attorney's office, a representative to the Illinois Congress, and the fourth African American and only black woman elected to the US Senate. President Bill Clinton appointed her ambassador to New Zealand and Samoa. She runs her own law firm and manages an organic, fair trade food company called Ambassador Organics. Her legislative career promoted education and environmental causes and the rights of women and minorities. On social issues, she strongly articulates progressive positions, while being more centrist on economic ones.

Yvonne Scruggs-Leftwich was deputy mayor of Philadelphia, the housing commissioner for New York State, deputy assistant secretary of Housing and Urban Development (HUD), a consulting vice-president in municipal finance, a professor at the National Labor College, and for ten years the executive director and COO of the Black Leadership Forum—a coalition of black civil rights and social organizations. She has been a creative voice on issues of leadership and urban politics. Her *Sound Bites of Protest,* published in 2008, illuminates the triple marginalization of women on the basis of race, gender, and class.

All four have family structures and formative race experiences that differ markedly from one another. Amiri Baraka grew up in a middle class family with both of his parents present. Clarence Thomas's father abandoned him at age two, and when he was six, his mother sent him and his brother to live with her parents. Carol Moseley Braun lived with both of her parents until their divorce when she was a teenager; subsequently, she resided with her grandmother. Yvonne Scruggs-Leftwich grew up in a middle class family with lots of attention from her parents, grandparents, and godparents.

All four experienced different levels of segregation. Baraka and Scruggs-Leftwich grew up in New Jersey and northern New York, respectively, and went to integrated schools. Thomas was born in the segregated South, attended a predominantly black primary school but a mostly white high school. Braun grew up in Chicago and attended mostly integrated public and parochial schools.

All developed stable and meaningful lives, emerging as successful leaders in their chosen careers.

Extended and Fictive Kin

Black leaders emphasize the critical influence of extended and fictive kin. Extended and fictive kin refer to those people beyond the members of the nuclear unit who participate in the daily life of a family. A nuclear family unit refers to a two-parent household and their children. Extended kin, then, would include grandparents, aunts, uncles, and distant relatives. Fictive kin refers to individuals who are treated like family members and are given familial names but have no biological or marital tie to the family unit, hence "fictive"; these people are often neighbors or close friends.[6]

Calling attention to extended and fictive kin networks reinforces the large body of literature frequently noted in black family research. Some scholars argue that reliance on a wide network of support beyond that of biological parents is rooted in African tribal family orientations in which elders (grand-parents) are integrated into daily life and form deep, personal relationships based on blood ties.[7] Others highlight the role of extended and fictive kin dur-ing plantation slavery, resulting from the inability of black families to remain together when some were sold to other masters. Some enslaved blacks, for example, developed strong ties with others on their plantation—either more distant relations or unrelated individuals who took on familial-like roles.[8] Research on modern black families often demonstrates the continued presence of extended and fictive kin who frequently help provide members with needed economic and social support such as money, food, childcare, and emotional support.[9] Even when controlling for socioeconomic status, extended living arrangements are twice as likely to occur in black households as in white.[10]

This should not be viewed as a reflection of dysfunction. Amiri Baraka, Clarence Thomas, Carol Moseley Braun, and Yvonne Scruggs-Leftwich offer numerous examples of the ways in which extended and/or fictive kin expanded their support systems, and functioned as teachers or role models.

For Amiri Baraka, in addition to his parents, it was grandparents and great-grandparent relationships that nurtured his sense of possibility. In his autobiog-raphy, he writes about the multiple times the family moved, the frequent changes in his father's jobs prior to his securing a position at the US Post Office, and the constant motion and misty confusion of his early years. How does a child make sense of moving four times before the age of six, the challenges of combining his father's lower-middle-class background with his mother's black bourgeois roots, the childhood play groups that became more race conscious with age, and the multiple race-based school experiences?

In Newark, his grandparents were omnipresent. For part of the time, when the family lived on Dey Street, the Russes (his mother's family) and Joneses (his father's) all lived together. When his mother and father both secured war-related jobs in the 1940s, his grandmother raised him and his sister "almost exclusively." It was she who taught him "practice makes perfect." She was his "heart and soul." It was her spirit that he claims "is always with us as part of our own personality (I hope)." "It never occurred to me that my grandmother (my mother's mother, *Nana*) could be anywhere or do anything but what I depended on for my under-standing of life and reality."[11] His grandfather, Tom Russ, also exerted a power-ful influence. For many years, he held a patronage job in an election warehouse in reward for his commitments to black Republican politics. He also served as president of the Sunday school and a trustee at Bethany Baptist Church. Tom Russ was "a name to conjure with" and was the "stabilizing center" of the house-hold.[12] His community presence had a strong impact on his young grandson: "I was used to seeing my own people, you know, in public kinds of situations. So I thought it was normal."[13] His grandfather also was a victim of racism, both in Alabama where his grocery store was burned by arsonists and later in Newark.[14]

While returning the short distance from his job as night watchman in the elections warehouse, he got hurt on his way home; he ended up silent and paralyzed. Baraka never quite believed the relatively benign story shared about the accident, and his grandfather's experiences clearly influenced Baraka's views about injustice and oppression.[15] For him, an extended family setting seemed normal: "I had the sense of a Jones-Russ life/universe that was an extension of everybody's. All the bloods mostly," he writes. It was a world that provided his basic foundation:

> The Jones-Russ orange-ish brown house was one *secure* reality and the scrambling moving changing colors and smells and sounds and emotions world at my eye and fingertips was something connected but something else. I knew that many of the kids I ran with did not have the same bulk of bodies and history and words and *articulation* to deal with what kept coming up every morning when I'd rise. There was a security to my home life....A security that let me know that all, finally, was well. That I'd be all right, if I could just survive the crazy shit I thought up to do. And the wild shit some wildass people thought up to drop on you.[16]

In addition to his parents, sister, and grandparents, there was an uncle named G.L. who also lived with the family. He earned his living as a Pullman porter—and therefore came and went, was the "exotic" personality in the house, and introduced Baraka to quality restaurants in downtown Newark, helping him feel "slick and knowledgeable."[17]

His parents were also there for him. They were part of a circle of educated friends, with an optimistic sense of possibility. His father knew Effa Manley, the woman owner of the black pro team Newark Eagles. He remembers fondly the outings with his father to Ruppert Stadium where "our baseball team" played. He remembers the pride of being with his father, the excitement of being in a place where black men played baseball, but even more importantly where a deep *political* message was transmitted that carried forward for the rest of his life.[18] And the ballet and piano teacher, from whom he and his sister took lessons, was a friend of his mother's. From his mother, he was exposed to "every kind of lesson you can imagine." In retrospect, Baraka understands that "she was emphasizing the arts for us. You know, we were going to be artists one way or another."[19] But it is clear that without the extended family, little of this would have been possible.

He learned about storytelling from his great-grandmother and his grandmother when he spent time with them in extended kin relationships. Baraka nostalgically remembers the magic of these moments:

> We used to sit out in the—in Hartsville, South Carolina, population of about three—and it would be getting late. The sun would

be going down, and it'd be my sister, myself and then my two first cousins...we would sit out on the porch, all four of us, and our great-grandmother...she'd be telling us all kinds of stories usually from the *Arabian Nights*. She loved the *Arabian Nights*.... [S]he would tell these stories and, man, they were fascinating. But what was *really* fascinating was that she could tell them like that...My other grandmother—my grandmother in Newark, she would tell you the tales coming out of the South, while the one in the South was telling me stories about, you know, Ali Baba and the Forty Thieves and, you know, the genie coming out of the lamp and stuff like that. I was—I think I've always loved stuff like that, you know, slightly science fiction.[20]

Baraka's world—both in terms of his basic sense of security and belonging and in terms of his fascination with language—was nurtured by his extended kin. His great-grandmother, grandparents, uncle, and cousins, in addition to his parents and sister, wrapped him in security. They taught him about loving relationships, modeled possibilities, and offered examples of a supportive family; they inspired his imagination.

For Rev. Calvin Butts, it was his Uncle Leon, the union organizer, and his Uncle James, the Mason, who educated him about powerful leaders in the world; even more important is that they imparted the sense that "they cared about you."[21] For John Lewis, it was his Uncle Otis, his mother's youngest brother, who came to live with the family when his own mother died, and who "more than anyone else said you've got to go to college, you've got to get an education."[22] For Diane Watson, the congresswoman from California, her great-aunt Pauline Slater who was the first African American teacher in the Los Angeles Unified School District inspired her to want to be a teacher.[23] Charles Rangel, congressman from New York, reflects that he "didn't know any blacks folks that had succeeded" and that "poverty was the motivating factor" in his life. Yet, on reflection, it was his grandfather, the elevator operator, that he most wanted to impress when he decided to study law after returning from the military.[24] Nikki Giovanni, the poet, was influenced strongly by her grandmother, Emma Louvenia Watson, who taught her about "giving back" and responsibility to others.[25] Over and over again, black leaders credit the role of extended kin in teaching values, modeling behaviors and possibilities, and embracing them with love and support.

Clarence Thomas also credits the role of grandparents as fundamental. He grew up in vastly different circumstances from those of Amiri Baraka, both because he lived in rural Georgia during segregation and because his biological father who "sired" him was absent from his life. Born in 1948 in impoverished Pinpoint, Georgia, he was the middle child of three. Until he was six, he lived in a "shanty" with an outhouse and no electricity in a house that his mother, Leola, shared with his great-aunt Annie. Rural poverty seemed "idyllic" compared to the "hell" of Savannah, when he and his brother moved to a one-room tenement apartment after "Sister Annie's" house burned down. "Overnight I moved from the comparative safety and cleanliness of rural poverty to the foulest kind of urban squalor," Thomas writes in his autobiography. His brother shared a bed with his mother, and he slept in a chair. In 1955, the family moved to a two-bedroom apartment while his mother struggled to provide basic support. Her father lived nearby in a modest but meticulously kept home. That summer, without explanation, young Clarence and his brother Myers moved the few short blocks to the home of his grandparents, Christine and Myers Anderson. "[I]n all my life, I've never made a longer journey," Thomas writes.[26]

His grandfather taught him about self-discipline and self-control. He was the model of "how you can live as an independent black man in the segregated South." This is the man, Thomas says, who "dominated our lives" and who ruled with an "iron will." He was tough and unforgiving. He was Thomas's anchor, his role model, and the "greatest man" he has ever known.[27] Myers Anderson had no more than a third-grade education and was barely literate. But through hard work and grit, he developed a small family business delivering heating and cooling materials—first wood, then coal and ice, then fuel oil. He also owned several rental homes. His income was enough to provide for his family and to be dependent on no one but himself. Life became full of responsibility, discipline, chores, church on Sundays, and Catholic School during the week.[28]

Clarence Thomas's family experiences were defined through extended kin networks. Dire poverty virtually guaranteed that others would become involved in the care of children as a means of survival. In Pinpoint, Georgia, most of his schoolmates were relatives of one sort or another and he lived with his great-aunt and mother. From the age of seven on, his grandparents became his surrogate parents. Those two people, Thomas writes, "gave me what I needed to endure and, eventually to prosper. They are the glue that held together the disparate pieces of my life, and hold them together to this day."[29]

People beyond the family also played a substantial role. When asked about family and neighbors, Thomas fondly remembers the close-knit relationships among black families in his community. He speaks to a type of "community parenting," where other elders act as caretakers and disciplinarians so that even when the principal guardian is not around, the child still receives adult supervision and familial-like care.[30] In his case, it was neighbors who functioned as "fictive" kin:

What they do is they reinforce....[N]eighbors tended to reinforce what you were getting at home, what you were getting at school, what you were getting at your church, the positive things, what you got at the Carnegie Library in Savannah. It was all the same message. And so my cousin Hattie or Miss Mariah or Miss Beck, Miss Gertrude, Miss Gladys next door, it was all the same message... It was consistent. They were my neighbors and, you know, and in the South, of course, when anybody could tell you what to do. You know, anybody could tell you to go to the store to buy some snuff, some Honey Bee Snuff or whatever they wanted at the time, some Stanback or some Anacin that they took quite frequently.... I remember one day, I was on East Broad and Henry Street just down a few blocks from our house, and we were cautioned never to cross the street against the light. And, of course, I'm a kid, so we crossed against the light, you know, there was no traffic so we ran across, and out of the back window of the bus, you heard this voice—"I'm going to tell Teenie on you." That was the worst voice ever to hear. That was Miss Gertrude. And before we got home—I don't know how she got the message to my grandmother—but before we got home, she'd informed her that we'd crossed the street against the light whereupon we were informed that "Your granddaddy will deal with you when he comes home"...And that's the worst threat you could ever have.[31]

Clarence Thomas

http://blackleadership.virginia.edu/05

Miss Mariah or Miss Gladys, although of no biological relation, felt a duty to look after Thomas and to recommend disciplinarian action to his grandparents. Likewise, Thomas was taught to treat these other adults with a familial respect, which makes the fictive kin network a positive functioning force in his life.[32]

In a similar vein, Yvonne Scruggs-Leftwich credits her extended family with reinforcing the most fundamental values about educational expectations, hard work, and feminism. Hers was a household in which women were expected to excel. Both her parents were college-educated. Her grandfather, a physician, wrote the book *Women of Distinction*. Her father was a "staunch feminist," too. Her cousins led the way in educational achievements and became important role models, reinforcing the notion that she could reach for the stars.[33]

But in addition to her nuclear and extended family, she recognizes the fundamental role of godparents. In fact, she mentions these godparents in the same breath as her parents. Speaking of her "wonderful, wonderful childhood," she reflects:

I had two godparents who had no children but me...here's this little kid who has four parents. My godmother was a homemaker. My mother worked. My mother taught and worked and did different things. And my godmother took care of me when my mother, when my parents were at work. And she would take me down to Niagara Falls, down to the falls with the little picnic lunch and we would have lunch there. So, I had a childhood during which I was the center of adults' attention.[34]

She also recalls the ways in which people trusted one another in her community. After her nuclear family moved from Niagara Falls to Buffalo, New York, she remembers traveling by train to spend time with her godparents—people with whom she spent every school vacation and several weeks during the summer. Her father, who had been a Pullman porter, was part of an extended community, and virtually thought of other porters as family members.

I started traveling by myself when I was eight or nine years old....This is something I think that just recently is being discussed again a lot about the network of the African-American community. But it was clearly understood that I was to respect this man [the porter] as though he were my father when I was on the train. He was going to look after me, make sure nothing happened to me. He was going to make sure that I was turned over directly to the hands of my godparents. So there was little risk. And so I was able to travel and do this kind of thing on my own.[35]

Figure 2.1 The Scruggs Family in 1955. Yvonne Scruggs is second from the left, seated on couch. Privately owned by Licensor.

Scruggs-Leftwich is critically aware of this extended kin paradigm in black communities as she refers to networks of African American communities, where families are intertwined and rely on one another. Close ties in black communities were reinforced to better cope with systematic and institutional oppression, low economic status, exclusion from white society, and fear of white discrimination and violence. The extension of who counted as family resulted in a bigger, broader safety net for adults and children alike.[36]

Carol Moseley Braun's description of family patterns is probably less typical in black communities. Braun's childhood memories are of a conscious progressive movement toward integration. Her father was deeply involved in political campaigns. He challenged the "Daley Machine" of Chicago. He helped blacks get more jobs, and fought for union rights. Her family consciously reached out to other like-minded people to create a larger, broader family composition—a family where Braun could learn about other types of people and cultures within a circle of trust. Generally speaking, fictive kin in black families, particularly in the 1960s, were other black community members. Carol Moseley Braun's parents, however, formed an interracial family:

> We had kind of an unusual household because…we were surrounded by artists and musicians and so people from a lot of different walks of life, so we always had an integrated household, but there was always discussion of race relations and the kinds of developments in the larger community and so even as a small child, I was really acutely aware of the efforts of people to build an integrated society…there were black people and there were white people in my family, in what I considered to be family. There were Asians in my family, and so I kind of grew up in this multicultural milieu and didn't really see firsthand the problems.[37]

For Braun, her "family" network—composed of Asians, whites, and blacks—provided a context where she could learn from and identify with multiple types of people and learn about racial reconciliation rather than acute race discrimination. Such values and attitudes became central to her future political leanings, and no doubt helped her reach out to multiple communities when she became the first black female US senator.

Baraka, Thomas, Scruggs-Leftwich, and Braun obviously grew up differently, yet at the same time they were all supported by extended and fictive kin, who helped with childcare and socialization practices. Other interviewees also comment on the importance of fictive kin in their lives. Oliver Hill remembers Bradford and Leila Pentecost, an upper-middle class couple with whom his mother and stepfather shared a house. But when his stepfather's business failed and his mother took a job at the Homestead, young Oliver continued to live with the Pentecosts from the time he was eight until he was 15.[38] Lucius Theus, a major-general in the US Air Force, credits Mrs. Adams, a neighbor in the small town of Robbins (outside of Chicago), who insisted that he come in and eat with the other children in the family. As one of nine children from a broken, impoverished family, he appreciated the way that people would "work together... and look after each other."[39] Douglas Wilder similarly recalls that people in his community "would feed you, they would care for you, just as they would care for their own."[40] Josephine, the mother of Mary Futrell, took in the children of her deceased good friend and raised them, despite her single-mother status, and her own economic struggle.[41] Mary Betsch, mother of Johnnetta Cole, brought a student from Edward Waters College home who never left. Cole says she grew up with an "adopted" sister and other friends and relatives who lived with the family from time to time. "[I]n this way," Cole comments, "my parents gave me an experiential understanding of the varieties of Black families as well as what Black familyhood is like at its best."[42]

Extended and fictive kin often serve as childcare providers for parents who cannot always be present. This situation was particularly true for low-income black families. Unlike many white, middle class families where a mother could afford to be home or employ a nanny, most black families had two working parents or a single parent with more than one job; such employment situations necessitated another means of adult supervision for their children. Through community parenting, children were watched over, were less likely to get into trouble, and could rely on other people in times of need. These extended family members also act as mentors and role models, providing different types of learning environments, contexts, and opportunities.

The four leaders featured experienced diverse nuclear family patterns. They enthusiastically embrace the role of extended and fictive kin in their lives and show us how flexible family networks can be viable and positive. Fostering a large, caring "family" can be productive and helpful for children, for the nuclear family unit, and for society. Mary Futrell, former president of the National Education Association and retired dean of the George Washington University Graduate School of Education and Human Development, also recognizes her childhood reliance on neighbors as her single mother worked full time to avoid welfare. Futrell notes the intense gratitude for her childhood experience: "And I've often looked back and I've thought about the fact that if I had not had that kind of extended family from the community, where would I be today? I don't know where I would be today."[43]

Racial Socialization

A primary duty of parental figures is the socialization of children—the preparation for them to be productive citizens in a larger societal context. Through socialization, individuals acquire personal identities and learn the norms, customs, social skills, and ideologies of their society. Racial socialization refers to the developmental process by which children identify with an ethnic group and learn the multiple facets of their racial identity. In the main, parental socialization patterns in black families parallel those in the larger society. However, racial prejudice and discrimination must be addressed so that they do not negatively affect the realization of positive self and group identities.[44]

Racial socialization messages are tricky to navigate. Scholars point to at least three types: racial barrier, racial pride, and non–race-specific.[45] Racial barrier messages teach about discrimination and unequal treatment; in black families, messages include lessons about appropriate behavior around whites, social expectations that one must not violate, and the inevitable daily and institutional racism one has to endure and combat. These lessons were particularly important during times of *de jure* segregation when Jim Crow laws prevailed. An inappropriate glance, the place one walked on the street, and assumptions of acceptance or familiarity could lead one to be badly beaten or worse, killed.

Many African Americans growing up in the 1950s and 1960s remember the story of Emmett Till.

A naïve black 14-year-old from Chicago, Till went to Money, Mississippi to visit his uncle for the summer. While in a store run by a white couple, he made what was considered an inappropriate remark to the female storekeeper. Shortly thereafter, he was seized from his uncle's home, brutally beaten, shot, and thrown into the Tallahatchie River with a heavy cotton gin fan tied around his neck. When the case came to trial, the all-white jury acquitted the two defendants in just 67 minutes of deliberation. This shocking murder in 1955, along with so many other brutal incidents from the civil rights movement confirmed for parents the crucial need to teach their children how to coexist in a world of white social mores and white justice. Racial barrier messages were crucial lessons for survival.[46]

Racial pride messages offer the counterweight to racial barrier messages. It is often the case that in order to balance negative feelings of inferiority caused by racial barriers, black history, black culture, black values, and black communities are celebrated. Teaching that racial hierarchies and discrimination emanate from power relationships and ignorance and have no justification in scientific and social theory is an important component of racial pride messages. To reinforce this reality, black families encourage hard work and striving for upward mobility, thereby proving that blacks are capable of being intelligent, successful members of society. Racial pride messages include denouncing whites' mis-understandings, emphasizing a deep sense of racial dignity, and setting high work ethic standards.[47]

Raising black children in a white dominant society requires teaching about race and racism in order to prepare them to overcome possible barriers.

Such teachings must not, however, focus solely on the negative implications of race but must also affirm the shared positive cultural strengths of blacks. Racial barrier messages alone can correlate with a sense of defeat. Providing only racial pride messages might lead to an unrealistic sense of opportunity and therefore a lack of preparation for discrimination and institutional racial barriers. Therefore, by combining a mixture of messages as appropriate given the context of race relations in one's community, a child can develop racial pride while recognizing the realities of discrimination.[48] Such racial socialization was critical in the world of Jim Crow where the indignities people suffered based solely on the hue of their skin were constant and palpable. The messages continue to be important today, because we do not yet live in a race-neutral world.

The third type of racial socialization message, non–race specific, centers on the equality of all people regardless of race. Carol Moseley Braun's father promoted such a message, when he consciously introduced his daughter to multiple communities, teaching the values of multiculturalism. Her family further inculcated this message by embracing peoples of many different ethnic and racial backgrounds.

For the concept of equality to have a substantial impact, however, a society must endorse it through laws. The first significant legal recognition of race equality came with the *Brown vs. Board of Education* decision in 1954, asserting that "separate was not equal." But it was only with the Civil Rights Acts of 1964 and 1965 that *de jure* segregation was struck down. As black and white Americans interacted across racial lines in public places and as voting citizens, they began to break down the embedded historical race hierarchies. Yet, within the family, racial socialization continues to be important, because race prejudice and race discrimination lingers in multiple ways today.

Families of the primary leaders under discussion spent significant time helping them understand their black identities. They provided their progeny with the tools and lessons necessary to navigate a white-dominated world. In some cases, modeling behaviors transmitted messages. In other cases, they came through direct conversations or by implication, through actions taken.

The mother of Amiri Baraka, for example, taught him about racism by confronting it head on. "I used to see my mother go up against these racists all the time," he says. One day, as a young child, he accompanied his mother to a grocery store.

> I remember one time we were in this store, my mother … said, "Give me a pound of those nuts." And the woman said, "You mean the Nigger Toes?" And my mother said, "Those are Brazil nuts, lady" and threw the nuts down on the thing and grabbed my hand and walked out. So I could hear that and I saw—that's the way you're supposed to act toward

that. You know, you're supposed to treat them with contempt and defiance, you know. Several times I saw her dealing with people like that around a racial thing. So I figured from early— that that's the way you deal with that. You know, you don't let them get away with anything, you know, whatever the consequences. You know, you take it up. Oh, she took those nuts and threw em down at—rolling all over the counter. So I said, "Well, that's the way you're supposed to handle that."[49]

Amiri Baraka
http://blackleadership.virginia.edu/06

This interaction taught Baraka two important messages: one, do not respect and interact with those who disrespect you just because of the color of your skin; and two, have enough pride in yourself to combat ignorance. Racial socialization, as the black family scholar Wade Nobles writes, requires "unique child-rearing techniques found in African American families…geared to prepare children for a particular kind of existence in a hostile racist environment."[50]

Baraka also reflects specifically on the racial pride messages he was given. Baraka's parents and grandparents continually reinforced a self-love that was to grow in spite of racism. He says:

But even in the more or less passive way, I still had the feeling that we were going to be able to penetrate this kind of, you know, racism. 'Cause I had been told that by my parents, my grandparents all my life…That those people were fools and that no matter what was said, that we were beautiful, that we were intelligent and that we were going to win—my parents always believed that.[51]

The centrality of self-love and self-confidence is necessary when there is a societal context of hate and racism. Baraka's parents' and grandparents' capacity to instill self-esteem was essential for his survival in a hostile environment. Even today, researchers claim, receiving racial socialization messages from parents and caregivers results in better coping strategies for African American children.[52]

The messages Baraka received reinforced a strong sense of black pride. Those messages translated into a defiant stand against racism through a more racialized view of culture. Baraka led an artistic revolution, the Black Arts Movement, which at its height spurred thousands to engage politically in transformational black power politics. He spawned a cultural movement based on a language of opposition rather than a language of submission.[53]

Now considered one of the outstanding intellectuals of the late twentieth century and an internationally recognized black protest writer of his generation,

Figure 2.2 Amiri Baraka (center) at the entrance to Spirit House, Newark, with musicians and actors of the Black Arts Movement, 1966. Courtesy of Moorland-Spingarn Research Center, Howard University Archives.

none of his achievements would have been feasible without a strongly centered sense of self. Baraka credits his family with those very strong racial socialization messages that ultimately led to an inspirational black aesthetic establishing a cultural basis for black autonomy.

Earl Graves, founder and publisher of *Black Enterprise* magazine, also shares stories that teach us about racial barriers and racial pride. He learned about the satisfaction of entrepreneurship and independence from his West Indian father, who regularly intoned that one should "own and not rent." His father, who unfortunately died at the age of 48, made it clear to his sons that success and family pride went hand in hand. But it was his mother who provided the "moral compass" in his family and who stood up to racism within the community.[54] He candidly recounts a story that reveals his mother's contempt for community policies at the YMCA. A supervisor attempted to restrict the young Graves from using the swimming pool, saying "there's a Y set aside for the colored boys." His mother traveled to the YMCA and confronted the athletic director, telling him that he should expect severe consequences should he try to enforce racial segregation of the pool. Graves remembers:

> Not only did I get to swim from that point forward, but that Y became integrated because my mother explained to him what he could expect

and the wrath of God that was going to come down on him if her son and any other black boys, as he called them—or called us—were not allowed to swim. I mean, those are vivid memories. My mother—I remember her telling me that you don't have to let anyone talk down to you... but you have to be respectful of adults, but not talk down to you. She made us very race conscious.[55]

Graves learned at a young age from his mother how to handle discriminatory institutions. She taught him to have pride in himself and to actively pursue what he wanted to do—his interest in swimming did not need to be confined to swimming at the "black pool" but swimming at the best pool available. Confronting community racism directly could be empowering, as Earl Graves witnessed through his mother's behavior. Ms. Graves's racial socialization messages to her son and his father's business drive appear to have been long lasting: Earl Graves is now a top executive and authority on creating successful black businesses. His book, *How to Succeed in Business without Being White*, can be seen as a business oriented reiteration of parental racial socialization messages.

Clarence Thomas's grandfather came from a fundamentally different background than Earl Graves's father. But his fierce independence in the face of little opportunity for black men of his region and generation transmitted a message of racial pride to his grandsons. Thomas says "there're lots of things, lots of insults and slights and injustices and unfairness that just sort of nipped away at him, just pecked at him the entirety of his life, and yet he showed us how to deal with all of that and continue on in a positive and constructive way.... To hold himself erect and proud and to achieve and to accomplish in spite of it all, and to figure out a way to get his boys to do the same thing." In the rendering of this story, one can't help but hear both racial barrier and racial pride messages; it was the racial pride messages that cause Thomas to view his grandfather as "that great model for me."[56]

Other stories by Robert M. Franklin and William H. Gray provide palpable examples of the two sides of racial socialization messages: Franklin speaks to racial barriers and Gray to racial pride. Franklin, former president of both the Interdenominational Theological Center and Morehouse College, recalls how his mother taught him how to negotiate his blackness in a white world at a time when the tragic experiences of Emmett Till were "very much in the air."[57] He tells this story:

My mother, on the other hand, really was the sort of mediator in terms of racism in Chicago and America and would talk about it, would warn.... I reflect on the way in which she and my grandmother sort of socialized us to be survivors on the mean streets of Chicago, both in terms of neighborhoods we shouldn't enter and interracial settings in which there's a certain etiquette and behavior we should display. Not to call attention to ourselves. To be polite and well-mannered in dealing with police officers and so on. This is all very practical wisdom about how to sort of negotiate touchy situations.[58]

Franklin's mother taught him about certain barriers that he had to face and gave him explicit messages on how to handle the racial hierarchy. This story, in particular, illustrates the parental work of analysis, comprehension, and preparation required to teach children about race. Similarly, Bill Gray highlights how much work by parents is required to encourage self-esteem when racism is present. His parents were people of distinction—his father, the president of Florida Normal College (later Florida Memorial) and his mother a dean. They embodied the importance of education and success. Their son learned his lessons well, becoming president and executive director of the United Negro College Fund, serving as a member of the US Congress, and a senior minister in Philadelphia's Bright Hope Baptist Church. Yet, as a child, he experienced overt discrimination, which could have been crippling. Born in the South in 1941, he witnessed *de jure* segregation first hand. His family helped him deal with it in ways that empowered him despite the societal restrictions:

I came from a very strong family background where I was taught, even when I was living in the South and had to ride in the back of the bus, and had to drink from the colored water fountain, and couldn't go to, you know, a white school, that I was as good, if not better than they were. And I had that drummed into me. I mean, there was no psychological damage that often happens. I mean, I had parents and grandparents who did that.[59]

Vernon Jordan received a very similar message racial pride message from his mother. Mary Jordan insisted that her children think beyond the slights of segregation and not allow themselves to be limited by it. In taking the bus through Atlanta, for example, to go the Butler Street YMCA, Vernon had to get on the streetcar and sit in the back. If he needed a bathroom or wanted water, he would have to go to the "colored bathroom" or drink "colored water." But, he says, "I was also trained by my mother to go to the bathroom before I left home, to drink whatever water I wanted so that I'd not—did not have to confront the insult of inferiority or a statement about inferiority." In this way, Vernon "got through it." The lesson was clear to him: "But I also remember this, Julian—my mother telling me that 'despite the fact that you're sitting in the back, you're as good as anybody on that bus.'"[60]

Like Baraka, Graves, Gray, and Jordan, Yvonne Scruggs-Leftwich was told she was intelligent enough to accomplish anything she desired. Her parents and godparents pushed her to achieve despite racism and sexism:

I was encouraged to try to do things that I was interested in. I had the feeling that there wasn't anything that I wanted to do that I couldn't do. And so, while people say, "I owe it to my parents," I really do. I had wonderful role models who mentored me actively because they—my parents and my godparents were born in the South, and they were all living in Niagara Falls. And they recognized that I was in an environment different from the one in which they had grown up. And that I could be given the tools to be able to cope and manage that environment....

So I had all of this reinforcement from the role model from my mother, but my father also, who was a staunch feminist, and his father had been. My grandfather who was the physician wrote a book published in 1893 called *Women of Distinction*....I had all of this history of the rights and the possibilities of women and the fact that opportunities ought to be made available. When the opportunity came, you...ought to take advantage of it.[61]

Yvonne Scruggs Leftwich
http://blackleadership.virginia.edu/07

Her parents' struggle in the more racist environment of the South made it clear to Scruggs-Leftwich that she should take advantage of opportunities that living in the North provided. In a similar vein, her family experiences encouraged her to embrace a feminist ideology that women could be leaders. Having parents and grandparents as successful role models reinforced these messages, and while they acknowledged racism and sexism they also emphasized a work ethic and belief in possibilities. Through the comparison with her parents' experiences in the South, she received both racial barrier and racial pride messages. Scruggs-Leftwich defied the barriers to and stereotypes of blacks and women and incorporated the racial pride messages to become the first executive director of the Black Leadership Forum.

Carol Moseley Braun processed the complex racial socialization messages from parents and grandparents who had different approaches to life. She describes her parents as opposites. Her mother was the "firesides and slippers" type—a person who argued that "you grow where you're planted." It didn't matter, Braun recalls her mother saying, "whether you're a street sweeper or the president of the United States, you do the best job you can at what you're doing and be proud of your work, so she was very much a 'This is the job, this is the task, focus on not having ambitions, not seeing a world outside of the home and the family as being all that relevant.'" The importance was to develop self-pride and not have many expectations of the larger society. In many ways, her mother was trying to protect her from the world in which she might experience racial barriers and to surround her with the security of family and home. Her father, on the other hand, was a social activist who took his daughter to Catholic Mass on Sunday but also to "everything from Buddhist temples and the Hindus temples; the Bahai Temple, of course, there in Chicago; Jewish synagogues, the Muslims, the Moslems, the Zoroastrians." He was teaching her about the wider multicultural world and the equality of all belief systems. At the same time, he arranged for her to meet Chicago's first black female alderwoman, Anna Langford, and Illinois's first elected black woman judge. It was a way of saying that she could be anything she wanted and that the world was full of possibilities. Similarly, her two grandmothers delivered different messages. One lived a calm, structured life and became a source of "great refuge and nurturing and comfort and guidance." The other was "hell on wheels" and an ardent black nationalist.[62] Putting together all these different messages must have been challenging. Nonetheless, Carol Mosely Braun had the benefit of exposure to both racial barrier and racial pride messages that fostered her own ambitions. Is it any wonder that she became the country's first black woman elected to the US Senate?

Congresswoman Barbara Lee credits her family, and especially her mother, with strongly feminist racial socialization messages. To be a successful black woman, it was necessary both to learn traditional skills and to break out of

Figure 2.3 Carol Moseley Braun (far left) with other women Senators and Hillary Rodham Clinton, 1993. Courtesy: William J. Clinton Presidential Library.

traditional roles. Barbara Lee's mother birthed three daughters and had two sisters of her own, so thinking about women's roles was central to her household "[F]rom day one," Lee said, "my mother emphasized going into non-traditional roles."

> For example, she emphasized that I needed to study so I could go to college to be whatever I wanted to be, but she also emphasized the fact—and she made me take piano lessons and she made me go to sewing classes and she insisted I learn how to type. You know what, she said, "You're going to need to learn how to type so you could figure out how to get through college so you can get the kind of job that you went to college to get," and so she was always very clear on learning all of the skills that we needed to learn and that women needed to learn so they could move forward in their lives, but also she...made sure I was involved in sports. I played basketball. She made sure that I was a cheerleader and part of the drill team. So she made sure that we did everything as a child, so myself and my two sisters as girls could grow up to be the kind of independent women that she thought we should be in a male-dominated and in a racist society.[63]

Racial socialization messages remain necessary in a society where racism exists. Black parents and extended kin carry a double burden: they must teach children to believe in their own potential to succeed, but they must also help them navigate through a society stacked against them.[64] In essence, effective racial socialization requires knowledge of a hierarchical, yet potentially fluid racial order. Such a reality has been part of American society since its beginnings, and only recently have we begun to chip away at our embedded restrictive hierarchies. Black Americans have been forced to live with a "double consciousness," as W. E. B. Du Bois recognized as early as 1903, when he asserted that the problem of the twentieth century would be the problem of the color line:

> this sense of always looking at one's self through the eyes of others, of measuring one's soul by the tape of a world that looks on in amused contempt and pity. One ever feels his two-ness,—an American, a Negro; two souls, two thoughts, two unreconciled strivings; two warring ideals in one dark body, whose dogged strength alone keeps it from being torn asunder.[65]

The struggle that Du Bois eloquently identified continues to be the motivating force behind racial socialization messages. By listening to the recollections of prominent black artists, judges, educators, businessmen, and public servants, we can understand how such messages took hold and influenced leaders' potential success. Baraka, who found his voice in writing, and Thomas, who became a Supreme Court justice, both grew up understanding the pride and pain of being black in America. They absorbed different messages about the facets of racism and how to overcome it, which each applied to his leadership philosophy. And for female leaders like Scruggs-Leftwich and Braun, these messages also include a gender component through the acknowledgment of sexism in society. Of course, understanding racism and sexism does not automatically result in the ability to overcome its obstacles, but recognition is a first step to combating its nefarious effects. As long as racial inequality exists, racial socialization as a familial strategy is a viable means to help prepare children of color for success.

Diligence

Communicating racial pride and dignity, however, is not enough. Effective racial socialization included a subtext about hard work—about a work ethic that is required to prove oneself, to prove that skin color does not have to determine social and economic status. Clarence Thomas addresses this aspect of racial socialization. His grandfather modeled entrepreneurial independence by being self-employed, thereby maintaining his own sense of racial dignity and pride. He believed that racial equality could be furthered when blacks raised their own standards and seized opportunities without the aid of whites. His was a message of self-help; he despised the notion of reliance on employers or the government.

Clarence Thomas's grandfather was a hard taskmaster. He made Thomas work with him in the business from the time he was in fourth grade and made his two grandsons work throughout the summers on family land.[66] At the same time, he insisted that his grandson cultivate his mind and use his intelligence instead of his physical strength to persevere. The race lessons he learned from this fiercely self-sufficient small businessman focused on the imperative of striving, the need to grasp opportunity, and the obligation to prove yourself. Once African Americans were granted rights previously denied—like the right to an equal education or the right to use a previously segregated library—they had an "obligation to measure up," Myers Anderson believed. "Don't shame me, don't shame the race," his grandfather would say.[67] Getting ahead required both autonomy and education:

> He was a man who thought that, you know, when you talk of freedom, he talked of independence—that is, the ability to do for yourself, the ability to grow your food. And he was a very active member in the NAACP. We went to meetings. We went there to four o'clock meetings

on Sunday. He would take us along…because we had to learn. He thought that we should learn how to read so that we weren't like him where he had to work with his hands. He wanted us to learn how to work with our minds.[68]

It seems that racial pride trumped the racial barrier messages. These values are ones that Clarence Thomas applies in his approach to law as an associate justice of the Supreme Court. Although his understanding of how to overcome racism is fundamentally different from many other leaders, his rise to a leadership position in his field was fostered by positive racial socialization messages from his grandfather—messages that sustained him through many racially motivated challenges.

Geoffrey Canada, the director of the Harlem Children's Zone, likewise remembers the work ethic that came from his grandfather. Like Thomas, Geoffrey's father left when he was an infant, and his mother was raising four boys by herself. His grandfather, a man with only a fifth- or sixth-grade education, became his male role model. He earned his living by selling fruits and vegetables.

> He just made sure he always worked for his family and he taught me how to work, I mean, how to really work, and it didn't matter what we were doing, that we had to do it well. You had to deliver quality to people and you had to have, I think, the tenacity to get the job done, so I got my work ethic from my grandfather. Sometimes he picked me up, six o'clock in the morning, we'd go down to the lower part of Manhattan to get the fish. We'd sell fish all day, cutting them and cleaning them and everything else and, you know, come home that night, I'd get a dollar, I was thrilled, like a whole dollar, and after a while, when I first started working, people would say like, wow, you work long hours, aren't you tired? I said, no way, cutting fish all day on your feet traveling around, I mean, that's a tough job. You're smelly. It's, you know, fish all over everywhere. . . . I always had some kind of job that I was selling newspapers, walking dogs, and . . . no matter what the work was, I always loved the idea of working and providing and helping my family with the money so that work ethic I think I got from my grandfather.[69]

In black families focused on the success of their children, there was always the need to deal with the race prejudices of others and to teach the principle of self-worth. That is why Edna, Carol Moseley Braun's mother, constantly told her to "do the best job you can where you're planted." It meant she had to work harder than anyone else, and it became the motivating mantra for her vision of leadership. "For me, the philosophy is back to Edna's advice," she affirms. "[E]very day you have to find something that you can be proud of and that you want to celebrate, and that's what I strive to do every day."[70]

For many, diligence messages were tied to educational achievement. In a society in which low socioeconomic status for blacks was the norm, education was seen as a primary route toward upward mobility and a positive representation of the black community.[71] African American education was a collective process; families aided one another by nurturing learning, setting standards, and helping with class work.[72]

Vernon Jordan remembers clearly the diligence messages delivered by his parents when it was time for him to leave for college. He chose to attend De Pauw University in Greencastle, Indiana, and was excited by the possibility of moving outside his black network. His mother, who had taught him not to be confined by race, was nervous about what he would face, and thought he might be better off at Howard University. This did not dissuade him, however, and when it was time to leave him at De Pauw, his mother handed him $50, and whispered "God bless you, son," with tears in her eyes. His father, on the other hand, delivered the tough love:

> My father shakes my hand and says, "You can't come home." I said, "What do you mean?" He said, "You can't come home." I said, "What do you mean, Daddy?" He says, "The counselor says that you're reading less than 200 words a minute and your classmates are reading between six hundred, eight hundred a minute. Which means when you're reading history of civilization, they'll be in Chapter 6 and you'll be struggling to get out of the preface. But you can't come home." He said, "In 1951 you used a plane geometry book that had been used by a white student in 1935. But you can't come home." So I said, "What am I supposed to do, Daddy?" He said, "Read, boy. Read." That's all he said. And that's how he left me before I went into that assembly at East College where I was the only black in my class. "Read, boy. Read." And when I graduated four years [later], my brother came and shook my hand, my mother, tears in her eyes, gave me $100. My father just walks up to me, shakes my hand, and says, "You can come home now." Just—I've never forgotten that. And that was—I mean, I understood what I had to do.[73]

Vernon Jordan

http://blackleadership.virginia.edu/08

From his father, Vernon Jordan learned the importance of determination, hard work, and diligence to overcome the stereotypes of inferiority.

For Scruggs-Leftwich, whose extended family benefitted from educational achievement, there was no question about the educational standard that she should attain. She remarks:

> And my father said to me any number of times, "You're going to finish school. I'm not going to have you marrying and having to be subjected to treatment that you don't deserve. You will finish school." When he said "finish school" he didn't mean high school. He didn't mean college. He meant graduate school.[74]

Reaching high was an important part of diligence messages in the families of black leaders. Scruggs-Leftwich worked toward a college degree at a time when many prominent colleges did not accept blacks or women. Yet, her family told her she would attend graduate school. Her empowerment, her belief in her right to attain an advanced degree, began with the standards set in her home.

Calvin Butts remembers the central importance of primary school education and the emphasis placed on learning well. He went to a little one-room schoolhouse, where the teacher

> taught us how to spell, how to read, and how to write, and how to use numbers...and we didn't know any better but to learn and were frightened out of our minds if we didn't learn because when we got home, if we didn't do what we were supposed to do, they'd go get a switch.

Diligence in learning was a necessity, not a choice.[75]

Henry Marsh, state senator from Virginia, also credits people who early in his life encouraged him to get an education.[76] For a few years of his childhood Marsh lived in an extended kin family with his aunt and uncle in rural Virginia. He recalls: "They raised me. They were strict disciplinarians. They sent me to a one-room school five miles away. And literally, I actually walked to school everyday, five miles, which meant in the early morning we had to leave about six o'clock to get to school."[77] Later in Marsh's childhood, he lived with his father and stepmother; he depicts his father as an impressive role model:

> While we were in school my father went back to college. He had stopped college to marry my mother. And we were in school and he was in college, working twelve hours a day as a waiter in a restaurant, continuing his education until he got his degree. So he didn't have to tell us to study. We saw what he was doing.[78]

School was a route toward knowledge, upward mobility, and racial equality. The familial emphasis on education and the diligence required to attain it was the same despite the differences in socioeconomic circumstances. Black leaders come from homes where black parents insist on and model serious educational attainment.[79]

Black families emphasized education as more than just a cultural value. They stressed the importance of education as a purposeful strategy to help their children overcome oppression; they recognized that education would prove instrumental in raising up their black children from the lower status imposed upon them.[80] Valuing education promoted multiple results: close relationships between families, schools, and communities; increased effectiveness of schools; children's success; fewer barriers for racial minorities in higher education; and more opportunities for African Americans.

But cultural attainment was also important. Baraka's parents encouraged diligence by broadening their children's horizons in the arts and cultures of their communities. Baraka's mother, in particular, stressed the arts as an integral part of his and his sister's childhood. When asked about the influential role his parents played, Baraka emphasizes:

> My mother made me do...I've had every kind of lesson that you can imagine. I mean, from piano, you know, drum and art, drawing, all those kind of things....And my sister...took ballet lessons, tap dance lessons. My sister was the only black girl in Newark at the time you'd see ice skating. Nobody else could ice skate. She would be down in the middle of the town ice skating...But that is the result of my mother in the main insisting—you know, insisting on that.[81]

Extracurricular activities were serious endeavors. Being diligent about them inculcated discipline, and ultimately spawned a love of the arts.

Diligence—working hard at whatever you pursue—is a means to overcome racial barriers and inculcate racial pride. Diligence creates focus, requires self-discipline, and internalizes personal expectations and self-worth. It is an indispensable part of the racial socialization messages transmitted by black leaders' families.

Conclusion

Black leaders credit their families for providing vital support systems. They were nurtured, taught, disciplined, and loved by extended and fictive kin. They learned about racial barriers while also developing racial pride, so that the discrimination they faced daily did not erode their self-esteem. They also learned that diligence and education must be revered as the crucial vehicles for upward mobility and successful lives.

Understanding the strategies used by black leaders' families—both structural systems and voiced and unvoiced messages—helps to overcome the stereotypes reinforced through public media and academic literature about "the black family."

This scholarly literature has a lengthy history, extending back to at least the 1920s, when Robert E. Park developed the fields of urban sociology and human ecology, founding what became known as the Chicago School of Sociology. Park worked closely with the Tuskegee Institute before going to Chicago, and was deeply invested in better understanding African American culture. Park influenced E. Franklin Frazier; they both challenged racial theories of inadequacy. While Park directed his attention to urban conditions, Frazier focused greater attention on the black family. He argued that slavery largely destroyed black masculinity, causing family dysfunction and both socioeconomic and cultural deprivation as black families failed to adopt the white paradigm of a nuclear family.[82] Both emphasized the disorganization within black family life.[83] They focused on the female-centered household so prevalent in African American families, arguing that black families would be healthier when they adopted the white-dominant two parent patriarchal family model. In 1944, when Gunnar Myrdal published the comprehensive study commissioned by the Carnegie Corporation, *An American Dilemma: The Negro Problem and Modern Democracy,* he lauded Frazier's 1939 work, *The Negro Family in the United States.* The recent book "is such an excellent description and analysis of the American Negro family that it is practically necessary only to relate its conclusions....," he wrote.[84] Only with the publication in 1965 of Senator Daniel P. Moynihan's *The Negro Family: The Case for National Action* (widely known as the Moynihan Report) has Frazier come under greater scrutiny and attack for his approach and his findings.[85] Moynihan described black families as deviant, perpetuating a "cycle of poverty and deprivation. At the "center of the tangle of pathology is the weakness of the family structure," he claimed.[86]

Black activists and scholars reacted strongly against these arguments, giving rise to a revisionist literature that emphasized the significance of extended families, reverence for the elderly, and consanguineal family ties.[87] By the 1970s and 1980s, new approaches to exploring black family structure and norms emerged with the publication by William Julius Wilson of *The Declining Significance of Race* (1978) and *The Truly Disadvantaged* (1987), emphasizing the greater importance of class as an explanation for life patterns.[88] Black families were not functioning well because the decline of low-skill job opportunities in cities reduced the numbers of employed and marriageable black men. The problems were not embedded in African American family culture. Rather, they were a reflection of societal culture and its implications for class status.

Books published around 2000 and after explore upper/middle class black families, the continuing significance of race and racism, class oppression, and/or the inadequacy of welfare and other government programs.[89] Yet, despite this serious scholarship, concepts of the "underclass" or "cultures of poverty" or "female-headed households" or "welfare moms" dominate the public consciousness with impressions of major dysfunction across black families in America. There is little understanding of the complexities of family situations that can lead to both despair and hope.[90]

Eleanor Holmes Norton, congressional representative for the District of Columbia, understands the importance of addressing black family needs at a national policy level. "[T]here are millions of black children who can't take advantage of [opportunities of the civil rights movement] because they don't have the nurturing of families," she asserts:.

> By families, I mean families of any configuration. We haven't had nuclear families as the only family.... it was also the rule to have extended families, which do not thrive nearly as much in urban settings and those children are raising themselves very often. Getting into this issue is very different from getting into a better education or the rest of it, but all of that may depend upon whether we get into this issue of surrounding children, if not with nuclear families, at least with proxies for those families.[91]

More than 25 percent of children in the United States today under the age of 18 live with one parent. The vast majority of single parents—over 85 percent—are women, and poverty is widespread. In 2010, single-mother households accounted for 75 percent of the homeless population. The poverty rate for single mothers in the United States was the highest among the 16 high-income countries studied. Government data reveals that 38.2 percent of blacks under the age of 18 live at or below the poverty line compared to 17 percent of whites. Nonmarital birth data reveals that 72.1 percent of black children in 2010 were born outside of marriage, compared with 53 percent of Latinos and 29 percent of whites.[92] Rates have risen dramatically in the last half-century.[93] Historically, blacks have been disadvantaged with resulting implications for employment, health, family stability, education, and income.

Positive family traits do not always overcome difficult barriers posed by discrimination. They cannot be expected to operate for all people exclusive of other societal dynamics. Nonetheless, the positive adaptive strategies of black family life analyzed above—those of extended and fictive kin, racial socialization techniques, and an emphasis on diligence—provided a foundation for success for a group of diverse leaders, and continue to influence black families throughout the United States. Given the trends in single-parent household and the continuing debilitating effects of poverty, the teachings imparted by black leaders seem all the more salient today.

> *I believe that we all live in one house. We all live in one house. So if we all live in one house, we all are one family. The American House is a house at peace with itself, where we care for each other. We don't forget about each other.... It seems like we have been saying, "You know, too bad, you're poor, you're a minority, you're just left out and you're left behind." But in the real American House, in that true American House, no one is left out or left behind.*[94]—John Lewis

CHAPTER 3

Education: Caring Communities

BOND: *Have you any idea of how we as a whole society, how can we foster, create and nurture leaders for the future? What can we do we're not doing now?*

BRAUN: *Education, education, education, education.... The whole ideal of quality universal public education is... very much at risk now.*[1]—Carol Moseley Braun

For blacks in America, no single issue has greater salience than that of education. At the same time, no goal has been more fractious and recalcitrant than that of educational equality in America. In a country that prides itself on concepts of opportunity, uplift through education has proved particularly thorny. If you are a person of color and/or poor, the odds for inequality increase. Equal educational opportunity provided through government-funded schools is more a myth than a reality, and in the twenty-first century, the solutions seem increasingly intractable. Our public schools are still segregated and unequal, more than a half-century after *Brown v. Board of Education* declared this unconstitutional. We know that quality education is fundamental to success, but we seem unable to provide it as a basic societal good across race and class.

In this chapter, six leaders share personal experiences that speak to the power of education to create positive identities and future opportunities. Some recognize the material and economic deficits of their segregated schools and the sacrifices necessary to access educational opportunities. All recognize the inspirational power of teachers, the instilling of self-worth and self-confidence, the ethic of caring, and the challenges of creating fully integrated classrooms. All understand how positive identity is nurtured through education. In their own career choices, they mirror some of what stirred them to succeed. Through those choices, they offer something of a blueprint for the future, even as they recognize that *Brown v. Board of Education* ultimately changed the education dynamic and contemporary solutions must account for that change. Each one is a participant in educational enrichment and is passionately committed to teach the next generation.

The six exemplars, in order of birth, are William Raspberry, Johnnetta Cole, Mary Futrell, Freeman Hrabowski III, Geoffrey Canada, and Rita Dove.[2] They come from different regions of the country—from Florida to New York to California and places in between. They grew up in small communities and in major cities. In their formative years, their economic circumstances ranged from poverty to relative privilege. They are both men and women. Some had parents who were very well educated; others lived with parents denied the benefit of schooling. Their educational opportunities chart historical and regional patterns in America. Remarkably, however, they share a set of values and commitments to education that are very similar and that reflect their own most positive experiences.

The late William Raspberry (1935–2012) hailed from the tiny town of Okolona, Mississippi in the heart of the Cotton Belt. It was the kind of town in which there were "two of everything...one for whites and one for blacks."[3] Black children in Okolona could access public education only through the tenth grade. Okolona College, an Episcopal Church–run school, existed because of Jim Crow laws that provided unequal education. On its campus was a four-year high school and a two-year college, with an enrollment of about 200 students. Raspberry was born on that campus, and he recognized that he had the enormous benefit of a rich learning environment. Both his parents were teachers at the school: his mother taught English and his father taught carpentry and masonry. His parents "loved learning so much themselves, we absorbed that.... they were able to instill in us, first, a love of learning."[4] The school was a safe haven in many ways. It was also a place where he was exposed to more things than other rural children would experience, creating a greater degree of cultural awareness. "[It] finally dawned on me," he says, "that at least a good part of what was happening at that little school didn't have to do with brilliant teachers or great facilities or any of those things but with kind of a network of caring designed to protect us and bring us along and let us be what we could be."[5] It was a formula for success.

In 1952, Raspberry left Okolona to attend Indiana Central College (now University of Indianapolis). He lived with his sister, pursuing a preministerial curriculum and graduating with a B.S. in history in 1958. Along the way, there were some bumps in the road, and he took some time off from college to earn money and to find an academic focus. In 1956, he accepted a summer job at the *Indianapolis Recorder*, a black weekly, where he learned the ropes of journalism. This "J school" opened up the possibility of a career path. He was drafted into the US Army in 1960, serving as a public information officer in Washington, D.C. By 1962, as more opportunities opened up, he became a teletypist for the *Washington Post* and within a few months began writing articles.[6] Three years later he won the Capital Press Club's "Journalist of the Year" award for his coverage of the Los Angeles Watts riot. By 1977, he was a syndicated columnist appearing in more than 225 newspapers. When he retired, he was one of the best-read columnists in America. He called himself a "solutionist" rather than a liberal or moderate. Particularly concerned with solving problems related to race and to class, he both wanted to find ways to lift those in poverty into the middle class and to demand that black Americans take responsibility for their own actions. This philosophy lay behind his writing and his altruistic endeavors.[7] As a writer, he was also a public educator.

Johnnetta Betsch Cole (b. 1936) was born in Jacksonville, Florida, to a prominent and economically comfortable multigenerational family of leaders. Her maternal great-grandfather, Abraham Lincoln Lewis, was well known in Jacksonville, Florida, for creating the Afro-American Life Insurance Company and for developing a black country club with beachfront property—the only beach then open to African Americans in the region. He was the first black millionaire in Florida and contributed generously to black colleges. Through him, Cole became acquainted with one of her "sheroes," the nationally prominent educational leader Mary McLeod Bethune.[8] Cole's mother was a professor of English at Edward Waters College, and her father owned businesses in town. It was, as she calls it, "*the* African-American family in Jacksonville." She grew up, she writes, as "a member of an upper-middle-class Southern black family" with access to high culture and fine material possessions.[9]

But despite this stature, no black child could grow up without a consciousness of the "tenacity of racism. Because there was simply no amount of money that could buy us out of Jim Crow-ism in Jacksonville, Florida," she says.[10] Young Johnnetta remembers being called "nigger" when she was only three or four, and understanding the insult intended. She knew that many places were closed to her and that she had to wait for service in stores even when she had arrived first. She recalls her continuing anxieties about driving with her family at night, fearing that they might get a flat tire and be subject to the terrors of the Klan.[11] Her educational options were limited.

When it was time for college, she chose to attend Fisk, but transferred to Oberlin when her father died. Ultimately, she earned a Master's and Ph.D. at Northwestern University, working with the distinguished anthropologist and founder of African American Studies, Melville J. Herskovits. Her fieldwork took her to Liberia for two years.

Cole's entire career has focused on ways to make learners more culturally sensitive and sophisticated—whether as a professor, college administrator, or director of a major public museum. Beginning in 1962, she taught briefly at UCLA and Washington State University–Pullman while a trailing spouse. In 1970, she joined the W. E. B. Du Bois Department of Afro-American Studies at the University of Massachusetts at Amherst, and soon developed a deeper interest in women's studies. Thirteen years later, she left U-Mass for Hunter College.

By 1986, she was appointed president of Spelman College, the esteemed black women's college in Atlanta, which she led for ten years. Upon completing her very successful term, she became a Presidential Distinguished Professor at Emory University (1998–2001). Between 2002 and 2007, she stepped up to a second college presidency at Bennett College for Women, where she again led a successful fundraising campaign, established an art museum and initiated new educational foci. In 2009, she was named director of the Smithsonian's National Museum of African Art. Promoting education through multicultural understanding is her passion.

Mary Futrell (b. 1940) began life in the small town of Altavista, Virginia. Her mother, Josephine, had been orphaned at the age of 14 and earned her living as a domestic. Her father was a construction worker, without insurance. He was seriously ill for a year and died when Mary was four. She and her siblings grew up on the edge of poverty. They moved to Lynchburg, where her mother worked for three different families, in addition to cleaning churches. Young Mary remembers walking to school barefoot when there wasn't enough money to pay for shoes, and being sent home by her principal as a result.[12] She never anticipated that college was an option for her; it was simply unaffordable. School administrators carried the same assumptions about her future trajectory, initially placing her on a vocational track. But several teachers in her community helped raise funds for her to attend Virginia State University, where she earned a degree in business education in 1962.

Upon completion of her undergraduate college work, Mary Futrell moved to Alexandria, Virginia where she taught business courses at segregated Parker-Gray High School. By 1965, as schools began to desegregate, Futrell was transferred, as a "floater," to the white George Washington High School.[13] While teaching, she enrolled in an M.A. program at George Washington University and earned her degree in 1968.

Futrell's engagement with statewide issues propelled her to leadership positions. When the traditionally black Virginia Teachers Association (VTA) merged with the Virginia Education Association (VEA) in 1967, she helped form a minority caucus to bring attention to the concerns of black teachers and administrators. When Alexandria city schools fully integrated in 1972, she became active in facilitating understanding. Her human relations skills were apparent, and in 1973, she was elected president of the Education Association of Alexandria (EAA), where she battled with the school board over teacher salary equity. With leadership skills honed in Alexandria, Futrell was elected president of the VEA in 1976. It was a difficult time for public employees in Virginia, because the state's Supreme Court handed down a decision banning collective bargaining at the same time that cuts in education accelerated. To support her fellow teachers, she rallied 7,000 educators for a march in Richmond to advocate for education funding and negotiations legislation.[14]

By the 1980s, Mary Futrell became a nationally prominent education leader. In 1983, just six months after the National Commission on Excellence in Education issued *A Nation at Risk,* she was elected president of the National Education Association (NEA), a position she held for an unprecedented six-year term. She became the highest-ranking black or woman in the US labor movement, assuming leadership of the largest teachers' union in the country during a very turbulent time.[15] With conservative William Bennett holding the position of secretary of education under Republican president Ronald Reagan, she led the NEA through an embattled period. In both 1984 and 1985, *The Ladies' Home Journal, Ebony Magazine,* and *Ms. Magazine* recognized her among the most important women in America. When her national administrative responsibilities eased, she became a doctoral student at George Washington University (GWU) at age 49. Yet, before she could focus entirely on this new venture, she assumed new international responsibilities as president of the World Congress of Organizations of the Teaching Profession. Still working on her advanced degree in education policy studies, she joined the faculty at GWU in 1992. In 1995, she was promoted to dean of the Graduate School of Education and Human Development, a position she held until 2010. She has been at the cutting edge of leadership dealing very directly with the racial politics of education and with the preservation of educational resources for all of America's children.

Freeman Hrabowski (b.1950) experienced his formative years in the cauldron of Birmingham, Alabama during the most intense years of the civil rights movement. He is the only child of middle-class parents who were both teachers, before his father took on three different blue-collar jobs to support the family. A precocious child, he skipped two grades in elementary school, entering high school at the age of twelve. While in his first year of secondary school, he participated in the Birmingham Children's March, spending a week in jail. Some of his leadership skills were honed there, since he had responsibility for a group of younger children terrified by the potential of abuse and violence. Somewhat like Johnnetta Cole's parents who insisted on her educational enrichment, Freeman Hrabowski's mother sent him to Massachusetts in the summers, where he lived with one of his godmothers, and experienced an integrated classroom. That gave him a comparative advantage and also put him in competition with a broader range of children. While still in high school, he was selected to participate in a mathematically based National Science Foundation program at Tuskegee University. This experience convinced him that he wanted to get a Ph.D. in mathematics.

Completing public high school in Birmingham at age 15, Freeman Hrabowski spent his college years at the historically black Hampton Institute. In 1970, at the age of 19, he graduated with highest honors in mathematics. One year later, he had earned an M.A. and by 1975, he completed a Ph.D. in higher education administration and statistics at the University of Illinois. His dissertation focused on strategies for effective college-level mathematics instruction for African American students.

Hrabowski's educational leadership opportunities evolved quickly. While still a Ph.D. student, he was named assistant dean for student services, focusing on Upward Bound programs for low-income high school students and on programs for minority students once they arrived at college. In 1975, he returned to Alabama, accepting a position as associate professor of statistics and research and as associate dean for graduate studies at Alabama A&M. Just one year later, he became a professor of math and dean of arts and sciences at Coppin State College in Maryland before rising to vice president for academic affairs.

In 1987, Hrabowski moved to the University of Maryland, Baltimore County (UMBC) as vice-provost, becoming executive vice president and then president in 1992. At UMBC, he initiated the extremely successful Meyerhoff Program that gained national attention for attracting minority students to the sciences. He was presented with the first US Presidential Award for Excellence in Science, Mathematics, and Engineering Mentoring. Freeman Hrabowski has focused his educational career on encouraging minority students to pursue and excel in mathematics and the sciences. He has built UMBC into one of the most diverse educational institutions in the country, and he is viewed as one of the most respected university presidents in the United States.[16]

Geoffrey Canada (b. 1952) experienced both the challenges of urban poverty and the encouragement of family members from a very young age. Four Canada brothers grew up in a tough, poverty-ridden neighborhood in the South Bronx where Geoffrey was exposed daily to the enormous dangers of the street.[17] His father, a chronic alcoholic, abandoned the family. His mother worked many odd jobs, and at times had to rely on welfare and food donations from charities. But she understood the importance of education, and encouraged him to read broadly.

During his high school years, he escaped the dangers of the South Bronx by moving to his maternal grandparents' home in Wyandanch, a black community on Long Island, New York. There, as a young male student, it was socially acceptable to avoid guns and violence. His high school football coach influenced him, infusing a sense of optimism and encouraging struggle for success. Both family and community mentors prepared him to step into the unknown and to excel.

Canada entered Bowdoin College in Maine as one of a handful of black students. He learned how to invest in academic excellence and then enrolled in Harvard University's Graduate School of Education, where he earned an M.A. degree. In the 1970s, he taught in Boston, Massachusetts, quickly rising to administrative positions.

But he wanted to return to his roots in the Bronx. In the 1980s, he became educational director and director of the Truancy Prevention Program at the Rheedlen Centers for Children and Families in New York. Within a few years he became president and CEO of Rheedlen and transformed it into the Harlem Children's Zone.[18]

Canada aspires to save the children of Harlem, providing all the educational and social support services necessary. To save the children, he believes it is necessary to rehabilitate communities with safe streets, employment opportunities, and social services.[19] He has received national and international recognition for his efforts, and he doesn't plan to stop until the job is done. His vision is vast.

Rita Dove (b. 1952) was born in Akron, Ohio, to two educated parents who had not been able to fully realize their career goals because of race. Her father, the first black chemist in the rubber industry, had spent years working as an elevator operator at Goodyear before the doors opened up and allowed him to be hired as a professional.[20] Her mother, a housewife, declined a scholarship to Howard University because her parents were fearful for her safety.[21] Dove's parents, however, offered her every opportunity to excel, and her teachers cooperated as well. She was on an experimental fast track in integrated middle school and high school. As a shy person, she chose somewhat solitary pursuits—playing the cello or writing poetry. She did, however, get involved in baton twirling, so she could engage with her fellow students. A stellar student, she was one of 100 students in the country to be named a Presidential Scholar.[22] In numerous ways, her early educational experiences illustrate the positive example of quality integrated schooling.

At the University of Miami in Ohio, she discovered she could be a poet. Nurtured by faculty, she applied and won a Fulbright Scholarship to Germany. Upon her graduation from college, she was accepted into the prestigious

Figure 3.1 Head Majorette Rita Dove leading Buchtel High School Band in 1969. Photo by Ray A. Dove ©1969.

University of Iowa's Writers Program. She discovered the power in the writing of Toni Morrison, who spoke directly to her as a black woman. Race role models for her writing came from the printed word, and they were extremely important.[23] Teaching appointments followed at Arizona State University and the University of Virginia.

Rita Dove won a Pulitzer Prize in Poetry in 1987 for her collection of inter-related poems, *Thomas and Beulah*, loosely based on the lives of her grandparents. She was named poet laureate of the United States and consultant to the Library of Congress from 1993 to 1995, and poet laureate of the Commonwealth of Virginia from 2004 to 2006. In 1996, President Bill Clinton presented her with the National Humanities Medal. In 2011, President Barack Obama honored her with a National Medal of the Arts. She has published many books of poetry, short stories, novels, lectures, and plays.[24]

These six people have built remarkable careers. Their educational journeys shaped their sense of possibility, their understanding of the ways that race affects opportunity, and their passion to effect meaningful change through leadership. For them, education is the great equalizer and the sine qua non for successful lives. In their zeal for educational advances, they, along with most interviewees, adhere to a long and rich African American resolve, extending back in time to prerevolutionary America.

Education Denied; Education Nurtured

My mother grew up in Little Rock, Arkansas. And her father grew up in Ozan, Arkansas, also born in the early 1900s, as was my grandmother. They had the same existence in the sense that slavery had ended in the fifty years before their birth, but they had relatives and friends who had been involved in slavery. They were in the middle of Jim Crow segregation… You couldn't go to schools unless they were segregated.[25]—Charles Ogletree

For black Americans, the quest for education follows a troubled trajectory. It is a story of education denied, education nurtured, education segregated, education desegregated, and education re-segregated. Before the American Revolution, laws passed in the Southern states prohibited teaching literacy skills to slaves. If people could not read and write, they would become more dependent on their owners and they would not be able to develop strategies of resistance through effective communication with one another.[26]

Some masters understood the advantages of allowing certain enslaved men and women to develop artisanal and literacy skills, because they could be more useful as workers on the plantations. And within the churches, some pastors thought it a Christian duty to teach the enslaved to read the Bible.[27] As a result, despite the prohibitions on reading and writing, even in the most oppressive of situations, there were a few who developed agency through literacy and used those skills to exercise leadership. For slaves who either bought their freedom or escaped to the North, many became abolitionists and teachers. Such familiar individuals as Frederick Douglass, Sojourner Truth, and Harriet Tubman, and the lesser-known Henry Highland Garnet, William Wells Brown, and Reverend Richard Anderson Sinquefield could write and speak about the evils of slavery as a result of the education they garnered while enslaved.[28] Long before emancipation, slaves valued literacy and education.[29]

With the coming of the Civil War and the postbellum period, newly freed African Americans hungered for learning opportunities. As Union army chaplains established schools for "contrabands of war," former slaves flocked to them.[30] They understood that literacy and learning were essential to freedom.[31] For black Americans, education denied meant subjugation; education acquired portended power and liberation.[32] In postbellum America, blacks perceived education as democracy's great equalizer.[33] They pursued education as an overriding objective dramatically reversing the illiteracy rates from 81 percent in 1870 to 43 percent in 1900.[34]

Black teachers were central to this mission. Along with ministers, they became the leaders in their communities. They approached education with a missionary zeal, believing they were critical to the advancement of their race. They earned the veneration of their communities and occupied positions of great prestige.[35]

In community after community, blacks took charge of education and tried to fund it as best they could, often accepting a system of "double taxation" that existed from before Reconstruction through the 1960s.[36] They frequently paid teachers' expenses and supported their salaries, while also providing funds for the building and maintenance of schools in their districts. And their teachers, drawn from their communities, provided extraordinary service. This cultural capital, centered on self-reliance, developed from within communities and provided a sense of empowerment in the face of white oppression.[37]

Philanthropic acts by Northern free blacks, with relatively high levels of literacy, provided funding for many schools in the South and for developing northern institutions of higher learning. Black clergy, largely from the African Methodist Episcopal (AME) and Baptist churches, supported these efforts, raising millions of dollars in support of schools and universities. Wilberforce University, incorporated in 1863 under the auspices of the AME Church, became the first institution of higher learning fully owned and operated by blacks. Black Baptists from the north supported over 107 private schools in the South by the early twentieth century.[38]

White missionaries and philanthropists also played significant financial roles. The George Peabody Fund, John F. Slater Fund, and Anna T. Jeanes Fund provided monies for teacher and industrial training. Julius Rosenwald offered monetary assistance to support African Americans' efforts to fund and build their own industrial schools in the rural South. He offered one-third funding if others (usually African Americans) came up with the remainder. In time, other support came from the Carnegie Foundation and the Phelps-Stokes Fund for higher education research and for libraries.[39] Often they came with strings attached and limitations that felt paternalistic.[40] Despite these well-meaning and laudable efforts, white philanthropic support never offset the discriminatory policies of states and localities. Teacher training funds, resources, and facilities remained woefully inadequate.[41]

Black Americans engaged in energetic discussion about what kind of learning would best lead to meaningful opportunity. The models proposed arose from different conceptual and intellectual ideologies aligned to assessments of power and politics. The best-known debate was between Booker T. Washington and W. E. B. Du Bois, drawing in Carter Woodson, John Hope, James Weldon Johnson, Alain Locke, Alexander Crummell, and Mary Church Terrell.[42] Washington endorsed an industrial/technical model of education for the postbellum world,[43] while Du Bois supported a more classical education that allowed blacks to fully compete with whites in qualitative educational learning so necessary for leadership.[44] The intense articulation of positions along an accomodationist/protest continuum illustrates how important these issues were within the black community and underscores the value placed on education.

At every level of society, black Americans embraced educational opportunity, debated how best to educate, sought ways to improve the quality of their own teachers, worked cooperatively with local officials and philanthropists, raised money from within their own communities, and actively lobbied when they could for improved conditions. Often stymied by economic deprivation and racist assumptions, they demonstrated when and where they could just how important education was for the future of the race.

Education Segregated

The lower grade schools were one-room schools. I mean on the one hand a good education because when you're in the first grade you hear the second-grade class and then you hear the third-grade class. So you know, you're really getting educated two or three times over. But they really were inadequate schools. The local public [high] school... was just not a good school.[45]—Julian Bond

These were people who were not extraordinary scholars or particularly gifted teachers, but they were so committed to rescuing, saving a generation of us in the heat of segregation that they really did transform our lives.[46]—William Raspberry

As a post-Reconstruction race dogma of white supremacy deepened and the courts institutionalized segregation laws in the late nineteenth century, two separate and unequal systems of education emerged. Many black leaders who grew up with race-based segregation inherited these deep disparities.

Inequalities between black and white educational systems increased with the loss of the black vote and black political power at the end of Reconstruction.[47] White Southerners viewed Booker T. Washington's vision of vocational education, reinforced by the creation of agricultural and technical schools, as appropriate to blacks' abilities and needs. Education for blacks existed to serve the needs of the white power structure. Both state-controlled curriculum and resource allocation reflected the reality of race-based castes in the American South.[48] This educational vision persisted until and beyond the 1954 *Brown v. Board of Education of Topeka, Kansas* Supreme Court decision declaring "separate but equal" inherently *unequal*. Many black leaders at the height of their careers today went to schools with these disparities.

Blacks and whites could not be totally separate, of course. To the extent that education was supported by taxpayer dollars, black teachers and principals needed to demonstrate their competencies to white superintendents to run their own schools, despite recognized disparities in opportunities for teacher training.[49] Black community members and teachers pleaded for additional resources for their children's education and for the expansion of a black professional class, thereby coming into contact with white supervisors, school board members, and occasional civic representatives.[50] Forced to accept inadequate pay and dreadful conditions within their schools, teachers nonetheless felt they needed to put the best possible face on their situation and appease white administrators during obligatory visits. At the same time, within the black community, black educators were viewed as middle-class role models and as race leaders of educational advancement. They had a set of impossible tasks: "Teachers were also expected to be public health workers, Sunday school teachers, home visitors, agricultural experts, fundraisers, adult literacy teachers, racial diplomats, moral examples, all-around pillars of the community, and general uplifters of the race."[51] As black resistance to the inequalities grew in the 1930s and 1940s, teachers often found themselves criticized within the black community for being unwilling to protest and suspect within the white community for teaching militant or radical ideas.[52] Black educators walked a fine line while they carried the burden of "double-agent."[53]

Conditions in black schools were appallingly bad. Around 1900, across the 16 former slave states, only one African American teacher was available for 93 black schoolchildren.[54] Schools were often one-room shacks, with inadequate heating. Usually, books were handed down from white schools, and black students too often did without books and supplies. Black teachers' salaries were a fraction of their white counterparts. Whites determined the length of the school year, and the school day for black children was often dramatically shorter.[55] Vast disparities existed between city and country schools, with rural schools—where most blacks lived—more independent and more forsaken.[56]

Until recently, we knew little about why people educated in these circumstances remember their schooling so fondly. From North Carolina to Alabama to Georgia and New York, local studies and oral histories—in both rural and urban settings—convey a common story.[57]

Put simply, education was revered. It offered a path for self-improvement, upward mobility, and personal enrichment. Schools, along with churches, were cultural symbols. They were central to the life of the community, and they fostered racial pride.[58] Within those schools, there were lessons to learn, drama and music events, debate and public speaking contests, dances, clubs, sports—the full array of activities that promoted a sense of belonging. At school assemblies, clubs performed and speakers motivated. Principals and teachers transmitted values of discipline, responsibility, and respect for elders. The curricular focus on African American history, literature, and philosophy inspired self-worth.[59] To this day, black leaders recall how their schools reinforced such values.

With very limited neighborhood resources, schools functioned as community centers. Parents, teachers, ministers, businessmen, and students gathered there for Christian and secular holiday events. The school often became the "cultural city of the segregated community."[60] Parents provided support through their labor or monetary resources. They purchased playground equipment, lumber, grass seed, instruments, and at times even school buses. They made food for special events. They helped build physical structures like gymnasia. In so doing, they interacted with teachers and principals. They knew their children's teachers and were known by them. Schools, then, were extensions of segregated communities that drew people together in common purpose.[61] Even without adequate resources, many segregated black neighborhoods unconsciously adopted the community schooling model that is currently deemed to be so successful in reversing the educational declines in stressed urban areas.

Beyond these often expected roles for parents in their children's schools, the tremendous disparities in educational needs motivated parents and community members to do even more. They took their role as advocates for their children's education to a higher level. They appealed to white school boards for transportation, creation of high schools, better facilities, and longer school terms so that their children would have equal opportunity. By the 1950s and 1960s, they protested for school integration.[62] They demonstrated how centrally important education was and how much they cared. Children received powerful messages.

But no group transmitted values of caring more than the teachers and principals themselves. Black teachers often offered adult education classes and directed literacy programs in their communities. Many lived within a few blocks of their schools and knew the parents of the children they taught. They saw their students in the grocery stores, in church on Sundays, and on the streets of the community. Their "ethic of caring"[63] extended far beyond the confines of their schoolrooms; they embraced their students with critically important values in the struggle to overcome racism.

Teachers' messages reinforced those of principals and parents: to succeed in a racist world, you had to be twice as good. You had to believe in the future, even when the present offered little.[64] There could be no excuses for home-work left undone, failure to complete assignments in a timely way, sloppy writing, bad grammar, inappropriate language, rude behaviors, and lack of respect. Teachers took responsibility for student outcomes and for their personal self-improvement. They held tutoring sessions, visited students' homes, and bought or collected clothing for their most needy students. They participated in black teachers' association meetings, took summer school classes to enhance their own skills, and joined professional organizations. Both state associations and the National Association of Teachers in Colored Schools (NATCS) proliferated in the late nineteenth and early twentieth centuries, offering thousands of black teachers the educational publications, networks, and knowledge of best practices.[65] Throughout the early decades of the twentieth century, teachers' skills improved markedly, and many school districts reported 100 percent participation in professional organizations.[66] In all these ways, teachers and principals modeled behaviors of how to overcome societal racism that denied equal education. They did so through values of interpersonal and institutional caring.[67] They engaged in a "pedagogy of love."[68]

Teachers also organized and protested. Septima Clark, a schoolteacher in rural South Carolina, promoted adult literacy through "Citizenship Schools" and sought to develop grassroots leaders throughout the South. From the 1920s on, she remonstrated against the inequitable salaries of black teachers and worked with the NAACP to demand the right for qualified black teachers to be principals in the schools of Charleston.[69] By the 1930s and 1940s, other teachers collaborated with the NAACP to bring suits against local school boards for salary equalization, funding to improve physical conditions in black schools, and transportation for black children. They were courageous, risking termination from their jobs in order to promote the larger good of their people.[70] Equality under the law was their goal.

The lessons teachers taught were subversive. Teachers who stressed African American accomplishments and taught black history and culture engaged in forms of protest and acts of resistance. Through their choice of texts, oratory, music and poetry, they nurtured an oppositional consciousness among their students.[71] The noted black author bell hooks remembers: "For black folks teaching—educating—was fundamentally political because it was rooted in antiracist struggle.... My teachers were on a mission."[72] Theirs was an "emancipatory" pedagogy that helped students recognize social injustice and fostered a sense of empowerment.[73] Every black teacher who demanded excellence was challenging the expectations of the larger society; every black teacher who promoted a classical curriculum was fighting against white claims of inferiority; every black teacher who fought for equalization of salaries or who testified about conditions in the schools was testing institutionalized racism. The black struggle for education was coincident with the black struggle for equality.[74] Teachers could not transcend their material environment, but they could transmit powerful messages of racial pride and uplift. On the front lines of the struggle for racial uplift—revered by some for their skill, criticized by others for their political caution or their shortfalls—teachers were race leaders, advocating for the liberating power of education.[75]

Six Leaders: Education Lessons

William Raspberry, Johnnetta Cole, Mary Futrell, Freeman Hrabowski, Geoffrey Canada, and Rita Dove grew up in dramatically disparate circumstances of personal security and comfort. From the Harlem ghetto to the middle-class neighborhoods of Jacksonville, Birmingham, and Akron to the more rural communities of Altavista and Okolona, they nonetheless shared some common educational experiences that illuminate the larger story of black education in America from the 1940s through the late 1960s. Five of them experienced the inequalities of segregated education, but also appreciate the ethic of caring within their schools.

Most grew up with segregated education, but often with forays into integrated classrooms. In their segregated classrooms, they had less than white children and they knew it. Nobody, for example, could hide the fact that black schools in Jacksonville, Florida where Johnnetta Cole lived were only open for half a day, while white schools operated on a full-day schedule. Her parents would not tolerate this imbalance of opportunity, and sent young Johnnetta and her older sister Marvyne to school in Washington, D.C., where they lived with their paternal grandmother. Leaving home at the tender age of eight, Cole remembers "hating racism" because "it" separated her from her parents.[76] After remaining in Washington for two years, she returned to Jacksonville, where she attended a private Methodist secondary school for "Negro girls" where teachers were predominantly white women.[77] It was one of two black high schools in Jacksonville.

Others also sent their children away to enhance educational opportunities. Julian Bond's parents, for example, chose the George School in Pennsylvania for him while his siblings went to Massachusetts. Although he describes his upbringing on the campus of Lincoln University in Pennsylvania as "idyllic" in many ways, he also recognizes how the inadequate primary and secondary education affected him:

> My parents wanted better for us....And my preparation was so poor I had to repeat my first year, so I was at this school five years. I had to repeat the first year and come back again because the work was just above me. I was smart. Could read, write and do all those kind of things. But I didn't have any kind of foundation to compete with these other kids who had had a superior education all along.[78]

Middle-class black parents looked for opportunities outside their communities to enrich the educational experiences of their children. Freeman Hrabowski, for example, attended summer schools in Massachusetts in integrated environments and came to understand the enormous differences in opportunity.[79] But while he was exposed to rigorous education, there were losses. But at the age of 13, he began to grasp the concept of the "Invisible Man" when he was ignored as the only black child in the class. The alternative was the Birmingham schools, where he had been made to feel "really special" in his smaller, less competitive school. His sense of self and his confidence in his ability to succeed was fundamental to his later accomplishments, he contends.[80] Although he was suspended for participating in the Birmingham Children's March, he recalls how his school principal held a school assembly and spoke of the leadership and courage of those who participated. Rather than being disgraced, he was honored for his leadership.[81]

Material conditions within segregated schools strongly disadvantaged black children. "There was so much about segregated schools that was shameful and dehumanizing," Cole recalls. Black children had to use "hand-me-down books White children no longer needed...." They were "restricted to using the colored branch of the library which was never stocked with as good a collection of books as were found in the White branch." They had few "extracurricular activities such as drama or band."[82] Likewise, Freeman Hrabowski remembers the "degradation of used, worn books" in Birmingham, Alabama.[83] In Lynchburg, and even Alexandria, Virginia, the same conditions prevailed. Mary Futrell recalls:

> We didn't have the up-to-date class books, textbooks. We didn't have the up-to-date equipment, and that was in simple Lynchburg. When I moved to Alexandria [in 1962] and started teaching, Julian, I was surprised that in Alexandria, the black kids would get the textbooks that were being used by the white kids, and then after they finished, we would get them. We would get the hand-me-down equipment. I remember one

year, we asked for workbooks so that our kids could have practical experiences, and we were told they couldn't afford them. But when we went to a meeting at the white school, there they were.[84]

Long after the *Brown* decision, unequal education persisted.

Geoffrey Canada left home to live with his grandparents in order to escape the violent, drug-infested "gladiatorial" Morris High School in New York. His high school experiences in Wyandanch, though still in a segregated environment, put him in touch with counselors and teachers who encouraged him to apply to college. He credits the role of chance for his educational salvation—the chance to escape the inner city that so many others did not have. It changed his life.[85]

Despite the deficit in physical and material resources, these black leaders felt the power of parents, community members, and teachers who strongly believed in education and in the possibility for success. Johnnetta Cole's first-grade teacher, "Bunny" [Bernice] Vance, refused to allow her to mumble and insisted that she respond to questions with strength and self-dignity. "We've got to remember the tremendous influence and power of a single teacher, at a given moment, in a child's life," Cole contends. "The Mrs. Vances of the world," Cole emphasizes, "made learning and going to school fun."[86] In the "colored schools of Jacksonville, Florida," she remembers:

> there were teachers who profoundly believed in us. First of all they believed that there was no such thing as an uneducable child....I was aware that the books were hand-me-downs. I knew that we didn't have enough gym equipment. I knew that across town in the white schools that they were enjoying many, many more material things. But I always felt deeply appreciated. I felt people telling me I was good and smart and that I could do things in the world.[87]

Geoffrey Canada knows that his mother, who always encouraged reading, and a first-grade teacher, who introduced him to Dr. Suess, unleashed in him the power of poetry and the joy of reading. His mother promoted education as a means to move beyond poverty. Her mantra: "reading is the key." Together, they compensated for the harsh realities of the inner city, unlocking the "great potential that people have inside of them." Canada claims that this teacher changed his life, opening his eyes to literature and poetry. With Dr. Seuss as a base, Langston Hughes, Countee Cullen, and even Geoffrey Chaucer became stepping stones to educational excitement.[88]

William Raspberry also credits parents and teachers for inculcating a love of learning and a lifelong commitment to education. His was a household in which both parents and children were "forever reading things." Beyond his household,

the community of teachers at the high school and technical college also reinforced educational values:

> The presence of that little school helped to transform our town into
> what these days we would call a learning community, at least for the
> black half of the town.... it was really quite extraordinary in ways that I
> didn't realize until I left the place.[89]

Raspberry particularly remembers his math teacher and the man who taught
him agriculture; they were people who took an interest in him and were willing
to engage him in personal discussions outside the classroom. "I worked hard in
school to please adults who cared about me," he reflected. Like so many poor,
segregated communities in the South, it was the teachers who could lift people beyond their "segregated and awful" conditions to build towards a brighter
future.[90]

The power of parents, extended kin, and community members to make a
difference is fundamental. Mary Futrell tells a story about how tough her mother
was on her, largely because she was determined to make her daughter succeed.
"Your circumstances do not control you," she liked to say. "You can be anything
you want."[91] Although her mother was rarely home, Mary knew she had to do
her homework. Neighbors helped:

> [They] looked after us not only to make sure we were well fed and that
> we were safe, but to also say, "You have chores to do, you have home-
> work to do. If you don't have homework, you have books you can read,"
> and...looked at our report cards, and if we did something wrong, they
> corrected us. They also would make sure my mother knew what we were
> or were not doing. And it wasn't like a tell-tale situation. It was trying to
> help us and trying to help the family.[92]

Caring communities fostered educational commitment.

Mary Futrell describes herself as a very shy child. Yet, by high school, she
had become a cheerleader, played on the basketball team, joined Future Business
Leaders of America, and participated in the student council. Such experiences,
she contends, "gave me a chance to grow and to open up and to have more confidence in myself...." As a child growing up in poverty, she could easily have been
bypassed, but teachers believed in her.[93] One such teacher was Miss Jordan, who
insisted that Mary learn self-discipline and stay focused on educational achievement.[94] Moreover, segregated Lynchburg was the kind of community that pushed
children to excel; it was a community in which the single black dentist, doctor,
lawyer, or minister—"the prominent people...were the teachers." They became
the role models, the people who could demonstrate that segregation would not

stop them from being successful.[95] She learned leadership skills that served her well:

> One was building confidence. Another one was the ability to work with people, learning how to work with all kinds of people, learning how to listen, learning how to appreciate different ideas and not look at the source of the idea but the quality of the idea. I think it was, how do I phrase it, being able to motivate people, because see, I became the captain of the cheering squad. And so being able to motivate, being able to lead, being able to get people to do things—I think a major part of leadership is being able to persuade people to do things, having the will and the ability and the desire to do things....Being in a school play. Those kinds of activities give you confidence and give you the ability to get up and do things that later you know, you take for granted. And I tell people all the time, "What I have learned and what I have done as a leader started back in Lynchburg. Started back in Virginia State College where I was given the opportunity or opportunities to be out front and to do things." I had to grow like anyone else. I was not—I don't think I was a natural leader. I had to acquire skills and I had to grow and so I was also willing to learn, willing to study, willing to listen. So those things helped me later.[96]

Collectively, these stories reflect the power of culturally relevant communities and culturally relevant teaching. In such an environment, the members of the community support and empower. Culturally relevant teachers actively seek to overcome the negative effects of the dominant (in this case, white) culture. They bring a strong sense of self and professionalism to their work, and they function as role models for the children in their midst.[97]

Freeman Hrabowski, for example, remembers his mother (a teacher of English and math) challenging him to perform both within and outside the classroom. At home, she introduced word problems to him, while also having him memorize Zora Neale Hurston.[98] She taught him to help others learn and excel. As a first and second grader, Freeman was asked to work with other children in the classroom who were not as far advanced as he.[99] He felt empowered to lead others.

> [What] teachers did for me in school—in elementary, middle, and high school—in saying I matter...It's amazing how we're all shaped by our childhood experiences.[100]

Mary Futrell's mother insisted on educational achievement. But she was not able to advocate for her child when some teachers targeted her for a vocational track because they assumed that she would never have the money to go to college. Nonetheless, other teachers saw her potential:

> And I remember when I was, I think it was, a junior in high school, they gave a test, and I came out number five in the class. And the teachers and everyone, they were shocked. And so then they switched me over to the academic track. But by then, see, I didn't have the background. But I also remember those teachers going out and getting me money to go to school. I did not plan to go to college. My mother simply did not have the money. And they went out and they collected the money in the neighborhood to send me to school. And I remember the night I graduated. They didn't tell me, they told my mother, but they didn't tell me—I assume they didn't tell me because they didn't know how much they were going to collect. And so the night that I graduated, they walked up on the stage and they gave me $1,500 to go to school. And I was flabbergasted. And I remember one of the teachers that said to me, "Apply anyway." And I was going like, "Why apply? I'm not going. I don't have any money. So why should I apply?" And she insisted, "Apply anyway." And so here were the administrators and other people telling me I couldn't. But here were my teachers telling me I could. And not only saying, "You can," but all along insisting that I do the best that I could with my studies and then saying "Here's the money to go. Now it's up to you."[101]

Mary Futrell

http://blackleadership.virginia.edu/09

Geoffrey Canada also grew up very poor in New York City. In addition to his mother and teachers, a person named Mike, himself a drop-out, saw potential in Geoffrey and pushed him to stay in school, perform, and rise above his circumstances.[102] By the time he got to high school in Wyandanch, where his grandfather lived, there were students who were college-bound who became role models. There were people who believed in him, who pushed him to succeed.

Both Mary Futrell and Geoffrey Canada, as poor children in black communities, experienced the effects of tracking. Futrell, herself, was a target of such tracking and Canada is painfully aware of all his classmates who never had a chance—either because they were deemed to be unteachable or because they ended up addicts or criminals. A sense of unfairness motivates both of them in their work and scholarship. For Futrell, educational transformation requires a serious look at the tracking system, which has such a negative impact on minority and poor children. In integrated systems, she believes, the system may be getting worse because fewer people know the students' potential.[103]

The ethic of *caring*[104] within their communities was fundamental to the success of black leaders. While they would never choose to return to segregated communities, they recognize their community's efforts to shield black youngsters from the worst abuses of racism. In primary grades, there were teachers and mentors who challenged, nurtured, and supported. As a result, these black leaders developed strong self-confidence with which they could confront and conquer the larger world. Being told both that they were special and had to prove it to a skeptical or hostile world by being twice as good provided armor for life.[105]

Being "twice as good" and absorbing messages of diligence and excellence came first and foremost from families, as we have already seen. It didn't really matter whether one was in a segregated or integrated school environment. And in some cases, there were integrated school environments where teachers cared deeply without regard to skin color. Rita Dove, for example, attended integrated schools in Akron, Ohio. She doesn't remember any significant discrimination from teachers:

> I had a remarkable education. I was really lucky to have teachers who believed in teaching, were dedicated. I had quite a few white teachers. My first black teacher was in fifth grade, Miss Ford, and I remember being tremendously excited to have my first black teacher. She was phenomenal. After that point there were others, but most of my teachers actually were white and didn't seem to show any kind of discrimination, so we were pushed.[106]

As a particularly capable student, Dove competed in accelerated classes from the seventh grade on. They were "tracked" in an experimental program that created a community among like-minded students. Her high school English teacher, for example, struck terror in the students "but she brought literature to life and she was absolutely dedicated to it." One Saturday, for example, she took interested students to a poetry reading by John Ciardi, demonstrating that it was viable to "be a poet in this world."[107]

Between her parents, community, and teachers, Rita Dove experienced the positive experiences that came from an integrated environment. She was not immune to racial slights from some children, and she had to wait until graduate school to find black writers who seemed to be speaking directly to her.[108] But in her integrated setting, she identifies the very same components that inspired other black leaders in totally different circumstances. Fundamental to her success were the values of parents, community members, and teachers. The very tracking system so detrimental to Mary Futrell and Geoffrey Canada—a system that too many black students still experience—allowed Rita Dove to excel because she was placed in the fast lane to achievement.

When Geoffrey Canada went off to Bowdoin College in Maine, when Johnnetta Cole transferred to Oberlin College in Ohio, when Freeman Hrabowski went to graduate school at the University of Illinois, when Rita Dove went to the University of Iowa, when William Raspberry went to University of Indianapolis or when Mary Futrell entered George Washington University, they did so armed with a belief in themselves that had been lovingly nurtured by parents, teachers, and mentors.

Crossing boundaries into integrated institutions could be somewhat traumatic. The color line existed then as it does today. But it was the love of education that sustained these leaders and encouraged them to exploit the opportunities in their new environments. Like many people of his generation, Geoffrey Canada was inspired by the *Brown v. Board* decision. He felt he was part of a "generation of firsts" in a "race to the top" to break down existing barriers. At Bowdoin, though, there was a whole new culture and set of expectations—an extreme immersion experience. By the time he graduated, he felt like a different person:

I had never been around even middle class African Americans so I went to Bowdoin and I found middle and upper middle class whites and I found middle and upper middle class African Americans and I had never seen anything like it before.... In the South Bronx when we were growing up, we had a certain culture of toughness, right...—so if we met somebody for the first time, it'd be like, "Yo, how ya doing?" And, you know, it was just like everybody'd be cool. You had to be—and so I was meeting these kids—"Hi, how are you?" And I was like, whoa, and I was saying, "Yo, what's up, how'ya doing?" And no one talked to me for the first six months and I was wondering, so later I asked my friends, I said, "Look, when I first got there, you guys treated me so bad." They said, "You were the most hostile person we had ever met...." But it was just the way we were sort of brought up and so suddenly I had to confront all of these issues. I'd never been around white people before...and so suddenly I'm surrounded and I'm finding out, hey, they're just people. They're just good, bad, individuals, people....I met some of the most brilliant African Americans I'd ever seen in my entire life...and I just said, I want to be like that and as a role model, it inspired me to take academics serious[ly] and to want to become a scholar....Here, there was a bar that everybody said you have to get to that bar and everybody around me was trying to do that and there was no escaping that and after a while, I just accepted that that was the cultural values of that school and I became that myself and then after a while, this was about how many A's you received in your classwork and not about whether or not you made the varsity basketball team or you were playing football or some of those other things and that—when I left Bowdoin and came back—I still understood the streets and I still understood— but I was also a changed person.[109]

In the crossing of educational boundaries from the disadvantaged black neighborhoods into middle and upper-class white America, Canada had to alter his speech patterns and his style of engagement. But needing to do this gave him another set of verbal skills that allowed him to compete more successfully. Canada clearly believes his exposure to white culture was an advantage:

> I actually thought this was an addition and not a subtraction, that the change allowed me to move from talking with a group of kids in the projects, be they black or white, and feeling comfortable walking through that neighborhood as well as it did going into a boardroom and talking to people about budgets and finance and those kinds of things.[110]

He credits Bowdoin for that education. Canada is one of the fortunate few who overcame the deficits of the South Bronx.

For William Raspberry, leaving the nurturing environment of Okolona to attend the University of Indianapolis was traumatic and somewhat overwhelming. He had to learn how to navigate a real city, figuring out the distinctions between black and white neighborhoods and the unwritten racial codes of access. He chose to attend an "overwhelmingly white" integrated college, and was "scared to death" to compete with both white and northern students. "I worked my buns off that first year to prove that I could [compete] and then really I lost a lot of interest in school."[111] It seems that Raspberry burnt out, needing to take time off to refocus and to earn some money. So, although his experiences in Okolona provided a basic love of education, making the transition to a larger world proved difficult. He floundered a bit, exploring a variety of majors, and eventually took a job at the *Indianapolis Recorder*—his "fifth major"—setting him on his career path.[112] Once again, however, there were teachers who cared and there were a handful of African American students who found one another. Eventually, he graduated in 1958 with a degree in history.

Johnnetta Cole also remembers the opening up of new worlds at Oberlin. At age 15, she had begun college at Fisk. But after her father died, she desperately felt the need to be closer to family. She transferred to Oberlin, where her sister was enrolled. Oberlin, she recalls "was a startling, intriguing adventure that showed me just how narrow and closed the South had been, where black is black and white is white."[113] At the same time, Oberlin was "cold. And white."

BOND: And rural.

COLE: And rural and absolutely fantastic. For a youngster—I'm sixteen—and to be placed in an environment that was so profoundly challenging, that was so diverse in comparison to the way that I had grown up. I think that I may have written somewhere that, you know growing up in Jacksonville, if someone had asked me about religious diversity, I thought that that would mean "Are you AME or CME? or one of the Baptists?" But that I would now go to school with individuals of the Jewish faith, of Islamic faith, with folk who were of Hindu faiths. I mean, this was, this was startling for a young southern black woman. It was also a place that was deeply challenging intellectually. And I don't want to, in any way, imply that Fisk was not. One of my strongest memories of Fisk is that I was intellectually set afire in that place. But Oberlin did nothing to put out that fire. In fact, it simply fanned it. They were good years for me. And I've always felt particularly fortunate to have had both the experience of a historically black university and of a major outstanding small liberal arts college.[114]

The challenges of graduate school, for people like Johnnetta Cole and Freeman Hrabowski, were more manageable because they had been reared in environments in which there was a "constant message of denial of second-classisms."[115] Living in middle-class parallel cultural worlds made it somewhat easier to cross racial boundaries for people like Cole and Hrabowski. For Cole, there was a direct motivational line from her first-grade teacher Bunny Vance to George Eaton Simpson (a white sociologist at Oberlin) and then to her Ph.D. advisor Melville J. Herskovits (a white anthropologist at Northwestern).[116] For Freeman Hrabowski, in addition to his minister John Porter, who gave him leadership opportunities, there were the examples of his mother as teacher, his principal George Bell (also a mathematician), the Ph.D. mathematician he encountered at the Tuskegee University's National Science Foundation program, his godfather (and black superintendent of schools) Dr. Hays, his high school counselor Rev. Rice (and father of his good friend, Condoleeza Rice), and Dr. Martin Luther King, Jr. who inspired him to participate in the Birmingham Children's March. They were all teachers: people who taught values, self-discipline, leadership, and risk-taking.[117]

These positive and formative experiences inspired black leaders. Johnnetta Cole taught Anthropology, Black Studies and Women's Studies—seeking to open students up to new and exciting ways of configuring knowledge. She views herself as a feminist comfortable with northern intellectual assertiveness. Yet, in 1986, she found herself back in the South, in Atlanta, president of the relatively conservative black women's college, Spelman. There, she worked to create greater intellectual vitality, generate openness to difference, and inculcate a mind-set of service.[118] Her educational lessons from family, teachers, and mentors propel her to leadership.

Similarly, Freeman Hrabowski thinks of graduate school and his lifetime career path as a continuation of his childhood experiences and motivations. His dissertation topic, focusing on effective strategies for teaching mathematics to African American students at the college level, continued a journey of math education he had begun as a child tutor. It was "...in many ways, the same problem I've been looking at now for almost four decades and that is—how do you get more people of color to excel in math and science and engineering? How do you get a society to believe they can do it?"[119]

Education Integrated; Education Resegregated

I think most observers would have to agree that if you actually look at the impact on our schools today, in many instances, it's had a limited impact, especially when you differentiate by class.... limited impact of Brown v. Board of Education *right here on a day-to-day basis, certainly. That's why I call it a statement of a vision but in terms of practical reality and impact, [we] haven't seen it.*[120]—Anthony Williams

When the *Brown v. Board of Education of Topeka, Kansas* decision was rendered by the US Supreme Court, it generated jubilation and euphoria in black communities in America. Finally, the highest court of the land understood that separate could not be equal. The challenge to the legality of segregation in schools meant that segregation elsewhere eventually would fall. Ending separate schools held out the promise that equal resources would flow to all schools, that white and black children would learn together, and that all Americans would have access to quality education.[121] Some black teachers and students were ambivalent, knowing that proud traditions and institutional connectedness would be lost.[122] Eleanor Holmes Norton attended the prestigious Dunbar High School in Washington, D.C., a college preparatory black high school where many of its black teachers held advanced degrees, and remembers that her teachers cried when the decision was announced, knowing that their beloved, excellent school would eventually lose its storied stature.[123] Still, ending the principle of "separate but equal" held enormous hope for equal opportunity in America.

Unfortunately, the reality of integrated education often has been otherwise. We know, of course, of the resistance to the *Brown* decision. Schools closed rather than integrate. Legislators used the law, as best they could, to circumvent the court's intent. Black children were taunted, spat on, and beaten. Freeman Hrabowski, for one, remembers the trauma to black students who tried to integrate high schools in Birmingham and had rocks thrown at them.[124] Violence erupted and racial hysteria prevailed. Bombings occurred; individuals died. Federal marshals were brought in to maintain the peace. While some people of goodwill welcomed the change, the vast majority did not. In major cities, there was white flight to avoid integration. In rural areas, there was active resistance and the constant threat of violence.[125]

When integration of schools finally occurred, often a good 15 years after the court ruling, many black teachers, principals, and administrators were eliminated. Black schools closed. The sense of pride, agency, and empowerment that had existed in many segregated systems could not be replicated. Between 1954 and 1965, 38,000 black teachers and administrators lost their positions.[126] Integration eroded the agency of teachers within black communities and undermined their critical function as mentors, role models, and disciplinarians. Desegregation abolished the place of teachers as anchors of the black community.[127]

The racial balance of the teaching force shifted and continues to decline. Students of color in primary and secondary schools make up close to half of the school-age population. Yet, the gap continues to widen with fewer teachers of color in the classroom. In 2014, only 18 percent of teachers were minorities, with fewer than 2 percent being African American males.[128] As a result of these historic changes, children no longer readily identify with same race teachers from their own communities. The effects of this have been particularly harmful for children of lower socioeconomic status.[129]

School integration created multiple harms for all its long-term good. Functional, intact communities were hurt when schools shut down. Black schools were less well equipped and often in greater states of disrepair; their doors were shut and their structures frequently razed as the white schools survived. The presumption was that there was nothing of value in the black community to preserve. The corresponding assumption that blacks would benefit simply by being in the presence of the dominant culture was demeaning.[130] The disruption to children and neighborhoods was palpable. The cost of the goal of equity in education (which rarely occurred in any case) was the erosion of cultural strength in African American communities.[131]

As black children entered schools controlled by whites, they often encountered white administrators with stereotypical views about black student performance. They were assumed to have poor academic skills and be less capable learners. For placement in academic programs, students took culturally determined tests in which they often performed at a lower standard. Many white administrators were unable to understand the cognitive styles, values, and traditions that were associated with black culture. Lingering myths of racial inferiority meant that black children often were placed in special education classes and expectations for their progress were low.[132] Those who performed exceptionally well were viewed as aberrations—"special" or "unusual."[133] High-performing blacks were separated from their peers and lived with the psychological burden of "difference."

Meanwhile, black neighborhoods in both the South and the North were torn apart and reshaped. Population shifts reconfigured social space, negating the potentially beneficial effects of *Brown*. During the 1940s and 1950s, more than 3 million blacks emigrated to the North. By 1970, close to half of all African Americans lived outside the South; three-quarters were in urban areas. At the same time, increasing numbers of whites moved to the suburbs. Professional and middle-class blacks did the same. With each passing decade, the income gap between city and suburb widened.[134] Socioeconomic and cultural values meant that schools quickly resegregated.

Urban schools increasingly became associated with failure as poor (and minority) students populated the inner city. There were fewer peer role models associated with successful academic performance, as the poorest black children lived in a world of "hypersegregation."[135] Bureaucratic educational policies made it especially difficult to implement programs for specific high-risk schools.[136] High school dropout rates for minorities rose. Where jobs existed, there were fewer low-skilled, living-wage opportunities. Unemployment rates in inner cities mounted, leading to frustration, crime, and incarceration.[137] Resegregated schools increasingly were class-based.

Of course, some African American students found that their educational opportunities increased as a result of national policies of inclusion. Science laboratories, arts-based programs, selective courses and academic programs, and sports programs offered some the opportunity to excel. In cities like Akron, Ohio, where Rita Dove lived, schools had been integrated in the 1930s, and educational opportunities offered greater equality. Neighborhoods organized themselves more along class lines and schools reflected class distinctions; natural segregations occurred as a result of zoning but Dove learned to interact with both white and black classmates.[138] Her experience demonstrates the ideal possibilities for integrated education.

Programs implemented in the 1960s and 1970s focused on affirmative actions to compensate for past wrongs. More magnet schools were created, more community-based programs existed to enrich the curriculum. College recruitment efforts expanded and more scholarships were available for people of color. National legislation ensured that qualified blacks would have equal access to jobs. For several decades of the late twentieth century, a growing black middle class attested to the change in tone in the country. But the benefits that accrued did not affect those who lived in inner-city ghettos or in rural poverty.

Black leaders witnessed some of these failures. In New York, where there were no formal Jim Crow laws, the poorest sections of the city were segregated de facto. That was the world that Geoffrey Canada experienced in the South Bronx, where he regularly saw his friends get in trouble, go to jail, and sometimes die. He wondered at age 11 or 12 where the adults were "to come in and save us." And he knew then that his life's work would be to "make sure the monsters don't get you."[139]

Canada believes that the educational system in the North gave up on many kids, making assumptions about their inability to succeed. On the basis of his own schooling, he could see that a tracking system was in place.[140] When he returned to New York City from Boston in the 1980s and became the educational director of the Rheedlen Centers for Children and Families, he noticed many more children were failing than anyone had realized. He thought he was working to get the 15 percent of the children at the bottom back into the middle of the curve, when he suddenly realized that "There was no middle. The middle had gone." By the mid-1990s, in places like Harlem, data indicated that 75 percent of children were falling behind, and that by eighth grade, the figures had jumped to 85 percent.

Sixty years after the *Brown* decision, approximately a third of all black children in the United States live in poverty, causing African Americans to wonder whether the promise of *Brown* was a mirage.[141] "Brown v. Board of Education is becoming a milestone in search of something to signify," Charles Payne contends.[142]

After heartening gains in educational achievement in the 1970s and 1980s, the gap widened. Hrabowski contends that most black and Latino children attend schools that are "underfunded, underachieving, and unequal." He focuses on data that shows African American and Hispanic 12th graders performing at the same level as White students in 8th grade.[143] Inadequate educational achievement means that minorities are more inclined to drop out of high school, and the drop-out rates for blacks continue to be higher than those for whites. Among those with no high school diploma, more than 50 percent are unemployed.[144] Deprivation and despair can lead to crime and imprisonment, and incarceration rates for black and Hispanic males more than doubled in the closing decades of the twentieth century. In addition, young black men and increasingly black women are targets of racial profiling. Is it any wonder, then, that more blacks find themselves in jail than in the workplace? More than 60 percent of people in prison in 2013 were racial and ethnic minorities.[145] Canada claims that one in fifteen of all people of color are in jail.[146]

Lower levels of achievement, even for those with high school diplomas, means that those who enter college do so with deficits. Freeman Hrabowski has used a 2000 study of first year students in California's public colleges that shows that 75 percent of all black freshmen needed developmental work in mathematics, and over 60 percent required developmental English classes.[147] The situation has not changed much; *U.S. News* reported in 2012 that only 23 percent of American Indian, Hispanic, and African American high school graduates tested for college readiness in math could make the grade.[148] Data from the US 2009 Census reveals that 19.5 percent of white people 25 and over have college degrees compared to 11.5 percent of blacks.[149] The situation is significantly worse for Hispanics at 8.7 percent. Mary Futrell is convinced that this is because public schools continue to segregate student populations through tracking. As long as this structure remains in place, she contends, "you're not going to meet the standards. And these children are going to look as though they can't learn. It's not that they can't learn. They're not being taught the basic math, the basic science, the basic English, the basic whatever. So a lot of it has to do with politics. A lot of it has to do with educational policies. A lot of it has to do with attitudes that we still have."[150]

Katori Hall, a young black playwright from Memphis, Tennessee, is painfully aware of the continuing impacts of tracking on her and her peers. Growing up in Martin Luther King, Jr.'s city, she recognized the disparities between the "haves" and the "have-nots." When her parents moved from a black neighborhood to one where she could have the benefits of a stronger education, she sensed the trade-offs:

> You know, I was very cognizant of, you know, what was being left behind and it being a place of poverty, but also a place of community, a place of home, a place where big momma took care of all the kids and it was like a daycare center, but then, if I would've stayed where big momma stayed, I wouldn't have been able to be in an optional program, have AP classes, and be really enriched artistically and academically. But there is a kind of trade....I think I still kept my sense of being an African American, a sense of "blackness," but there is a sense of always being the only one in the room and having that huge responsibility to defend your race...Or to represent your race, and to work harder than your other white counterparts because you have to prove to them that you deserve to be there, that you should be there. That is a lot of emotional weight.[151]

America's school-age populations are becoming increasingly minority. In October 2008, 43 percent of students from elementary through high school were nonwhite.[152] If the educational disparities by race and ethnicity continue, and there is no reason to suppose otherwise, the consequences for the nation will be disastrous. An undereducated population will impact our domestic economy, standard of living, ability to provide basic services to the populace, security, and class and race differences.[153] The problem of educational disparity is urgent and requires bold interventions.

What Is To Be Done?

In 1952, Horace Mann Bond pointed out that the word "integration" derives from "integer"—a mathematical concept. With remarkable prescience, he warned against the "delusion of automatic progress where social and racial relations are involved." He did not welcome integration if it took the form of an "absorptive swallowing" that would disregard black culture and tradition.[154] People, he asserted, are more than integers, and human personality is complex. In thinking about policies related to integration, he counseled, "...we have to do with a physical man, and a biological man, and a psychological man, and a sociological man, as well as with a purely abstract mathematical man."[155] The restrictive vision of a mathematical solution prevailed, failing to take into consideration the sociocultural and economic histories of black communities.[156]

We also know that there are approaches that work, if we have the collective will to implement them. Interviews with black leaders illuminate that high self-regard and strong group pride, parental and community involvement, quality teacher training, respect for diversity, expectations of educational achievement, and equality of resources will level the playing field, making it possible for all students to have a fair chance.[157]

Black education leaders are dedicated to implementing such systemic approaches. They know that quality education is critical for leadership. William Raspberry looked homeward to make a difference. His small, segregated community of Okolona, Mississippi, benefitted from the four-year high school and two-year Okolona College. Yet when integration occurred, the college closed. Okolona lost its foundational base for educational excellence. Now the town is mired in poverty without the means to propel people forward in the same ways he experienced. Its estimated median household income in 2011 was $17,715 compared to $36,919 in Mississippi. Almost 70 percent of the town's 2,800 residents are African American.[158]

Creating *Baby Steps* is William Raspberry's way to contribute to the next generation's success. *Baby Steps* teaches parents how best to prepare children from at-risk families to be socially and educationally prepared for kindergarten. The program focuses on preliteracy skills and language development skills for infants and toddlers, with the parents being the primary educators.[159]

Research shows staggering disparities based on class and income level in how many words children hear from parents in home environments. A poor child, on average, will have heard 30 million fewer words than a child from a professional family.[160] That translates into language acquisition, which then translates into early success in school. *Baby Steps* exists to level the playing field. Raspberry explains:

> But you know, you ask what we do, what we teach them. Sure. Attitudes are among the things that I think are critical. The beginnings of a new belief in themselves as parents and their own efficacy. But there're specific things that they can be taught to do. Talk to your kids. Talk to your children. It can be quite astounding to watch how little conversation happens between parent and child at some of the lower income levels. Studies have been done on this that as you come down the socioeconomic ladder, there is less conversation between parent and child...you spend time with a middle-class mom or dad and their toddlers, there's

this incessant chatter that's going on both ways. This is language formation. It promotes reading readiness although that's
not what it's meant to do.... Reading to their kids
every night is something they can do. Using stuff
that's around the kitchen to teach initial letter
sounds is something they can do and enjoy learning to do.... if you can help people to believe that
what they do will make a difference for their children's life chances, you can get their attention.[161]

William Raspberry

http://blackleadership.virginia.edu/10

Geoffrey Canada focuses his efforts on a much larger community—that of
Harlem, New York—but similarly understands how attitudes must be taught
and community-wide needs must be met. Serving children from kindergarten
through high school, the Harlem Children's Zone now encompasses close to
100 blocks in central Harlem and reaches more than 8,000 children and 6,000
adults.[162] The budget is over $75 million.

Canada has grown the Harlem Children's Zone over time, because he knows
that to level the playing field, he can't "play along the margins." He wants children in Harlem to have the same opportunities as those in Scarsdale:

It gets back to education. It gets back to—are we making sure these
young people have an education where they can compete and what's
stopping that from happening? And to me, that's what this whole thing
is about and for some poor kids, there're a lot of things stopping that
from happening. It's not just whether or not the schools are equitably
funded and whether or not the schools are integrated. You've got all of
these other barriers that you have to remove before these young people
can get an education.... So people come and they say, "oh, you provide
health care." We have a health clinic. Mental health, we have psychia-
trists, social workers. "You do education?" Yes, we run our own schools.
"You do all the social—recreation." Yeah, we have great recreation, great
culture, great arts, and they're like "isn't that great," and I think, no,
it is simply average. That's what the average middle class kid gets in
America. There's nothing great about that.... No. This goes on all over
America. It just doesn't happen in poor communi-
ties and so what we're trying to do is just simply
provide for what happens in other places in the
country.... [W]hat would you expect in Scarsdale?
Well, you know what, we should have that for poor
children and no one should think that that's like
some great big thing that we're providing for them
because that should be their right as Americans, in
my opinion.[163]

Geoffrey Canada

http://blackleadership.virginia.edu/11

Canada's overriding goal is to change the odds for the poor by creating an interlocking web from birth to college that rebuilds community.[164] Only with such a systemic approach will he be able to stop the devastating cycle of deprivation and death.[165] His audacious goal has been to develop a programmatic system that can be validated and replicated nationally.[166] HCZ now includes a Baby College with parenting classes for expectant and new parents, charter schools Promise Academy I and II and Promise Academy High School, Academic Case Management for children in public schools, Employment and Technology Center, Truce Arts and Media initiative, College Success Office, and numerous after school, summer camp, and fitness initiatives. But HCZ is not focused on education solely. There are also parent support programs, literacy initiatives, Community Pride (focused on tenant and block associations and community engagement), Single Stop (for legal, financial, social service advice), health and wellness initiatives (focused on asthma, obesity, drugs and preventive health care), and foster care and truancy prevention programs under contract from New York City.[167] These programs represent both a "conveyor-belt strategy"—a system from birth to college—and a "contamination strategy"—exposure to specific outreach programs for those unable to access the charter school systems. Canada's intrepid intent is nothing short of changing Harlem's culture.[168]

For Geoffrey Canada, there are multiple measures for long-term success of the system-wide safety net programs of HCZ. But since education is fundamental to

Figure 3.2 Geoffrey Canada with children from Harlem Children's Zone. Courtesy of Harlem Children's Zone.

his mission, one important measure is the number of college degrees generated. For 2010–11, 254 students were accepted into college, representing 90 percent of HCZ high school seniors.[169] In his own life, he knows that he is a survivor, and that chance played a big part. He wants to minimize the role of chance for others by providing the tools to live healthy and productive lives with the capacity to nurture the next generation of children. Nothing short of that will break the cycle of poverty. He wants to end the conversation about whether it is possible to "take large numbers of poor, disadvantaged students and get them in and through college and on the path to success" and he wants "to prove it so convincingly that this won't be a question of whether or not it can be done." That, he hopes, will be his leadership contribution.[170]

Other black education leaders seek to make a difference on the collegiate and graduate school levels, making sure that research advances understanding of underrepresented minorities and that all individuals have an opportunity to pursue their dreams. Freeman Hrabowski initiated the Meyerhoff Scholars Program at The University of Maryland Baltimore County in 1988 to demonstrate that the STEM (science, technology, engineering, math) disciplines are fully teachable and accessible to minority students. It all goes back to his experiences in learning and helping others learn mathematics. "I want them to dream like I did," he says. "I want them to know that they can earn a master's and doctorate. I want them to know that they are special..."[171]

Figure 3.3   Freeman Hrabowski with Meyerhoff Scholars. Credit: Jim Burger/UMBC

Initially, the Meyerhoff Scholars Program targeted African American males who wanted to obtain Ph.D. degrees in math, engineering, and science. The first class of 19 students received financial assistance, mentoring, research opportunities, and advising. By 1990, the program expanded to include African American women. Then, in 1996, it opened to all minorities seeking careers in science and engineering fields. Over time, the program has become more and more ethnically and racially diverse. For 2013–14, 290 students are enrolled; 53 percent are African American, 22 percent are Caucasian, 18 percent are Asian, 6 percent Hispanic, and 1 percent Native American. As of February 2013, alumni have earned 132 Ph.D.s, 31 M.D./Ph.Ds, 187 M.S. degrees, and 106 M.Ds. 300 more students are in the pipeline. The program boasts over 800 alumni. Research demonstrates that students in this program are 5.3 times more likely to have graduated from a STEM program or be pursuing such a program than those who chose to study elsewhere. Based at one of the most diverse universities in the country, this program is succeeding in changing the racial balance of STEM professionals in America.[172] In the process, UMBC demonstrates how community can empower new leaders.

Like the Harlem Children's Zone, the Meyerhoff Scholars Program is systemic, stressing cooperation, community engagement, and the pursuit of excellence. Study groups, mentoring, advising, living arrangements, and faculty engagement are core components. Students in the program tutor others at both the K-12 and college levels. Parents are kept informed of students' progress, invited to counseling sessions, if necessary, and included in special events.[173] The emphasis is on creating a caring and supportive community—the kind that Freeman Hrabowski knew as a child in Birmingham, Alabama:

> I have no doubt that people watch what presidents of colleges do all the time and those actions from leaders have an impact on other people.... Leaders can do so much more through their actions than they can through their words.... I do know that large numbers of colleagues, faculty and staff, have said to me over the years.... " We shouldn't just assume that it's okay to walk by people without connecting in different ways," and that a part of this community that's important, a really important part of it, is relationships. The importance of connecting with students and other colleagues to let them know that what they do is important and that they matter.... It's amazing how we're all shaped by our childhood experiences and my point for today and the University is that I know my colleagues care about these students. I see it all the time.[174]

President of UMBC since 1992, Freeman Hrabowski is a national educational leader. Over 13,000 students attend his university. It is one of the most racially diverse universities in the country. Hrabowski wants to empower every-one to achieve to his highest potential. It is an ethical and philosophical commit-ment for Hrabowski:

> One's philosophy is, from my perspective, the ethical core of the person. What is it that you value? What is it that is critical when you think about themes that help to shape who you are? If someone were to ask me the question what is my philosophy of life, what is my philosophy of education, I could very easily say that my philosophy focuses on build-ing relationships with people characterized by trust and authenticity and my believing in the fundamental goodness of people—that we can bring from people that goodness, that we all have all kinds of sides and can be all kinds of things or people if we're not encouraged to be our best, whether in education or in life.[175]

To lead, one has to be authentic, honest, and open. These values are critical to Hrabowski's way of thinking. For him, leadership requires constant self-examination. For him, authenticity means openness to all people and a willingness to engage in frank dialogue about race.[176] For him, building caring community requires his outreach to others to encourage their self-reflection about personal values and assumptions. For him, support for a diverse America means that all students must feel empowered to seek the American dream. Educational oppor-tunity is a key to leadership, but success also requires caring families, nurturing communities, support networks, and personal determination.

To level the playing field, stepping up to leadership is fundamental. Mary Futrell began her career as a teacher of business subjects in a segregated Alexandria, Virginia, high school in 1963. She ended up as Dean of the School of Education at George Washington University. In between, however, she assumed major lead-ership positions in state and national education associations, becoming a role model for black women and challenging establishment norms.

Mary Futrell grew up poor. She experienced both the negative and positive effects of segregated southern schools. She saw the inequities built into the school systems. She was subjected to the unfair assumptions of classism, alive and well even in segregated communities. Yet, within her community, there were those who believed in her. She knows they helped create the opportunity for her to become a leader.

Important models for organizational leadership existed within the black uni-versities and throughout the Commonwealth of Virginia. In Futrell's youth and into adulthood, both the state and national teachers' associations were strictly segregated. Black teachers had first formed associations on the state level as early as 1877. When black voters were disenfranchised, such organizations focused exclusively on teacher training and educational support, sponsoring teachers' institutes and summer schools. But their resources were extremely limited. From the 1920s on, as organized labor groups expanded and as more black high schools were created, the Virginia Teachers Association (VTA) grew from fewer than 200 members to 3,000 by the decade's end. John M. Gandy, already president of Futrell's future college, Virginia State University, was the force behind this enormous growth. He published a quarterly bulletin, created parent–teacher organizations, established an employment service and a speakers' bureau, and carried out survey research. He modeled leadership for black empowerment.[177] Mary Futrell remained sensitive to the potential marginalization of black educational issues after the merger of VTA and VEA.

National education lobbying groups also began as segregated institutions but eventually merged, creating opportunities for broader discussion of critical learning issues. The National Association of Teachers in Colored Schools (NATCS) was the main lobbying force for black education. Renamed the American Teachers' Association in 1937, this organization merged with the National Education Association (NEA) in 1966—14 years after the *Brown* decision. In 1983, only five years after heading the integrated VEA, Futrell was elected president of the NEA at age 37.

Futrell has spent her career working at the organizational level to integrate systems in equitable ways so that everyone has a fair chance. She worked tirelessly to protect teachers, administrators, and students from racism, sexism, and classism. During her tenure as NEA president, she continually sparred with Secretary of Education William Bennett over tax policies, teacher certification, school vouchers, teacher salaries, class size, and teacher testing. She urged greater teacher self-governance and wanted to see a more prominent role for teachers on the National Board for Professional Teacher Certification. She also wanted to serve minority and female children more effectively and was disquieted by the waning number of minority teachers. She helped launch NEA's Operation Rescue to combat dropouts and looked for systemic answers to education's complex problems. When President Ronald Reagan accused the NEA of "brainwashing America's schoolchildren," Futrell countered that he had treated education as a doormat. When Bennett blasted the NEA for its "lack of accountability" and its unwillingness to support proposals by his office to measure teachers' abilities and to set national standards, Futrell insisted that the NEA would not sacrifice the needs of children to "wall-chart charades." When she stepped down after an unprecedented six years in office, widely viewed as the most popular and effective leader in NEA's history, she assigned a D to Bennett's performance as secretary of education.[178]

Futrell claims that her formative experiences created an inner toughness:

> you learn how to survive. You learn... that if you believe in something strongly enough, that you're willing to go back and keep trying....And

when you grew up in a segregated society like I did, you learn how to fight early. And so, when I look back on all the things I experienced in Lynchburg, and Virginia State, and other places—I had learned at Virginia State to be a fighter, to stand up. I had learned in Lynchburg, unknowingly to stand up. And so, you don't let defeat stop you. You come back and you keep trying.[179]

Futrell worries about the loss of black teachers. Without a racial balance in the schools, both black and white children suffer, she contends, because imbalance denies black students positive role models and gives white students a distorted view of the world. She is equally concerned with the tracking of black students, which denies them full educational opportunity. "We owe all students a vision of the racial, ethnic, and religious mosaic that is America—a vision of the diversity that is our strength," she wrote in 1989—the year she stepped down as NEA president.[180]

As a faculty member and then dean of the School of Education at George Washington University (GWU), she continued to advocate for these causes. Her goal was to build a pluralistic society that inculcates high educational standards. She became one of the codirectors of the Center for Curriculum, Standards and Technology at GWU. CCST, founded in 1992, trains teachers to be leaders of educational reform, and researches and proposes reforms in curriculum standards, national teacher certification, and effective teachers' professional development.[181]

In every phase of her career, Mary Futrell has worked for systemic change. Her vision for education emanates from a larger belief in the American dream—a dream of full equality. She wants integrated schools to focus on the educational potential of each and every child. They must work with parents to motivate their children. They must eliminate systemic tracking. The ethic of caring must become part of the national infrastructure of education. Only then will society overcome the debilitating impact of class-isms. Only then will justice in education prevail.

Like Futrell and Hrabowski, Johnnetta Cole has spent much of her career at institutions of higher education.[182] She brings her life experiences to her educational philosophy. Growing up as a child of black privilege, she knows how much she benefitted from her exposure to the arts and music, to foreign cultures, and to integrated higher education of superior quality. She also knows that despite her privileged background, she had to "overcome the images that others...projected" onto her; as a result, she feels an "enormous responsibility not to project myths on others in turn."[183] She was drawn to study and teach those subjects at U. Mass-Amherst, Hunter College, and Emory University that increase sensitivity to cultural diversity and empower minority groups. While president of Spelman, she sought ways for students to expand their intellectual horizons. While president of Bennett College, she oversaw the opening of an art

Figure 3.4   Dr. Johnnetta Betsch Cole standing in front of the statue *Toussaint Louverture et la vieille esclave (Toussaint Louverture and the elderly slave)*. Photo credit: Jessica Suwaroff, Smithsonian's National Museum of African Art.

museum and initiated programs in global and women's studies. In each context, she recognized the importance of being a committed mentor to students.

The battle to achieve full equality continues. Cole believes that Americans have never fully confronted slavery and the damage it inflicted on the psyche of African Americans.[184] Education, therefore, is critical to nurturing self-awareness and to promoting equality. Self-awareness is critical to self-realization and personal liberation. Writing for her sisters at Spelman, she defines liberation:

> I mean liberation from all the "isms" previously discussed: racism, sexism, provincialism, and the individualism that prevents us from building sturdy Black bridges.[185]

Even at esteemed black women's colleges like Spelman, students can be narrow-minded to cultural differences. During her administration there, Johnnetta Cole is most proud of making the climate more hospitable to Muslims, lesbians and bisexuals, feminists, and to a service mentality of responsibility to others.[186]

Education is far more than book-learning, according to Cole. Education must be socially responsible. It must expose students to the larger world and must lead them to appreciate the "multiplicity" of competing "truths." She writes:

An education grounded in a social responsibility for making the world a better place hinges directly and completely on a deep, studied, and ongoing education about the complexities of human diversity and culture in all the neighborhoods of our nation, on all the continents of our world.... The histories of the poor and the powerless are as important as those of their conquerors, their colonizers, their kings and queens.[187]

Teachers are profoundly important in this process. Johnnetta Cole reflects on the role of her own teacher in insisting that she fulfill her highest potential and regrets the human tendency to make assumptions about achievement based on color:

Our task is to socially reproduce the Bunny [Bernice] Vances. But there are so many non-Bunny Vances. So many teachers who really have decided that the easiest way for them to get through a day is to color-code their kids. And so the brown ones and the black ones will never achieve what the white ones will. And so out of a kind of least common denominator of thinking they begin to give off the signals to these kids as to who can and who cannot.[188]

Johnnetta Cole

http://blackleadership.virginia.edu/12

Our educational challenge as a nation is to treat all children equally, to nurture their capacities, and to instill an appreciation for cultural diversity.

In her role as director of the Smithsonian's National Museum of African Art, Cole has a platform to educate internationally. Her very ambitious goal is to increase the visibility of the museum and expand its range of visitors. This is education in the public realm—education that enhances cultural understanding.

Coming from a very different set of experiences than either Canada, Futrell, or Hrabowski, Cole nonetheless ends up in the same place. They passionately believe in the centrality of education for leadership. Quality education provides opportunity. Education raises people up through knowledge. Worthy educators teach the highest American values.

Rita Dove also had the benefit of growing up as the child of well-educated parents. Living in Akron, Ohio, rather than Jacksonville, Florida, meant that she had the advantage of integrated schools and educational resources that provided opportunity. As a poet in the creative writing program at the University of Virginia, she sees her role as an educator of all potential poets. Poetry is a means to connect us to our own humanity and to engage emotionally. Although she is aware of how black poets helped her to realize her own career goals, and although she knows that race is part of her self-definition, she writes poetry for the human race:

> Whenever I talk about poetry, whenever I read poetry in front of a group, I feel that I am opening myself to them and when I say myself, I don't mean just all of my tiny frustrations or anything like that. I mean a very complex mix of every interesting and complicated emotions that human beings have. I mean me as a black person, as a woman, as a human being, as an American. All of these things, but I'm saying here it is. Now, can you—Is this something that relates to something in you and that's intensely personal....And I also feel—I think that for me to have someone, a perfect stranger say, that they have felt the same way, too, and this perfect stranger may be a white man from rural Texas. That's an incredible victory for the human race and for civil rights and all of that to acknowledge, to realize that different skin colors, different classes, we're all human beings. This is where civil liberties and mutual respect begin.[189]

As poet laureate of the United States, Rita Dove loved the opportunity to connect with children, and to help them overcome their fear of poetry. "Poetry is about life. It's not about books," she said.[190] It is within all of us.

Rita Dove will go anywhere to deliver the message that poetry is an educational vehicle to help people get in touch with their emotions and to learn more about themselves—to Sesame Street, to schools, to public poetry readings, to concert halls. She is aware that "race gets sidelined" in poetry, and she is conscious of the need to take that on in her own work. At the same time, even as she seeks to transcend race and to connect through the written word with all people, she knows there are continuing impediments within the broader society:

> being conscious of race is a natural part of my DNA and I have looked at society as an African American woman, an African American poet, and seen how race gets sidelined and my race gets sidelined, and so naturally I've taken an interest in that kind of rub against, let's say, history with a capital "H," history with a small "h," which formed the basis for *Thomas and Beulah*, for the story about an African American couple as their interior lives as it's reflected against the larger backdrop of American history in the 20th century...I would hope that as people read...it would open some eyes to what happens racially in this country in terms of people's perceptions and also open their eyes to how we're all connected rather than being separate. If, however, you would ask me

or insist that there were a leader that transcended race at this time, I would say that it's something I always hope and I'm proven wrong and I think Obama was elected in an incredible wave of race transcendency, let's say, and he in fact conducts the Office of the Presidency that way. I think it's exceedingly important but the actions of Congress and the Tea Party and these groups show that we have not transcended race, that there are forces which are just as virulent.

I think that personally as a poet I at times think that my work and my example has transcended race and then I'm brought up short and reminded...that, no, we haven't transcended race, not yet.[191]

Rita Dove

http://blackleadership.virginia.edu/13

Education has always been a vital route toward upward mobility. Almost all black leaders know that there is a long way to go to provide fully equal public education. Politician and lawyer Carol Moseley Braun believes that "The whole ideal of quality universal public education is very much on the bubble, very much challenged, very much at risk now" both because preschool education has been scaled back and the costs of higher education have grown astronomically.[192] Civil rights attorney Elaine Jones likewise recognizes that we need to "get these quality schools for our kids and help our kids to dream. Our kids—too often, their dreams are dashed. Kids, you know, are inquisitive and creative—we—that's beaten out of them, and then the circumstances beat them down. So, we're on the right track when we stick with this whole question of quality public education. If we lose that, we've lost it."[193]

What our leaders learned from their own educational experiences is that schools are implicated in the moral life of their communities. Morality *precedes* knowledge. Educational reform and educational excellence are grounded in the need to create a racial literacy that values every individual equally.[194] That is what inspires our leaders in their educational efforts. Their values, collectively, should inspire educational reform in America. They teach us that educational excellence in America is possible at all levels. But it takes a caring, committed society.

CHAPTER 4

Networks: Role Models, Mentors, Organizations

It takes a whole village to raise a child.—African proverb[1]

I don't think during my high school years I really fully comprehended the vastness of leadership, the integrated nature of it. But when I finished law school and came back and became a part of the community and began to take part in civic and political activities, I could see the value of the network, the value of talking to people.[2]—Vernon Jordan

* * *

My father...was a Mason, a Shriner. He was the head of the Masons and the head of the Shriners. And he would go to these conventions and he was an Elk and he was an Odd Fellow... [A]nd the way that people went to conventions in those days—this is interesting—is that there was this network of homes because you couldn't stay in the hotels if you were African American. We had a home that had rooms in it that my mother made available to conventioneers. And so the network grew because you would meet people who were from other places who would stay in your home and everyone knew they were staying in your home. They were like family. And they were treated like family....I think that my mother was involved with the companion organizations of the Masons...Daughters of Isis. She was also a Lady Elk....[B]ut she helped found the sorority, branch chapter of Iota Phi Lambda in Buffalo. So we had all these tangents that right,—that helped me and my brother and my sisters as we ventured forth....There was always somebody you called when you went to another city...And somebody that my parents knew. "Call up Mrs. So-and-So and tell her you're, tell her you're my daughter. And let her know that you're there." Even when I went to college...my family doctor...called up a physician in Durham who was a friend of his and said, "We've got Yvonne coming down. I want you to look after her." And so when I got to Durham I called them up....That pattern sort of continued. When I went to the University of Minnesota, Carl Rowan was in Minneapolis writing for the paper there. Carl Rowan's wife is from Buffalo. She was the daughter of—or is the daughter of a family, a large family the sister of which was the head of the Urban League and the brother of which family was my mother's physician. So when I went to Minnesota, I called up Carl Rowan because Vivian was his wife and "I'm from Buffalo. Mother said to call you up."....There is this network, and it developed because two things. Because we did not have access to the major support, commercial institutions that people— that non-black people, white people and other people—relied on when they moved from city to city. And because it was dangerous. It could be dangerous out there.[3]

Yvonne Scruggs-Leftwich sums up the multiple ways in which networks and connections, both personal and institutional, provide grounding and safety. In some cases, the relationships are deeply personal and demonstrate the power of mentors or role models. In other cases, positive identity is nurtured through group associations. Group memberships may be voluntary or involuntary, but the lessons learned often create lifelong values and habits that lead to productive and successful lives. The networks and connections that exist beyond family and beyond educational structures, illuminating the "village" ideal of community, dominate in this chapter.

Five black leaders—Dorothy Height, Elaine Jones, Vernon Jordan, Robert Franklin, and Bobby Rush—illustrate the central importance of networks and connections in their evolution to leadership.[4] Whether the goals were personal empowerment, community advancement, political organizing, or spiritual growth, these leaders developed strong personal confidence along the way. A sense of self was fundamental to their emergence as leaders. But their self-esteem was deeply rooted in a sense of place. The leaders highlighted here explain how their households and communities functioned and how individuals and institutions protected them from the *anomie* so characteristic of modernity. In numerous ways, these black leaders were products of their "villages."

Hillary Clinton brought national attention to disparities faced by children in America with her 1996 best-selling book, *It Takes a Village*.[5] She focused renewed energy on how we might level America's playing field so that all children can grow into resilient and productive adults. She did not deny the fundamental role of parents and family members in child-rearing. But she also recognized the need to create healthier communities so that responsible adults can do their jobs. Theologian Robert Franklin focuses on the African American community specifically in his book, *Crisis in the Village*. He examines the contemporary crisis in families, schools, and churches—those institutions which he maintains "have played a heroic role in serving black communities in the past."[6] For both Clinton and Franklin, village implies shared communal purpose and intimacy.[7] They call attention to those fundamental "anchor institutions" that create stability and offer healthy, nurturing experiences.[8]

While there are some ways in which networks and connections are distinctive to black communities, the experiences that shaped the lives of individuals in this sample can be generalized beyond race. The value of healthy networks and communities is not color-coded. Neither is it class-coded nor gender-coded. Of course, the opportunity to establish functional and healthy communities does not exist in equal measure across socioeconomic categories. Racism and discrimination impact psychic development and economic well-being. Yet, within the communities of so many black leaders interviewed—whether integrated or segregated, whether middle-class or poor, networks and connections nurtured them and provided the foundations for future successes.

Formative experiences for many black leaders who came of age in the late twentieth century occurred in the context of racial marginalization. White neighborhoods and white schools were often off limits. When they moved through these spaces, they were forced to drink from "colored" water fountains, to use "colored" bathrooms, to sit in the back of the bus, or to give up their seats to white passengers. Returning home was a means to access a safe space, one in which they were segregated but comfortable. Although these places were limiting and confining, they also functioned as healthy, nurturing communities. The networks and connections forged alliances among people that helped them overcome the daily bigotry individuals experienced when they ventured outside their communities.

Political theorist Melissa Harris-Lacewell contends that "everyday spaces" and "everyday talk" in black communities create a ripe environment for stories to circulate and identities to develop as people "link their individual experiences to group narratives."[9] Collective definitions of political interests and potential actions also emerge from such everyday talk.[10] Put another way, networks and connections catalyze leadership opportunities around community interests.

But how, precisely, are such positive identities nurtured? What formative influences do leaders draw upon? And how do they transfer those experiences into their own leadership paradigms? Five people help us better understand the meaning and power of networks and connections. Dorothy Height, the president of the National Council of Negro Women for over 50 years and the *grande dame* of the American Civil Rights movement, formed her initial networks in the northeast in a largely integrated environment. Elaine Jones, a Virginian, grew up in the strictly segregated community of Norfolk and encountered integrated education only after she was accepted as the first black woman in University of Virginia's Law School. Vernon Jordan experienced his formative years in the urban center of Atlanta, Georgia in the deep South—a neighborhood that also was strictly segregated but was an epicenter of African American business, education, and activism. Robert M. Franklin's earliest experiences were in southside Chicago—a troubled neighborhood in a vast metropolis—but one where his family created a small village environment. Bobby Rush moved from small town Albany, Georgia to a different section of Chicago, where he experienced both the positives and some negatives of inner-city life. Born between 1912 and 1954, spanning communities from the Northeast to the South and Midwest, these five individuals personify shared core values that undergird their leadership trajectories.

These leaders stress the rich and productive relationships that were key to their personal development. Some of these relationships emerged from within their homes; some arose from interactions with teachers, community members, and institutional leaders who were consistently engaged in their lives. Together, these influences created the textured quilt of self-esteem and positive identity. Leaders were empowered by their associations.

To best illustrate the salience of networks and connections, I follow leaders' stories through ever-widening arcs. In some cases, individuals learn to engage networks and organizations by observing their parents or other family members. This analysis returns to family, but only to emphasize the ways in which family members modeled relevant behaviors. Educational institutions, discussed in the previous chapter, created critical community connections. I focus on those less here; their centrality to leadership development has been addressed. As circles broaden, community mentors, churches, and fraternal organizations raise up black leaders. Many credit non-race-specific experiences in scouting, the military, and international living for creating the connections so fundamental for their broader understanding of leadership. Their personal journeys follow different paths, but reveal similar truths.

Role Models

Leadership begins with values learned at home. Black leaders acknowledge how primary family members established the foundational principles for their lives, adapting to the communities in which they lived.[11] In fact, family members modeled how to be effective participants in networks and communities.

Dorothy Height, for example, credits her mother and her father for her involvement in organizations. Both her parents had been twice widowed by the time she was born, and they decided to leave Richmond, Virginia, in 1916 to seek a better life. Young Dorothy was four when they moved to the small coal mining and steel manufacturing town of Rankin, Pennsylvania. The town, located eight miles south of Pittsburgh, had a population around 6,000 people. It was a place of great diversity with many foreign-born and first-generation Americans. She grew up with Italians, Croatians, and Germans.[12] Her father was always self-employed as a highly skilled building contractor. He was active in both politics and in the Knights of Pythias, an international nonsectarian fraternal organization and secret society founded in 1864 to promote national healing in the aftermath of Civil War. He was also both choirmaster and superintendent of Sunday schools for their Baptist church.[13] Her mother, a trained nurse, was unable to find work in hospitals once they moved to Pennsylvania, and ended up doing "household work." Eventually, she was able to use her nursing skills to take care of private patients.[14] In the self-help mentality that black Americans had to adopt to survive, her mother became deeply involved in organizations, especially the black women's club movement.

That movement was still relatively young. In 1896, with the inspiring Mary Church Terrell as president, the National Association of Colored Women's Clubs was formed. With the motto "Lifting as We Climb," the NACW created a cohesive communication network of black women in the country. The NACW's primary goal was to promote uplift as a means to end racism. Local clubs focused on many of the same issues that white women's Progressive organizations tackled. With a "talented tenth" mentality, these middle-class and elite black women took on such issues as the convict lease system, lynching, Jim Crow laws, kindergarten education, fair labor practices, and women's suffrage.[15] In so doing, the NACW became a leadership laboratory for women.[16]

Height understood well the purpose of such women's groups both for her mother's generation and her own:

> those groups I always said often furnished for our community what the white community had taken for granted. Everyone had a project of feeding the poor, feeding the hungry, home for homeless girls. You had to have a specific service in the community. And it also was that you had to see what you could do with those who needed it most. And I don't think anyone realizes the way in which those clubs—they sold pies, they baked cakes, they sold chitlin dinners, or fried chicken, or whatever, but always the money was raised to help someone. They gave baskets at Thanksgiving and things of that sort, but over and above that, they sustained programs.[17]

Dorothy Height

http://blackleadership.virginia.edu/14

From her parents, she said, she "understood the value of organization[s]."

From her mother, Height learned other values. She learned that she "could not just strut around and be proud" because she had a "responsibility to other people." It was her mother who helped her "relate to needs in a community and to people."[18]

No wonder, then, that from such role models, Dorothy Height sought out organizations as a way to focus on societal uplift. In Rankin, she was active in school, in church, in the Pennsylvania Girls' Clubs, and in the NAACP. Once in college at New York University, she connected with the United Christian Youth Movement of North America in addition to the NAACP. But she and her colleagues also formed new organizations, like the Harlem Youth Council, the United Youth Committee against Lynching, and the Ramses Club. In so doing, she worked with Kenneth Clark, James Robinson, and Juanita Jackson. They made their own networks:

> we found each other and we kind of made our own little group....And we gathered together. We weren't seeing ourselves as a caucus. We were seeing ourselves as needing to find ways to get more understanding of who we were. And so when we had Dr. Du Bois just sit and talk with us, or Langston Hughes, we just felt we'd had the best time in the whole world.[19]

When she began to work, she did so through organizations. She found mentors in Mary McLeod Bethune and Eleanor Roosevelt. Subsequently, she came to head one of the most important national black women's organizations in America, the National Council of Negro Women. She also spearheaded interracial initiatives like Wednesdays in Mississippi at the height of the civil rights movement.[20] Grounded in African American networks and having role models who could navigate the racial divide, her leadership trajectory follows her formative experiences.

Robert M. Franklin was born in the year of the *Brown v. Board of Education* decision. Societal values had shifted some since the youthful days of Dorothy Height and would shift more radically during Franklin's youth. Yet, the formative lessons learned at home were surprisingly similar to those of Dorothy Height. Unlike her, his family lived in the huge urban metropolis of Chicago. Unlike her, he lived within an extended family structure with grandmother, uncles, and aunts all around him. The role models at home transmitted core values that created a life philosophy, which in turn defined his career and his style of leadership.

Robert Franklin's family were migrants from Mississippi. They spent years on Chicago's south side near the stockyards before moving in 1962 to Morgan Park, right on the dividing line between white and black Chicago. His grandmother, Martha McCann, and her twin sister, Mary, purchased two houses next door to one another.[21] There, in the middle of urban Chicago, his grandmother and the extended family recreated the village life they had left behind in the small towns of Mississippi. It felt, he writes, "as if we lived in our own Southern compound tucked inside the big city. When we entered the extended family compound, we felt that we were in the safest place on earth."[22] There was lush foliage and a marsh where children could catch tadpoles. His grandmother planted a garden in an empty lot and grew all sorts of vegetables. The garden, he realized later, was a means to resist the "dehumanizing effects of urban living" and to have a means to extend her ministry to a larger community.[23] There, he experienced the power of an extended family in an always crowded household:

> Two of Grandma Martha McCann's six sons and two daughters (one of them my mother) plus my father all lived together in a dynamic working unit. Nearly every day one or more of my other uncles came by to visit or eat. That's six adults, all of whom worked and pooled their resources.[24]

In this context, Franklin learned about building community, taking care of others, and a strong work ethic.

Both his mother and grandmother found meaning and purpose in church-based activities:

> they were sort of pillars of the local church in a church that didn't ordain women. These were women without title, but with significant portfolio, and they ran all sorts of youth programs and they organized recreational activities. They encouraged mentoring and after-school tutorials and so on. So they kept us very busy and tried, in some ways I think, to insulate us from the racism in Chicago and the larger nation.[25]

His grandmother's bicultural and charismatic qualities exerted the largest single influence on him. She represented the "staid and proper existence of the church world." Yet, she also could span multiple worlds. Robert recalls how some of her sons—his uncles—were "tough guys" who would drink on weekends on their front porch. Together with the women from the church, in their finery and nurses' caps, were the neighborhood winos, "all on that porch together enjoying fried chicken, collard greens and sweet potato pie." He realized that his home was more inclusive than the church. His grandmother's cooking was a means of outreach to community. Sometimes, she would load all three grandsons into the car to deliver collard greens and corn bread to the inner city from which she had escaped. She also had the capacity to stride into the middle of potentially violent arguments among gangs and "talk those boys down." She could do so without risking personal harm because she had "moral authority" in her extended community. She was a "bridge figure" who brought people together. She had earned her moral authority by her life commitments. To Robert, she modeled a "style of leadership that has a high threshold of tolerance for difference and different practices and inclinations."[26]

Grounded in church-based communities and social justice outreach, Franklin became a theologian, teacher of ethics, and institutional leader. His leadership is manifest through the many years he served as president of the Interdenominational Theological Center (ITC) in Atlanta. He also held a distinguished professorship of social ethics at the Candler School of Theology at Emory, before being tapped to become president of Morehouse College in 2007. In 2013, he accepted the position of director of Religion at the Chatauqua Institution, working to bring people together across religious persuasions. Robert Franklin's values were nurtured at home, where his primary role models taught him daily how to envision the world as networks of people working together for common purpose.

Other black leaders also speak of strong role models who taught them about the power of wider networks. Elaine Jones, the child of a Pullman porter and a school teacher, grew up in Jim Crow Virginia. Her father, after all, belonged to "the first black trade union." Sometimes, A. Philip Randolph came home with him for dinner and appeared in her family's kitchen. "You know," she says, "Pullman porters were close...and Daddy...was very active and vocal and people gathered around...."[27] Jones remembers the intense debates around "a very active dinner table." As Jones recalls, "the food was secondary. You know, it was the conversation that was primary. And, I mean, from the earliest I can remember, that happened. And so, when I was growing up in the segregated South and I saw the wrongs, the palpable wrongs—because we lived the wrongs—I said to myself, 'I have to do something about this and I can do it.'" She determined that she would be a lawyer (at a very young age), and her parents never discouraged her from those ambitions.[28] Because of the rich conversations at the dinner table, and the interactions between her family and her community, Jones "had the confidence as a child, 'Well I can make a difference.'"[29] From her father, she learned about the power of African American networking and met one of the most powerful African American leaders of the day.

Vernon Jordan also became a lawyer, as well as a writer, political advisor, fundraiser, organizer, and public speaker. Born in 1935, his primary experiences were in the deep South in the completely segregated city of Atlanta, Georgia. His family life and his community were strong, offering lots of examples of how to make one's way in the world. In his memoir, he writes:

When I think about the early part of my life and how it helped make me the man I have become, it is so clear to me how lucky I was to have been born and raised in a world of structures. There was the structure of my family, the structure of the St. Paul African Methodist Episcopal (AME) Church, the Gate City Day Nursery, my schools, the Butler Street Colored YMCA. But above all else, I had my family.[30]

His father provided stability even though he was somewhat constrained by the prevailing mentality that convinced many African Americans of their limited opportunities in life. Vernon walked to church every Sunday morning with his father—a weekly ritual that took him and his brother to Sunday school, while his father participated in a Bible study group.[31] The Church offered a safe place to interact with others.

Vernon's mother was his inspiration, modelling for him how to engage networks. She lived in a segregated world, but that world did not define her aspirations. As the owner of a well-respected catering business, Mary Jordan knew both how to introduce her son to the world of white people and to shield him from it. Working for his mother's business gave the young Vernon his first real exposure to wealth and power. Serving food and drink to his mother's clients, especially at the Lawyer's Club in Atlanta, Jordan "got to see how you do things."[32] By observing a world of white privilege, he developed the ability to build networks cross-racially and to interact with people whose wealth or position afforded them power. But more fundamentally, his mother's entrepreneurship and work ethic afforded her a basic position in the Jordan family, a position that left its mark in terms of her son's commitment both to business and to civic service and community development.

> She was sort of the CEO of our family. She was in charge of the money. She was the entrepreneur and she was in charge of the structure of our lives from church to school to choir rehearsal to piano lessons to the Butler Street YMCA to the Gate City Nursery. In addition to that and running her business, she was the president of every PTA of every school I attended: E. A. Ware, Walker Street, David T. Howard. When I was in high school, my youngest brother was in elementary school, she was president of both PTAs. So that was—that was a lesson, number one, in leadership; it was also a lesson in community service.[33]

Mary Jordan modeled for her son how to build and engage networks to enrich community. These core values would be enormously important in his leadership choices down the road.

Bobby Lee Rush, like Robert Franklin, left the deep South for Chicago. Born in Albany, Georgia in 1946, he moved with his mother and four other siblings. He recognizes that his father wanted to do better in life, and was "frustrated as a black man." That frustration led to a lot of "anger" and "rage," disrupting family life. His mother, a beautician, had the courage to act in the interests of improving the conditions for her family. He admires his mother's willingness to take risks and attributes his own risk-taking as something she had ingrained in him.[34] Chicago offered Rush opportunities for networking and for climbing out of dire circumstances. Those connections, however, came from beyond immediate family figures.

Community Mentors and Role Models

In current literature, mentors and role models are often differentiated. Mentoring creates tangible relationships through intentional connections and recognizable structures. Role-modeling emerges out of less formal and frequently inadvertent links.[35] Mentors are usually older than their mentees (or protogés); they are individuals who know and understand the culture that the junior person wishes to access.[36] Such relationships can be formal or informal, long- or short-term. In segregated black communities, natural mentors emerged through churches, neighborhoods, and schools. They encouraged, guided, and emotionally supported youth and adolescents, allowing them to develop autonomy from parents while still having adult support.[37] But with fewer coherent neighborhood institutions, less natural mentoring occurs. The number of caring adults available to youth is reduced. This is especially true in urban centers where fewer middle-class adults who traditionally served as community leaders now reside.[38] As a result, planned mentoring programs have taken the place of natural mentors. But planned mentoring only is effective if it can be sustained over time. Otherwise, more harm than good may occur.[39]

Black leaders talk about the powerful impact that mentors had on their lives. In general, they profited from natural mentors. These were people in their schools, communities, churches, clubs, and organizations who they met in the course of their daily activities. In fact, the mentors and the institutions often could not be separated. Very frequently, mentors and role models were indistinguishable and emerged out of family and community relationships. The associations formed were rich and enduring. Nikki Giovanni, for example, talks about the lifelong relationship with Miss Delaney, her English teacher, with whom she stayed involved until Delaney died in her mid-eighties.[40] Mary Frances Berry speaks of her relationship with Ms. Minerva Hawkins, a high school teacher, who "spent a lot of time teaching me about things" and who "was for all my life my best friend until she died."[41] Such connections made school far more meaningful and inculcated a love of lifelong learning in their respective fields. Bobby Rush remembers the role of a teacher, Marion Smith, whom he met when he first moved to Chicago and felt very out of place. At Franklin Elementary School, she recognized his love of reading and helped to nurture that habit. In an integrated school in Chicago, Miss Smith lifted him from the "scorn and ridicule" of his classmates, who saw a "country boy with a southern slang" in his voice. She "saw something" in him. She helped him realize "that in spite of attitudes and opinions, you should strive to be the best that you can be. You should strive to understand who you are and move forward...." Coming from a single family household in which his father was absent, Bobby Rush could well have been at risk as he struggled to find his identity. But his teacher-mentor validated his own inclinations and fostered a positive personal identity.[42]

Vernon Jordan, on the other hand, grew up in a stable neighborhood with role models and mentors that surrounded him. The individuals he saw in his community offered a sense of possibility for engaging the world. He talks warmly of Alonzo Moron, the manager of University Homes—a housing project where he and his family lived:

> The manager of University Homes was Alonzo Moron who was a Harvard Law graduate. He was from the West Indies. He ended up as president of Hampton Institute. And Mr. Moron... lived in the housing project, too, though he was the manager. And he walked with authority. He wore a shirt and tie and he was—he was a leader.[43]

For Jordan, growing up in the first public housing project in Atlanta whose residents represented diverse socioeconomic levels was an advantage. It was a place where one could find prosperous businessmen and teachers, as well as the occasional street hustler. "We got to see black people get up and go to work every day in a wide range of occupations.... They were in my life on a day-to-day basis, flesh and blood. I could talk to them."[44] They were, in effect, both mentors and role models.

University Homes also had the benefit of being adjacent to the Atlanta University Center complex. Jordan's daily activities allowed him to observe eminent leaders at Spelman, Morehouse, Clark, Morris Brown, and Atlanta University. The atmosphere of the university community, with homecoming parades, track meets, and important intellectual activity was a "huge source of inspiration" to him. He saw such towering figures as Benjamin Mays, the charismatic president of Morehouse College. Young Vernon would imitate his walk and his carriage so that one day he might be as successful.[45] The Butler Street Y was also a place where he could go and find himself surrounded by impressive individuals. He developed a strong civic pride in his own community and saw the possibility of emulating people he knew and respected. "I was shaped, formed by Atlanta," he says. "The Butler Street YMCA is in my will. It means that much to me."[46] These black leaders and these places where black people gathered unknowingly provided a kind of roadmap for his future. His neighborhood was strictly segregated, but within it, role models and mentors who were community leaders surrounded him.

Jordan benefited from networks and connections as he moved from his neighborhood to the larger world beyond. He was only 26 years old when Ruby Hurley hired him to be regional director for Georgia of the NAACP. In that position, he sometimes had to pick up black leaders at the airport and drive them back to Macon, Georgia. "And so, two years out of law school you have Roy Wilkins hostage, actually, to your questions and to your inquiries." The people who were his mentors at that early stage of his career constituted a "huge, informal training ground."[47]

Ruby Hurley, his boss, showed him how an individual can influence a group. In 1950, Walter White, then executive secretary of the NAACP, asked her to coordinate membership campaigns in five southern states. By 1951, Mrs. Hurley became the regional secretary of the Southeast Region of the NAACP.[48] Among other tasks, she investigated racially motivated murders. In 1955, the NAACP assigned her the Emmett Till case, and she became a bold and fearless advocate in the cause of civil rights.[49] Jordan worked closely with her as field director: "She taught me about the mechanics of organizing. She taught me about how to give leadership to people who were afraid, how to make them feel comfortable in their leadership.... Ruby Hurley taught me how to manage dissent and how to be a leader."[50]

Twenty-five years earlier, in Washington, D.C., as a young woman of 25, Dorothy Height forged a lifelong relationship with Mary McLeod Bethune. Height was already a woman of distinction for her time. She was a graduate of New York University (NYU), president of the New York State Christian Youth Council, chair of the Harlem Youth Council, and vice-chair of the United Christian Youth Movement (UCYM) in the American Youth Congress. In 1937, she was selected as one of ten youth delegates and the only African American to represent the United States at the World Conference on Life and Work of the Churches held at Oxford University in England. The delegation, chaperoned by Dr. Benjamin Mays and his wife Sadie, came to be "like a big, forty-member family." There, she met Richard Tawney and John Macmurray, Reinhold Niebuhr and Paul Tillich—powerful intellectuals who inspired her to think more deeply about equality and justice. It opened up a world to her that she "didn't even dream of before."[51]

Not long after her return, she was offered and accepted a position as the assistant executive director of the YWCA Harlem branch.[52] One month later, Mary McLeod Bethune told her she was needed at the National Council of Negro Women (NCNW) and promptly appointed her to the resolutions committee.[53] Height recognized it as a significant turning point. "On that fall day, the redoubtable Mary McLeod Bethune put her hand on me. She drew me into her dazzling orbit of people in power and people in poverty."[54] Height grasped that she had a unique mentor. "She had so much wisdom to impart. She helped me feel that the philosophical and spiritual dimensions of our work mattered as much as its material impact. Her guiding principle was: 'Make something of everything you have—head, heart, and hand are equally important. Learn to use them together.'" The bonds were intimate, and those in her inner circle "became like daughters and sons to her."[55] Height writes: "The very essence of Mrs. Bethune fortified me."[56]

The relationship between Mary McLeod Bethune and Eleanor Roosevelt was very strong, and Dorothy Height was tapped to work with Mrs. Roosevelt on the World Conference of Youth in 1938. Height was one of ten people who went to Hyde Park to spend a day discussing the conference. Her "inner resources" were "nurtured and strengthened" because she was able to live so fully "in the relationship" of "such wise elders." Height went on to serve on the national board of the YWCA; in 1947, she was elected national president of Delta Sigma Theta sorority, a position she held until 1958; and in 1957, she was elected the fourth national president of the NCNW.[57] Almost a half-century after Bethune's death, Height wrote in 2003: "Her radiance still gleams, illuminating my life as it shone throughout her own."[58]

Teachers, community leaders, and supervisors served in multiple ways as mentors. They played a profound role in their development of black leaders. They bequeathed a deeply personal impact not over months or years, but decades.

Institutions within the Black Community: Business, Fraternal

Individuals, although fundamental as role models and mentors, cannot sustain leadership modeling without structures and institutions behind them. Within black America, institutions created the structures for implementing shared visions of freedom and equality and for insisting that the country live up to its values. They were centers of oppositional consciousness to identify injustice and to promote change, consistent with democratic values.[59] Within these structures, networks formed to create a new generation of leaders.

For Vernon Jordan, such structures and institutions existed within the neighborhood. There, the community network of black-owned businesses and local nonprofit institutions instilled a "self-contained confidence about education, preparation, community service." It was here that community leaders and community members gathered and organized. Black people in Atlanta had little choice where they could live and with whom they could create networks and connections. But they knew they could cultivate racial pride and racial uplift in the context of their own communities. Jordan believes his community offered a type of collective mentorship through its successful institutions:

> It was a source of confidence that you could do business. There was a Young's barber shop. They did their business. There was the Butz grocery store, the Johnson grocery store. These were all black businesses serving the black community. And then when you got to go the Butler Street

Y on the other side of town, you saw the Mutual Federal Savings & Loan, you saw the Citizen's Trust Bank. There was WRD, the first black radio station. There were these huge churches on Auburn Avenue—Big Bethel, Wheat Street and Ebenezer. And then there were the nightclubs.... As a kid going to the Butler Street YMCA, we would see all of the talented tenth leaders—the businessmen, the doctors and the lawyers, the social workers.... I am so grateful for those institutions that my parents exposed me to and the individuals in those institutions. They were great role models for me.[60]

Vernon Jordan

http://blackleadership.virginia.edu/15

For his parents' generation, church was the place to go "to achieve dignity and status." Black people might be subject to demeaning attacks and might have to work in jobs for which they were overqualified, but when in church—the black church—they could be somebody. "On Sundays, America's second-class citizens had somewhere to go to get spiritual nourishment and to feel like whole human beings."[61] He recalls that church was "the bedrock of life in my public housing project." There, he learned to speak, to protest, and to lead:

> I intuitively understood that speaking well was highly valued. The very roots of the African Methodist Episcopal (AME) Church and other black denominations sprang from blacks' determination to be able to speak freely, passionately, and persuasively. Blacks were not allowed to do that in most of American society. Our voices were largely ignored when they weren't completely stifled. But not in the black church.[62]

Learning "to speak in a way that influenced people" was critical to his future leadership.[63]

The Black Church was one of the earliest and most important institutions for African Americans. Founded in the late eighteenth century by free blacks, churches became the locus of their spiritual and secular well-being.[64] Within church walls, preachers sought to lift parishioners from the drudgery of their daily lives. They embraced a theology that combined Afro-Caribbean spirituality and American Christianity.[65] The theological message was focused on future salvation. But true salvation could not come without total freedom to serve the heavenly master. That, in turn, required liberation from the constraints of daily life. Many black people achieved that liberation through an emotional and spiritual catharsis at Sunday services. But during the week, one could only hope to reach toward freedom through communal effort. In black churches, freedom was heralded as the highest value of the black sacred cosmos. To achieve freedom, individual destiny was tied to the destiny of the community. Church-based

programs focused on mutual responsibilities within communities. Black liberation theology meant both spiritual and secular liberation.[66]

Through church-based communal organizations, African Americans
spawned schools, low income housing units, banks, and insurance companies. In
church spaces, they talked about and organized political activities. Churches were
the locus for advancing freedom and opportunity long before secular institutions (like black sororities and fraternities, the NAACP, and the National Urban
League) were created in the early twentieth century. Churches also were cultural
and learning centers for programs in music, drama, and art.[67] In the basements
and halls of black churches, people talked about children who needed additional
support, about educational aspirations, and about drugs. In this holistic way,
church activities created social capital for entire communities.[68] Black churches
were places of worship, but they also provided moral authority, social control,
education, and culture.[69]

Churches and black religious institutions inspired collective action and a
yearning for change. The Bible said that God and Jesus were on the side of the
oppressed. As the biblical Christ fought for social issues and died to save humankind, so too did black men and women of faith who believed they were obli-
gated to work for change and for local, national, and worldwide liberation. Not
all churches embraced this message, but those that did emphasized the need to
"stand up" and to exercise moral integrity.[70] The church and spirituality provided
a "way out of no way" in the face of uncertainty and oppression.[71]

Robert Franklin contends that too many preachers in America have lost
touch with those living on society's margins. The poor, homosexuals, immigrants, those with AIDS, and the imprisoned lose out to clerical greed and materialism.[72] Meanwhile, one-fourth of the black community continues to live in
poverty.[73] It is, Franklin claims, a "crisis of mission." He would like to see the
black church return to its historic mission to empower the downtrodden and
oppressed.

Robert Franklin's leadership was powerfully influenced by his own pastor,
Bishop Louis Henry Ford. Ford rejected the notion that the church be a place of
detachment from the larger world. "He said, 'No, . . . we have to be moral agents.
We have to be change agents." Bishop Ford raised money for scholarships; he
spent time with his young congregants, and helped them establish connections
that would allow them to lead productive lives. Involved in local politics, he
worked with the "Daley machine," and brought businessmen and politicians to
his church for serious dialogue with young people in his congregation. He also
took black youth out to the wider community, challenging them to recognize the
interrelated nature of the world in which they lived and to network with people
they might wish to emulate.[74] Ford's approach became the model for Robert
Franklin's theological ethics, his view of the role of the black church in society,
and his commitment to "pastoral capital:"[75]

He certainly made me feel that it was important to understand the language of the larger polis, the larger city and the language of business, the language of politics, the language employed in higher education. And not simply to know one's own idiom in the African-American community and more specifically, in the black church. He pushed us to be open, to cross barriers....And he again, I think, was trying to expose us to a larger world and saying, "You can participate. You have the confidence to do that." So it was an interesting way in which he was sort of building our own self-esteem, promoting us, getting us out there.[76]

Robert Franklin

http://blackleadership.virginia.edu/16

Bishop Ford was Franklin's personal guide to church leadership. But in Franklin's youth, there were also many other "giants in the land" like Dr. Martin Luther King Jr., Elijah Muhammad, and Malcolm X. Witnessing such provocative speakers who could mobilize people, Franklin says, "was very important in my own understanding of leadership."[77]

Religion has had a profound influence on many black leaders who combined active pastoring with other kinds of leadership. Bill Gray, Floyd Flake, and Calvin Butts similarly view the black church not only as a place of spiritual retreat from the world, but as a place to inspire active engagement in the world. For them, the church is an institution that serves their communities spiritually, socioeconomically, politically, and culturally. It grounds individuals in their communities, merging the sacred and the profane.[78]

The late William H. Gray III (d. 2013), the son of a Philadelphia Baptist minister, held leadership positions as the president and chief executive officer of the United Negro College Fund (1991–2004), member of the U.S. House of Representatives (1978–1991), businessman, and senior minister at Bright Hope Baptist Church in Philadelphia (1972–2007). He recognizes the strong historical role of black preachers as "the independent force of leadership in the black community" involved in the "whole ministry."[79] He witnessed that in his life, making it possible to blend so many different roles together simultaneously.

So I grew up around a group of ministers who taught me that ministry was not just simply something you do on Sunday morning. It's something you do in the streets, it's something you do about housing, it's something that you do about economic justice....And finally, my senior year, I decided, "Stop fighting it. That's really what you want to be. That's really what you ought to be, and that's what God called you to be." And so, I stopped fighting it.[80]

While senior minister at the Bright Hope Baptist Church, a position he inherited from his father's pastorate, he became involved in community civic engagement. He considers it the job of being a minister—one he had witnessed growing up:

> Every time I saw an example of a black minister who was really, really relevant, it was not just preaching. It was not just visiting the sick. It wasn't simply baptizing and those things. It was also helping the community with the basic issues, you know, good news. What's good news to the poor? A job, you know. What's good news to the homeless? An apartment, or a house to live in. And so yeah, we immediately immersed ourselves in that kind of a ministry. We became the focal point for the formation of a development corporation, the Union Development Corporation, that took on the city's relocation housing. The city of Montclair was doing its first urban renewal project, and a bunch of ministers, we got together and said, "We're not going to let it be urban removal."....And so, we said, "We'd like to be the housing authority and insist upon good, safe, decent housing," and built a housing project there.[81]

William Gray

http://blackleadership.virginia.edu/17

Two other black leaders interviewed, Floyd Flake and Calvin Butts, built these types of "prophetic" churches in different areas of New York City. These organizations operate with dual roles—nurturing the spiritual life of their members, while encouraging their involvement in political and community affairs.[82] Rev. Floyd Flake's Greater Allen AME Cathedral of New York boasts over 18,000 members and a history that spans 180 years. The church ministers to the community. Since the 1980s, the church community rehabilitated local stores and homes, created a Senior Center, operated a K-8 school for 30 years, and established a health center. It distributes free meals and free clothes to the needy. Flake has created a church community in which there is a symbiotic relationship between its spiritual and secular missions.[83] For Floyd Flake, broad connections between the church and the community can effectively engender change. His leadership revolves around a pragmatic understanding of networks and connections, and their role in raising people out of poverty and into self-directed lives.

For Floyd Flake, religion and politics are inextricably interconnected. To suggest otherwise, he says, would be "foolish."[84] Feeding the hungry, providing housing, dealing with both physical and spiritual needs, creating circumstances for increased dignity and status are ultimately political acts because political power accrues to those who are mobilized for action.[85] Flake's church is centered on this dual mission. Not surprisingly, in 1986, Floyd Flake ran successfully for the U.S. Congress and served until 1997 (without relinquishing his church leadership). For him, institutions are interdependent, and his "bi-vocational" leadership is centered on making things happen to promote community-wide progress. His is a bootstrap, self-help philosophy emphasizing self-reliance.[86]

Similarly, Rev. Calvin O. Butts, III serves simultaneously as the pastor of the Abyssinian Baptist Church in New York, president of Old Westbury College of the State University of New York, and founder of the Abyssinian Development Corporation (ADC). The ADC emerged out of the church congregation in 1989 as a nonprofit corporation dedicated to the rebuilding of Harlem. It has generated over $600 million for housing and commercial development. Over 1,000 rental units for low-income residents, Head Start programs, the Thurgood Marshall Academy Lower School are some of the ways that ADC improves the quality of lives for people in Harlem.[87]

Calvin Butts sees no conflict between these various roles: they all emanate from his Christian vision to "see the valleys exalted and the mountains made low and all of God's children stand on an equal plane." Faithfulness to his calling means that he can't separate the pastorate from the presidency:

> Both the college presidency and the pastorate are callings and the struggle for me is to... provide... the kind of leadership that helps people to move forward, so... if I'm working on building housing for working families, that empowers the working family. That provides them with some of the life, some of the pursuit of happiness, and on here, if I am trying to get Julian Bond to become a faculty member at the State University of New York because I think that he imparts wisdom and experience and intellectual acuity to the students, it's the same thing. I'm helping those young men and women grow by exposing them to the best. If I'm building dormitories, particularly at a public college, I'm empowering poor people who can't afford to pay $20,000 a semester for tuition... one of the interesting and compelling things about the public university is that it is accessible, that the people I'm called to serve can get there, so $40,000 a year as opposed to $17,000 a year. So, I'm called to be faithful to that.[88]

Calvin Butts's vision expands constantly, and now extends to a pan-African goal of uniting all people of African descent. "Charity starts at home, but now we've got to reach out and try to unite as much of the world, particularly the African world as we can," he said. His youth minister has approached him to create a black church-based NGO for development in Africa, which Butts sees as the Holy Spirit at work.[89] His Christian vision, implemented through the black church, draws upon a huge interlocking web of networks and connections that unite spiritual and secular institutions for the improvement of the human condition.

Carol Moseley Braun, in her successful candidacy for the U.S. Senate from Illinois, capitalized on an oppositional consciousness central to black networks and connections. She used the church to network with ministers, labor organizations, and civil rights organizations. Meeting with clergy from the Chicago area, she also invoked religious symbols. She talked about Jesus's exaltation of the weak over the strong, and referred to the story of David and Goliath to remind listeners that black political actors could reverse the power dynamics of the political system—and that women could transcend gendered stereotypes. Braun used the church to host receptions, activate voter-registration drives, and provide grassroots workers for her campaign. She portrayed herself as a person who was doing God's work to challenge societal oppression.[90]

Other institutions also helped and continue to shape black leaders. Important fraternal organizations include the Masons, Elks, Odd Fellows, Eastern Star, Shriners, Daughters of Isis, and the Knights of Pythias. The Colored Brotherhood and Sisterhood of Honor, the African Legion, and the Grand United Order of Galilean Fisherman were among the exclusively black fraternal organizations.[91] These nonsectarian groups nurtured solidarity and communal responsibility across religious denominations. They supported communities economically, sponsored civic and political activities, and struggled for civil rights. These institutions melded individuals into larger communities and provided avenues for leadership and training.[92]

Figure 4.1 Elaine Jones and Delta Sigma Theta Sorority. Ms. Jones is the fifth woman (from left to right) in the front row. Bison Yearbook, 1965. Courtesy of Moorland-Spingarn Research Center. Howard University Archives.

Black intercollegiate fraternities and sororities are also critical to the development of black leaders. Nine intercollegiate black Greek-letter organizations are dedicated to racial uplift through social action.[93] The networks are wide and deep. Charles Hamilton Houston and Thurgood Marshall were Alphas; Elaine Jones and Dorothy Height were Deltas.

As early as 1913, the Deltas marched for women's suffrage and later supported the NAACP, National Council of Negro Women, and the National Urban League. Dorothy Height served as national president of the sorority and emphasized its social action agenda. Later, when she and Anna Hedgeman were the sole women who helped organize and plan the 1963 March on Washington, she experienced the "blatantly insensitive treatment of black women" when no woman was allowed to speak.[94] Yet, she knew she could count on the active participation of her Delta sisters in the march. Mary Futrell also recalls how her Delta sisters supported her aspirations: "When I ran for local president they networked to make sure that people knew I was running. When I ran for state president they sent the word out that a Delta was running and needed support. Even when I ran as a national secretary-treasurer, then later as a national president, they sent the word out. Everything from being a contact or raising money to being there when I needed them."[95] Together with women's church-based groups and women's clubs, these black sororities were part of a broad spectrum of networks and connections working together to create resilient communities. They supported community members when there were no social services to do so. They helped people feel they could overcome the circumstances which ground them down. They created racial pride and racial purpose. They emphasized the importance of service. No doubt, they laid the foundations for community engagement used so effectively later on by the major civil rights organizations.[96]

Extensive connections existed among and between organizations. Congressman Sanford Bishop remembers that the deacon in his church, Mr. A. J. Dickerson, was also a Boy Scout executive in the all-black troop which he joined. As Bishop matured, he recognized "the wisdom of associating and affiliating with such organizations and realizing the historical place that they play and have played in our history and our culture and our success."[97] Church, fraternal organizations, and scout troops were all part of a social fabric that helped nurture leadership skills and create successful lives.

In many ways, the all-black Boy Scout troop served much the same purpose as did the black fraternal organizations for older men. Bishop went on to become a member of the Order of the Arrow, a "brotherhood of honor campers," which taught him "service and self-sacrifice."[98] For Bobby Lee Rush, scouting taught the value of accomplishment. Rush describes his scout leader, Alex Outerbridge, as a "magnificent man," who served as a male role-model in lieu of his absent father. Outerbridge took the boys in his troop on camping trips and to parades. Through the structure of the scouting program, Rush "learned how to set goals.... I wanted to excel and I picked that up also through the Boy Scouts."[99] He worked for badges and honors and achieved leadership positions. He learned self-discipline and experienced the joys of achievement. Calvin Butts likewise remembers scouting as an organization that inculcated pride and developed character.[100]

Some leaders honed their skills through black organizations that reflected the growing anger of a younger generation. With the evolution of the civil rights movement, new organizations developed that embraced the message of Black Power. Bobby Rush joined the Black Panthers as a means of channeling his anger in ways he deemed productive for the larger society. He got to know Stokely Carmichael, Robert J. Brown, and Huey Newton, and admired their mentorship: "Even in the Panther Party, Huey told us to be involved in electoral politics."[101] They spent a lot of time on the "streets," and Mayor Richard Daley often tried to recruit them as precinct captains in the neighborhoods they frequented. It was a kind of training for the position of Chicago Alderman. But when he got out of school and tried to find a job, many doors were shut in his face as a result of his former association with the revolutionary Black Panther Party. Rush knew that he liked politics. That was something he could do, because he had experience as a political organizer. The Black Panther Party had been his training ground, and he eventually was elected to office as part of the Harold Washington sweep in 1983. He has been a member of Congress ever since.[102]

Institutions beyond the Black community

The African American experience was a part of me, and I knew it and was part of it and it was home and I was rooted in it. But I knew there was a bigger world. There's a larger world out there, and in order to function in it you've got to be exposed to it, you've got to.[103]—Elaine Jones

Organizations within the black community fostered an awareness of the self and the mutually supportive relationship between the individual and the group. But there was a wider world that beckoned. As they matured and gained self-confidence, black leaders also moved beyond their communities.

Military training often helped create leadership skills. Bobby Rush, for example, cites it as formative to his development. It was the time in his life when he was forced to deal with his adolescent anger. He rebelled against his battery commander, who used "every opportunity to suppress my efforts to be a black man." Rush was disciplined, but feels he benefited from the structure of Army life: "You know, iron sharpens iron." He was "forced... to stand up for what I believed in and not to retreat from it...."[104] Other black leaders accepted the rules more readily, and profited from the opportunities for leadership development and advancement. The late Major General Lucius Theus (d. 2007) spent 36 years building a career in the US Air Force and retired as a major general—one of only three members of the esteemed Tuskegee Airmen to receive that rank.[105] He believes the military was at the forefront of treating people equally without regard to race. "We used to look at the military as a place where—if anywhere, a person could get equal treatment and they could go forward and be rewarded for their work, for their efforts and so forth. Now we don't think about that too much. Now the battle is in the industrial, in the business arena, and so forth.... "[106] Earl Graves, the founder and publisher of *Black Enterprise* magazine and highly successful business entrepreneur, says the military "gave you an opportunity, on an equal footing, to prove you were as good as the next person, and we did that with a vengeance. We did it in Korea; we did it in Vietnam, in terms of showing the metal we were made of."[107] It was all about performance. And the self-discipline and skills it took to perform were the same as those required for leadership in business or any other field. In the Army, Graves said: "I led by example.... I just knew I wanted to be the best. I inculcated that into my people... I wanted them to know that if you want to be good, you have to start with a baseline of where you're going to be and then set a goal for yourself. And what I tell people today, and I've written it in my book, in order to be successful, you really do have to have goals for yourself."[108]

Elaine Jones, Dorothy Height, and Robert Franklin all talk about the power of stepping outside of their comfort zones. For Elaine Jones, that opportunity came as she completed her undergraduate work at Howard University. She decided to go into the Peace Corps and requested a placement in Turkey. She explains her reasons for doing so:

> On the Peace Corps, it's just—I think my growing up in my environment, which was warm and wonderful but was all African American, all African American. My college was predominantly, at that time, overwhelmingly African American.... But I knew there was a bigger world.... I think my father traveling to Salt Lake City and all over the place and coming back, talking about the things that he'd seen, had an impact on me. I also knew that the world was not an African American world, you know. I said, "Elaine, you have to be exposed to whites in America. You have to. You have to, because you want to function in a larger society and because the system has to change."[109]

Elaine Jones

http://blackleadership.virginia.edu/18

From that experience, Elaine Jones came to see how a black American was viewed abroad. "It was tough," she said to be a black American in Turkey. They believed she was an Arab, because "Americans were blond and blue-eyed and were not me...." And there was no love between Turks and Arabs at the time. But white Americans were also struggling with a strong wave of anti-Americanism in the late 1960s, so for different reasons, both she and her white colleagues had to overcome negative stereotypes. She learned during those years about how to be comfortable with being herself.[110]

She also came to appreciate the wider world and saw that she could function very well in it. She decided to apply to law school at the University of Virginia and was the first black woman to be accepted. She organized overlapping groups of black and female law students so that she would not feel so isolated.[111] Both support networks were important to her. She developed her own ability to work with multiple groups, a quality that served her well when she subsequently assumed the leadership of the NAACP Legal Defense and Education Fund. Although that organization exists to protect the legal rights of African Americans, Elaine Jones claims that she could not do that job without the support of other communities:

> I cannot do it by myself, without other communities in this country buying into that notion. White America, you know—Latino America, Asian America. At LDF our cases not only impact on African Americans. They help white Americans—I can give you example after example— white Americans, Latinos, Asian—because it's the law. And once you've changed and impacted on the law, it impacts on all of us....I mean we're completely diverse. And I said,... "make sure I have white lawyers on my staff. It's my affirmative action program." I mean I have to, you know. I don't have to have white lawyers on my staff, but they bring something to LDF that's valuable.[112]

Similarly, Robert Franklin came to a larger self-understanding by living abroad and transcending his local environment. In his junior year at Morehouse, he applied for a scholarship and went to Durham, England. He found himself at an 800-year-old university, being asked to interpret the American antiwar movement, civil rights, and black power. Like Elaine Jones in Turkey, he came to feel like an ambassador abroad. The experience "deepened [his] awareness of [his] own kind of inner world." It provided an opportunity to "slow down" and to retreat from what the theologian Howard Thurman called the "busy traffic of life." He felt the tug of religion as he reflected more on the meaning of life for him. It wouldn't have happened, he said, had he stayed at Morehouse, which had become too comfortable as "a family, a network, a village:"

> I was still, perhaps by virtue of being outside the United States, keenly aware of cultural differences and curious about them, and curious about religious difference...But it sort of happened in the context of encountering other cultures and religious traditions as well.[113]

Thereafter, he travelled to Catholic Spain and Muslim North Africa and then to the Soviet Union. Eventually he returned to Morehouse, completed his Political Science degree, and almost by accident applied to Harvard Divinity School. Franklin had learned that he wanted "a vocation that would involve service and communicating with the masses and not simply a kind of scholarly literary classroom-based existence."[114] He had developed the confidence through his community-based networks that eventually broadened nationally and internationally.

Broad exposure to networks and connections beyond one's comfort zone impels people to reach beyond themselves and beyond their communities of origin. The foundational communities initially provide the personal grounding—the self-confidence and security—to take risks. Gaining self-confidence, our black leaders were able to test and clarify their personal values. As they ventured into new territory and new experiences, they expanded their understanding of humankind and honed new leadership skills.

Leadership Lessons Applied

Dorothy Height (d. 2010) built her life and career through organizations. President of the National Council for Negro Women (NCNW) from 1957, she led and developed that organization for 50 years, making it a formidable force for the rights of women, children, and civil rights. (In 1985, when the NCNW celebrated its 50th anniversary, there were 4 million members.) But long before she was chosen as the president of the organization begun by her mentor, Mary McLeod Bethune, she participated in national organizations for community empowerment and racial uplift. She joined the staff of the Harlem Young Women's Christian Association (YWCA) in 1937; between 1944 and 1947, she was a member of the YWCA's National Board and directed the integration of all its branches in 1946. She remained involved with the YWCA for more than 30 years, establishing and directing its Center for Racial Justice from 1965 to 1977. Between 1947 and 1958, she was president of Delta Sigma Theta, a public service sorority of African American women. Between 1958 and 1974, she was a member of the New York State Board of Social Welfare. In 1971, she helped found the National Women's Political Caucus with Gloria Steinm, Shirley Chisholm, and Betty Friedan. In 1986, she organized the first Black Family Reunion on the National Mall, an annual celebration that continues to the present.

Her organizational positions provided a set of networks and connections that she used to work for interracial and interclass cooperation, with a primary determination to advance the interests of black women, their families, and communities. She travelled extensively to promote these causes. As early as 1952, she went to the University of Delhi, India, as a visiting professor in their School of Social Work; trips to Asia, Africa, Europe, and South America followed for leadership training assignments. In the 1960s, she served on the Council to the White House Conference "To Fulfill These Rights." By 1974, she was a delegate to UNESCO's Conference on Women and Her Rights held in Kingston, Jamaica.

Conditions in America related to race and gender remained at the epicenter of her concerns. She was a member of the Council for United Civil Rights Leadership, a group of African Americans called upon to advise US presidents that included A. Philip Randolph, Martin Luther King, Jr., Roy Wilkins, Whitney Young, James Farmer, and John Lewis. She was the only black woman on the speaker's platform when King gave his "I Have a Dream" speech, but not allowed to speak—a reality that helped spark the women's movement. During the Freedom Rides and Freedom Schools, she went to Selma, Alabama, and places throughout the South to advocate for civil rights during voter registration drives. Along with Polly Cowan, she founded Wednesdays in Mississippi to represent the needs of children in Freedom Schools.

For her tireless devotion, intrepid and fearless determination, and unflagging courage in the cause of racial justice and civil rights, both Democratic and

Figure 4.2 President John F. Kennedy hands pen to Dorothy Height after signing Equal Pay Act, June 10, 1963. Credit: Abbie Rowe. White House Photographs. John F. Kennedy Presidential Library and Museum, Boston.

Figure 4.3 Dorothy Height with President Lyndon B. Johnson and Civil Rights Leaders, Cabinet Room of the White House, April 5, 1968. Credit: LBJ Library photo by Yoichi Okamoto.

Republican presidents recognized her achievements. In 1989, President Ronald Reagan presented her the Citizens Medal Award for distinguished service. In 1994, President Bill Clinton awarded her the Presidential Medal of Freedom. In 2004, George W. Bush gave her the Congressional Gold Medal. President Barack Obama delivered the eulogy at her funeral, remembering her involvement in issues of health care and unemployment in the final months of her life.[115] She was a major force and change agent, furthering both the causes of women and of civil rights.

In 2003, at the age of 91, Dorothy Height said: "I think it was the fact that my family exposed me to so many activities in church and the YWCA that I have had a high purpose all of my life. I think many young people shy away from organizations. But the real value of being a part of groups that have purpose is that they help shape you and help you understand who you are."[116]

Elaine Jones, born in 1944 in Norfolk, Virginia, witnessed the power of organizations and networks at her kitchen table where her father brought home so many powerful figures among the Pullman porters. When she graduated from Howard University in 1965 and left for a two-year stint in the U.S. Peace Corps, she was expanding her horizons through international networks and learning about organizational behavior to improve the conditions of the less fortunate. She returned home, armed with the capacity to step outside her comfort zone, and applied to the University of Virginia School of Law, never expecting to be accepted as the first black woman. In 1970, she rejected tantalizing offers from Wall Street law firms to join the staff of the NAACP Legal Defense Fund, the organization founded by Thurgood Marshall in 1940. The NAACP LDF fights for racial justice in America through litigation, advocacy, and public education. Its goals are to promote equal pay for equal work, to increase equity in education by removing racial barriers, to end racial bias in the criminal justice system, and to protect voting rights for all citizens.[117] The LDF is the legal arm of the ongoing civil rights movement. It was the LDF that orchestrated the landmark Supreme Court ruling in *Brown v. Board of Education* and pioneered the concept of public interest law. In 1972, only two years out of law school, Elaine Jones was the counsel of record in *Furman v. Georgia*, the Supreme Court case that abolished the death penalty in 37 states. She went on to argue numerous employment discrimination cases among some of the nation's largest employers. She left the LDF only briefly, from 1975 to 1977, while she worked as a special assistant to then U.S. secretary of transportation, William T. Coleman, Jr.

In 1977, when she returned to the LDF, she initiated the position of legislative advocate in the D.C. office. She provided briefings and expert testimony to congressional staff and committees, monitored and worked to confirm or defeat judicial appointees, bridged the civil rights movement and women's issues, and furthered the expansion of civil rights through legislation. She played a key role in passage of pivotal legislation, including the Voting Rights Act Amendments of 1982, the Fair Housing Act of 1988, the Civil Rights Restoration Act of 1988, and the Civil Rights Act of 1991. She became the first African American elected to the American Bar Association Board of Governors in 1989. By 1993, she became director-counsel of the LDF—the first woman to hold that job. She headed a staff of 80 employees and over 30 lawyers, administering a budget in excess of $10 million.[118] She knows how important it is to create networks so that the LDF can be as effective as possible. "I want us to expand, so we're no longer limited to courtrooms and briefs," she said. "We should be appearing before school boards and senate committees." She recognized the importance of forming coalitions like the Puerto Rican LDF or the West Dallas Coalition for Environmental Justice, a necessary "power move."[119] She sees her job as one of breaking down barriers wherever they exist.

Her life experiences taught her about the power of networks as a means to achieve something. It started with observing how Pullman porters were able to pull together; it expanded to her contacts at Howard University, where she took classes with Stokeley Carmichael or got to know Jim Nabrit, Jr., or became involved with her sorority, the Deltas. Then during her time in the Peace Corps, she came to see how people working together can make a difference in the international arena. Ultimately, she came to feel that none of what she accomplished at the LDF could have been possible without a capacity to engage the widest possible network of people.

Figure 4.4   Vernon E. Jordan, Jr., Atlanta, GA; in voter education project of the Southern Regional Council. Credit: Library of Congress, Prints and Photographs Division, USN&WR collection; LC-U9–17566, frame 5–5A.

Vernon Jordan earned his law degree at the historically black Howard University after receiving an undergraduate degree at the predominantly white De Pauw University. He has the capacity to move comfortably between the white world of privilege while never forgetting the meaning of the civil rights movement. Such abilities emerge from his experiences in Atlanta; at De Pauw in Greencastle, Indiana; at Howard University in Washington, D.C.; from his time as field director of the Georgia NAACP. By the mid-1960s, he assumed the directorship of the Voter Education Project of the Southern Regional Council, increasing voter registration by more than two million people.

In 1970, he became the director of the United Negro College Fund, and increased its endowment by $10 million. During his ten-year tenure as president of the National Urban League (NUL) between 1972 and 1981, he was able to act as a bridge between white corporate executives, politicians in Washington, and the urban poor. The NUL opened 17 new affiliates, while Jordan spoke out strongly against policies of both the Nixon and Carter administrations. For more than two decades, he has been one of the most visible and outspoken advocates for the plight of African Americans. In 1982, he stepped down to become a senior partner in the law firm of Akin, Gump, Strauss, Hauer, and Field. A close friend of Bill Clinton, he became co-chair of his transition team in 1992.[120]

Some have criticized Vernon Jordan for leaving public service, for unabashedly making lots of money, and for joining the ranks of corporate America. For him, however, there is no shame in making money and living well because it is important that black Americans network with the rainmakers in America and be perceived as successful. In any case, he is not leaving the civil rights movement. "I'm not a general, but I'm still in the Army....I am not so assimilated that I have lost my sensitivities to the basic inequities confronting minority people in this country."[121]

Robert Franklin's whole career focuses on the effort to balance the social, personal, and spiritual. He believes in a transformational leadership that marries religion, education, and social ethics. It was what he learned from his mother, grandmother, and critical teachers along the way. At Morehouse College (B.A. 1975), Harvard Divinity School (M. Div., 1978), and the University of Chicago Divinity School (Ph.D., 1985), he focused on political philosophy, social ethics, and justice. In 1986, he returned to Harvard as a visiting lecturer in ministry and Afro-American religion. Short-term teaching positions and writing followed, before he went to the Ford Foundation as a program officer for the Rights and Social Justice Program. In 1993, *Ebony* magazine conducted an extensive media poll of influential black Americans and chose him for their Honor Roll of Great Preachers. He has the unusual ability to draw attention to the salutary responsibility of the black church to lift up the downtrodden. The civil rights movement provided the model for authentic and lasting liberation and Martin Luther King, Jr. modeled for him the morally integrated person.[122]

In 1997, Franklin accepted the appointment of president of the Interdenominational Theological Center (ITC) in Atlanta. Chartered in 1958, the ITC is a graduate school of theology bringing together six different Christian denominations and educating both men and women to serve both church and society.[123] The ITC's mission is to produce public theologians and its vision is to be a national resource emphasizing the role of the black church in the renewal of American society.[124] Over 500 students and approximately 25 percent of American black ministers are trained there. For Franklin, ITC is a model for ecumenism and unity despite differences. He served as ITC president until 2002.

Between 2004 and 2007, he was appointed Presidential Distinguished Professor of Social Ethics at the Candler School of Theology at Emory. In 2007, he returned to his alma mater, Morehouse, as president for a five-year term. Following a year as scholar-in-residence at Stanford University's Martin Luther King, Jr. Institute, he became the director of the Department of Religion at Chatauqua Institution.

Robert Franklin has lived his personal and professional life building networks for religious understanding and for societal transformation through religion. His theological education, he maintains, "began on [his] grandmother's knee."[125]

On his congressional biography page, Bobby Rush writes about his "American story," describing the family's migration from Albany, Georgia to Chicago, Illinois. "At the time, most of American society held no expectation that the son of a single mother, growing up on Chicago's west side, would someday become a powerful national and international leader. But Bobby Rush didn't know that." He claims that the "struggle to fulfil the constitutional promise of equality for all would define [him] and his life's work." His personal story acknowledges support he received from his mother, teachers, and scoutmasters. But his political training and most formative networking experiences that helped him to see the deep disparities of race realities in America came during his high school years. He dropped out of high school in 1963, joined the U.S. Army, and got involved in SNCC. In 1968, he cofounded the Illinois chapter of the Black Panthers, engaged in acts of civil disobedience, was jailed for six months in 1972 on a weapons charge, and remained involved with the Panthers until 1974. He operated the Panther Party's Free Breakfast for Children and coordinated a Free Medical Clinic, helping to develop the first national mass sickle cell anemia testing program. But he also went back to school, earning his B.A. in 1973 from Roosevelt University, M.A. from the University of Illinois at Chicago in 1974, and a second M.A. in theological studies from McCormick Seminary in 1978. At the same time, he became more involved in Chicago city politics as a black militant. In 1983, he was elected alderman during the mayoralty of Harold Washington. In 1992, Rush defeated incumbent Charles Hayes, and became the US representative to Congress from Illinois. Discovering Christianity as a force for personal salvation, he resumed his education in the 1990s, and received a master's degree in theology. Since 2002, he has been the pastor of Beloved Community Christian Church in the Englewood neighborhood of Chicago.[126]

As the long-term Congressman for Illinois's first district, Rush has been concerned with the "most vulnerable" in society. From his very first year in office, he claims, he "focused on issues of importance to low-income and middle-class families and communities." He considers the economy and jobs, energy, and public safety to be major focal points. Having lost a son to gun violence, he is very active on issues related to firearm registration, crime, and economic hopelessness. He has authored bills to provide for research and services for individuals with postpartum depression and psychosis, and for nursing relief for disadvantaged areas. He also initiated a program to help low-income working Chicagoans receive federal tax credits. He has been particularly vocal on eliminating the death penalty, protecting the Voting Rights Act, and curtailing gun violence. He publicly expresses disappointment in President Obama.[127] His goals remain clear—to be a strong voice for the disadvantaged and to use the political process to correct the worst abuses.

Rush sees a "continuum" from the past to the present. "I'm a product of all my experiences," he said, from the Boy Scouts to the Black Panthers. His networks and connections made him who he is.[128] But what sustains him most is the need to fight against injustice and reverse the pandemic of violence.[129]

Conclusions

In his acclaimed psychological study, *Leading Minds*, Howard Gardner argues that leaders embody and relate particular stories—stories "about themselves and their groups, about where they were coming from and where they were headed, about what was to be feared, struggled against, and dreamed about." Ultimately, their stories are about identity and fall into three major categories: stories about the self, the group, and values and meaning.[130]

The five leaders highlighted in this chapter reflect diverse communities of descent, socioeconomic circumstances, family structures, and opportunities. Overcoming the odds of racial restrictions and race stereotyping was neither easy nor typical. Yet all of them emphasize the relationship of the self to the group, and the ways that networks and connections created value and meaning for their lives.

The existence of such linkages has a deep history tied to African philosophies and African religions. A people survives, first and foremost, through its "tribe." Members of a community learn about duties and responsibilities through others, who operate with a sense of collective responsibility and collective destiny. Each individual represents the whole.[131] Networks and connections, then, are the means to forge a collective unity.

Even within the context of *de jure* segregation and an America insensitive to its own racism, black families, neighborhoods, educational institutions, and communities offered support necessary for African Americans to gain leadership skills and lead highly effective lives. They transmitted messages that built confidence and self-pride. These networks and communities existed in intersecting and ever-widening circles that exposed people to ideas and to experiences that deepened their self-awareness and knowledge, and that raised their aspirations. We should consider these stories not just as inspirational anecdotes but as a blueprint for the inculcation of future leaders.

villages are the neighborhoods and communities in which all Americans reside. In the final analysis, we all live in villages and we all should aspire to transform them into beloved communities.[132]—Robert Franklin

CHAPTER 5

Law and Social Change: Catalyst for Leadership

Brown... became immediately an icon, a symbol, of America's commitment to justice, to racial justice and to being the best of a multiracial democracy... Brown stands for more than just segregation or desegregation.... [W]e made a commitment as Americans that we were going to change and that's what Brown signaled.[1]—Mary Frances Berry

Douglas Wilder, the first African American elected black governor of Virginia (1990–1994), was a recent veteran of the Korean War when the *Brown v. Board of Education of Topeka, Kansas* decision was announced in 1954. Returning to the United States only a few months before, he had "literally given up on what they called 'the system.'" He had fought in a war for other peoples' freedom but came back to a country in which his own sense of opportunity and self-determination was severely curtailed by race. He was demoralized and disillusioned.

> And when *Brown v. Board of Education* came down I said, "God have mercy the system works! You mean nine white men have said that they were wrong? I'm in the wrong field! I better get into law, I better get into something of this social engineering." So it literally turned my life around.... *Brown v. Board of Education* was sort of like a rebirth for me.[2]

In 1954, the US Supreme Court asserted the dramatic principle that race could no longer be a legal basis for differential treatment in the field of public education. *Brown v. Board of Education* reversed the "separate but equal" clause of *Plessy v. Ferguson* that had mandated racial separatism since 1896. While Chief Justice Earl Warren cast the case narrowly, the legal architecture

LAWRENCE D. WILDER
Editor

School of Law
Bison Staff

Left to right: Lawrence D. Wilder, Editor; Mrs. Harriette W. Batipps, Faculty Advisor;
William Gladden

Figure 5.1 Douglas Wilder, Editor of Law School Yearbook section with other staff; Bison Yearbook, 1959. Credit: Courtesy of the Howard University Archives, Moorland-Spingarn Research Center.]

for discrimination by race had cracked. Once segregation in public education ended, other public facilities would have to follow. The decision of nine justices on the Supreme Court, informed by legal arguments and mounting cases brought by brilliant black lawyers, created an initial sense of euphoria, hope, and vindication within the African American communities of America. The case came to be known as *Brown I*. The principle that segregation in education was illegal awaited an implementation plan.

In 1955, in *Brown II*, the Court granted authority to federal district courts to determine the timetable for desegregating public schools, urging "all deliberate speed." This incredibly vague and cautious phrase meant that those opposed could drag their feet and find numerous ways to subvert the decision. Most would argue that *Brown II* reaffirmed the systemic problems with American society, which still have not been resolved.

A long and continuing struggle followed. While lawyers and judges could interpret the meaning of the US Constitution, individuals needed to comply. When they refused, pressure and resistance from social and political activists spawned the civil rights movement. *Brown I* and *II* and "the movement" cannot be separated in historical reality. However, they created very different kinds of leadership opportunities.

This chapter explores how the lawyers responsible for *Brown* and the decision itself inspired others to use the law and the political process to work for social change. Legal actions and reactions catalyzed civic action and reaction, leading to a sea change in engagement. Across generations, *Brown* and its memory stirred millions to fight for social justice and to fight against racial oppression through legal and political means. Some worked on the front lines, adjudicating the initial case. Others watched the process unfold, understood its enormous potential, and became lawyers themselves. Still others, not yet born, were inspired by the stories they heard, the history they read, and the strength of their ancestors. In the process, new leaders were born in response to momentous historical circumstances.

Five leaders, all trained in the law, help us to trace the relationship between *Brown* (and by extension the power of law), civic action, and social change. Oliver White Hill, Sr., drew his inspiration from Charles Hamilton Houston with whom he studied at Howard Law School in the 1930s. He became the lead counsel for *Davis v. County School Board of Prince Edward County*—one of the state cases consolidated with *Brown*. Hill's legal prowess inspired a young man from Richmond, Henry Marsh, who followed in his footsteps and eventually became his law partner, the first elected black mayor of Richmond, Virginia, and a long-serving senator of the Commonwealth. Charles Ogletree, the Jesse Climenko Professor of Law at Harvard and director of the Charles Hamilton Houston Institute for Race and Justice, was drawn to the study of the law by witnessing the incarceration of Angela Davis and fighting to get her acquitted. Benjamin Jealous, the youngest executive director of the NAACP, became very familiar with legal processes when he worked at the NAACP Legal Defense Fund. It actually changed his mind about pursuing the law as a career, but at the same time, it made him aware of the other avenues to effect social change. Bakari Sellers, both a lawyer and congressional representative in Georgia, grew up at the knee of Cleveland Sellers, who also was unfairly incarcerated as a young man.[3]

The Meaning of Brown

The impact of *Brown* was transformative precisely because its initial promise seemed so large. *Brown* heralded meaningful action to correct existing educational disparities in American education. By extension, the concept that separate facilities are inherently unequal had dramatic implications for dismantling the racial hierarchies in America. Moreover, *Brown* challenged and loosened the legal underpinnings of racial discrimination. Roger Wilkins remembers thinking at the time that "...we were going to have a country of laws....*Plessy* was gone. And I thought the law was a great teacher. And I thought the American people would fall into line behind this....I thought this meant massive change."[4] If a band of black lawyers, aligned with rank and file citizens, could accomplish this, it meant that it was worthwhile to step up and fight. The legal triumphs were critical, but so too were the profound changes in race consciousness and race activism.

The *Brown* decision also demonstrated that the law does not work in a vacuum. Before the integration of schools could occur, the largely white population of America had to acquiesce. Before that happened America would erupt in ugly racist turmoil. Courts can alter the law of the land, but they can't transform popular opinion.

As the promise of *Brown I* waned under mounting white resistance, blacks determined that civic action through the popular press, local organizing, and even at times civil disobedience was necessary.[5] The generation of the 1950s created the leaders of the 1960s. The leaders of the 1960s inspired those of the 1970s and beyond. *Brown v Board*, the civil rights movement, the Civil Rights Acts, the Black Power movement, and the election of increasing numbers of black Americans to political office are part of a leadership trajectory that defined the long twentieth century. The intergenerational impact of *Brown* on leadership was enormous. Congressman Sanford Bishop claims that *Brown I* established "the foundation of equality through the 14th Amendment and I believe that through that, all of the other gains that we've been able to make in terms of race relations, whether it's the Voting Rights Act, the opportunity to participate, whether it's equal housing, public accommodations—all of that really came from the writ jurisprudence established in *Brown*."[6]

First came a euphoric sense of victory. Bill Gray, the future head of the Negro College Fund, a minister and a congressman from Pennsylvania, remembers his boyhood feelings:

> I remember being jubilant. I remember, you know, the feeling that, "Hey, a great thing has happened," you know, "We're on the way to the Promised Land—inevitably, things are moving in the right direction."[7]

Johnnetta Cole, then a freshman at Oberlin:

> I remember just extraordinary jubilation. I remember, I remember folk thinking that this was a victory of unusual consequences....I think that I thought that at that moment, like many, many others, that this was the great victory that would lead to enormous progress.[8]

Vernon Jordan, also a freshman at De Pauw University, viewed *Brown I* as

> an affirmation of what I heard in speeches from A.T. [Austin Thomas] Walden to Thurgood Marshall and local NAACP meetings that one day we will win.... It was nine men on the highest court of the land affirming black aspirations and black hope for their future.... It was about victory.[9]

Somewhat akin to a test of physical stamina and prowess, others use sports analogies in remembering the thrill when *Brown I* was announced. Congressman John Conyers, talking about the profound national impact, says "... it was like a victory. This was like a Joe Louis in the ring. I mean, we won."[10] And Roger Wilkins links the importance of Jackie Robinson in 1947 who became a symbol for black Americans' sense of possibility with the *Brown* decision of 1954 which was "in some way like winning World War II."[11]

The *Brown* decision was exhilarating because of its impact on peoples' aspirations. Ending the concept of legal segregation in America generated the will and determination of thousands to work toward its actual elimination.

The capacity of black lawyers to change America through the legal system persuaded greater numbers of African Americans to become civil rights lawyers. The *Brown* decision, for example, prompted Elaine Jones, future executive director of the NAACP Legal Defense Fund, to pursue the law as a career. She lived with the indignities foisted on her community: the segregated water signs, the all-white police power mongering, and the rules of public transport reflected a profound racism. It seemed never ending. But Thurgood Marshall's legal prowess led to her epiphany that law could change societal norms. The courts, more than the executive or legislative branches of government, could occasionally get a "semblance of justice."[12]

Many of Jones's generation came to "consciousness" at that time. They were inspired by the possibility of opportunities they never before had imagined. Eleanor Holmes Norton, a civil rights lawyer and now a member of the US Congress, was deeply affected by *Brown*. She was a high school student in 1954 at the prestigious but segregated black Dunbar High School in Washington, D.C., known for its rigorous education. Although her principal announced that their school would now be illegal, and although many teachers cried at the prospect of its disbanding, Norton felt hope. Her own father was a lawyer without much opportunity to practice. She grasped what *Brown* might mean for young people like herself: "It seemed to me that there was an understanding of young people in my generation that we were at a unique moment in time for our people, for black people, when for the first time the Supreme Court of United States said separate but equal is unconstitutional." For young people like herself, the future was all about change.[13]

Brown I catalyzed the ensuing civil rights movement, partly because its promise was sabotaged by white Americans who were not yet prepared to accept an integrated America. *Brown II*, allowing the integration of schools to proceed "with all deliberate speed," really meant that communities could drag their feet with every conceivable delay. Slow implementation or outright contempt for school integration highlighted the distinctions between rhetoric and reality and confirmed how deeply racism was embedded in American society. Massive resistance to *Brown I* helped reshape the civil rights movement, altering its trajectory from nonviolent to violent protest. New role models emerged, inspiring yet other people to become involved. Eleanor Holmes Norton remembers:

> I was driven by the fact that here was this important movement. There was much to be done. I mean, all right, the Supreme Court declared separate but equal and do it at all deliberate speed. Everybody could fathom from that that somebody was going to have to go ahead and make that happen through the law, even as the *Brown* decision occurred through the law. But more than that, it was—remember, the civil rights movement broke out because *Brown* was not self-executing in lifting segregation from this country. For example, in employment and housing, everything remained the same, actually, after *Brown* and even if the schools had been integrated all over the United States, everything else would've been the same in where you could be employed, where you could eat—and so the need to break through that and the fact that the law had broken through it as nothing else had.[14]

Those already trained in the law, like Roger Wilkins, knew it was time to step up at the point the South began to resist. "And I called Thurgood [Marshall] and I asked him could I come work for him that summer? My reaction was, 'Well, work needs to be done and I'll volunteer to do the work'....So I researched all those teacher tenure laws and wrote a memo on each one of them trying to provide guidance for the lawsuits that were sure to come. But then, at this point,...I knew we were in for a long haul."[15]

Disappointments, frustrations, and anger with the country's failure to implement the law of the land prompted new resolve. Dorothy Height, born in 1912, and deeply involved in the civil rights movement through her work with the National Council of Negro Women and the YWCA, recalls her exasperation. The failures of *Brown* propelled her to new resolve:

> I had to work harder to try to make its objectives realized....It gave a new base, however, for working, because at least we had a way of saying...there is no such thing as "separate and equal." And I think the elimination of that laid the base for all the work that we could do. Until

then I think we were working hard, but we were really up against some-thing that was impossible because segregation was legal....

But I have to say, often those who challenge you are, like President [John F.] Kennedy told the civil rights team, he said, "Bull [Eugene] Connor will prove to be your best friend because...he brought out that which is subtly hidden all around him." Well, I think sometimes those who challenge you are helpful because they make you have to test to what extent is this vision related to something that is real.... [I]it also makes you have to say to yourself that "I have to try a new behavior. I have to come another way. I have to see who else is ready to work with this." It makes you—it, in a sense, it really strengthens leadership if you can survive it.[16]

Black leaders and black organizations, recognizing that the law mandated a new set of possibilities, challenged local conditions through boycotts and marches. The Southern Christian Leadership Conference, under the leadership of Martin L. King, Jr., inspired thousands of people to make a difference through nonvio-lent protest. Black college students, beginning in Greensboro, North Carolina, recognized that they could make a difference by desegregating lunch counters and public places. The Student Nonviolent Coordinating Committee, under the inspired leadership of Ella Baker, Fannie Lou Hamer, John Lewis, and Julian Bond, among others, brought blacks and whites together to become an army of change agents. They played important roles in the Freedom Rides, and demon-strated the power of numbers to facilitate nonviolent change. The Mississippi Freedom Democratic Party (MFDP) challenged the status quo of Democratic Party politics and white supremacy. Other groups, like the Black Panthers, under the leadership of Eldridge Cleaver, Huey Newton, and Bobby Seale, reached out to the neediest black communities with social programs focused on alleviating poverty and improving health, while also delivering angrier and more volatile messages of armed resistance.

Still others, too young to participate, watched the resistance and counterresis-tance on their television sets. They saw the police dogs, the high-power hoses, the angry whites who spat on children trying to enter schools. They heard the white supremacist statements of George Wallace, Orval Faubus, and Bull Connor. They also saw the determination, courage, and resilience of those fighting back. They saw that people could resist by boycotting segregated buses and by sitting-in with nonviolent tactics in lawful assembly. Blacks and whites could resist together by participating in Freedom Rides and people could resist by going to jail or sup-porting those unfairly jailed. And they, too, were inspired.

The long arc of the civil rights movement extended beyond the generation who marched and protested. By the 1980s, the children of participants heard the stories and met the lifelong friends of their parents. Many came to understand

the dangers and sacrifices that had been incurred. Nurtured on the values of public service and public protest, they were empowered by the law and challenged
by its failures.

Five Leaders: Law and Social Change

*people move forward in activities to correct things and unquestionably,
circumstances make leaders, but also leaders make movements.*[17]—Oliver
Hill

Oliver W. Hill, Sr. was born in 1907 in Richmond, Virginia. He attended the
famous Dunbar High School in Washington, D.C., where he studied with
Ph.D.s unable to get jobs in white educational institutions. He entered Howard
University while still uncertain of a direction. But as a sophomore, his stepfather's brother, Sam, died of a cerebral hemorrhage. Sam was a part-time lawyer
in Washington, D.C. His widow gave Hill a 1924 United State Code Annotated,
piquing his interest in the law. That was when he first read the Thirteenth,
Fourteenth, and Fifteenth Amendments, and learned that "it was the Supreme
Court that had taken away our rights."[18]

> I couldn't understand why...segregation laws didn't violate [the amend-
> ments], so I went down to Congressional Library and read the cases
> that were cited as being where the Supreme Court had interpreted these
> amendments. And I read about *Plessy*, and I just thought they lost their
> cotton-picking minds with their decision, so—at that time...the big
> issue for the NAACP was anti-lynching law and you couldn't get a law
> through Congress making it a crime to lynch a Negro. So I decided the
> only thing for us to do was for somebody to carry a case back to the
> Supreme Court and convince them that they ought to reverse *Plessy*,
> and somebody ought to do it, so I didn't see why I shouldn't be the
> somebody.[19]

He was able to enroll in a combined program at Howard, using his first year
in a professional school to satisfy the grade point requirements for his last year
of college. In 1930, he began law school, earning his B.A. in 1931, and his law
degree in 1933.[20]

Hill was one of the 11 students to receive a degree at a time when the law
school at Howard was aggressively restructured to meet the very highest standards.[21] He regularly studied most afternoons in the law library along with his
classmate and friend Thurgood Marshall. They became the protogés of Law

School Dean and scholar Charles Hamilton Houston.[22] Hill graduated second to Marshall, with whom he would collaborate for decades.

Hill came of age at a time when his teachers and mentors were challenging the Jim Crow laws. He remembers studying law under Charles Hamilton Houston and learning that "we had to be social engineers or else we were parasites."[23] At Howard Law School, students worked on legal briefs under the tutelage of their mentors. They accompanied Houston and other faculty members to court and witnessed how their work played out in real time.[24] Hill learned how to use the law to challenge social inequality. Unlike some of his powerful legal associates, Hill claims that he did not venerate the law but saw it as a tool to promote social change. The Constitution was his guide, and the law had to be brought into conformity with it:

> I had sufficient faith in the Constitution to believe that they meant what they said, and that we ought to do something about it.... [T]he big difference between Thurgood and me was that I was an advocate for social change. I had no great regard for the law. Just like I think about law and religion. They're about the same. It all depends on who's administering it. [B]ut I...always had as companions people like Thurgood, Spottswood Robinson, and S.W. Tucker—they all had high regard for the law. They had a love for the law. I didn't have this.[25]

After graduating from Howard, Oliver Hill practiced law in Washington, D.C. and Richmond, Virginia, for the rest of his very long career, except for brief periods of military service during World War II and government service during the administration of John F. Kennedy.[26] He became a member of the black Washington bar in 1934, the only professional association open to him. In 1940, Hill won his first civil rights case, *Alston v. School Board of Norfolk*, establishing equal pay for black teachers. That same year, he became chairman of the Legal Commission of the Virginia NAACP, a position he held for 21 years. In 1942, he helped found the Old Dominion Bar Association for black lawyers, an organization that still exists to provide leadership training and support networks for African American lawyers.[27] In 1948, he became the first black elected to the Richmond City Council and served for two years. He was learning how to combine the law with other forms of civic engagement.[28]

Oliver Hill was a man of principle and a man of courage. He was not afraid to engage in civil disobedience to retain his self-dignity. He and his wife, Beresenia Walker Hill, were prominent people in the community and used their stature to picket large department stores like Miller and Rhoads and Thalhimers. His wife, a Richmond schoolteacher, persuaded people in her social clubs to join in. "We had all those people out there. We took the lead, other people followed," he recalls. "I didn't have any problems about breaking the law. As a matter of fact, in 1940, I decided I wasn't going to ride Jim Crow any more, and I didn't." Somehow, he did not get arrested. He modeled for others that segregationist laws that did not adhere to the Constitution had to be challenged.[29] It never occurred to him that he would work on anything other than race equity issues:

> There's no way to deny race when I was coming along, 'cause everything had racial overtones. We were fourth-class citizens most of the time. Occasionally we get bumped up to third class, but from time *Plessy* was enacted and from time they removed troops from the South, we were fourth-class citizens.[30]

Hill was part of a small but tight group of civil rights lawyers that included Thurgood Marshall, Jack Greenberg, James Nabrit, Jr., Louis Redding, Bob Carter, William H. Hastie, and Charles Hamilton Houston, and his law partners Samuel W. Tucker, Spottswood Robinson III, and Martin A. Martin. They worked closely to establish strategy and policy with strong civil rights organizations like the NAACP.

Oliver Hill was one of very few black lawyers in the South. As he traveled the region, he met many courageous citizens who wanted to use the courts to challenge the inequalities they lived on a daily basis. As he tells the story, he received a phone call in April 1951 from Barbara Johns. She was a senior at Moton High School in Prince Edward County, Virginia, and the niece of the nationally known civil rights Baptist preacher, Rev. Vernon Johns.[31] She spoke with Hill about a student strike they were staging in order to get better educational facilities. Involved in a similar case in South Carolina, Hill was not all that interested. But Johns was persistent, and Hill agreed to talk with the students and their parents. Once there, he informed them of a change in NAACP policy: the organization no longer wanted to argue cases in behalf of separate and equal facilities; they sought to challenge segregation per se. Ultimately, the parents decided to support the goals of their children, and Hill and Robinson agreed to represent the students in *Davis v. County School Board of Prince Edward County*. This suit, initiated in 1951, became one of the five-paired cases that combined to form the *Brown v. Board of Education* landmark decision.[32]

By the time of the decision, Hill had been recognized nationally. In 1952, President Truman appointed him to the Committee on Government Contracts Compliance where Hill worked to enforce antidiscrimination clauses written into government contracts with private firms. Subsequently, he took on cases that dealt with equalization of salaries in public schools, desegregation of buses and trains, black citizens' rights to serve on juries, and the desegregation of public assembly and recreational facilities. *The Washington Post* once estimated that Hill's

ATTORNEYS FOR NEGRO PLAINTIFFS—Left to right: Thurgood Marshall, Oliver W. Hill and Spottswood Robinson III. (Harold Boulware, another attorney, is not shown.) This picture was taken at the Virginia hearing, at which Marshall, Hill and Robinson appeared for the plaintiffs.

Figure 5.2 Published in Southern School News, August 1955. Courtesy of the Library of Virginia with permission of Vanderbilt University.

team won more than $50 million in higher pay, better schools, and resources for black teachers and students.[33]

Following the initial jubilation of the Supreme Court decision in the *Brown v. Board* case, Hill and his colleagues quickly came to see that their work was far from done. Virginia, along with the rest of the South, resisted the ruling. In some Virginia counties, local leaders closed their schools rather than integrate them. Massive resistance had the support of Governor Thomas B. Stanley, Attorney General J. Lindsay Almond, and Virginia senators Harry F. Byrd and Garland Gray.[34] Hill remained at the forefront of the fight to assail the tactics of white supremacists, using both legal and political means to do so.

It became the overarching focus of his career:

We always had to fight to keep the movement going. Massive resistance. Next thing we got was [Southern] Manifesto, telling people to use every legal means to violate the law. How you going to violate the law by some legal means?....There never was a time, right to the present day, where there's been an enthusiastic effort to bring on desegregation. They used to put one Negro into the school and talk about integration. That was nonsense. I told them that at the time. As a matter of fact, even when we were arguing for under the separated but equal doctrine, I went before the circuit. I told them if you build from the same plan, build one school for whites and one school for Negroes, side-by-side, equip them the same, put equally qualified teachers in the same, you still would have unequal, inequality. Because you can't—there are certain things you get from a community that you can't get unless you're part of the community.[35]

Oliver Hill

http://blackleadership.virginia.edu/19

Young blacks were watching lawyers like Oliver Hill. One of them was Henry Marsh. Although he had been born in Richmond, after the death of his mother he was sent away at age five to live with a variety of relatives. His earliest schooling occurred in Isle of Wight County near Smithfield, Virginia. He walked five miles each way to a one-room school where one teacher instructed 70 children.[36] When his father was able to reunite the family, he returned to Richmond. There, as a high school student, he rode the bus to school with his sister, personally experiencing the effects of humiliation:

> When she had to get up to give her seat to a white man because they had gotten to that point on the bus, it infuriated me. I mean, I was disgusted by it because I knew she had to get up because she was black. I didn't like getting up myself. But when I saw her get up, it really bothered me.[37]

In high school, Marsh learned of the work of Oliver Hill and Spottswood Robinson. Until then, without professional role models, Marsh thought that he would become a truck driver. He recalls:

> When I was in high school I heard about Oliver Hill in Richmond. And I was curious. And a bunch of us went down to a court case in Richmond where he was arguing—he and Spot Robinson were arguing a case. And I was impressed. I decided then that, "Hey, that's what I'd like to do!" As I continued, when I got to college I saw him again. I decided, "I *know* that's what I want to do." That's when I decided I wanted to be a civil rights lawyer.[38]

From 1952 to 1956, Marsh attended Virginia Union University. These were positive years, but it was impossible even while enrolled in a historically black university not to experience racism in the larger society. He describes a trip:

> When I went to Miami, Florida, for the first time with my fraternity brothers, it was in 1954....On the way down there when we stopped

in a service station to go to the restroom, the owner said, "Nigger, niggers don't use these restrooms. Get out of there. Don't you go in that restroom."[39]

Assaulted by such affronts, Marsh looked for role models, like Oliver Hill, who in 1955 remonstrated publicly against legislators' efforts to subvert the Supreme Court ruling. Marsh, then president of Student Government at Virginia Union, enlisted in the effort to combat the massive resistance of whites. He remembers a transformative moment:

> I was a senior in college. Virginia was—a year and a half after *Brown*, Virginia was in the middle of this massive resistance effort. And I read in the paper that the General Assembly was going to consider a plan to frustrate desegregation. So I went down and testified. I was the only student, and there were thirty-six adults. I represented the student government of Virginia Union University. Mr. Hill represented the state NAACP—state conference. He was masterful. He was already at his best. I mean, there was one hundred and forty legislators, all men, all white men, all elderly white men. No women, no young people. And they were assembled in one room in what they call a Joint Session. Mr. Hill stood there and shook his fist and dared them to pass these laws. And I was frightened frankly. I said, "What is he doing?" And then when he'd bang his fists on a desk and said, "If you do this, we're gonna beat you," I looked for a place to hide because I knew they were going to haul him away. But he was intent and his temple was throbbing. And whenever Oliver gets excited his temple starts throbbing. It was a masterful speech. So I got up and made my speech on behalf of the student body. When I finished Oliver came over and patted me on the shoulder. Said, "Good talk, young man." Said, "What are you going to do when you grow up?"....I said, "Well, I want to be a lawyer." He said, "Well, why don't you come and work with me? I need some help." I was a college student. I said "Okay," and we shook hands.... Little did I know, that was my future law partner.[40]

Henry Marsh
http://blackleadership.virginia.edu/20

Many steps lay ahead before that partnership was sealed. First was law school. Marsh enrolled at Howard, where so many of the powerful black civil rights lawyers were trained. He attended "dry runs" for Supreme Court cases and listened to Thurgood Marshall, James Nabrit, Jr. and others present their arguments.[41] The discussions were exciting, the atmosphere was electric, and the times seemed

Figure 5.3 Samuel Tucker, Henry Marsh III (in middle), and Frank Reeves at work to reopen the Prince Edward County School system, June 18, 1964. Courtesy of Richmond-Times Dispatch and the Virginia Historical Society.

so ripe with possibility. Marsh earned his law degree in 1959, and following his military service, he joined Oliver Hill's Richmond law firm in 1961.

Quickly, he began to learn how the law and social activism were intertwined. He was sent to Atlanta to work with Vernon Jordan, Grace Hamilton, and a "bunch of very enlightened white people" at the Southern Regional Council. Involved in the Voter Education Project, he learned that there was a "tremendous need for black elected officials."[42] After he returned to Richmond, he followed the example of his mentor, Oliver Hill, and successfully ran for the Richmond City Council in 1966. Unlike Hill, he served on that council for 25 years.

Still a lawyer, Marsh worked on desegregation cases in Virginia and elsewhere in the South.

But the law was painfully slow. Marsh became disillusioned with the pace of change:

[I]n 1968 Mr. Tucker and I took *Green v. New Kent* up there [to the U.S. Supreme Court]. And finally they said, "Now means now. Dismantle it now." But I mean, root, branch and burrow. But it was '68 as opposed to

'54. They had fourteen years—the Supreme Court gave the South to get ready for *Brown*. That was one reason why I decided to go into politics because the legal process was so slow, and I felt frustrated that we finally had a decision and the Supreme Court keeps giving them more, and more, and more time. So I said, "This stuff will never end this way."[43]

Marsh labored within the Richmond City Council to root out those resistant to change. He encouraged other black leaders to be less timid and more liberal.[44] From 1970 to 1977, he served as vice-mayor of Richmond. And in 1977, he broke racial barriers and was elected mayor of Richmond, the first African American ever to hold this position. As mayor, he brought people together across the racial divide, created a new civic organization called Richmond Renaissance, supported a new shopping mall that bridged communities, rejuvenated Richmond economically, and provided blacks a piece of the economic power base in the inner core of the city. More controversially, he divided Richmond into nine wards, giving more political power to black Richmonders.[45]

In 1991, following 25 years in Richmond city government, Henry Marsh was elected to the state senate, where he has served ever since. Maintaining his legal connections to the firm of Hill, Tucker & Marsh, he devoted his greatest energy to public office. The work of the frontline lawyers who toiled for decades to challenge *Plessy* and segregation allowed Henry Marsh and many others to run successfully for political office. Following the lead of his "hero," Oliver Hill, he embraced the law and politics to promote meaningful societal change.

By the early 1960s, younger college students, tired of waiting for white supremacists to abide by the laws of the land, began to create their own civil rights organizations. They demanded change and drew attention to those who had no voice. They focused on access to public places, on voting rights, and on unfair incarcerations. They became more insistent and more strident as time went on. One of them, Angela Davis, assailed the criminal justice system. In the early 1970s, in California, she became heavily invested in the case of George Jackson, one of the Soledad Brothers.[46] The times were violent. She bought a gun for self-protection. One day, Jackson's younger brother, Jonathan, walked into a courtroom with the gun registered in Davis's name. A shootout occurred, leaving the judge and young Jonathan dead. From her previous encounters with the law, Angela assumed that she would be picked up and probably brutalized in jail. She fled, becoming one of the "most wanted" by the FBI. When she was captured, she became an international celebrity. "Free Angela Davis" was a rallying cry for young activists around the globe.

Angela Davis's case was the transformative catalyst in Charles Ogletree's decision to become a lawyer. Ogletree was a young college student at Stanford from 1971 to 1975. An activist, he hung out with black nationalist supporters.

When Davis was arrested in New York and sent to the Women's Detention Center in Palo Alto, she was just a few blocks from the Stanford campus. White and black students organized the Stanford Students for the Defense of Angela Davis and Other Political Prisoners. Only a sophomore, Ogletree became the "self-appointed" editor of a Black Panther publication called *The Real News* and attended much of her trial in San José. He was fascinated by the courtroom theater.[47] Her case persuaded him that lawyers could be a positive force for social good:

> When I saw Angela Davis—I met her when she was in prison, talked to her about her trial, told her what we were doing. And I saw lawyers working for justice. I said, "Wow, this really makes a difference!" ... [S]eeing her trial made me think about, "Gosh, lawyers can make a phenomenal difference." And I saw four lawyers do that. I saw them take the government's evidence and turn it on its head. I saw them have a client like Angela Davis actually participate in the trial. She was not a potted plant. She actually played a role giving part of the opening statement, examining witnesses. I saw the true dream team, a diverse team of women and men, black and white, defending someone against charges that could have resulted in a punishment as serious as the death penalty. I saw it at a time, when...Reagan was the governor, Nixon was the president, and there was this war on crime, and certainly war on someone who would be labeled as a communist, as Angela Davis was. She was in the worst possible circumstance, and I saw lawyers save the day. And I said if I ever had the opportunity and privilege to do that, that's what I'd like to do. I'd like to become a lawyer and try to serve the community and try to save the day.[48]

Charles Ogletree
http://blackleadership.virginia.edu/21

While the Angela Davis trial provided the trigger for his career path, his life experiences imparted his values and sensibilities that drove his leadership trajectory. Time and again, he witnessed the distance between promise and delivery. Time and again, he saw the multiple ways in which race mattered in America, despite the rhetorical claims of equality.

Charles Ogletree grew up in Merced, California, in "abject poverty." His grandparents had moved from Arkansas to California in the 1940s, hoping for opportunity. His parents met at a migrant labor camp and married in 1951. Willie Mae, his mother, was 18; Charles, his father, was 42. Willie Mae bore her first child at age 16, ending her formal education.[49] Five more babies would follow while she was still in her twenties. Charles, Jr., born in 1952, lived with grandparents, parents, brothers, and sisters—all crowded into one house. His father physically abused his mother. Periodically, she called the police, who arrested his father, took him away, while young Charles watched with humiliation and sadness. In 1960, when he was eight years old, his parents separated and his mother went on public assistance. He moved from place to place, living in homes without bathtubs or showers, sharing a bed with his brother, and wearing the same clothes for days.[50] "From the time that I was born," Ogletree writes, "until I left home to go to college eighteen years later, we moved constantly, always facing poverty."[51]

Charles, Jr., was two years old when the *Brown* decision was rendered. *De jure* segregation did not exist in California. De facto segregation, however, was defined by the railroad tracks, "the dividing line between blacks and whites, between opportunity and despair."[52] In his city school, the student body was predominantly black and Hispanic; all the students were poor and working class. Ogletree remembers fondly his black fourth-grade teacher, who paid for him to get a haircut. This was a school where serious nurturing and disciplining took place, and where his principal stressed racial and ethnic pride. He loved his experiences there and felt empowered.[53]

By the time he got to high school, another African American teacher, John Heflin, introduced Ogletree to black literature. Heflin encouraged him to read Harriet Beecher Stowe's *Uncle Tom's Cabin,* Claude Brown's *Manchild in the Promised Land,* and Richard Wright's *Native Son*—books that "awakened a consciousness" in him.[54] He read about the plight of the black man in America, talked about, and reflected on it: "it sort of radicalized my whole thinking about race," he said. It helped him to understand the world, and allowed him to see how race matters in America.[55]

Dr. Martin Luther King, Jr. was assassinated while Ogletree was still in high school. Older people tried to maintain calm and said God would resolve the matter, but he and his friends were angry. Disgusted with the hypocritical rhetoric about integration, equality, and justice, they formed Operation Get Together, the precursor of the Merced High Black Student Union. Two years later, Ogletree became the first black president of the student body at Merced High School.[56] As a high school leader, he went to Washington, D.C. in 1970 to attend the "presidential classroom for young Americans." It was his first trip outside California. In his senior year, Ogletree's guidance counselor suggested he apply to Stanford for college—a place he had never heard of.[57] It was a distance of 135 miles between Merced and Stanford. But it might as well have been a different planet.

Charles Ogletree grew up intimately aware of the political and social turmoil gripping America. Every day he saw the fundamental inequity engendered by poverty and race:

there were two Americas—one black, one white. They were separate and unequal. That was it, and that everything flowed from that, whether it is a relationship between the community and police, whether it's a relationship between employment opportunities and a lack thereof, whether it was the opportunities for a meaningful education, whether it was health care. It was—everything was, in a sense, influenced by your race. And it was condition at birth that determined not your aptitude but your altitude, where you could possibly go.[58]

But every day, Ogletree also read about the struggle for equality and justice and the aspirations for the children born after *Brown*. He recalls:

we were hearing about Governor [Orval] Faubus in Arkansas not let-ting black children go to Central High. In the 1950s, we heard from Governor George Wallace, "Segregation today! Segregation tomorrow! Segregation forever!" And we would learn about the Southern Manifesto that our Congress was saying that "we will fight against integration," using the term that people attribute to Malcolm X, "by any means nec-essary." That's what the southern segregationists were saying, that they were going to fight this effort, and it was amazing to us that we thought a law had been decided, and people had to follow the law. But what we saw on the news and heard on the radio and read was that people were willing to give their lives to resist integration. And on the other hand, African Americans were dying with their white supporters when they were trying to promote integration in places throughout the South.[59]

For Ogletree, the meaning of *Brown* was that the court had ruled that separate was inherently unequal, but Americans refused to accept the law of the land. The aspiration of *Brown* was toward a color-blind America; the reality of *Brown* was that Americans held on to their race prejudices. It was not just in the South. When Ogletree entered Harvard Law School in 1972, he witnessed the vicious busing crisis going on in South Boston. Integrating America's schools would be a violent and arduous process. He was profoundly disillusioned and uncomfortable to be living his privileged life as a Harvard law student while being aware of the violence on the streets nearby.[60]

For Charles Ogletree, the history of *Brown v. Board of Education* and civil rights' struggle remains very personal. He knows he is a "direct beneficiary" of the *Brown* decision, enabling him to go to Stanford and Harvard Law School. He also feels an obligation to "steadfastly challenge the system" and to lead in the struggle for equality.[61] More than one hundred years after W. E. B. Du Bois announced that the problem of the twentieth century was the color line, Ogletree contends that racism and segregation still persist in America.[62]

For many years, Ogletree served as a public defender in Washington, D.C. After joining the Harvard faculty, he wrote on restorative justice and educational opportunity, becoming an ardent champion of reparations payments to help the poorest people in America. In 2004, he chaired the American Bar Association's Commission on *Brown v. Board of Education.*

Ogletree's mission is to resist injustice and fight back. Fighting back has a personal connotation for him. Fighting back means looking back toward Merced, and never forgetting your roots; it means spending twenty years of your life supporting a childhood friend, Eugene Allen, who was unfairly framed and sent to San Quentin. Fighting back also means supporting poor children in Merced with scholarships. For personal sustenance, fighting back requires returning to Merced because it is there that the real world of class and race exists, and that is where the faces of family and childhood friends become most clear.[63] "There is no way that we can't find a way to take the social engineering principles of [Charles Hamilton] Houston and apply them to our professional lives and our personal lives," says Ogletree.[64] Clearly, his predecessors have had a profound influence on him; they modeled how the law and civic engagement can advance racial equity.

In 2001, Charles Ogletree received the Charles Hamilton Houston Medallion of Merit by the Washington Bar Association. He received the award in honor of his lifelong work promoting social justice and equality. In accepting it, he said: "I will fight with you, I will fight for you, and if necessary, I will fight against you to ensure justice in the 21st century."[65] That is what leadership means to him.

In 2008, Benjamin Jealous assumed the position of president of the NAACP, the country's oldest civil rights organization. He was 35 years old, and the youngest person ever to hold this prestigious office. It was the 100th anniversary of that esteemed organization. Jealous is neither a clergyman nor an elected official—training and skills that previous presidents possessed. But he is deeply rooted in civil rights advocacy and has a strong background in fundraising. Julian Bond, then the national chair of the NAACP Board, fought hard for his election, seeking someone who would continue the traditional focus of the historic organization.[66]

Jealous credits both foundational family experiences tied to civic engagement and an activist disposition for his personal leadership trajectory. His African American mother integrated her high school in Baltimore at age 14. An early member of SNCC, she helped desegregate lunch counters in southern Virginia. His father was among the very few white people arrested at antisegregation sit-ins. When these two activists decided to marry, his father's blue-blooded New England family disowned him.[67] "Being radical is not new for me," he wrote. "I was born out of resistance to Jim Crow when my mom and dad married despite their union being illegal in many states."[68] Personal stories about family histories mingle in his mind with the events and images of the civil rights movement.

These stories shaped the childhood of Benjamin Jealous and were "transformative," he claimed. "You know," he told Julian Bond:

> between my grandmother's stories and my parents' stories... [and] events like *Eyes on the Prize*, my imagination as a child and increasingly as a teenager was very much captured by the continuity of social movement in this country.... [T]here was just a notion that there was nothing more noble that a person could do than to help finish the American experiment and really create a pluralistic democracy that worked for everybody. There was also, and especially in my grandmother's stories and my mom's kind of spirituality and some of the conversations with Bill Starr, a notion that we were surrounded at any given moment by our ancestors, that there was a indebtedness that wasn't simply whatever you chose, however you chose to perceive it, but that there were actually real spirits that were judging you. And that sense—sort of metaphysical sense—of sort of responsibility and possibility, that on the one hand you had to continue the work that generations had started and on the other hand, that great changes were possible, led me to a place where I really have considered no other path.... I just kind of looked for how I could just help change the world for the better as quickly as possible.[69]

Benjamin Jealous
http://blackleadership.virginia.edu/22

For Benjamin Jealous, activism was integral to his family history and to family values. His maternal grandmother taught him the "dignity of being defiant."[70] Friends of the family challenged him to debate and to argue, preparing him for his own engagement. By age seven, he claims, he told his family that he wanted to become a civil rights lawyer.[71] At age 14, he was going door to door to register voters during Rev. Jesse Jackson's presidential bid. In high school, he spent a semester in Washington, D.C. as a page in Leon Panetta's office and as an intern to Congressman Sam Farr.[72] He learned how systems worked, and how to effect meaningful change.

The civil rights movement shaped his decision about college. A family friend and black judge from Baltimore, Robert B. Watts, insisted that he go to Columbia University in New York. "Why?," inquired Ben. Watts replied, "'because you want to be civil rights player, right?' and I said, 'yeah.'" Watts continued: "'Well, Jack Greenberg is the dean so that's where you're going to school.'"[73] Jack Greenberg had argued before the US Supreme Court in forty different cases, including *Brown v. Board of Education*. He became Thurgood Marshall's handpicked successor at the NAACP Legal Defense Fund (LDF), and worked there for 35 years. In 1989, he became dean of the College at Columbia.[74] Since young Ben wanted to be a civil rights lawyer, attending Columbia seemed the smart thing to do. "That's why I came to Columbia," Jealous recalled. "I literally came looking for Jack." In fact, he did get to know Greenberg, who arranged an internship for Jealous at the LDF.[75]

Mentors at Columbia exerted a powerful influence on him. They linked the civil rights movement, activism, and positive change in his mind. He took courses with political science professor Charles V. Hamilton, who had coauthored *Black Power* with Stokely Carmichael. He got to know Father Bill Starr, the longtime Episcopal minister on campus, and Rabbi David Saperstein—"spiritual leaders of anti-war protests with the Berrigan brothers." Jealous especially credits Starr as someone who "really encouraged me to develop, I guess, a spiritual base to sustain myself.... [H]e allowed us to see the Bible as just a place of refuge for people who were committed to social change." Starr emphasized the commandment to love your neighbor as yourself and to treat others with dignity. These concepts shaped his attitudes and actions when he fought for the rights of inmates incarcerated in Mississippi prisons.[76]

During his first two years at Columbia, Ben Jealous spent a lot of his time in organizing activities. He became president of the Black Student Organization, worked with the LDF, founded the Harlem Restoration Project Youth Corps, protested the Gulf War, advocated for need-blind financial aid at colleges and universities, and championed the preservation of the Audubon Ballroom (where Malcolm X was assassinated). When his protests morphed into disruption, he and six other students were suspended for a semester by the very Jack Greenberg he had so admired.[77]

Like the student founders of SNCC during the previous generation, activism for societal change seemed more meaningful to Jealous than reading books and taking exams. He treated the suspension in his junior year as an opportunity. He went to Jackson, Mississippi, and worked as a community organizer for the NAACP. He helped keep three historically black colleges open and funded. He became a reporter for a weekly black newspaper, *The Jackson Advocate*, and worked closely with the paper's courageous founder, Charles Tisdale in behalf of African Americans and poor whites.[78] He eventually became the managing editor of this controversial newspaper, putting himself in danger while learning how to mix journalism with advocacy.[79] He exposed corruption of high-ranking officials at the Mississippi State Penitentiary—also known as Parchman Farm—and helped acquit a small black farmer wrongfully accused of arson.[80] Like Julian Bond before him, he came to understand the importance of the press in communicating truth to power.

After two years in the Mississippi trenches, Jealous returned to Columbia to complete his undergraduate work. Mentors Carlton Long, Judith Russell, and Father Bill Starr encouraged him to consider applying for a Rhodes Fellowship.[81] He turned his college record around, won the Rhodes, and spent a year studying comparative social research at Oxford University in England. His readings focused not on civil rights in America, but on human rights globally.

By the time he went to Oxford, Jealous knew that he did not want to become a lawyer. Like Henry Marsh, he had come to feel that the law was a painfully slow way to reshape society. He recalls that all the cases that he worked on at the NAACP Legal Defense Fund "were older than I was." He felt he had been "sold a bill of goods" when he realized that cases like *Brown* took decades to adjudicate and enforce. His work in Mississippi taught him that social action could be more efficacious than legal strategies.[82]

Each step prepared Jealous for the next. Between 1999 and 2002, he was the executive director of the National Newspaper Publishers Association, a trade organization representing over 200 black community newspapers. Afterward, he became the director of the US human rights program for Amnesty International and the president of the Rosenberg Foundation. Along the way, as director of the US human rights program at Amnesty International, Jealous became deeply involved in the Troy Davis murder case.

In 1989, Davis was convicted of murdering a police officer in Savannah, Georgia. No physical evidence linked him to the crime. Seven of the nine witnesses either contradicted their testimony or recanted, and six more eyewitnesses identified another killer. Jealous found a way to get Davis a new evidentiary

Figure 5.4 NAACP President Ben Jealous and Amnesty International Executive Director Larry Cox surrounded by sign waving supporters at a press conference in Savannah, Georgia before evidentiary hearings in the Troy Davis murder case. June 23, 2010. Photo by Patrick Rodgers. Courtesy of *Connect Savannah*.

hearing, even though Davis had exhausted his appeals. When the US Supreme Court granted his request, Jealous was jubilant. He believes that a key to his success was "a big media strategy and a local community organizing strategy." In his view, "change in the court of public opinion" will move the legal system.[83] Activist strategies, he is convinced, often yield faster remedies than legal ones. (Unfortunately, despite worldwide pressure, Troy Davis was executed by lethal injection in Georgia on September 21, 2011.)

Born in 1973 and coming of age in the 1990s, Benjamin Jealous was deeply affected by the *Brown* decision and the subsequent civil rights movement. He felt impelled to act, embrace Jesus' commandment to love your neighbor, and develop a comprehensive vision for leadership:

> Vision, in my experience, is what you feel compelled to do…Vision, you know, and calling to me are very spiritual and often spontaneous or inspired, and in my experience, come with a sense of being compelled…It's the vision that compels you to follow through.[84]

As president and CEO of the NAACP, Jealous felt an "obligation…to extend the ladder of opportunity."[85] He sees a continuous line between the leaders of the civil rights movement and his own mission. In his view, *Brown* remains "a great sore on the American consciousness" because it has failed to insure "that all children have access to a quality education and can go to any school they want to."[86] For Jealous, "our biggest victory of the 20th century is also our biggest shortcoming."[87] Achieving quality schools is a human right, he contends. Originally motivated by the possibility of using law to catalyze social change, Jealous came to see the need for other ways to change American hearts through the broader focus on human rights.

Jealous views himself as a child of the historical civil rights and human rights movements that go back to the time of slavery. He still sees a wide gulf between the opportunity provided to him as a child of "The Dream" and the thousands of his peers who are killed or incarcerated.[88] It is that unfulfilled dream that drives him. Defying the status quo, he wants the NAACP to "dream bold dreams, break them down into achievable steps, practice discipline and pursue them until you win…."[89] By organizing, promoting social action, nurturing racial pride, and employing the law, he hopes to exert leadership and achieve his mission—the same mission pursued by the heroes—both recognized and unrecognized—of the civil rights movement.

Bakari Sellers, born in 1984—a decade after Ben Jealous—also defines himself as a child of the 1960s. He claims that February 8, 1968, though it was nearly 20 years before his birth, was the most important day of his life.[90] Cleveland Sellers, Bakari's father, was arrested and jailed that day as a result of a demonstration that occurred at South Carolina State University in Orangeburg. Tension had been brewing for days as students tried to desegregate a local bowling alley. After several failed attempts, students organized a bonfire on the campus of their black university. Like Kent State two years later, the police overreacted, leaving three students dead and 27 wounded in an event that became known as the Orangeburg Massacre. Cleveland was injured, while attempting to help others. Although only an observer that day, he was suspicious to the FBI because of his efforts to organize resistance to the draft and his overall militancy.[91] When his friends urged him to go to a hospital to get medical attention, the police seized him. They accused him of "arson, inciting to riot, assault and battery with intent to kill, destruction of personal property, damaging real property, housebreaking, and grand larceny."[92] They took him to the state penitentiary in Columbia, and set bond at $50,000. Cleveland Sellers remained in federal prison for more than four months, missing the birth of his first born as a result.[93]

Prior to this tragic event, Cleveland Sellers had been active in the movement. At age 19, he participated in the voter registration drives in Mississippi during the Freedom Summer in 1964. He became the national program secretary for SNCC, working closely with Stokely Carmichael, Julian Bond, John Lewis, and Ella Baker. There are pictures in the family home showing Cleveland Sellers with Stokely Carmichael, Elijah Muhammad, the Rev. Martin Luther King, Jr., and Rev. Jesse Jackson.[94] Bakari grew up hearing stories of the movement, feeling a sense of intimacy with its leaders. It is a legacy he cherishes.

His favorite picture, however, is one from 1993, when he was eight years old. It is a picture of his father with his arms draped over Bakari's shoulders at a memorial at S.C. State on the 25th anniversary of the Orangeburg Massacre. Their heads are bowed and their eyes closed.[95] Deeply affected by his father's life experience, Bakari reflects:

> I think that I'm angrier about February 8th than he is. I think he's come to some reconciliation within his own heart about that day, but it was a day that will forever stain the history of our great state and the state I love.... [Y]ou had a powerful group of youth who decided that they were going to break down ... the last vestige of discrimination and Jim Crow's final hiding place—and just that gumption or that courage, that audacity ... just showed the strength of that generation, that young generation. And then how they were met with just brutal lethal force when they attempted to do so by people who had cast themselves in a light that was something other than that.[96]

Bakari feels that his "father and others ... have kind of molded and ordered my steps."[97] What he means is that he has been inspired by their commitment and that he seeks to make the same kind of difference through public service leadership.

Bakari Sellers grew up in the tiny town of Denmark, South Carolina; in 2000, the town had a population of 3,328 people. The racial makeup of the city was 86 percent African American and the median income for families was $22,000 per year. Thirty-five percent of the population lived below the poverty line, with 51 percent below the age of 18. Bakari knows the debilitating effects of poverty. Like Charles Ogletree, he experienced the intimacy of rural life, and he also breathed its limitations. There was no Boy Scout troop, no YMCA, and no exposure to high culture. But there was the Denmark Recreation Center, built by his father and others in the community, where he learned about soccer, baseball, basketball, and football. There were full-day summer programs, housed in two cinderblock rooms. No one was turned away.[98] Denmark, South Carolina, was a tight knight community with little knowledge of the issues affecting the outside world unless, of course, you had exposure through your family.

When it was time for college in 2001, Bakari Sellers chose Morehouse. He knew he would be held to high standards there. He also knew that some of the most influential African American leaders had been trained there. Anticipating he would go to medical school, his experiences at Morehouse altered his trajectory. He was elected president of the Student Government Association. In that capacity, he sought to "bring leadership beyond the gates" by initiating voter registration drives, raising money for tsunami relief, and holding political forums about the 2004 election. Serving as an intern for Atlanta mayor Shirley Franklin and then for U.S. congressman James Clyburn acquainted him with the challenges of political leadership.[99] As campus president, he also had the chance to attend the annual conference of the American Israel Public Affairs Committee (AIPAC). There, he learned more about world affairs and met some members of Congress. They were people, he said, "that one day you knew you wanted to grow up and be like."[100] His professional path was set.

To succeed in political life, Bakari believed he needed to have legal tools at his disposal. He viewed the 1954 *Brown v. Board* decision as a landmark in *his* own life:

I think that it broke down barriers, substantial barriers, to growth and development. I think it gave the opportunity for blacks and whites to sit down together and have the dialogue and even more importantly, I think it shattered the theory that was established by *Plessy*, that you had to be separate and that was still equal, so I was, even though it was twenty-nine, thirty-some years before I was born, I think that was the landmark case in my life and whenever I speak, I often use Chief Justice Warren's opinion in which he said that segregation causes a sense of inferiority by placing children in environments not conducive to learning—I oftentimes use that as a point whereby I begin to talk about where we have come from and where we go from here.[101]

He understands how powerful a tool the law has been as a means to overcome marginalization. His examples go right back to the early civil rights movement:

> in South Carolina, we're talking about 1949 *Clarendon County Briggs versus Elliott* and—then we have Sara Mae Fleming in 1954, who sat in on a bus, then we have the Orangeburg Massacre in 1968. And we're rooted in struggle.... The young people then, they created a change that we have today. So... I just figured it was incumbent upon myself when I see that my generation is, once again, becoming marginalized, doesn't have a voice.[102]

He also believes that his father's mistreatment at the hands of the law pushed him to want to be able to use the law as an effective, rather than abusive, tool. Looking back to the events of the Orangeburg Massacre, he said:

> he stayed on campus that day and he wasn't a organizer, *per se,* of what was going on,... but he did get shot and arrested. And I think that egged me on just a little bit in my legal career because I kind of understood how the judiciary system kind of yanked him around and the criminal justice system didn't quite do him justice until about twenty-five years later, when he got pardoned.[103]

As an intern in college in James Clyburn's office, he also saw that so many people who worked on Capitol Hill had law degrees. He saw that this path could open doors, even if one were not a practicing attorney.[104] Following college, he enrolled at the University of South Carolina Law School, knowing that he wanted to come back and serve his own state.

But while still in law school, he decided to run for legislative office in 2006. He passionately wanted to make a difference, so he jumped in with both feet, challenging the Democratic incumbent Thomas Rhoad, Jr. He won at age 21—the youngest person ever to hold that position in the South Carolina legislature. Rhoad was 82 years old; he had been in the State House for more years than Sellers had been alive. Bakari saw the deep poverty within the district that included Bamberg County. He saw the great divide of the railroad tracks. He knew about the schools that had unequal resources.[105] He simply didn't have the time to wait until Rhoad was ready to retire.

In his current position as a legislator, he has focused on economic issues that go beyond race. Every child in America should have the chance for health: Bakari seeks to get vending machines that sell unhealthy snacks out of schools. That, he feels, will begin to deal with the issues of obesity. Every child in America must have the right to equal education: Bakari fights for improved funding so that South Carolina education will be competitive. Only then, he believes, will the state begin to address its high unemployment rate. In the scope of his vision and his determination to act, he calls himself a "New Democrat."[106]

Gwen Ifil thinks of Bakari Sellers as part of a "breakthrough" generation, distinguishing his issues from those of his father's generation. The main difference seems to be that his politics and public service look beyond race.[107] In reality, however, his passion for change and his belief in the possibility of change come directly out of his familial connection to the events of a previous generation. He also recognizes the continuity from his parents' generation:

> I think that we are a breakthrough generation, but I don't want that to be misconstrued as we're a generation that stands on our own. We're a generation that stands on the shoulders of those that come before us, but we're a breakthrough in terms of the thought.... My goal is not to end segregation and Jim Crow. My goal is so that every person, no matter their race, creed or color, has access to quality education because now we have blacks and whites, thanks to *Brown*, who go to the same school but the school is still poor and struggling, so my goal is to uplift that school as a whole.[108]

Bakari Sellers
http://blackleadership.virginia.edu/23

The "chip on his shoulder" that he carries with him in his legislative duties relates to his responsibility to carry forward the mission and goals of the three who died in the Orangeburg Massacre.[109] Moreover, his inspiration comes from those he came to know who were fundamental to the civil rights movement:

> It has to start with my parents. There was no other direction I could've taken, but I used to go everywhere with my father. I would be on his leg, and you know, whether or not we were going somewhere to see you [Julian Bond] or whether or not we were hanging out with Reggie [Robinson] or even at Morehouse, they always used to tell me, they'd say, "Your uncle is here." "My uncle?" They said, "Yeah, your uncle is sitting in your office." I'd say, "My uncle?" And it would be Willie Ricks sitting in the office, and just growing up around these people—when I pick up the phone and it's Kathleen Cleaver on the phone, a lot of people don't have those experiences, so my network was a little bit more expansive and just, you know, Judy Richardson, being able to just walk up and hug her and there were a lot of people from the former chairman of SNCC to SNCC activists and Rita [Schwerner] Bender—great friends.... [T]hese people, they are heroes and sheroes, and I get to touch them every day and talk to them every day—Connie

[Constance] Curry, Bob Zellner, who is a fool, who I love—you know, you just learn so much from these people and it's just an awesome experience that I've been blessed with and those people who gave up so much for social justice, who am I not to do those same types of things?[110]

His path to leadership is not all that surprising. His father, Cleveland Sellers, said that in his household "politics was front and center" and his son was "always encouraged to be involved in political action and political movement."[111]

Bakari's own sense is that the events of the 1960s were "epic." "We need more of that boldness now," he claims. Perhaps it is the understanding that people, acting in concert, can change the world that creates his confidence. "Of course, I wake up and believe I can change the world...I guess I just don't know any better."[112]

* * *

Law operates as a means of social organization and social control. The denial of the basic right to freedom and protection of the law for persons of color occurred before there was an America, with the legal importation of slaves. Despite the right to life and liberty, enshrined in the Declaration of Independence, slavery existed in the United States through the Civil War. Once it became illegal, Jim Crow laws barring persons of color from basic rights, replaced the hierarchies of race embedded in the US Constitution. Overcoming race inequality in America has been a constant struggle that persists. And the struggle has been engaged from the very beginning of the nation's history.

The *Brown v. Board of Education* case did not initiate the forces of resistance to flawed legal premises. But it did galvanize actions and reactions. Because the Supreme Court of the United States declared the principle of segregation illegal, *Brown* achieved a kind of transcendence as a core value for American society. It became a reference point for making America better.[113] For those who wanted to hold on to the race paradigm of inequality, it became a justification for manipulation, brutality, and murder. The battle over race became charged in ways it had never been before. In that sense, the principle of *Brown* was transformative.

Law and social change are inextricable.[114] The law is a tool that establishes a set of social realities. To change those social norms, lawyers respond to individuals who are wronged and seek redress. Generations of such people had been working at that redress long before the five cases that constituted *Brown* came along. The trenches were filled with individuals and organizations whittling away at the status quo. We could start with unnamed people who resisted slavery through song, or those who worked along with Harriet Tubman on the Underground Railroad. We could trace the history of the abolitionist movement, or recall the writings of Frederick Douglass, or those of W. E. B. Du Bois. We could point to the formation of the NAACP at the turn of the twentieth century. There is no dearth of heroes and front-line challengers.

Yet, the fact that a cadre of superbly trained black lawyers from black institutions were able to get the US Supreme Court to reverse the concept that race separation could equate to equality was an enormous breakthrough. These lawyers did not act alone, of course. There were some white lawyers in support. There were also black individuals in every community across America who were willing to stand up and be counted in this struggle. Charles Hamilton Houston, dean of Howard University's School of Law and the first black man to serve on the *Harvard Law Review*, could not do this on his own. Thurgood Marshall, Oliver Hill, Spottswood Robinson III, and James Nabrit, Jr. could not do it alone. They needed people like Joseph Albert Delaine, the AME minister from Clarendon County, South Carolina, who was ultimately driven out of town as a fugitive from justice, and the 20 other plaintiffs who supported him.[115] They needed women like Septima Clark, who fought to equalize pay in Charleston schools, and once fired, helped set up Citizenship Schools across the South through the Highlander School.[116] They needed Barbara Johns, a high school student, willing to walk out of her school and lead a demonstration for better facilities. They needed the hundreds of forgotten individuals who agreed to be the named parties in legal suits across America.

It was the implementation of *Brown* and the resistance to it that also spawned a movement. The struggle did not end with *Brown I*; in fact, it continues for unimaginable decades as a result of white supremacist efforts to circumvent and sabotage *Brown II*. Yet, the very need to hold on to the promise of a more equal America spawned new leaders who took their place either as lawyers or as civic activists. The students in Little Rock, the church members in Birmingham, the women who baked and who talked about what was going on in their kitchens and beauty shops—all of these people had an impact on future leadership. Before the resistance for basic integration and civil rights was felled, they needed the fighting power of members of SNCC. They needed the religious support of SCLC.

The people highlighted in this chapter point to particular individuals who motivated them toward careers in law and public service, thereby expanding the army of civil rights warriors. They underscore how individuals can be leadership models for people they do not know and will never meet. They illustrate how inspiration flows from shared values. They demonstrate how social change occurs.

I think that, in the largest sense, every advance we've made has been based on Brown. Every single advance. Nobody would have thought about doing some of the things we've done—not SNCC, not SCLC, not NAACP, not the Freedom Riders—had it not been bolstered by Brown. Because it took a while for the consciousness to spread through the community that this was the death knell of segregation. It could no longer exist. The question then became How long? Under what circumstances? What steps must be taken to speed it along?[117]*—Benjamin Hooks*

Benjamin Hooks

http://blackleadership.virginia.edu/24

CHAPTER 6

The Civil Rights Movement: Grassroots Leadership—Living "in struggle"

And then the civil rights movement.... You call me to come to Mississippi to do a show....I was there because my friend called me, because I knew the beauty of the movement. I didn't know the movement was going to have the effect that it had on me.[1]—Dick Gregory

* * *

Oh, Lord, let me tell you. My heart was pump, pump, pump. The only thing that kept us going...I was singing those songs—"Let nobody turn me around, turn me around." It was just amazing and that gave you courage to keep going, but you get up there and there's this guy with this red face—ooh, I remember, ooh—And he said, "What do you want, little nigra?" Oooh, I'm just shaking. "Suh, suh," as in sir, you know, "We want to kneel and pray for our freedom." And that's when he spat on me. Yes, he did. He spat on me, picked me up. Just pushed me towards the paddy-wagon and they threw us all into the paddy-wagon....He was so angry and he was also angry because there were people taking pictures, you see, and it was embarrassing his city and all that.[2]

Freeman Hrabowski
http://blackleadership.virginia.edu/25

Freeman Hrabowski was a young boy in May 1963 when he joined the Birmingham Children's Crusade. His story, in which one can still sense his fear, is one of millions of recollections of those who fought for racial change in America.

One year later, Bob Moses became the unsung architect of Freedom Summer— organizing thousands of young people, black and white, who came to Mississippi to facilitate voter registration drives. He believes that his experiences with the courageous African Americans who worked at the grassroots level within their communities coalesced with his earlier study of the works of Albert Camus, inspiring his own life philosophy and commitment to living a life "in action":

Camus...outlined a kind of philosophy...of walking this line—that you had to be engaged but you didn't want to be a victim but you didn't also want to cross the line and become an executioner. And so how to walk that line was the way I thought about the work that we were doing...how to do that work so that I'm not in the role of a victim but I'm also not trying to cross it and somehow be an executioner....How do you build a bond in action of actual relation—how does real relation happen in an action—in the action which is living—the idea of living with purpose. And I think that was reinforced by Amzie [Moore] and C.C. [Bryant] and E.W.[Steptoe]...and certainly Ella [Baker]....But Amzie, C.C. and E.W. are living it in communities, in families, right, but still really living a life of struggle. So, I think that's the thing with Camus cause he's writing about people who live a life in struggle, so how do you live that life in struggle and balance it...so I got examples of that through Amzie and C.C. They did it in different ways. They had figured out how to live a life of struggle in the country and in some sense that's who I think really has made my own life have some kind of sense to it—right—that it's a life in struggle that I first learned about living such a life through the movement.[3]

Robert Moses
http://blackleadership.virginia.edu/26

So many participants in the civil rights movement envisioned a society beyond race—a society of equal opportunity and equal justice.[4] To reach for their dreams, they accepted leadership roles both large and small. Their aspirations, although not fully realized, inspired generations.

Diverse leadership styles allowed multitudes to see a role for themselves. There was the prophetic leadership of Rev. Dr. Martin Luther King, Jr. and the Southern Christian Leadership Conference (SCLC); the consensual leadership model promoted by Ella Baker and embraced by the Student Nonviolent Coordinating Committee (SNCC); and the militancy of the Black Panthers and Malcolm X. All these leaders and organizations charted unknown territory and broke new ground.

Three well-known leaders of the civil rights movement featured in this chapter, attracted to the individuals and groups mentioned above, developed their leadership philosophies and styles as college students during the 1960s and early 1970s. John Lewis embraced the prophetic leadership philosophy so central to the black church. Julian Bond emulated the consensual leadership model associated with SNCC. And Angela Davis adopted the radical philosophies of the black left, associating at different times with SNCC, the Black Panthers, and the Communist Party. As young people caught up in those heady times, they learned about leadership through their engagement. They also came of age at a moment in time that built upon previous successes they could advance.

They didn't start out thinking they would be leaders; the movement propelled them into their roles. As young people, they found a place in the movement consistent with their philosophical predilections. They developed leadership styles modeled by *their* mentors—leadership styles and values they passed on to others. Lewis, Bond, and Davis were three young people who knew and engaged with one another. In time, they went off in different directions. Never forgetting the power of those years and never losing their commitment to the cause of social justice, they become models for future generations. Their continued engagement, public exposure, and principled commitments to the cause of social justice kept the memories of the movement alive.

Beloved Communities

the '60s changed my life forever.... It made me committed to the discipline and to the philosophy of non-violence, to this concept of the Beloved Community, that love is stronger, more powerful than hate, that non-violence is a much better way, a more excellent way than the way of violence.... I'm more committed to the philosophy and the discipline of non-violence now than ever before.[5] —John Lewis

John Robert Lewis turned to religion at an early age for solace and guidance. His parents were sharecroppers and devout Christians in rural Pike County, Alabama. In his hometown of segregated Troy, poverty surrounded him. There were few opportunities for enrichment. His church and his school were central to his life beyond family. There, he found models of leadership:

Teachers, ministers; these are the people that I came in contact with. During the week in school, then [on] the weekend; at church on Sunday. The religious leaders, the school teachers. These were the leaders. These were the pillars in the community.... They got in the way... They could bring people together.[6]

As a child, he was drawn to preaching. When his parents gave him the responsibility of taking care of the chickens in his yard, he practiced on them, seeking their reactions to the sound and cadence of his voice. Through this childhood experience, leadership qualities emerged that would again surface during the civil rights movement: "patience, compassion, nonviolence, civil disobedience and not a little bit of willful stubbornness." Those 60 chickens became his followers, and he was drawn to their "absolute innocence." The henhouse was a "holy place" and his responsibility for those chickens felt "spiritual, almost religious." His response to a childhood job for the family foreshadowed how he would think of responsibilities to the movement. His inclination to prophetic leadership developed further when he began preaching while still in high school at local Baptist churches. Religion and faith would be the foundations upon which he built his life's work.[7]

Lewis's passion for uplift through church-based activities and spiritual values came out of a long African American tradition.[8] Called "a nation within a nation," the church provided a grounded center for socializing, community engagement, prayer, and belief in a better future.[9] Throughout American history and across religious practices, black Americans associated freedom as a communal concept tied to liberation and salvation. To serve the master of the universe, one could not be enslaved to another.[10] The structure, organization, language, and rituals of the black church were central to the civil rights movement.[11]

Preachers could set the tone for the values of the church community. Some preachers, like the itinerant preacher from Montgomery who showed up once a month in the Macedonia Baptist church of John Lewis's youth, adopted a priestly, otherworldly message of forbearance. Eventually, God would liberate His people and true freedom would reign. Until such time as freedom came, accommodation and survival were the best you could hope for. John Lewis's parents absorbed that lesson and believed in this path.[12]

Other preachers, especially after World War II, adopted a prophetic message emphasizing the this-worldly role of the church and its members.[13] Godliness means making a difference in the political, educational, and eventually economic realities of peoples' lives. Godliness, according to Martin Luther King, Jr., means creating Beloved Community through nonviolent means. Godliness, according to King, means adopting the *agape* love endorsed by Mahatma Gandhi. It was this concept of love that elevated nonviolent resistance and became a tool for social transformation.[14]

Still in high school, John Lewis heard the broadcasts of Martin Luther King Jr.'s sermons on a radio gospel show. He was inspired:

I was fifteen years old and I heard Dr. King's voice on an old radio station, on WRMA. It was a soul station in Montgomery. I heard him preaching and I just felt like he was preaching to me. I felt like Martin Luther King was saying "John Lewis, you, too, can do it." And I listened to him move me and I knew he was speaking to me.[15]

Dr. King related the teachings of the Bible to earthly problems—the very problems that he could see around him. John Lewis felt he was "on fire with the words I was hearing."[16]

The first in his family to complete high school, he went to Nashville and enrolled in the American Baptist Theological Seminary (ABT) and Fisk University in 1957. The seminary opened his eyes to preachers and teachers who made him think—people like James Bevel from Mississippi and Bernard Lafayette from Florida, both of whom became close friends.[17] But during that first year, deeply homesick, he thought about transferring to Troy State, a white school closer to home. Something impelled him to want to integrate the college, as Autherine Lucy had tried to do at the University of Alabama. Midway into his first year of college, he sent an application. It was ignored. He took the bold step of writing to Dr. Martin Luther King, Jr. for advice and help, and he began a correspondence with Fred Gray, King's attorney. In late spring, King sent him a round-trip bus ticket and invited him to come to Montgomery, where he met with Gray, King, and Ralph Abernathy. Just 18 years old, he was petrified:

I saw Dr. King and Ralph Abernathy standing behind a desk. I was so scared. I didn't know what to say or what to do. And Martin Luther King, Jr. spoke up and said, "Are you the boy from Troy? Are you John Lewis?" And I said, "Dr. King, I am John Robert Lewis." I gave my whole name. And we started talking about my going to Troy State, and he told me how dangerous this could be, my folks' home could be burned or bombed.[18]

They seemed "genuinely concerned, troubled even." But if Lewis really wanted to bring suit against Troy State, King and Abernathy would see him through and cover his legal expenses, they told him. He was exhilarated, returning on the bus to Troy as if in a dream. He had just met the inspirational Dr. Martin Luther King, and was about to take a stand.[19]

Ultimately, he stayed in Nashville. His mother and father were very fearful about the consequences of his potential action and he could not risk their personal well-being. He wrote to King to explain his decision, heartbroken.[20]

The choice to remain in Nashville changed his life because he had direct access and exposure to black intellectuals and theologians engaged with the nascent civil rights movement. Home to Fisk, Meharry Medical College, Tennessee

State University, and ABT, black Nashville nurtured future leaders, teachers, and scientists.

His fellow students constantly argued about how to apply the meaning of such scriptural verses as those found in Matthew, when Jesus says "Think not that I come to bring peace but a sword."

> in a sense, if we were going to be true to our calling, in our mission, we had to be part of disturbing things. . . . I had [James] Bevel one semester as a roommate and then Bernard Lafayette probably a year, and we were always talking to each other, we always were preaching to each other, trying to convince the other one that this is the right thing to do, this is what we had to do, that it was not enough to go out and pastor a church—and that is good—but you have to move before, beyond a little church in the countryside of Tennessee or outside of Nashville. You just cannot be limited to four walls. You have to get out there in the larger society and the larger community. So that was a real struggle and we would argue about that and sometimes at three or four o'clock in the morning.[21]

At Fisk, he met W. E. B. Du Bois and listened to inspirational speakers like Rev. Fred Shuttlesworth, Dr. King, Roy Wilkins, and Thurgood Marshall.[22] At ABT, he studied with powerful men like Dr. Rev. John Lewis Powell.[23] He attended the First Colored Baptist Church, was moved by the progressive sermons of Reverend Kelly Miller Smith, and arranged to study with him at ABT. When Rev. Smith became the first president of the Nashville branch of the Southern Christian Leadership Conference (SCLC), he brought to his church James Lawson, a local field secretary for the Fellowship of Reconciliation (FOR). From Lawson, Lewis learned about the great world religions, Mahatma Gandhi, nonviolent protest, civil disobedience, and the concept of redemptive community.[24]

With Nashville becoming a focal point of the integration movement, Lawson organized trial sit-ins in some of the city's department stores. Lewis joined in the struggle—a young boy from Pike County suddenly thrust into the center of black-led organizations promoting nonviolent direct action and New Testament pacifism.[25]

> And the day came when a small group of black and white college students and some foreign students went downtown to one of the large department stores, and went in to the restaurant or the lunch counter, and took our seats, and which established the fact that this particular store, that the restaurant and the lunch counter would refuse to serve us. That's all we wanted to establish and we were denied service. We got up

in an orderly fashion and left. And a few days later we went to another department store and did the same thing. The same thing happened. We got up and left. And we continued the non-violent workshop.... We had two test sit-ins and we were ready. And we started sitting in on a regular basis.[26]

Lewis believes that "deep-seated religious convictions" coalesced completely with the civil rights movement:[27]

I think many of us saw getting involved in the civil rights move-ment during those early days as an extension of our faith—that we couldn't be true to our faith, we couldn't be true to our calling unless we somehow in some way got out there and pushed to deseg-regate the South, but we also had individuals like Martin Luther King, Jr., and maybe even Jim Lawson before Dr. King in Nashville talking about the Beloved Community. That is the essence of the kingdom that—we talk about bringing the Kingdom, creating the Kingdom here on Earth as it is in heaven, so if you're going to create the Kingdom, you've got to create the Beloved Community. You've got to create a community at peace with itself. When you forget about race and color and see people as people, as human beings, as sisters and brothers, as part of the wholeness of humanity. So it was very much, I think, an extension of our faith. And religion also gave us this sense of hope, that—this sense of, "Yes, you may beat me, you may arrest me, you may jail me, you may shoot and kill me, but in the process—in the process—we're going to redeem the soul of America." And that's what Dr. King preached about on many occasions. We're going to change America. We're going to redeem the soul of America. We're going to make America something different, something better.[28]

John Lewis
http://blackleadership.virginia.edu/27

The 1960s, Lewis claims, changed his life forever. It gave him a "sense of direction, a sense of purpose...something to hold onto, something to believe in."[29] The belief system, religiously inspired, provided the courage to risk physical harm. It created the will to "get in the way" and to "disturb the order."[30] The power to lead, the power to build the American House, as he calls it, where no one is left behind, comes from the Great Teacher and the Good Book.[31] It comes from Jesus, but also from Gandhi, Thoreau, and King. John Lewis was their willing student.

Figure 6.1   John Lewis (second from left), SNCC field secretary and later SNCC Chairman, and others pray before demonstration in Cairo, Illinois in 1962. Credit: ©Danny Lyon/ Magnum Photos.

The philosophy of nonviolence tied to self-emancipation allowed Lewis to endure the contempt and hostility of white segregationists.[32] For Lewis, civil disobedience and the ensuing arrests were righteous acts:

> I just felt....that it was like being involved in a Holy Crusade. I really felt that what we were doing was so in keeping with the Christian faith....we didn't welcome arrest. We didn't want to go to jail. But it became...a moving spirit....it became a religious experience that took place in jail.[33]

He went to jail multiple times for the cause. The spiritual and secular were joined in a messianic crusade of black struggle.[34]

John Lewis led in many ways. In 1961, participating in the Freedom Rides, angry mobs beat him. "I thought I was going to die," he says. "But if I had died, Dr. King probably would've said it was better to die a physical death than to die a psychological or a spiritual death."[35] In 1963, at age 23, his friends at SNCC elected him chairman, a position he held for three years. While the prophetic philosophy of SCLC sustained his religious and moral convictions, he wholeheartedly adopted the consensual leadership strategies of SNCC. That same year, he became one of the "Big Six" leaders of the civil rights movement, called upon to be a keynote speaker at the March on Washington in August 1963.

Figure 6.2 SNCC Chairman John Lewis speaks from the steps of the Lincoln Memorial at the March on Washington, August 28, 1963. Credit: ©Danny Lyon/ Magnum Photos.]

He wrote a fiery speech, incorporating the righteous indignation of the emerging movement, asserting "if we do not see meaningful progress here today, the day may come when we will not confine our marching on Washington, but we may be forced to march to the South the way Sherman did, nonviolently." His elders in the planning group objected to what they saw as its inflammatory rhetoric, and he was forced to tone it down.[36] It, too, became a lesson in building consensus for a movement. In 1964, he participated in Mississippi Freedom Summer, helping to organize voter registration drives, again putting himself in danger. And in 1965, he led over 600 peaceful protestors across the Edmund Pettus Bridge in Selma, Alabama, where state troopers brutally attacked them. There, he said:

> I thought I saw death. I thought I was going to die. I thought it was the last protest for me. But it's—I don't regret standing there, taking the blows, giving a little blood. In the process, I'm a better human being.[37]

With immense courage, he took the violent blows, serious physical injuries, and the jail sentences—always sure that he was answering to a higher master.[38]

After losing reelection as chair of SNCC to Stokely Carmichael in 1966, Lewis served the movement in other ways. He directed the Voter Education Project (VEP), adding nearly 4 million minority voters to the rolls. In 1977, after losing a race for a seat in Congress, President Carter appointed him to ACTION, the federal volunteer agency, where he oversaw more than 250,000 volunteers. In 1981, he successfully ran for the Atlanta City Council. Then, in 1986, he ran again for the Fifth Congressional Seat against his good friend, Julian Bond, and won. He has been in Congress ever since, continuing to fight for social justice.[39]

In Congress, John Lewis speaks eloquently and often about social justice in America. He remains committed to the principles of Beloved Community and nonviolence that he absorbed from King and Lawson. In 1991, his Democratic colleagues named Lewis one of three chief deputy whips for the Democratic Party, a position of real power, and in 1992 he seconded the nomination of Albert [Al] Gore for vice president of the United States at the Democratic National Convention. In his remarks, he referred again to the inspiration of Dr. King, suggesting that Gore was also committed to the Beloved Community: "an all inclusive community of justice, a community of opportunity, a community at peace with itself."[40] In 1995, he stayed away from the Million Man March because he thought Louis Farrakhan's message was inconsistent with the notion of interracial democracy and beloved community. In 1998, in a public speech on the floor of the US Congress, he called for public forgiveness for the transgressions of President Bill Clinton before the impeachment vote:

> You have to believe in forgiveness; you have to believe in the process of redemption; you have to believe that people who make mistakes can grow and change. Let those without sin cast the first stone. We're all in the same boat. We're all saved by the grace of God.[41]

Subsequently, he supported gay rights for civil marriage, writing: "We all live in the American house. We are all the American family."[42] In 2004, he argued against mandatory minimum sentencing, using the case of Marcus Dixon in Georgia to demonstrate that "equal justice" was not served.[43]

On June 25, 2013, The Supreme Court of the United States invalidated key provisions of the Voting Rights Act of 1965, allowing nine southern states and other municipalities to change their election laws without prior federal approval. Chief Justice Roberts contended that the country had changed, making those earlier safeguards unnecessary. For those who had put themselves in harm's way and who had dedicated their lives fighting for access to the political process, the Supreme Court decision, as President Obama said, was deeply disappointing. The very day of the decision, John Lewis issued a press release to exhort the country and the Congress toward a remedy:

> Today, the Supreme Court stuck a dagger into the heart of the Voting Rights Act of 1965, one of the most effective pieces of legislation Congress has passed in the last fifty years. These men never stood in

unmovable lines. They were never denied the right to participate in the democratic process. They were never beaten, jailed, run off their farms or fired from their jobs. No one they knew died simply trying to register to vote. They are not the victims of gerrymandering or contemporary unjust schemes to maneuver them out of their constitutional rights.... I disagree with the court that the history of discrimination is somehow irrelevant today. The record clearly demonstrates numerous attempts to impede voting rights still exist, and it does not matter that those attempts are not as "pervasive, widespread or rampant" as they were in 1965. One instance of discrimination is too much in a democracy.[44]

On July 17, 2013, John Lewis presented testimony before the US Senate Judiciary Committee to urge Congress to act in behalf of the Voting Rights Act. Yet again, he recalled the struggles of the civil rights movement so central to his life: "In a democracy such as ours, the vote is precious; it is almost sacred. It is the most powerful non-violent tool we have. Those who sacrificed everything—their blood and their lives—and generations yet unborn, are all hoping and praying that Congress will rise to the challenge and get it done again."[45]

In the 1960s, John Lewis modeled a kind of leadership that stirred people. His leadership was based in faith. It emanated from the foundational structure of the black church. The teachings of ministers and pastors to become God's servants in creating a liberated world on Earth inspired Lewis. Through his example, John Lewis inspired others to become part of the effort to build beloved community.

His courage, conviction, and self-dignity in the face of provocation and brutality demonstrated to America and the world that he—among thousands of others—was willing to sacrifice even his life for the cause of justice and equality. The "mountaintop"[46] experiences he had in his twenties have sustained him throughout his long public career. In the process, the memory of the 1960s has remained alive.

Consensual Communities

[SNCC] convinced me of the necessity for involving everyone in making a decision...—we're all in groups and groups make decisions about things that they're going to do.... That principle, for me, comes out of my SNCC experience.[47]

The group grew, shrunk, grew, shrunk, shrunk. Why did I carry on in this? I think those of us who carried on, saw early on, victory. We won. We integrated the lunch counters in Atlanta. I don't think we realized how tough the rest of it would be but we said to ourselves, "Hey, we won this one. We can win the next one." It was that early victory that made us see what possibility was.[48]—Julian Bond

Julian Bond embraced a group-centered leadership philosophy of consensus. Born into a distinguished black family, raised on a university campus, educated by Quakers, exposed to Morehouse traditions, and drawn to Ella Baker and SNCC, Julian Bond learned about the concept of consensus in multiple ways. His values are secular. His mantra is "Speaking Truth to Power." From the 1960s to the present day, his ability to persuade through the written and spoken word and his willingness to speak out and work for social justice is basic to his leadership.

Julian's path to leadership began with his childhood experiences. His father, Horace Mann Bond, was president of Fort Valley State College in Georgia from 1939 to 1945 and the first black president of Lincoln University in Pennsylvania from 1945 to 1957. A distinguished leader in the struggle for desegregation, Horace Mann Bond earned his Ph.D. from the University of Chicago. Young Julian grew up on university campuses, where such leading intellectuals as W. E. B. Du Bois, E. Franklin Frazier, and Albert Einstein came to his home for dinner.[49] He sat on Paul Robeson's knee. At age three, his father and Dr. Du Bois gathered in the kitchen of his boyhood home, cracked open a bottle of champagne, and held a mock ceremony consecrating Julian and his sister to a life of scholarship.[50] Julian's childhood was infused with intellectual stimulation, black pride, and civil rights activism.

Julian's parents insisted on quality education for their children. They sent him and his siblings to boarding schools. Julian went to the Quaker-run George School in Bucks County, Pennsylvania, an elite preparatory school opened in 1893. Although he was the only person of color who lived at the school, he remembers it as a wonderful place (despite an abiding loneliness).

At the George School, he absorbed the Quaker principles of building consensus through persuasion when he attended the required religious chapel:

> The religious service doesn't have a minister. You can get up and speak. I can get up and speak. Joe, Mary, Frank, anybody can get up and speak if we think we have something to offer. That kind of democratic thought, I think, had a great deal of effect on me at an early age, and of course I wasn't processing it quite in this way. I think it's something I began to realize later on.[51]

At the George School, he also learned about "speaking truth to power" and the importance of peaceful resistance to violence and inequality. The phrase became more popular in the mid-1950s, with the publication of a Quaker treatise urging a nonmilitary approach to the Cold War based on faith in human integrity and conscience. "We do not end violence by compounding violence nor conquer evil by destroying the evildoer," the authors wrote. The treatise called for a "sense of community, of mutuality, of responsible brotherhood for all men everywhere."[52] Bayard Rustin was one of the authors, unacknowledged at the time. While the main focus was on the international community, the concept could so easily be applied to internal American society. It was not lost on the young Julian Bond:

Here in the United States this same tradition of—you know, the combination of non-violent aggression, if you can put those together—that we're going to resist. If we see something we don't like we're going to do something about it. We're going to do it peacefully. We're not going to shoot or maim or burn or kill. We're going to do it peacefully. We're going to do it, and it doesn't matter what you do to us, we're going to keep on doing it. We'll be back. We'll be back. We'll be back. That had an enormous effect on me. It wasn't until the civil rights movement came along and I got engaged in that that I really put this together. But at the time I was absorbing it and taking it in.[53]

Julian's concept of "speaking truth to power" had no metaphysical or spiritual implications.[54] He interpreted it directly and literally. It became part of his life philosophy that he applied when part of the leadership team at SNCC, as an elected official in the Georgia legislature, leader of the NAACP, public commentator, and university professor.

At the George School, Julian also learned that all people can and must contribute to the general welfare of the society. It was a principle based in egalitarianism:

You had to work. Not work to pay your tuition. You just had to work. So for example one year you might work in the kitchen where you would serve the food.... Or you worked cleaning an office.... These jobs rotated and it was sort of the luck of the draw.... I think it showed me that nobody's too good to work. It doesn't matter who you are—you're going to work. I went to school with some rich, rich kids who had never done anything. Never worked in a kitchen ever before, and it was an experience for them and it was an experience for me. But it was this kind of ethos of Quakerism that everybody is somebody. Everybody's got something to offer, something to share. That made a big impression on me.[55]

Armed with a commitment to educational excellence and the Quaker ethos of egalitarianism and pacifism, in 1957 Julian went to Morehouse College, the distinguished all-male black institution in Atlanta, Georgia. The South was Julian's new reality. Morehouse was the institution of Benjamin Mays and Dr. Martin Luther King, Jr.—a place to network with the black leaders of the future and to absorb the race lessons of the past. At Morehouse, he met young people eager to resist Jim Crow laws and racial oppression. He, too, was searching for a focus.

In 1955, just one year after *Brown*, the Montgomery bus boycott challenged the segregation of public transportation facilities and inspired new initiatives to confront discrimination in public restaurants, at water fountains, and in stores. In 1959, Nashville students began learning about and experimenting with tactics of nonviolent civil disobedience. In February 1960, four students attempted to desegregate the Woolworth's in Greensboro, North Carolina. The student phase of the civil rights movement had begun.

Julian stepped up to leadership in 1960 when Lonnie King, a student at Morehouse, approached him and asked if he thought the movement could spread to Atlanta. Almost an accident of time and place—as Julian tells the story—he began speaking to people with the intent of integrating lunch counters. The Atlanta movement began on March 15 with coordinated sit-ins by college students at ten different lunch counters and cafeterias. Quickly, the movement expanded to a city-wide civil rights group named the Committee on Appeal for Human Rights (COAHR). Julian understood that he had become part of a "small cadre" in which leadership was a shared responsibility. [Lonnie King] "was the leader, but we knew we were leaders, too. . . . I was a leader of the Atlanta sit-ins." They began with restaurants, but quickly realized this would be an ongoing struggle:

> There were movie theaters. There were bus stations. There were—a world out there was segregated and we could use what we'd done in this instance to attack it in these instances, too. So there was going to be more. So this is going to be a longer struggle than we thought. I knew I was going to play a role in it. Wasn't sure what that role would be.[56]

In April 1960, representatives of the sit-in movements throughout the South came together to coordinate strategy. Bond went to the meeting at Shaw University as a representative from Atlanta. There, he met the remarkable Ella Baker, whose "group centered" or consensus leadership became the hallmark of SNCC.

A long-term social and labor activist in New York, Baker strongly believed in leadership from the bottom up. With the Montgomery Bus Boycott of 1955, she saw the opportunity for a nonviolent southern movement modeled on the northern Fellowship of Reconciliation (FOR). Together with Bayard Rustin and Stanley Levison, the idea for SCLC emerged. Reluctantly, she became its executive director and organizer of a Crusade for Citizenship to jump start voter registration efforts. But she quickly came to dislike King's preacherly speech and his "cult of personality" leadership style.[57] When King authorized $800 worth of SCLC funds for her to bring together students of the sit-in demonstrations, she had an opportunity to shape the future of the movement. Four months after the meeting at her alma mater, Shaw University, she left SCLC to work with SNCC members. She endeared herself to the students because she allowed them to take the lead while she honored the notion that each person had a contribution to make, gently prodding them with her questions.[58]

Ella Baker built upon her mother's activism in black Baptist women's groups.[59] Her thinking about social change evolved further in Harlem during the 1920s. A founding member of the Youth Negroes' Cooperative League, she helped develop a five-year plan for economic empowerment; by 1931, she was its national director. At the same time, she became involved in journalistic activism, writing for the *Negro National News,* the *Pittsburgh Courier,* and the *Norfolk Journal and Guide.* She came to see the power of grassroots activism as she continued organizing efforts in the American Labor Party, and later within the NAACP as a field organizer.[60] It was this philosophy and skill that she brought to SNCC. She linked past and present for young people with a short sense of history.[61]

Ella Baker encouraged individuals to listen and talk until consensus was reached. She taught people how to subsume their individual differences and to encourage collective action. She was not concerned that the young people involved in SNCC might err; rather, she claimed that they had the right to make their own mistakes, and that the movement was their own. She was a fine listener and a shepherd, always reflecting the view that individual opinion should be respected.[62] Deeply suspicious of King's cult personality leadership, she argued that real leadership was a form of teaching, and that success could be measured in terms of process. What mattered was the ability to pass on strategies for change—to be a *fundi*—as Bob Moses later said and as Joanne Grant eulogized at her funeral in 1986.[63]

SNCC would not have existed in the form it did without her – she was both its physical and psychological anchor.[64] And in turn, she found in SNCC an organization that could reach out to women, young people, and those in rural areas.[65] SNCC became the organization that best reflected her values of "group-centered leaders" rather than "leader-centered groups."[66] Bob Moses found her distinction fundamental to his own understanding of how to lead. He did not see himself participating in the sit-ins or Freedom Rides, but he did find a role in escorting people to the polls to register to vote: "it's the difference...that Ella identified between helping people into leadership versus being the leader." And he was inspired to work with people in rural communities at the grassroots level—people like Amzie who were "real."[67]

Baker's message also resonated strongly with Julian's proclivities. She was, he said:

a remarkable woman...who had a long career as an organizer of protest and who had worked in the budding cooperative movement during the Depression in Harlem forming economic co-ops to buy milk and groceries and so on. She developed—or these co-ops developed—the

notion that there's one vote per person. Not one vote per share. One
vote per person. You might have ten shares, I have one, but our votes are
equal because each of us is a person. She brought
that. She didn't tell us that. But she brought that to
us early on. She was one of our adult advisors. We
didn't trust older people. Ms. Baker...was in her
late 50's and very much the distinguished lady. But
we trusted her and always called her Miss Baker.
I know some of the women called her Ella, but
I could never call her Ella. She was always Miss   Julian Bond
Baker to me.[68]   http://blackleadership.virginia.edu/28

He was far more impressed with the leadership style of Ella Baker than that of
Dr. King.[69] His SNCC years convinced him of "...the necessity for involving
everyone in making a decision depending on what the group is that you're in."[70]
The leadership style so attractive to him resonated with the "Quaker meeting of
all those people sitting in a room and everyone knowing that each person has the
right to stand up and speak truth to power."[71]

Following the initial meetings of SNCC, Julian Bond returned to Atlanta for
further coordination with Lonnie King and COAHR. In August 1960, he was
one of the founders of the *Atlanta Inquirer*, an alternative newspaper that publicized the work of civil rights activists. His comfort with writing and with speaking out allowed him to begin to fill the void in publicizing the roles of students
and of those working on the front lines of the movement.[72]

Julian Bond's leadership role coalesced well with consensus building. He
became SNCC's communications director from 1961 to 1966. He edited SNCC's
newsletter, the *Student Voice*.[73] He participated in voter registration drives, and he
wrote about them in news releases. He worked in the central office, under primi-
tive conditions, to get out bulk mailings. He struggled to get reporters to distinguish between SNCC and SCLC. SNCC public relations campaigns focused
directly on the dreadful standards of living for blacks in the rural South. In so
doing, they garnered more and more favorable press.[74] In 1963, when John Lewis
became the chair, he spent most of his time at protest sites. Bond's job was to be
in touch on a daily basis, so that he could pass on the information about plans
and numbers of people involved to the press. There was a constant stream of press
materials. Bond increased the staff in order to keep the focus on key activities and
conditions.[75]

By August 1963, SNCC had a presence in over a dozen communities in
Mississippi; additional projects existed in Georgia, Alabama, Virginia; and
Arkansas. There were 12 paid staff, 60 field secretaries, and 121 full-time volunteers.[76] From time to time, Bond needed to travel through the South to SNCC
projects, where he would set up press conferences and write releases. When crisis

Figure 6.3 A young Julian Bond on telephone at work in SNCC civil rights activities, with Cordell Reagan on right, responding to inquiries and working with news media in Albany, Georgia. Civil Rights Documentation Project records. Credit: Courtesy of Howard University Archives, Moorland Spingarn Research Center.

struck, he would need to deliver audiotapes of events happening on the ground or make calls to radio stations. The more publicity SNCC got, the better. He became masterful at responding from the Atlanta headquarters to what was happening in the field. He also often was at the center of information to report on missing persons, or broken down cars, or attacks on freedom riders, or details of voter registration activities.

He constantly generated ideas so that the work of SNCC members would be reported in every major newspaper in America. As a result, more and more students were drawn to SNCC activities.[77]

During Freedom Summer 1964, a communications office opened in Greenwood, Mississippi. Bond remained in Atlanta, helping to coordinate state projects and training new volunteers in communications. Regular news releases went out, reporting on voter registration campaigns as well as police violence.[78] The national media was out in force, fascinated by the dedication of so many young people. They were also clamoring for answers when Mickey Schwerner, Andrew Goodman, and James Chaney disappeared. Violence lurked constantly just below the surface. The attention of the country had been garnered.[79]

Julian Bond was at the nerve center of information essential to insiders and critical for outsiders. He had to make the decisions about what to release and when to release it. Through his actions and reactions, SNCC's reputation was formed. Handling this huge responsibility with sensitivity and awareness of the booby traps all around him was fundamental to the success of SNCC.

He pulled no punches. His words could be sharp and biting. He spoke truth to power. He spoke truth to anyone who asked. In 1962, he told Thomas Rose—a student writing his senior thesis at San Francisco State College—that he was disappointed in Martin Luther King, and that he believed more would become disillusioned with him over time. He considered him "just another preacher who knows how to talk well, who has a flair for publicity and is a nice fellow."[80] He remembers feeling that "in the scale of militants and aggressive behavior, and again we're talking about in a non-violent context, but on a scale of aggressive behavior we were first. He was maybe second or.... [m]ore cautious. And that you couldn't do this by caution. You had to be bold. We were bold and he was not."[81]

His very good looks and his quick wit only added to his allure. Despite his efforts initially to stay out of the limelight, he was soon followed in the media as "Horace Mann's boy." He quickly distinguished himself as an independent thinker, as a person willing to speak the "truth" as he understood it, and as a young man with composure and gravitas. It made him an important part of the SNCC team; he was a young leader with enormous charisma. If John Lewis stirred people, Julian Bond impressed them.

As SNCC evolved, its members moved away from racial integration, becoming more focused on black nationalism. During 1964 and 1965, SNCC leaders became more suspect of support from white workers, believing that the movement had to be black-dominated. Tensions arose over the 1964 Mississippi Freedom Summer campaign and the Vietnam War.[82] In 1966, Stokely Carmichael replaced John Lewis as SNCC chairman.

With young children to support at home and an unsustainable salary from SNCC, Bond knew he would need to find other paths to reshape American society. Successful voter registration drives (after passage of the 1964 Civil Rights Act and 1965 Voting Rights Act) meant that blacks could be elected to positions previously unimagined. SNCC leaders looked for candidates to support. In 1966, Ivanhoe Donaldson, Ben Brown, and John Lewis pushed him to jump into the race following reapportionment of state legislative districts.[83] Bond and seven other blacks ran for the Georgia Legislature and won. He was 26 years old.

A protracted battle ensued before he was sworn in. His colleagues in the Georgia legislature called him a traitor to the United States and refused to seat him. Julian had publicly supported SNCC's statement opposing the Vietnam War. That statement said, in part:

We believe the United States government has been deceptive in its claims of concern for freedom of the Vietnamese people, just as the government has been deceptive in claiming concern for the freedom of colored people in such other countries as the Dominican Republic, the Congo, South Africa, Rhodesia and in the United States itself.

We know for the most part, elections in this country, in the North as well as the South, are not free…

We are in sympathy with, and support, the men in this country who are unwilling to respond to a military draft which would compel them to contribute their lives to United States aggression in Vietnam in the name of the "freedom" we find so false in this country.[84]

Julian did not draft the original statement. But he remained true to his pacifist principles, publicly admiring the courage of those who would burn their draft cards.[85] A grilling by *Meet the Press* commentators Herbert Kaplow, Robert Novak, Max Robinson, and Tom Wicker demonstrated that the 26-year-old could hold his own under fire with incredible grace and clarity.[86] It only added to the admiration felt by the growing number of people opposed to the war.

The legislature ignored the popular will and refused to seat him, despite winning the election on three different occasions. To defend his first amendment rights, he appealed to the courts. Finally, the US Supreme Court ruled the actions of the Georgia House unconstitutional and he was sworn in for the January 1967 session. As difficult as the battle was, it exposed the hypocrisy of his opponents. Julian Bond always believed that his civil rights activism was behind it all.[87]

Once in the Georgia Statehouse, Julian's colleagues derailed his every move and mocked his every word:

The House years were not happy years. It was in the House that I was expelled from. My nemesis, Sloppy [James H.] Floyd, was still there. Whenever we'd get sworn in every two years he'd always walk out of the chamber. He wouldn't be sworn in with me. He had a small, a very small cadre of friends who were always hostile people. That was not a happy time.[88]

"If I had gotten up and said: 'Motherhood is great, and I've got a resolution promoting it,' they would have said: 'No way,'" Bond recollects.[89] Nonetheless, he continued to serve his constituents between 1967 and 1975. The outrageous behaviors of those who fought against the progress of civil rights had the unintended consequence of bringing more attention to the movement. And Julian Bond continued to be at its forefront.

Despite the efforts to stymie him within the Georgia House of Representatives, Bond continued to lead with increasing national exposure. In 1968, he led a challenge delegation from Georgia to the National Democratic Convention in Chicago and, unexpectedly, became the first African American to be nominated for the position of vice president by a major political party. Too young to accept, he graciously declined the offer. He had become a nationally recognized leader, renowned for his strong anti-war positions and his calls for economic and social justice.

Julian Bond speaks out and acts on the principles and values that have guided him since his youth—egalitarianism, honest speech, pacifism, social justice. In all his roles, he models consensual community-building and speaking truth to power. While still in the Georgia House, he became the first president of the Southern Poverty Law Center, an organization incorporated in 1971 to seek justice for the nation's most vulnerable citizens. In 1973, he became president of the Atlanta branch of the NAACP and served in that role until 1987.

In 1974, Bond successfully ran for the Georgia Senate and served there until 1987. Those were much better years in government leadership, because he was given the opportunity to chair committees, to pass bills, and work collectively with his colleagues. He really liked the challenge of leading by building bridges to other senators:

> There were fifty-six of us, so if I get twenty-eight people to agree with me and I'm the twenty-ninth, then I've won. I can carry the day. And I loved that idea that you always knew: these people would vote no matter what it was...These people might if you explained it to them. These people were a little tougher because you had to really explain it to them. These people you could trade with. I'll vote for you on this, if you vote for me on this. So I liked putting all that together and very much enjoyed that.[90]

Unlike his years in the Georgia House, he was able to lead in the Senate through a consensual model.

Finally ready to move on to Washington, D.C. as a representative of the Fifth Congressional District of Atlanta, he lost in a bitter fight to John Lewis, his close friend from his SNCC days. It was disheartening when Lewis announced after Bond had declared his intention to run. It was hard to hear some of the things John said about him personally and about SNCC:

> He began to talk about himself as a different kind of personality than I was. I was a slacker, lazy, non-successful. He was brave, courageous, strong and true....And he said, "You know, Julian Bond worked for me."...And in SNCC nobody worked for anybody. We all worked—we were all equal. We all worked together. Nobody worked for anybody else. There were no bosses in SNCC. That was just awfully painful for me.[91]

Effective leadership requires the capacity to recoup and to regroup, while still remaining true to fundamental principles. The loss to John Lewis came at a low point—both personally and professionally. [92] He had to find new avenues for his consensual-style leadership.

Familiarity with the media and with public speaking opened up some opportunities. In 1987, Julian Bond narrated the immensely popular and powerful 14-hour documentary, *Eyes on the Prize*. His voice was reintroduced to millions of Americans on their television screens. He hosted his own weekly television show, *America's Black Forum*. He appeared as a commentator on *Nightline*, narrated untold radio and TV documentaries, and lectured all over the country. Universities engaged him to teach, and he offered courses at Drexel University, Williams College, the University of Pennsylvania and Harvard. Permanent positions followed at the University of Virginia and American University, where he has taught thousands of students over more than two decades.

Julian Bond seized the opportunity to lead the NAACP, the nation's oldest civil rights organization. In 1998, he was elected chairman of the board and held that consensus-building position for 12 terms until 2010, overseeing a board of 63 people. Once again, his skill was to build consensus in an organization that could be unwieldy:

> The big challenge has been to keep moving forward and to keep improving and...to keep pushing and pushing and pushing. It's not easy to do because the board is so large. The organization is so large, and the organization is so democratic, small "d" democratic. People have said it suffers from an excess of democracy, because at every step the leadership is elected: The local president's elected. The state president is elected. The regional president is elected. The board is elected. We're all elected.... So it's a tough, tough—it is the toughest job I've ever had— and it's not a paying job. [93]

He brought the NAACP back to a position of great stature nationally and locally.

Leadership, for Bond, means staying true to principles of openness and fairness. It also means being willing to speak your mind:

> Everybody has to have a say. On the NAACP Board that means 63 people. I'm the 64th.... They have to have their say or their chance at a say. And that there's got to be transparency, which is the modern word for openness. There's got to be openness in—organizations that depend on public support have to be transparent.... I think people have to see you the leader as someone who adheres to principle.... I want to treat other people the way I want them to treat me. The old Golden Rule is – I really believe in that – Treat me the way you want me to treat you. If you do that we can get along, we can be okay.... I believe in fairness. I

don't mean in big, racial terms. I believe in it there, too. But in personal terms I believe in fairness. "Let's be fair with each other.... We are each due the same level of respect."[94]

Julian's proclivity to "speak truth to power" sometimes put him in difficult spots, but it allowed him to maintain his own integrity. While still in the Georgia legislature, he publicly disavowed the candidacy of Jimmy Carter for president. In 1970, he published an article in *Playboy* magazine in which he wrote of black resistance to the "domestic imperialism waged by white America...all aimed at getting the white man's foot off the nonwhite's neck, the white man's noose off the red or black or brown throat."[95] Throughout his life, he has held fast to the principle of tough speech. It is not surprising, therefore, that the 2001 NAACP convention's theme, over which he presided as chairman, was "Speaking Truth to Power." In the opening statement of his convention address, he defined what that maxim means: "It means at all times following your highest sense of right, whatever the consequences, however lonely the path and however loud the jeers.... It is holding on to the power of truth when everyone around you is accepting compromises."[96]

Along with this willingness to speak with a barbed tongue came another quality. Julian was courteous. He was easy to get along with; he was a team player. In the turbulent 1960s, he brought to the table a persona that reflected composure, refinement, courtesy, determination, and defiance. His leadership in SNCC was based both on bold speech and on an ability to build consensus with others.

The civil rights movement propelled Julian Bond into consensual communities and consensual leadership. For him, those were the heady days.[97] The very nature of the group experience empowered him, and empowered a lifetime of activism:

> in my life there's never been anything like it.... this was the most intense in my life. First of all I'm surrounded by other people my age who are running—we're running this thing. We're in charge. That's awful heady to be 22, 23, 24, 25 and running this thing. We were running it. We were in charge. There's no older people saying do this, or don't do that, or so on. We did it ourselves. We raised the money. We did the work. We did a fabulous job. And the people with whom I'm working...these people are my closest friends today...most of it, it's a rough life and a life way down on the income scale. Living in communal houses, 10 guys living in a house, sleeping in bunk beds and so on. So it's not an easy life.... But it's intense. And you become so close to the people with whom you work that you are bound to them for the rest of your life.[98]

The 1960s lives on through people like Julian Bond. His leadership training and associations in SNCC translated into the roles of elected public servant in Georgia, public speaker on social justice and civil rights, media personality/ spokesperson, university teacher, and national chairman of the country's oldest and most distinguished civil rights organization. Through these multiple leadership positions, he has been an exemplar to generations of others. As Julian is fond of saying, "It happened then, and it can happen now."[99]

Radical Communities

My vision has always been that of a better, more just, more egalitarian world and, of course, I spent many years as an activist in the Communist Party. I'm no longer in the Communist Party but I still imagine the possibility of moving beyond capitalism to some kind of democratic socialist arrangement. I don't know if I can succinctly describe what my philosophical approach is, but I will say that it is—if I were to try to succinctly describe it, I would talk about a critical posture towards everything. Learning how to raise questions, even about that which one assumes is unquestionable and that this is what I've learned from my philosophical studies, from critical theory, that we have to be willing to test even that which—even those categories we use to try to understand the world.[100]—Angela Davis

If John Lewis is strongly motivated by prophetic community, and if Julian Bond is drawn to consensual leadership, Angela Davis looks to other philosophical and political ideologies. Five years younger than Julian Bond and John Lewis—she was born in 1944—that difference represented a generation in the lifetime of the civil rights movement. By the time Davis was in college, more radical impulses took center stage—impulses she recognized from her childhood experiences.

The eldest child of college-educated parents who were trained as teachers, Davis grew up in the race-based cauldron of Birmingham, Alabama. Both her parents were leftists, determined to make a difference in the racial politics of the American South. After briefly teaching high school, Benjamin Davis, her father, owned a service station, and her mother, Sallye Bell, continued to teach. When she was four years old, her family moved to a white neighborhood, where she endured the stares and hostility of neighbors.[101] A year later, another black family moved to the neighborhood, igniting a series of Klan house bombings that caused the area to be known as Dynamite Hill.[102] In the midst of this turmoil, Angela lived a middle-class existence, taking dance and piano lessons and joining the Girl Scouts. She could not, of course, sit in the front of a bus, or go into the white movie theater near her father's service station. Such affronts became more visible and more confusing to her by comparison with her frequent jaunts to New York in summers with her mother, who was pursuing a master's degree in education at New York University.[103]

Both in New York and in Birmingham, she vaguely experienced the discomforts of being followed. She was too young to understand the national hysteria about communism and communist sympathizers in the early Cold War. Her mother was a major figure and officer in the Southern Negro Youth Congress (SNYC) and had close friendships with many black leftist women affiliated with the Communist Party, USA (CPUSA). Even though the SNYC disbanded in 1949, her mother continued to be suspect to anti-communist groups.[104] In Angela's mind, when FBI agents followed people either in the North or South, it was hard to distinguish whether they were suspect because of their race or something else. When she was six years old, she remembers being followed in Birmingham by the FBI.[105] Those experiences occurred again in New York, where her mother and her siblings lived and interacted with prominent communist couples like Dorothy and Louis Burnham and Herbert and Faye Aptheker, along with other leading black and white radicals. One of them was James Jackson, a Birmingham family friend, who had gone underground during the McCarthy period, and the police were looking for him, following his children and others who knew him. "I understood only what my eyes saw: evil white men out to get an innocent Black man."[106]

All around her in Birmingham she witnessed the deep disparities between the resources allocated to black and white children. Her elementary school was incredibly dilapidated; her playground an empty dirt bowl. Her textbooks were "old and torn, often with the most important pages missing," there was no gym, and her friends often came to school hungry and in tattered clothes. She learned about class differences and about the disparities between the black and white schools. In grade school, however, she also learned about racial pride and the courage of African American leaders. She noticed the differences between the white and black national anthems—one of them focused on freedom; the other on resistance.[107] "I think that my teachers in elementary school and high school gave us all a sense of pride and gave us the tools with which to resist the imposition of racial inferiority."[108] But in her all-black high school, which she entered as the civil rights movement was heating up, she became aware of the growing anger among her classmates, often turned inward, "because we did not yet know how to struggle against the real cause of our misery."[109]

Life in Birmingham was filled with signs of race hatred and race disparity. Her parents could not shield her from that reality. In 1956, the Rev. Fred Shuttleworth's house was blown asunder. Friends were constantly harassed by the police. Elsewhere in Alabama, there were reports of horrible violence in the aftermath of the *Brown* decision. And her high school was not providing an enriched education.

At age 14 and a junior in high school, she had a choice—either apply to Fisk University early or enter a program sponsored by the American Friends Service

Committee in which black students from the South attended integrated high schools in the North. With some trepidation, she chose the latter. She lived with a white Episcopalian minister, Rev. Melish, who had used his pulpit to preach against the witch-hunting tactics of Joseph McCarthy. Having lost his pulpit, he had moved with his wife and three sons to Bedford-Stuyvesant, a black neighborhood in Brooklyn.

Davis went to Elizabeth Irwin High School, a small school on Bleecker Street in Greenwich Village, where most of the teachers had been blacklisted for their communist activities. Her parents knew about the school because of the network of black radicals and their New York connections. At this school, she had a real political awakening. She learned about socialism and read the *Communist Manifesto*. Marx's message struck her "like a bolt of lightning."[110] Now, she had a clear explanation for the incredible economic disparities that surrounded her—both in Birmingham and New York. Blacks—southern blacks especially—were the proletariat of America. She embraced a lifelong mission to change the American system.

While in high school, she became involved with political causes and organizations that linked the personal with the political. Bettina Aptheker invited Angela to a youth organization called Advance. Advance supported peace movements and civil rights activities, and affiliated with the Communist Party. The multiracial youth organization often met in Bettina's home, where Bettina's father Herbert Aptheker, was already a prominent Cold War intellectual who had been blacklisted in academia because of his Communist Party membership. Angela and Bettina became close friends.[111] They "picketed Woolworth's every Saturday because of the policies of segregation in the South…and marched across the George Washington Bridge. It was all quite fun, too," she recalled.[112] She was learning about political activism.

As a young woman, Angela did not fully recognize how her mother's commitments and networks shaped her life. But as she matured, she acknowledged:

Well, it's taken me a long time to recognize the extent to which I walked down a path that was carved out for me by my mother, because I always saw myself resisting my parents, as children often do, but my mother was an activist. She was a member of the Southern Negro Youth Congress. She was actually an officer of the Southern Negro Youth Congress. She was involved in the NAACP. She was involved in the campaign to free the Scottsboro Nine. And as a child, I had the opportunity to spend time with black communists who had come to Birmingham to help organize there, to help organize the Southern Negro Youth Congress, so I—you know, I often tell people that later when I joined the Communist Party, it was a difficult decision because I always considered the Communist

Party to be so conservative. It was my parents' friends, you know, I wanted to do something more interesting and more radical, but I do think that both in terms of my career as an educator and in terms of my life as an activist, I'm following in my mother's footsteps.[113]

After high school, Angela attended Brandeis University and studied abroad, establishing further the intellectual foundations of her radical approach to social action. At Brandeis, she was one of only two black women undergraduates. During her junior year, she chose to study in France. Shortly after her arrival, in September 1963, she experienced a sense of devastating isolation when the bombing of the 16th Street Baptist Church in Birmingham occurred, killing four young girls she knew well.[114] The reaction in France to this violent tragedy with personal meaning seemed terribly muted. The shock and horror that she experienced alone, she said, "made it impossible for me not to lead a life that would be dedicated to social justice... [T]hat reinforced the importance of building communities of struggle. Because I knew I needed to feel—I needed some place to feel at home with people who had the same kind of emotional response that I did... and I couldn't find anyone.... [T]hat was a pretty devastating moment. That was a really devastating moment in my life."[115]

Angela Davis
http://blackleadership.virginia.edu/29

At the end of the year, upon her return to Brandeis, she wanted to read more deeply in philosophy—to find a way to make sense of the disturbed, painful world in which she lived. Remarkably, she was able to work independently with Herbert Marcuse, the renowned radical philosopher, who mentored her and allowed her to enroll in his graduate seminar on Kant.[116] After graduation, she went to Frankfurt and attended lectures and seminars by Theodor Adorno and Jurgen Habermas. Inspired by this "intensive learning experience,"[117] she also gravitated toward groups struggling against the inequities and social contradictions of their own societies. Although far removed from the United States while Watts was burning, black militancy was emerging, and SNCC was beginning to embrace the philosophy of black nationalism, she could join the German Socialist Student League (also known as S.D.S.), and participate in student demonstrations.[118] In Franklin and Berlin, she learned about effective organizing in an international context.

In the United States, the civil rights movement shifted in the mid to late 1960s as disappointment and disillusion set in with liberal reform. Black nationalist activists were impatient with unmet promises to deal with entrenched poverty in America's ghettos. They railed against state-sanctioned violence toward protestors.[119] James Meredith led the March against Fear in Mississippi only to be sprayed by bullets. Nonviolence had lost its effectiveness, they argued. Stokely

Carmichael replaced John Lewis as the head of SNCC; and the Black Panthers wore black, armed themselves, and declared war on white, racist America. The urban, militant, angry image was vastly different from SNCC's collegiate, well-bred aura.[120]

Angela Davis's interests in philosophy, sociology, and political theory drew her back to the United States. She enrolled in graduate school in 1967 at UCLA, working with Herbert Marcuse—her undergraduate mentor. She studied philosophy to give her the "tools and conceptual approaches and methodologies...to better understand the world." Teaching on the university level seemed an attractive path because it was a way to "encourage people to develop independent and critical modes of thinking that might lead them to the conclusion that they need to do something to make a difference in the social world."[121] Much happened in the intervening years before she could accept her first position.

The very year she entered graduate school, Huey Newton was shot, arrested, and denied bail in Oakland, California. For her, it was confirmation that black men in the United States who challenged the system were viewed as political prisoners and readily denied basic rights. Davis became increasingly involved in campus and California-based grassroots organizations.[122] Protesting the Vietnam War, forming the Black Student Union, creating the California-based SNCC, working with the Black Panther Political Party drew her into radical activities; often, she too landed in jail.[123] Her study of philosophy and her activism were completely intertwined—each informed the other. She saw her role primarily as that of an activist teacher:

> I think I imagined my role as being that of a teacher and so when I worked with SNCC, I was the head of the Liberation School Project. When I worked with the Black Panther Party, I was working with the Political Education Project. I always did work that involved teaching and I think that that would've been the role that I imagined for myself.[124]

She worked ardently to spur the "collective consciousness" of her people and to empower them to protest in the name of social justice for radical change.[125] She focused especially on the black urban poor. In July 1968, she became a card-carrying communist by joining the Che-Lumumba Club, inspired to do so by Charlene Mitchell, who ran for president on the CPUSA ticket.[126] Fearing the police, facing considerable risk, and experiencing gender threats from male comrades, she focused more attention on protecting herself. She went out and bought a gun.[127]

Through all of this, she tried to remain engaged as a student and also as a teacher. She passed her Ph.D. qualifying exams and began work on a dissertation prospectus. In 1969, with her dissertation in progress, she accepted a teaching position at UCLA, only to discover a little known clause barring the hiring of communists. Ronald Reagan, then governor, would not allow communists to teach at state universities. The Board of Regents fired her, turning her into a "minor celebrity."[128] Although the courts subsequently declared the rule unconstitutional, she felt the growing provocations and violence against her and her race.

Davis discovered that her commitment to communist ideas made her less attractive to many in the militant movement. Revolutionary Marxism was the ideological foundation on which to fight against multiple forms of oppression. To many black Americans, however, communist ideology was distinctly European, and they wished to establish their own agenda.[129] She found herself looking for ways to be true to her own values and her own ideas, while not separating herself from the cause. The Soledad Brothers case—and especially that of George Jackson—gave her the opportunity to work within community to draw attention to criminal injustice in America.[130]

George Jackson had been arrested at age 18, a passenger in a car while an acquaintance robbed a service station. Sentenced from one year to life, he was sent to Soledad prison along with John Clutchette and Fleeta Drumgo. When a prison demonstration led to the death of a guard, all three were charged with his murder. To Angela Davis, it seemed as if innocent black men were being framed yet again, and she wanted to right this wrong. She became very close to the family of George Jackson, and virtually adopted his younger brother, Jonathan, as her own kin. In multiple hearings and trials of the three men, she sensed a mockery of justice. One day, young Jonathan snapped. On August 7, 1970, using a gun registered in Angela Davis's name, he attempted to free some prisoners. Several people, including Jonathan and Judge Harold Haley, were killed.[131]

Suddenly, Angela was wanted as an accomplice to murder. She believed she was doomed if she allowed herself to be arrested. Her entire life experience had taught her that. She fled California, went to New York, and lived in hiding from August until October 1970. Placed on the FBI's Most Wanted list and charged with murder, kidnapping, and conspiracy, she was arrested in December and extradited back to California where she faced the death penalty.

For two years, as a fugitive in New York, and then a prisoner both in New York and California, Angela Davis became the public face for black anticapitalist and feminist protest. Supported by tens of thousands of Americans demanding "Free Angela Davis," she became a cause célèbre. She was an international celebrity. Public statements and appeals and thousands of private letters came from politicians, religious leaders, academicians, writers, poets, political prisoners, women's groups, and unionists both in America and around the world. Nikki Giovanni turned her published poetry into a broadside in Greenwich Village and gave the proceeds to Angela's sister, Fania, in support of a fund for her legal expenses.[132] Local networks, like those in black Birmingham, supported her cause with total commitment.[133] But to really accomplish the goal of justice, it took far more. People like James Baldwin, Ronald Dellums, Coretta Scott King, Reverend Ralph Abernathy, Reverend Jesse Jackson, Herbert Aptheker, the Women's Secretariat of the African National Congress, dozens of women from the United Arab Republic, and thousands more protested and wrote in her behalf.[134] Her childhood friend, Margaret Burnham, with whom she had lived during her summers in New York, quit her job to work full-time on Angela's defense. This coming together of so many different civil rights groups on her behalf demonstrated the power of the movement, activated by many of her own networks:

> I've come to think of that moment as a kind of collective empowering that demonstrated to us that we had hope and that we could make change in the world, so I have to be the beneficiary of that and I continue to see myself as the beneficiary of this amazing movement.[135]

In 1972, after 22 months in prison, she was acquitted on all counts, free to resume her life.

Davis's ideas and activism tie her to generations of militant activists for social justice. The Marxist patois of Du Bois, the 1930s activism of black unions and of those who sought to work on behalf of the Scottsboro Boys, the racial uplift ideology of black militants like Huey Newton, Bobby Seale, Eldridge Cleaver, and Malcolm X, and the attention to anticolonialist international liberation movements are interrelated.[136] As she was awaiting trial in 1972, Julian Bond wrote: "There is a line from Du Bois to Seale to Jackson and to Angela Davis; a chain exists linking the dark 'army of the wronged' that has marched from the loins of black America for the past 350 years. But these named...are but the tip of an iceberg, a crag of black bluehard coldness so massive it could sink America."[137]

Davis also recognizes those intergenerational connections. Reflecting on her lifelong focus on the inequities of the justice system—from the 1950s to today—she says:

> I guess the overwhelming majority of my life has been devoted to work around issues of prison and imprisonment and, of course, when I went to jail, it was around the campaign to free the Soledad Brothers so I was already doing work around political prisoners and around prison in general, but I don't think I would've imagined then that this would've been my calling, that I would devote my life to this work, but then I think of my mother working on the Scottsboro Nine and I think that this is a way in which to challenge injustice at its core.[138]

From then to now, Angela Davis speaks and works for the unknown oppressed. She writes on topics of social justice, imperialism, capitalism, and feminism. Called upon frequently to speak on prison reform, she never wavers in her commitment to help those ensnared by systems she views as corrupt and racist. She remains convinced that the quest for justice and equality must be found in socialism.[139] America cannot be redeemed without drastic reform.

Leadership, for Angela Davis, is a collective endeavor:

> I like to think of leadership not as a series of qualities that prepares one to lead or to give leadership to people in the world, but I like to think of the best kind of leadership as emerging from social movements as reflecting collective ideas and collective aspirations.[140]

The 1960s were so powerful for so many, she reflected in 2007, because "[t]here was always a sense that the measure of your success was to a large part one that was linked to community advancement."[141] She definitely sees whatever leadership people ascribe to her as the result of the movement and the untiring work of others. She can accept the iconography that continues to surround her—the t-shirts, the buttons—and the popularity that follows her only because these are opportunities for others, particularly women, to gain strength.

In her role as teacher—the role she most envisions for herself—she resists the notion that she is a leader of minds. From 1980 to 2008, she held teaching positions at San Francisco State University and the University of California at Santa Cruz. In the best of circumstances, she doesn't transmit knowledge. Rather,

> I think that the best teachers, the best quality a teacher can have is the ability to assist someone to discover his or her own passion. And rather than concentrate on guaranteeing that this person knows this and that and whatever, I like to teach my students how to formulate the kinds of questions, particularly questions about that which they tend to take for granted, that will lead to real change in the world.[142]

The struggle continues and it continues in ever-expanding ways, Davis contends:

> I think the most effective black leadership will be leadership not simply for black people but leadership for all people and I'm convinced that engagement with issues of race, of gender, which is a lot more complicated today than it was because we not only have to talk about people who identify as men or women but transgender expression and issues of sexuality. What has been so fulfilling, I think, in terms of my own history has been the awareness that we've developed ever-more capacious visions of what it means to be free, and so in the beginning, if we thought about race as the barrier to freedom or racism as the barrier to freedom, we had to learn that racism doesn't exist on its own, that it's

connected with and crosshatched with sexism and gender discrimination. And then we have to learn that it's more complicated than that—that there's class there, and then we learn that gender is not binary, you know, that there's much more there than we ever thought and then we learned about sexuality. So it means that our sense of freedom becomes vaster and more interesting. And rather than go backwards and talk in terms that excluded people of color, that excluded women, that excluded transgender people, that excluded LGBT communities, then I think we have to find a language that is all embracing.[143]

Davis strongly believes that leadership comes out of a set of convictions. Her leadership is expressed through her teaching, her challenging of assumptions, and her writing. She has remained true to a revolutionary agenda that would transform America. The author of numerous books, she has written mostly about issues of class, race, and gender. She has been called upon as a public speaker, and she continues to take on the very issues that inspired her as a young student radical. They still need attention and she is indefatigable.

The leadership of John Lewis, Julian Bond, and Angela Davis illustrate the possibilities for multiple kinds of engagement during the "classical" phase of the movement. Although they became known for specific leadership styles during their twenties, they were primed for leadership by their formative relationships, historical knowledge, and awareness of both traumatic and triumphant events during their youth.

These three people, along with so many others, came of age at a specific moment in history ripe with the possibility of change. They benefitted from the "long civil rights movement," inspired by previous leaders.[144] Throughout their history in America, African Americans knew they were part of an imagined community struggling to become full citizens of their nation.[145] Collective consciousness existed through myriad aspects of the organic black community, including its fraternal organizations, religious communities, burial associations, and self-help societies.[146] Black leaders as diverse as Booker T. Washington and W. E. B. Du Bois wrote and spoke about the power made possible by African Americans' sense of community.[147] The many leaders who arose during slavery, emancipation, and the Jim Crow era spoke up for freedom and for the "redemptive value of citizenship."[148]

Civil rights leaders of the 1960s and 1970s could look to the ideas and the courage of Frederick Douglas, Sojourner Truth, W. E. B. Du Bois, Mary McLeod Bethune, Thurgood Marshall, Spottswood Robinson, Oliver Hill, Rosa Parks, and Ella Baker—all of whom were commemorated in black historical memory or were active mentors. They knew the history of resistance that characterized their people.[149] They knew the stories of unionized black workers who fought to reform the South and marched on Washington in 1941.[150]

Some surely knew about the "Double V" campaign to fight fascism abroad and racism at home during World War II and the deep alienation faced by returning veterans. They saw the rise of revolutionary nonviolent black movements in Africa in the 1950s and the growing international focus on the exploitation of colonized peoples in Africa and Asia.[151] Lewis, Bond and Davis—and many others of their generation—grasped their indebtedness to the multiple generations of black activists and intellectuals who "waged guerilla warfare on the infrastructure of Jim Crow" and challenged the injustices of American political and economic systems.[152]

In the 1950s, when John, Julian, and Angela were impressionable children, they saw the best and worst of America's racial justice on TV screens and in news media. Local reactions became instant national and international news.[153] Emotions gyrated from hope to despair and sometimes back to hope. All eyes were watching. They found the events riveting.

The *Brown v. Board of Education* Supreme Court decision especially resonated. Angela's parents were teachers in the deep South. Julian came from a family of educators, and his father worked on Thurgood Marshall's research team. These families immediately grasped the implications of *Brown*. Angela—only ten at the time of the decision—remembers thinking "...that this probably is going to be the beginning of a new era...I remember in my house and in our community there was a major celebration."[154] Julian recalls talking about the decision with his parents: "I was fourteen years old when this happened....I remember this feeling my parents had of great joy and optimism about it. I don't think they had foolish optimism. I don't think they thought things would change overnight. But they thought this was a sign of change. Change was going to occur. Things were looking up, looking better."[155] John, also 14, was attending the all-black Pike County Training school and read about the *Brown* decision in the black newspapers in his high school library: "I was so happy, I was so pleased....I felt for the first time I would be attending a desegregated school. I would no longer have the hand-me-down books or riding on a broken-down school bus passing the white school...."[156] He felt jubilant, thinking that "Come fall I'd be riding a state-of-the-art bus to a state-of-the-art school, an *integrated* school."[157]

One year later, in May 1955, the US Supreme Court delegated the responsibility for implementing the *Brown* decision to district courts, mandating that integration be carried out with "all deliberate speed." Such a vague requirement provided white supremacists the leeway to sabotage the Court's ruling for decades. The tactics evolved district by district and state by state. Disillusionment, but a growing determination to fight through renewed legal action, pervaded black America.

In the midst of this still hopeful atmosphere, virulent racism raised its ugly head. In August 1955, Emmett Till was murdered in Money, Mississippi. Images of Till's horribly mutilated body appeared in black publications such as *Jet* and the *Chicago Defender.* Lewis remembers being "shaken to the core:"

> I was fifteen, black, at the edge of my own manhood just like him. He could have been me. *That* could have been me—beaten, tortured, dead at the bottom of a river. It had been only a year since I was so elated at the *Brown* decision. Now I felt like a fool.[158]

Bond, living in a very different place with very different life experiences, had the same reaction:

> Seeing the corpse of this young, innocent boy, tortured and savagely beaten almost beyond recognition before being killed—all on account of some minor perceived transgression of southern racial etiquette—we all thought: it could easily have been me.[159]

The graphic pictures, along with future examples of Little Rock and Greensboro, inspired Bond's lifetime of activism.[160]

Five months after Emmett Till's funeral, grassroots activism spawned the Montgomery Bus Boycott, thrusting Martin Luther King, Jr. into the national spotlight. Boycotting the buses in the wake of Rosa Parks's arrest brought the bus company close to bankruptcy. Within a year, responding to a suit filed by the Montgomery Improvement Association, the Supreme Court invalidated segregation on Montgomery's buses.[161] The "foot soldiers for democracy" proved their collective power.[162] Again, hope.

For many future civil rights leaders, the catapulting of Martin Luther King, Jr., onto the national stage and the remarkable success of the boycott were transformative. Julian Bond remembers being drawn initially to King largely because he seemed willing to take risks.[163] For John Lewis, King's social gospel message was powerful. Listening to King on the radio station they received from Montgomery, he was drawn in by his voice, cadence, and passion. But even more important was the realization that biblical teachings could be applied to "...the earthbound problems and issues confronting a community and a society." 1955 was a "watershed" year for him: "I don't think I've been the same person since," he subsequently reflected.[164] Hope, despair, hope again.

When nine students tried to enter Central High School in Little Rock, Arkansas, in 1957, only to find their way blocked by National Guard troops ordered there by Governor Orval Faubus, new disillusionment set in.[165] Yet, three weeks later, failure seemed to turn to success when President Eisenhower ordered the 101st Airborne Division to Little Rock and took federal control of the Arkansas National Guard. This time, the ordeal of the students was covered nationally by *Time, The New York Times, Jet, Ebony, Sepia,* and *Colored.* They became national celebrities.[166] Television covered their tribulation. Some, like Julian Bond, felt this was a coming of age for him. He was "profoundly affected" by these young people, so close in age to himself, who possessed "grace and courage under great pressure."[167] Hope and despair created an emotional tension made all the more palpable by media images that portrayed the ugliness of racial hatred and the quiet, dignified resistance of ordinary black Americans.

What became more and more clear was that individuals could make a difference in the quality of life for black Americans. There were risks to be sure, but there were also rich rewards. Young black Americans and some white Americans from all regions of the country—but especially from the South—on the cusp of their own adulthood watched as lawyers, ministers, Little Rock high school students and Montgomery adults stood up on behalf of basic constitutional rights. Such was the background in which civil rights leaders came of age.

Taking stock of how the civil rights movement of the 1960s served as a catalyst for black leadership requires that we move beyond the examples of a few individuals. The era was so powerful because it was a movement of unprecedented scale that insisted that America be true to its founding principles. At first polite and nonviolent, and later demanding and militant, young people demonstrated their willingness to take enormous risks to move America toward justice. They would put themselves in harm's way. They would deny themselves basic comforts and turn away from rewards because they believed so passionately in their cause. They would go to jail, if necessary. They would use every means at their disposal—their bodies, words, strategizing, organizing, and protesting—to bring about results. They worked within the political system; they worked outside the political system. At the end of the day—through their concerted collective efforts—they showed both black and white America that significant, meaningful change in the contours of racial equality could happen. They could—and did—topple Jim Crow. In doing so, they generated enormous hope for the future of America.

They also modeled courage through conviction. Progress requires struggle, because "power concedes nothing without demand," Frederick Douglass said. Civil rights leaders modeled how power can pass to others with resolute and determined action. When they went to prison for their beliefs, they modeled courage not just to their own generation, but to those who would come later. Some, like John Lewis, found the imprisonment liberating. Surviving the dreaded incarceration helped him overcome his fear.[168] When Julian Bond spoke "truth to power," and when he discovered that he could be denied his legislative seat as a result, he demonstrated the courage to fight back—and he won. If the Georgia legislature would refuse to seat him, he would challenge the decision all the way to the Supreme Court. Such attitudes in the aggregate created an enormous psychic buzz, revealing that accommodation was passé.

On a practical level, the movement taught people skills. They learned how to work cooperatively with one another, developing numerous leadership strategies and models. Within the early years of SNCC, the model was group-centered, consensual, and egalitarian. People learned how to share responsibility and empower others. Sometimes, the model was based on specific ideologies; sometimes, it was centered on practical strategic results. They learned by doing. They developed the knowledge of how to prod, push, and provoke American political systems and sociocultural attitudes.

These passionate, determined black men and women bonded with one another, forming lifelong friendships and networks.[169] Their relationships, built upon non-bureaucratic self-empowerment groups, were fundamental for the struggle.[170] John Lewis recognizes that "SNCC served as an incubator in a sense, to help grow and develop my leadership ability." It was the support of others that convinced him that he could be an effective leader.[171] Angela Davis knows that she was the beneficiary during her 22-month imprisonment of continued focus for her cause. Julian Bond knows that his initial election to the Georgia House was a result of partial SNCC organization. While so many in the civil rights movement chose diverse paths for their future leadership, their engagement with one another was a constant source of support. For many, their ability to move from protest to inclusion was affected by this vast interlocking web of relationships.

The young, impassioned leaders inspired legions of followers. Local residents—almost invisible to the media—nurtured, housed, and fed the outside activists. Local women cooked meals in churches and communities, keeping a low profile yet serving as role models for their own children. Unknown individuals in small towns around the South felt the psychological empowerment that came from taking a stand.[172] The civil rights movement included liberal and radical leaders; religious and secular leaders; those with advanced degrees and those with hardly any formal schooling. It included the young, the middle-aged, and the elderly; gay and straight people; blacks and whites; men and women; peoples from all regions of the country. It included those who believed in the capacity of the political system to change and those who believed it had to be overthrown. But they all shared a vision of a more just America. Together, they forced Americans to examine their moral compasses and propelled America to a better place.[173]

Black leaders today were among those inspired by their experiences and memories of the civil rights movement. Many of them were a part of it in one way or another, although they were not at the time recognized as its "leaders." Those just a few years younger than the student leaders saw the possibilities, got involved in their own communities, and became motivated for the rest of their lives. Bobby Rush, for example, awakened to the movement in 1968 when he was 22 years old:

I remember going to my first political convention. There was a CORE convention in Columbus, Ohio and that was the convention where Roy

Innis ultimately took over CORE, but that was my first political convention, and I was just wild-eyed and, man, it was just – you know, I found my niche.[174]

Barbara Lee, born in the same year as Bobby Rush, was inspired by Shirley Chisholm, but had also found her own engagements as part of the civil rights movement before that:

> Bagging groceries with the Black Panther Party. I started my own community mental health center.... Working with the Black Panther Party helping to start their school in Oakland, California. Protesting, getting arrested protesting apartheid in South Africa, being very involved in the End the Blockade movement against Cuba, so there've been so many movements that weren't necessarily part of my political life that I have been involved in that I guess kind of were stepping stones.[175]

The path to leadership is through engagement, and Barbara Lee wants to see more "street heat" today. Leadership means that "you can't abandon the people." That is what the civil rights movement taught her. "If it weren't for the Black Panther movement, the civil rights movement, the peace movement, the movements that I've been involved in for social justice—personally, I'm not sure what I'd be doing now so I think that's the path," she said.[176]

Barbara Lee
http://blackleadership.virginia.edu/30

Born just a few years later in 1950, Freeman Hrabowski was 12 years old when Dr. King and the SCLC began to recruit children for marches and civil disobedience. The moment was powerful: Freeman forced his parents to let him participate, but he was as scared as he could be. Organized by James Bevel, the Children's Crusade saw more than 1,000 children march to downtown Birmingham on May 2, 1963, to talk to the mayor. The next day, as the numbers increased, Commissioner of Pubic Safety Bull Connor turned high-pressure fire hoses, police dogs, and clubs on them. Hrabowski was in the lead of one of the groups, and Bull Connor spat on him before arresting him and many others. He learned from that moment that "you really don't have to be traditionally courageous to do something that has some meaning."[177] Stepping out to participate led to unanticipated leadership opportunities:

> I was fortunate to be—have been born at the time that I could be a part of that experience, to observe, to watch, to participate, and to do a small part. Just, I mean—it was very important. And so you see, after that event, people used me to talk about the experience because many of the children who were in jail were from the projects. There weren't

a lot of middle class kids who had had the advantages of educated parents who went.... When I went to Hampton, the president wanted me to talk about that experience.... They'd take me to New York to speak and so I was having all these experiences throughout high school and college.... This is what leaders do, if you think about it. We talk about what we really believe and we try to pull people into that work.[178]

Gwendolyn Moore, born in 1951, sees herself as a 1960s person—as someone formed by the movement and the spirit of resistance to oppressions of every kind:

in the '60s, I guess, things weren't right unless something was wrong. And I went to meetings every night as a teenager and I thought about other people. I thought about the condition of the world. I think that things that we did in the '60s—the African Americans have led the greatest civil rights movement on this planet. I think that we are or could be an example to the world. We look at all the conflicts around the world. I am so committed, Chairman Bond, to making a difference literally in the world. And some of the experiences that I've had during the '60s—the non-violent reconciliation of difference, the bringing folks together, things that the NAACP taught me, the things that I learned from a church and from community, the things that I learned during the Great Society, that we're all in this boat together and that it's our responsibility to look out for each other—I think this is a model for the future and I think it's a model for the world.[179]

Gwendolyn Moore
http://blackleadership.virginia.edu/31

For leaders of the arts, as well, the civil rights movement was formative. Bill T. Jones, born in 1952, founded Arne Zane/Bill T. Jones Dance Company with his white partner. Through the dance, they broke new ground in representations of sexuality and race. He credits the 1960s and the civil rights movement for the ideologies that made his own liberation possible:

We were following the blueprint of the 1960s. In order words, I am not my body. Any distinctions between people because of race are illusory. Anyone if they work hard enough can be the president. All of these things we were taught, you know, that "free at last, free at last, freedom."[180]

The memories of the movement inspired new generations, born long after it was possible to participate. People like Benjamin Jealous and Bakari Sellers, discussed earlier, harbored the stories of the movement shared by their parents. Still others read about it in books or met veterans of the movement along the way.

The civil rights movement opened a new channel of hope. The highly visible young people who were America's "new abolitionists" unleashed a torrent of idealism.[181] Their energy, commitment, and courage were obvious to those who watched the movement unfold. Well-dressed and respectful black students who participated in sit-ins at Woolworths; the dignified and self-controlled response of young blacks to police dogs and hoses; the sea of faces at marches to change the status quo slowly impinged on the larger American consciousness and challenged old stereotypes. Nationally recognized leaders demonstrated that black Americans in community could change the laws of the land in essential ways. Outsiders could become insiders; the previously powerless could have power.

They did not fully realize their dreams, but few would argue that black and white Americans alike are not better off as a result of the ideas, actions, and accomplishments of "*the* movement."

The civil rights movement was immensely important for fostering black leadership in America because it changed the nation's consciousness and the nation's memory.[182] Memories of the movement supplanted the representations of an American South nostalgic for plantation life, the Confederacy, and servile blacks with images of black agency and assertiveness in the face of white domination.[183] The insistence that America live up to its values of equality and freedom wielded cultural authority and moral power, and created intergenerational identities that linked the past and the present to new realities. Collective memories of the movement became tied to new national identities and national possibilities.[184]

Barack Obama drew upon the collective consciousness of the movement when he went to Selma, Alabama in 2008 while a candidate for president. Forty-two years after the violence that occurred at the Edmund Pettus Bridge, John Lewis asserted: "Barack Obama is what comes at the end of that bridge in Selma."[185] The civil rights movement was a catalyst for transformational black leadership. The hope that some day a black person could be president of the United States, now turned into reality, is what has inspired both those who participated and those who followed. The power of that decade transcends generations.[186] Even today, the memory of the civil rights movement shapes our sense of possibility.

the inspirations of the Malcolm Xs and the Garveys and the Adam Powells and the Kings, that's not in our street today. I felt that all around me . . .

. . . people like you said you were ready to risk your lives and the televisions came and the dogs came and the bombs came and circumstances came and then people said enough is enough and turned it around.[187]—Charles Rangel

CHAPTER 7

Leadership Lessons

BOND: *Mr. Hill, let me ask you—what are the qualities a leader has to have?*

HILL: *Well, I think the first thing ought to be honesty, and they ought to have confidence in their own ability. And they also have respect for the abilities of others, and as I say, I'm high on personal esteem. And also, I think people should be kind of low on ego. That causes a whole lot of problems. Ego gets in the way... and they also should have feelings of brotherhood or sisterhood for your fellow human beings. You don't necessarily want everything for yourself and nothing for the other folks. You know... when I was kid, I was taught to avoid people who their prayer was, "Dear Lord, bless me, my wife, our son John, his wife, us four, no more." Think in terms of community. Think in terms of children. You think the village should protect and raise the children, and you also think of communities of ours as providing for the benefit and health of everybody.*[1]—Oliver Hill

More than 50 black leaders answered specific questions about leadership preparation and potential; leadership vision, philosophy and style; and leadership and race. They shared their perspectives on how they, as black Americans, have succeeded as leaders. They forthrightly addressed whether one can yet speak about race-transcending leaders. They considered whether black leaders carry specific race-based moral obligations. They commented on whether leaders are born or made. They spoke about what it takes to sustain leadership.

These men and women are both direct and indirect leaders. Some have constituencies they must satisfy; they are accountable through public election, board selection, or congregational mandate. They might be members of Congress, mayors of cities, presidents of corporations, presidents of colleges and universities, or ministers of religious congregations. In exercising leadership, they balance their own goals and values with the demands of others and against possibilities of the moment. Knowing how to engage diverse needs and interests is fundamental to their success. Others exercise leadership in oblique ways. They have followers by virtue of their ideas. They are intellectual, cultural, or artistic leaders. They might be legal theorists and lawyers, poets, playwrights, journalists, choreographers, media personalities, and professors. There are no delimited terms of office, no electorate to satisfy, no geographic or community parameters. They use the power of written, spoken, or visual language to persuade and to enrich the larger society.

Yet the black leaders who follow such varied career paths, come from different parts of the country, represent diverse socioeconomic backgrounds, and experience potential race barriers in disparate ways offer remarkably similar lessons on leadership. Previous chapters traced the formative and developmental experiences that led to leadership. This chapter focuses on leadership strategies and values.

Lesson #1—Preparation Matters: Find Role Models Who Nurture Self-Esteem

Are leaders born or made? How does one learn to be a leader? How are careers chosen? The vast majority of interviewees, reflecting on their personal journeys, emphasize the crucial importance of role models and mentors. Those who built up their self-confidence, helped them overcome fear, encouraged risk-taking, and modeled success nurtured their capacity for leadership.

Role models and mentors can come from virtually anywhere. Parents, grandparents, teachers, fellow students, community elders, ministers, club leaders, other political or professional figures, and historical actors—all can have an influence in shaping choices about careers and modeling leadership behaviors. Knowingly or unknowingly, they prepare the next generation to be effective leaders in their chosen career paths.

Parents and grandparents help shape career interests by virtue of their own work, their life experiences, and their needs. Little might her family have imagined that Vivian Pinn's interest in medicine came from her role as a very young child administering insulin injections to her grandmother while her parents were at work. Or that she learned how to speak up and become more assertive at Memorial Hospital in New York when her mother was hospitalized for bone cancer.[2] Such are the early training experiences that inculcate responsibility and spark both interest and confidence. She also credits the local family doctor, Ralph Boulware, who made house visits. His presence seemed to make people feel better, and she was inclined to emulate him. Despite the fact that no black female doctors she knew practiced in Lynchburg and opportunities for black female physicians would be limited, her parents did not discourage her ambition. Both life experiences and family values influenced her career choice.

Earl Graves, founder of *Black Enterprise Magazine* and CEO of Earl Graves Associates management consulting firm—a media mogul—is involved with publishing, marketing, radio, and television. He credits his father, a self-made salesman of Jamaican descent, with modeling the entrepreneurial values and work ethnic indispensable to his own success. His father's charismatic salesmanship is what he carries in his head: "...where I get most animated and involved at the company today goes back to watching my father convincing some lady that that yellow coat that she had was just the thing that worked for her." While he manages a considerable portfolio of properties and is one of the most successful black businessmen in America, he reflects that he is best at being a salesman. His father also repeated frequently, "Never rent, always own," and Earl Graves knows that this has been an important lesson passed on to him.[3]

Other leaders reinforce Graves's view that leadership is learned from their parents' example. Yvonne Scruggs-Leftwich says she "learned politics from the age of five, right from the grassroots"—from her mother, an elected official in the Republican Party in Buffalo, New York. Yvonne followed her around and learned how to think politically. She also learned how African Americans functioned inside largely white institutions. Watching closely, she saw forms of gender discrimination.[4] Observing her mother, she learned to work collegially, assess political reality, and be assertive when necessary.[5]

As young people move through life, they acquire experiences that become a form of leadership practice. They observe responsible adults as teachers, librarians, scoutmasters, ministers, doctors, lawyers, and they imperceptibly shape their own aspirations and sense of possibility. Mentors and role models are all around you, says Representative Sanford Bishop of Georgia. You might not recognize them at the time, but their influence seeps into your life:

It's all in the experience, in the practice. When I was in junior high school and high school, our teachers and principals at assemblies day in and day out would say, "Young people, what you ought to be, you're now becoming,"....and as I participated, unknowingly I was gaining experience, confidence, and the kind of skills that it would take to, whether I was negotiating with my ninth grade class or my twelfth grade class or the student body and the administration at Morehouse over these conditions or ultimately Tom Murphy and the Governor and the General Assembly. These kinds of experiences prepared me for it as did my leadership participation in the Boy Scouts, starting off as a Tenderfoot going to 2nd Class, 1st Class, Star, Life, Eagle and then Senior Patrol Leader which is a leadership position where you have to lead other younger Scouts. In the Order of the Arrow, being head of the ceremonial team and the top person.... It's a learning experience, a growing experience and you get to have mentors and you get to see people with whom you can try to pattern yourself and so you—I'll give you a perfect example. When I got to high school, there was a young man—I was tenth grade, he was twelfth grade. He was student government president.... He was on the P.A. system every morning.... He was giving the announcements, including the menu for the day in the cafeteria. He was articulate, so articulate that everyone and particularly me, wanted to emulate him, wanted to talk like him and be like him and by the way, that was Dr. James Raphael Gavin III, the immediate past president of the Morehouse School of Medicine. He was my SGA president when I was in tenth grade and he was the guy that I wanted to be like.... [H]e was the guy that really inspired me and whom I tried to emulate.[6]

Although these experiences provided local leadership models, Bishop was also influenced by more distant ones, like Dr. Martin Luther King, Jr., Malcolm X, Nelson Mandela—people who spoke forcefully and delivered messages of societal transformation.[7] Dr. King spoke at Morehouse while Bishop was an undergraduate there, and because of King's inspiration, Bishop applied both to Crozier Theological Seminary and to Emory Law School. Ultimately, he believed that law would allow him to establish a "ministry of public service."[8] Frustrated while litigating a case about Georgia prisons, he ran for Congress so that he could exercise a more profound influence on his community and his state by helping to pass laws in Washington, D.C.[9] His story illuminates that mentors can be relatives and friends as well as powerful national and international figures.[10]

History also provides its own role models for some of our leaders. Richard Allen, founder of the AME church, was the leadership inspiration for Floyd Flake's ministry. Rev. Flake continues as senior pastor of the 18,000-member AME Cathedral Church in Jamaica, New York:

if you look at my dissertation, and you realize the emphasis I put on the role that Richard Allen played and buying his own freedom out of slavery and then being able to found a denomination where he was thrown out of a white church in Philadelphia... because on a certain Sunday morning they refused to stay in the balcony, but came down to the altar. That has been guiding in my life.... [W]hat we have lost in the denomination is that spirit of Richard Allen of—the self-help spirit of Richard Allen. And what I'm trying to do is demonstrate that this was a good model two hundred years ago. It's still a good model today.... [W]e're still trying to solve problems of trying to empower and enhance the capabilities of people to be able to do things for themselves.[11]

Some of our leaders remember specific people who inspired them and taught them the tools of their trade. Barbara Lee's life trajectory was altered when Shirley

Chisholm came to Mills College tin 1972. Lee, then Black Student Union president, had invited Chisholm to speak—without realizing she was running for US president. Inspired by her message, Lee joined Chisholm's northern California campaign. Thereafter, Chisholm became a lifelong mentor and role model. Lee loved Chisholm's style and message.[12] She also looks to Ron Dellums, Carlton Goodlett, and Maudelle Shirek, whose independence, toughness, spirit, inner strength, and candor gave her the tools for leadership.[13] For Armstrong Williams, it was Strom Thurmond, Clarence Thomas, and Robert J. Brown who served as mentors; for Eleanor Holmes Norton, it was Judge A. Leon Higginbotham and Pauli Murray; for Charles Rangel, it was J. Raymond Jones and Percy Sutton.[14]

These leaders recognize how mentors and role models have influenced their values and habits. They know they were helped by others, but their success also depended on honing personal qualities. Nikki Giovanni, for example, acknowledges the influence of her grandmother, Emma Lou Watson, on her core values.[15] But when it comes to her poetry, she insists that her inspiration doesn't come from others; it comes from her dreams. Her goals are to take risks and to explore where poets have not gone before. Her penchant for risk-taking, however, is something she acquired from the powerful women that surrounded her.[16] Her role models taught her how to dream; dreaming inspired the originality of her work as a poet.

In general, the lesson we derive from these stories is that leadership can be nurtured. It involves dreaming, risk-taking, and modeling. Black leaders were shaped by the love, discipline, ambition, and aspirations of others. Often, they did not realize the impact of those around them. Other people can have a profound influence on values, capacities, and styles. If you wish to make a difference, look around, reach out, and help someone climb the next rung to leadership.

Lesson #2: Attitude Matters: Philosophy of Inner Strength

Resist Personal Diminishment; Defy Adversity

Black leaders repudiate the boundaries of race. Simply put, they refuse to be diminished by circumstances or to be defined by others. They develop inner strengths that transcend and shatter the straight-jackets society imposes.

Sometimes, groups adopt an oppositional culture, reacting to injustices and inequalities through strategies of resistance.[17] "[B]lack people have always tried to remind America of its night side, of the barbarism lurking underneath its self-congratulatory rhetoric of universal freedom and equal opportunity,"[18] Henry Louis Gates contends. Oppositional ideas can be embedded in music, prayer, ritual, oratory, prose, and poetry. Voluntary associations, churches, schools, and neighborhoods inculcate these ideas. Subordination and oppression may lead to submission, but it can also catalyze a strong collective identity, an "injustice frame," and a willingness to resist the status quo.[19]

Eleanor Holmes Norton, congressional representative for the District of Columbia, says that growing up in segregated D.C. caused her to feel superior to many whites. She attributes this to the aspirations nurtured in her community:

> The sense I think that came particularly to young people was that whatever segregation was about, it was not about being inferior, because we felt we were surrounded by mediocre white people or southern white people who didn't seem to be striving for as much education as we, had not gone to a high school like Dunbar, had not sent their children away to all the best schools on scholarship, so what is this about inferiority? I never remember feeling in the District of Columbia that segregation had anything to do with inferiority.[20]

Washington, D.C. differed from the deep South, she explains, because there were no signs on water fountains and other public places that served as a form of humiliation. It was what happened within the community that mattered.

Johnnetta Cole grew up in Jacksonville, Florida, in the 1940s and 1950s. She remembers a kind of quiet protest that did not involve sit-ins or marches:

> I remember the protest that took the form of the dignity of black domestic women workers. I think about protest simply in the form of my mother saying, "No, you can't go to the symphony, but we can listen to a symphony here."[21]

Protest and resistance against diminishment begins with a mental state. It is born of a sense of self, nurtured by family and community members who model self-worth, dignity, and accomplishment.

Eleanor Holmes Norton and Johnnetta Cole hail from middle class families, with parents who supported their education and provided economic stability. Many other leaders interviewed, however, remember growing up in circumstances of economic poverty and deprivation. But they could see beyond the privation that surrounded many of them.

Charles Ogletree grew up in dire poverty. "From the time that I was born," he wrote, "until I left home to go to college eighteen years later, we moved constantly, always facing poverty." Yet, there was no "poverty of values" in his home.[22] His grandmother, barely literate, read to him every day from the Bible, reflecting aloud on life in the next world and on the possibility of realizing a better life here on Earth. From these Bible stories, Essy D. Reid drew parables: "A lot of them were about overcoming slavery, overcoming segregation, overcoming the whole sense of despair and poverty, by having not a poverty of values, but a set of values that...empowers your ability to think and respond." Hardships could be overcome, she thought, if you focused on higher values.[23] From his grandmother Ogletree learned that perseverance was determinative, that the suffering in one's own life was not a permanent condition, that a new generation could remake the world. She taught her grandchildren to resist the diminishment that came from economic deprivation. "We didn't know we were poor," Charles Ogletree contends.[24]

Floyd Flake, like Ogletree, grew up poor in segregated Houston, one of 13 children, living in a two-bedroom house with no running water. His parents had fifth- and sixth-grade educations, but minimal education did not limit their ambition or define them. He recalls that his father worked at least three jobs, including that of a nighttime janitor. He remembers a supportive childhood with his parents, coaches, teachers, and ministers prompting him to do better, to develop the inner strength to resist being stereotyped. One powerful memory relates to the need to drop out of Wilberforce University for lack of funds. Working as a parking lot attendant in Houston, Texas, a young white woman approached him claiming that she had been short-changed at the car park. He explained the company policy, but she was dissatisfied. She returned with a white policeman, who arrested him. On the way to the police station, he remembers the effort to humiliate him:

> So, on the way to the station, you know, the window was open. I put my hand in the window. The policeman said, "Nigger, get your hand out of that window." And you know, I did that. And I got down to that police station. Fortunately, the company lawyer was there to meet me within a few minutes just as they were about to book me...And I said to myself that very day, "The day is coming when I'm going to make more than that white cop. I'm going to do better than he could ever imagine doing in his own life." And that drove me for a long time. For a long time, the image of his face could not be erased from my mind. And every time I found myself getting discouraged or coming to a place where I thought I might want to quit doing something, the image of his face would flash before me. And that's when I realized that I'm going to keep on moving and I'm going to keep on driving.

Floyd Flake

http://blackleadership.virginia.edu/32

For Flake, this attitude has turned into a philosophy for overcoming those who would diminish him: "every time I've run into racial incidents, for me, it's been an inspiration to just perform better, to do more, to prove that I have the ability to do more than most of the people who would try to reduce me or limit me or neutralize me based on my race."[25] It provides him with an effective armor for leadership.

Other leaders echo Flake's views. Carol Moseley Braun vividly remembers the effects of her parents' separation on herself, her brother, and her mother as they moved from relative comfort to a Chicago neighborhood known as the "Bucket of Blood." There, she encountered dire poverty and hardship, precipitating her brother's death. She saw the "degradation that came of the kind of grinding poverty that the urban ghettos represented . . . with people piled in tenements and rats running around biting babies and kids getting shot on the street corner." While she does not suggest that an optimistic or positive view can change the truly negative aspects, indeed the related tragedies, of this experience, she does argue that she refused to allow these realities to define her. She learned from the experiences. She saw firsthand "the effects of . . . economic oppression." She made a "life commitment" to "push back" against those negative forces. She frames a grim and tragic story as a "temporary condition . . . one from which I could learn something."[26]

Amiri Baraka, the prominent playwright and poet and the founder of the Black Arts Movement, recalls having *Dutchman* panned by critics on opening night. Although the play won the Village Voice OBIE Award for Best American Off-Broadway Play that year, he could not have known that at the time. The multiple negative reviews from five or six newspapers attacked his use of language and his values. He would not allow them to define him—quite the reverse:

> And my take on all that was finally, well, they want to make me famous, I see. . . . [I]n some kind of not really miraculous, but surprising, fashion to me, there came down at my head this fierce understanding of responsibility. I never had that before. I was like a wild, young Bohemian. You know, I would do whatever was happening. But then suddenly this feeling "Oh, now you're gonna make me famous? I see. Now, you're going to pay for that." Then I'm going to say everything I ever thought, everything I ever heard, everything my Momma, my grandmother, my father, my grandfather, all those people in the ghetto. Now is my turn to run it. See? And I felt that very clear. I mean, that was not a vague thing. That came into my head clear as a bell. You understand? "Now I'm going to get you."[27]

Baraka chose to see the situation as a call to action, an incitement to speak that much louder for himself and a vast community of people whose voices were not being heard. Like other leaders, he found a way to deflect criticism and turn it around, to reconfigure events into stories that do not weigh him down but inspire his imagination and determination.

Leaders must be able to face challenges and overcome fears. Elaine Jones recalls visiting a dentist's office without her parents' permission, and being called to court to settle a dispute over the bill. Her parents did not go with her, although she was accompanied by a family friend. She was all of eight or nine at the time, and remembers facing the judge herself and being "very intimidated." Yet, at the end of the day, the judge dismissed the case, and she learned from this experience that she could face the challenge and prevail.[28] In another instance, she talks about the later experience of working as a young black woman lawyer in courtrooms of the deep South. When confronted by armed bailiffs who said "move, lady—this is for the lawyers," she was able to face down a man twice her size carrying a gun or stand before a white male judge.[29] Her life experiences prepared her for these challenges. And they also prepared her for leadership as president of the NAACP Legal Defense and Educational Fund, where she had to approach her job with strength:

> Every day I wake up, it's a challenge. I mean, it's a challenge. It is—the job I have is a tough job. It is. And the only way that I can make it and do this job the way I think it should be done is I have got to be energized by adversity. It can't be—it can't subdue me. It can't cause me to have self doubt, it can't cause me to go away in depression and despondency. It's there for me to fight. It's a challenge. And so that is the way I deal with it.[30]

For Jones, her attitude and her ability to transmit that to others was fundamental to her leadership.

Many black leaders derive strength from faith traditions. Barbara Lee turned to her Catholic faith for sustenance when she decided to vote against the use of military force after the 9/11 attacks in 2001. The only member of either house of Congress to oppose President Bush's request, she believes that her reading of Scriptures bolstered her resolve:

> You go to the Scriptures and read those Scriptures that undergird what you have done and give you the strength to stand. There's a scripture in Ephesians that I always go to.... it talks about when all around you is falling to pieces and going to hell and when there's confusion and wars and *boom, boom, boom,* what do you do? You just stand. You just stand and you have faith, and you just stand there until all this stuff kind of fades away. That's what I had to do. You stand.[31]

Floyd Flake also finds sustenance in his religion. He believes he is guided by God's will and purpose for him. He therefore doesn't know what doors open or how to handle unforeseen challenges, but he believes that if he stays "in the will of God," there will be future accomplishments. And when there are failures, that, too, is God's will:

> But with every failure, I've considered that as a part of the process of the purging and pruning that is necessary to get rid of the dead weights that all of us carry in life, so that as I move forward, I'm able to be even more productive than in the past. John, Chapter 15, Verse 1, talks about how God sometimes prunes us, not to hurt us, but merely so that we'd be more productive. So I take my purgings as a part of God's process-ing. And it's allowed me to continue to move in spite of whatever things happen in my life.[32]

Throughout their careers, black leaders—notwithstanding their very differ-ent leadership styles—resisted those who sought to belittle them. In fact, in their struggles to overcome adversity, they often felt empowered. The same events will impact people differently, but the story each person chooses to tell helps us to understand the way these individuals' stories may end.

In all these cases, black leaders transformed discouraging incidents into opportunities for self-growth and personal inspiration. The process begins with a mental attitude and requires seeing beyond the immediate circumstances. It necessitates a vision for some future goal. Gwen Moore calls this process seeing with a "third eye."[33] William Raspberry says it's an ability to understand the internal barriers to success.[34] Vivan Pinn, head of the NIH Women's Health division, advocates a philosophy of overcoming.[35] These attitudes and men-tal processes define most black leaders. The messages are relevant not only for African Americans but for all those who feel any sort of social restriction. They carry important meanings for those in our ghettos, for those suffering from poverty, for those whose life circumstances have made them feel lesser. Or out-siders. Or marginal. The collective message from black leaders is clear: Resist diminishment; invoke the positive voice within; don't write yourself out; learn from adversity.

Lesson #3: Action Matters: Strategies of Moving Forward

Understand Race Realities, but Don't Let Them Constrain You

The vast majority of black leaders interviewed believe that race still matters in America. We do not yet live in a color-blind America. Despite the election of Barack Obama in 2008 as the first African American US president, a postracial America still awaits. But the leadership lesson that emerges is that one must not let this be a form of constraint. If the civil rights movement taught us anything, it is that much is possible if you push toward it. Black leaders are conscious of race. Some are well aware of race disparities, race prejudice, race discrimination—either in the past or the future. They will not, however, allow it to constrain their own sense of possibility and opportunity.

Leaders who directly lived segregation and came of age during the civil rights movement believe race consciousness continues to be a reality. Mary Frances Berry is a constitutional scholar, lawyer, and professor. She contends that talking about race is not something black Americans do by choice to highlight their status: "we talk about it not because we decided to talk about it. We talk about it because it's the condition we were put in that we try to overcome."[36] Charles Rangel, US Congress representative from Harlem since 1971, doesn't believe he will see the day when color is ignored: "I think we have to always constantly remind ourselves that this country's not going to let us forget our color."[37] And the late Benjamin Hooks, executive secretary of the NAACP, Baptist minister, practicing attorney and judge, asserted that "You can't talk about America without admitting there was slavery and second-class citizenship."[38] Race consciousness continues to exist, and vigilance to combat race inequities remains necessary.

Economic disparities remind us of the continuing race-based societal needs. Barbara Lee points to the tragedy that occurred in New Orleans during hurricane Katrina as an example of continuing race disparities.[39] And Gwen Moore, serving in the Wisconsin legislature since 1989 and elected to the US Congress in 2005, would like to be thought of as a race-transcending leader, but one who is sensitive to the disadvantaged. It just happens that African Americans, along with many other minority groups, fall into that category.[40] Representative Charles Rangel argues, "I see who's poor so whether you're Hispanic or black, I'm very conscious of [race]." Many black leaders use these examples of race inequalities to argue that it is not yet time to look beyond race. Race-transcendent leaders, they claim, can arise only when we have made greater progress in eliminating an American race-based underclass.

Younger black leaders seem more comfortable with the possibility of transcending race in their leadership. Bakari Sellers, elected to the South Carolina legislature at age 22, hopes to be a "transformative race-transcending leader." He points to President Barack Obama for confirmation that the country is ready for a black person to represent the free world. His view of race transcendence, however, seems to refer to opportunity rather than personal identity. While he claims he represents all South Carolinians in his district, he also asserts that he wants to be more like Julian Bond than Barack Obama. He wants to be perceived as one who will fight first and foremost for civil rights and the needs of the disadvantaged within society.[41] His commitment emanates from his own very strong identification with his father's unjust imprisonment following the Orangeburg civil rights protest. His knowledge of family history and direct connection to leaders of the civil rights movement motivates his own ambition and coincident race consciousness.

Benjamin Jealous, elected president and CEO of the NAACP at age 35, argues that there have been leaders—like Edward Brooke of Massachusetts—who transcended race. It is "racism that defines race," he contended. Once you get rid of racism—which he clearly believes is possible—race will disappear.[42] Jealous calls race a "cultural bias" and believes that black leaders can transcend race. At the same time, he is very aware that he is black, and that he "never wanted to be anything else." He strongly identifies with his family's life history in which the interracial marriage of his parents led to a family rift not healed to this day in which extended family members disowned his father. He claims the events surrounding his parents' wedding were "transformative" to his understanding of American society, and he feels that he is surrounded by ancestors. It may be possible to transcend race in terms of public leadership, but personal histories matter profoundly. Yet, for people like Jealous and Sellers, there is a greater sense of possibility to "live beyond race."[43]

Despite generational nuances on the possibility of race transcendence in America, our leaders agree on the strategies for excelling in a race-conscious world.

First, **carpe diem**. Don't wait for the perfect opportunity. Just do it. James Clyburn recalls when his mother told him that he could not always wait to take the next step in life. Sometimes, you just have to jump in. That conversation, he recalls, was a defining moment for him: "Every now and then I think about how I want to do something, and I think about that. You can't wait until you see it through. If it's in your gut, launch it. Things'll work out."[44] Douglas Wilder, Virginia's first black governor, describes his style of leadership in a similar way: you need a philosophy and a vision, but the endgame will not always be clear. So, he says, just "do it":

> Don't talk about it. Do it. Vision in the absence of implementation is nothing. Philosophy is beautiful to expound and to discuss and to have drinks over, but style in encompassing those two things means you're doing it, getting it done. Now how do you do it? You just do it! You don't talk about it. Now, is it going to be right? It might not be. Is it going to be proven? It might not be. Will it work? You will never know. You've got to try to do it.[45]

Earl Graves agrees: "[Y]ou don't say to yourself every day 'I'm a leader.' You just get on with it."[46]

Many leaders took advantage of unexpected opportunities, moved beyond racial stereotypes, and stepped into leadership opportunities. For African Americans, often denied access available to whites, taking risks allowed them to traverse paths that opened up a wider world. For Elaine Jones, it was deciding to study law at a southern university that had regularly denied access to black students. For people like Dorothy Height, Robert Franklin, Angela Davis, and Aaron Williams, it was a willingness to travel abroad to experience other cultures and to test one's own ideas. For Vernon Jordan, it was the desire to step outside of the black community to attend De Pauw University. For Bobby Rush, it was the Black Power movement—itself a radical step in its own day—that then opened up politics as a career path. Leadership found them because they were willing to seize the moment.

Second, **be tenacious.** John Conyers, congressional representative from Michigan, emphasizes: "When we talk about leadership, the first thing that I put down is: 'How tenacious are you to reach the goal or the objective that you've set out to get?' Because if I can measure that in a person, in a cause, in an organization, I can guesstimate how likely they are to be successful."[47] Barbara Lee, also a member of Congress, sees herself as being in a war fighting passionately for the causes in which she believes. You can't allow yourself to get tired, she insists: "if you stay on track and if you really believe in what you're doing, I ain't in no way tired, you know, you just keep going."[48] Douglas Wilder agrees. The most defining quality of his leadership vision, he says, is

never resting. Never believe that you've made success of it. Because success is something you continue to work at.... Develop to the highest possibility your potential. At my age now, I never would have thought that I would still be tapping into that development.[49]

Douglas Wilder
http://blackleadership.virginia.edu/33

Race matters. But real leadership involves transcending the constraints of race. Strong leaders overcome resistance through action charged with determination and tenacity. They seize the moment and they won't give up on the cause.

Lesson #4: Goals Matter: Stand Up and Lift While You Climb

Look beyond Yourself

Leadership is about making a difference in the world. It is about implementing change. Geoffrey Canada, executive director of the Harlem Children's Zone, insists that you cannot be a leader if you are focused on yourself. "Leadership...comes not only from hard work and study but also from service and you never forget who the client is and the client is not you and your leadership skills or your, I think, celebrity." He intends to prove that neighborhoods of poor, disadvantaged children can be transformed by providing educational systems and support services, allowing them to become successful adults. Proving that will be his greatest accomplishment as a leader.[50] For James Clyburn, leadership requires living the second commandment: "do unto others as you would have them do unto you."[51] For Sanford Bishop, leadership exists to "make a difference in the quality of life that humankind can enjoy."[52] For Mary Frances Berry, leadership entails a willingness to respond to unfairness and to open the windows of opportunity for those who have been dis-served.[53] "My vision," she says, " is simply a world where barriers, where discrimination, invidious discrimination, doesn't exist and where specious rationales are not presented for denying opportunity and where people can sort of decide what they want to do...."[54] And Freeman Hrabowski, president of UMBC, aims to lift others up by implementing an "access imperative" to "increase substantially the numbers of students of all types who excel academically."[55]

In the African American community, leadership is all about service. Standing up means challenging the system, not only on one's own behalf but in behalf of others. Standing up is a metaphor for creating a more just and more caring world. Standing up ennobles and strengthens; for African Americans, it reflects both personal pride and race pride.

The relationship between service and leadership is a virtual credo among black American leaders. Johnnetta Cole, for example, remembers the lessons absorbed from her great grandfather, Abraham Lincoln Lewis, the son of slaves who became a millionaire and gave generously to a number of educational institutions.[56] He taught his children and grandchildren that position and power alone don't equal leadership. Service to others was a requirement, an obligation:

> My great-grandfather was a race man. In the classic sense of a race man. He was a very, very close friend of a great race woman, Mary McLeod Bethune, who indeed gave the eulogy at my great-grandfather's funeral in 1947. So I grew up with these things being said constantly: "Doing for others is just the rent that you pay for living on this earth." Mary McLeod Bethune was quoted incessantly: "You may climb, but remember to lift others as you climb." So I remember a very conscious effort on the part of folk in my family to say "Now look 'a here. You may have a little more money than anybody else. But let me explain to you what that means is greater obligations, more responsibility than perhaps other folk have."[57]

"Paying rent for the space you occupy" is a common trope of African American leaders. The Rev. William H. Gray cited it as part of his faith-based philosophy that he applied to every position he held. Doing the "Lord's will" means saving souls and bodies. To do so "means taking on systems—public policy systems, educational systems." He tried to do this when he served as a congressman and as the president and CEO of the United Negro College Fund. "I've just always been taught by my folk, parents, grandparents, that service is sort of the rent you pay for the space you occupy." A leader, he insisted, is someone "who really believes that the struggle for human dignity is never over, and that no matter how many times we may celebrate the victory, there's always a little way further to go, some more mountain to climb....And so, what I've tried to do is direct my life toward service based on faith and commitment and social justice."[58]

Benjamin Hooks also combined the role of minister with that of public servant. He was a lawyer, a judge, an ordained Baptist minister, and a social activist. Born in 1925, he served in World War II before becoming active in the civil rights movement, sitting in to desegregate lunch counters and speaking out against Jim Crow laws. In 1965, he became the first African American criminal court judge in Shelby County, Tennessee—displaying enormous courage. From 1977 to 1993, he served as the executive director of the NAACP. Rev. Hooks insisted that black leaders have a particular obligation to help others—especially other black people He, too, used the "rent paying" metaphor: "...the service we render is the rent we pay for the space we occupy on God's earth." We are born, he said, to make the world a better place: "[A]ll of us have some obligation to help others as we move along."[59] By advancing race-based issues, we advance society as a whole, he insisted, because "no chain is any stronger than its weakest link."[60]

Standing up and lifting others means looking beyond one's own financial success. Benjamin Hooks remembered working in private practice, doing well, and deciding to take the job of public defender when no one else would do it because "we've got to make this progress." Had he been white, he predicted that he never would have accepted that job, or the subsequent offer of a modestly paid judgeship. "I made certain decisions based on the fact that I...[wanted] to break down the walls of prejudice."[61] Lifting others requires self-sacrifice.

For Barbara Lee, "lifting up" reminds her of a commitment she made when she was 13 years old. Leaving El Paso, Texas, where she had witnessed the grinding poverty of blacks, she wrote in her diary that she had to do something to help her people. That was in 1960—38 years before going to Congress. African Americans, she says, have a "unique niche, you know, because of our history of slavery, Jim Crow segregation. Who else has the moral standing to deal with this stuff and to take on all of those issues that we have to take on to make not only America better for African Americans but for everyone?"[62] Her vision has not changed since she was that young 13-year-old in Texas.[63]

Mary Frances Berry attributes her activism—her willingness to stand up—to childhood experiences and to innate tendencies. Her deep "inner core" translates into a need to fight against the wrongs that she perceives. She saw those bad things happen to people firsthand, living a "hard scrabble existence."[64] For a while, she lived with her brother in a dreadful orphanage. She still hears his haunting cries of hunger. Later, when her mother brought her children home, Berry remembers the motorcycle cop who sadistically harassed young black children playing on their lawns. Then, there was the white woman for whom she worked as an 11-year-old who chastised her harshly for listening to a classical music album that was in the family's home. To this day, when she hears that music, Berry thinks about the woman telling her Beethoven was not for blacks. "Maybe," she muses, "...some of these things, the accumulation of them in some way, had something to do with the sense I have of injustice needing righting in the world....."[65]

Although Berry's assessment of her motives take stock of the hardships she experienced, other leaders feel an obligation to give back because of their relative good fortune. Julian Bond says his father insisted that "You had to pay back, and you paid back by being involved in good works. And the good works could be the kind of scholarly studies that he did. Or they could be the kind of NAACP work that Walter White did. Or they could be the kind of political work that Paul Robeson did. But you had to do something."[66]

Similarly, William Raspberry learned how to help others from the example of his own teachers. The people who taught in Okolona, he recalled, were "...so committed to rescuing, saving a generation of us in the heat of segregation that they really did transform our lives."[67] After a successful career as a syndicated columnist at *The Washington Post*, in 2008 he initiated the program *Baby Steps* back in Okolona where 35 percent of the population live below the poverty line. His program seeks to empower parents and help lift their children by preparing them for kindergarten.[68] Recognizing that he benefitted enormously from his own formative experiences in Okolona, he wanted to do the same for another generation:

> That experience of observing at first hand what a few committed people can do to lift the sights of people who didn't have much previous reason for lifting their eyes—that's also part of what drives the *Baby Steps* effort....in our own little way, *Baby Steps* hopes to get people thinking about creating once again a learning community in our town.[69]

That is also what drives leaders as different as Vivian Pinn and Armstrong Williams. They like mentoring young people and giving them the tools to excel in their lives. Pinn loves to hear from people she advised or mentored 10, 15, 20, or 25 years ago. She says this means more to her than any honor or award.[70] Likewise, Armstrong Williams is extremely proud that his public relations firm, the Graham Williams Group, has nurtured over 150 young men, even though it didn't add to his bottom line financially. Williams taught those young men core values:

> We developed their work ethic. We helped them buy and own homes for the first time. We gave them a lease and we gave them something

that money cannot buy—character, self-respect, and dignity and we stay in touch with them.... That's what leadership does because when you raise a young man up, especially when they've just expected to die by the time they're 21 years old and you make them to believe in themselves, it's amazing what they can become in life and how they can change their community because, see, look I can't save the world. All I can do is change the community where I am. And if everyone adopts that attitude, the world will change.[71]

For some leaders, involvement in the civil rights movement strongly reinforced their sense of responsibility to "lift others." Gwen Moore speaks of an organizing principle "that probably came from being a child of the '60s."[72] She feels a responsibility to help the poor and to reach back to those less fortunate.[73] A lot of people in this world suffer, she says, because "folk advance themselves and then pull up the ladder behind themselves...."[74]

Roger Wilkins was born in Missouri in 1932 and educated at the University of Michigan. He chose a career in government, worked as a journalist, and became a university professor. President Lyndon Johnson appointed him assistant attorney general and he won a Pulitzer Prize for his work on the Watergate scandals. But nothing in his life meant more than his participation in the civil rights movement where he acquired a lasting commitment to racial justice and to uplifting the underclass:[75]

My concern about the underclass comes from my parents and my experience as a welfare worker in Cleveland and then my work in the U.S. government. I think it's a continuation of the civil rights movement. I don't think the civil rights movement ever died. It never—didn't accomplish everything that it wanted to accomplish. And I don't think that just because you make some money and are lucky that you can sign a separate peace. The people in the worst precincts in this society—their ancestors came over in the same slave ships that my ancestors came on. The only difference is that I am luckier. And if I go through my ancestry, I can look at the points at which—from my great-grandfather, who was born in slavery in Mississippi—in which the Wilkins family just, my strand, just lucked out. And all of a sudden, here I am on this earth no better than some of my cousins who were left back in Mississippi except that we were lucky and they were not. Well, I might have used that good luck just for me. I don't think so. I don't think that is the right thing to do. I think that you use your leverage that your good fortune gave you to help save other people.[76]

Roger Wilkins
http://blackleadership.virginia.edu/34

For Wilkins, as well as for others,[77] the civil rights movement was transformative. Changing America's culture through racial uplift was its central goal. The satisfactions that came from that substantial accomplishment persist.

African American history and culture embodies a powerful mythos of survival and resistance born out of struggle and oppression. Leadership through the ages has been based on prevailing over subjugators. While much progress has been made, the strategies embedded within black communities continue to provide leadership lessons for the future. Those lessons emerge out of formative experiences at home, movements, or the larger history of struggle.

The struggle continues because legality and justice remain far apart, and sometimes the distance between them appears to be growing. Black leaders know that there is never a time to give up on the dream of a just and equal America. They are buoyed by the examples of those who came before:

> If someone had not fought for equal education opportunities, to desegregate the schools, and establish programs to provide an education to black children and for women, I would not be here today. If someone had not fought for fair housing, I would not be able to live where I live today. If someone had not fought for rights for women, I would not be here today. I am here because black people stood up and fought. Because poor people that I don't even know stood up and fought. When Martin Luther King, Jr was out there putting his life on the line every day, he didn't know me. When Sojourner Truth stood up and said, 'Ain't I am woman?,' she didn't know me. But I am their beneficiary.[78]—Mary Futrell

And just as the leaders from previous generations inspired so many that followed, the leaders featured in this book should in turn inspire the next generation. Their lessons may emanate from the African American experience, but they are valid for all times and all peoples.

Appendix A: Interview Questions

The University of Virginia
EXPLORATIONS IN BLACK LEADERSHIP
An oral history videotaped initiative
Sponsored by:
The College of Arts and Sciences
The Institute for Public History

Co-directors: Julian Bond and Phyllis Leffler
Website: www.blackleadership.virginia.edu

Explorations in Black Leadership is an important and inno-
vative exploration of issues centered on African American
leadership in America. Through in-depth analytic interviews, we focus on the myriad ways in which African
American leaders have emerged in the American landscape
and play a decisive role in American life.
The following questions form the basis of the inter-
view. The interview will proceed as a discussion, so this order may not be followed exactly.

Brown v. Board of Education

- What did the Brown case mean to you at the time of the court decision?
- What did you think it was going to mean?
- What has it turned out to mean?
- How has it impacted your life?

Background and Education

- Who are the people who have been most significant in helping you develop
  your talents?

- What led you to choose your career?
- What parts of your education were instrumental in developing your leadership skills?
- What historical events or episodes do you particularly remember hearing about? What impact did they have on your larger consciousness and on your personal growth?
- As you look back over your life, at what point did you begin to think of yourself as a leader?

Leadership Philosophy

- What do you see as the difference between vision, philosophy, and style? Will you describe the interaction between the three for you?
- Do you have a vision that guided your work? Has it changed over time? Why?
- Some categorize the making of leaders in three ways: (a) great people cause great events; (b) movements make leaders; (c) the confluence of unpredictable events creates leaders appropriate for the times. How would you characterize your path to leadership?
- Do you see your legitimacy as a leader grounded in your ability to persuade people to follow your vision or in your ability to articulate the agenda of a movement?
- Do you have a general philosophy that guides you through life? How has it sustained you through challenges or moments of alienation?

Black Leadership

- How does race consciousness affect your work? Do you see yourself as a leader who advances issues of race or society or both? Is there a distinction? Is there such thing as a race-transcending leader?
- Do you have a different leadership style when you deal with groups that are all black, mixed race, or all white?
- In *Challenging the Civil Rights Establishment*, the authors quote William Allen who writes of a danger in continually "thinking in terms of race, or gender... Until we learn once again to use the language of American freedom in an appropriate way that embraces all of us, we're going to continue to harm this country" (Conti and Stetson, 45). Is there a danger of further divisiveness when we focus on the concept of black leadership?
- Do you feel that black leaders have an obligation to help other African Americans? Is there a point at which that obligation ends, and one can pursue his or her own professional ambitions?

- What do you see as your greatest contribution as an African American leader?
- In his book *Race Matters*, Cornel West writes "[the crisis of leadership is] a symptom of black distance from a vibrant tradition of resistance, from a vital community bonded by ethical ideals, and from a credible sense of political struggle." (37) Do you see a crisis of leadership in black communities today? If so, what contributes to this?

Leadership in the Future

- What kind of leaders does contemporary society demand? How will future problems demand different leadership styles?
- As a society, how can we foster the most effective leaders for the future?

Appendix B: Glossary

For biographical information on individuals interviewed in *Explorations in Black Leadership,* see www.blackleadership.virginia.edu.

16th Street Baptist Church: The church was founded in 1873 as the first black church in Birmingham, Alabama, and became a social center, hosting such notable black figures as W. E. B. Du Bois and Mary McLeod Bethune. It was an organizational center for many of the meetings and rallies of the civil rights era and was bombed by racially motivated terrorists in 1963, killing four young girls.

Abernathy, Ralph (1926–1990): Abernathy was key in organizing the Montgomery bus boycotts alongside Martin Luther King Jr. He was also a cofounder of the Southern Christian Leadership Conference and was later president of the organization. Abernathy assumed direction of the SCLC Poor Peoples' Campaign after the assassination of Dr. King, his very close friend.

Abyssinian Baptist Church of New York: The church was founded in 1808 and has been a center for African American culture and worship. It advocates for civil rights and equality. Located in Harlem, the church's leadership had included such famous preachers as Adam Clayton Powell, Sr. and then his son, Adam Clayton Powell, Jr. From the Harlem Renaissance to today, the church has been a major site for black gospel music.

Adorno, Theodor (1903–1969): Adorno was a highly influential German philosopher, sociologist, and musicologist in the post–World War II era. He is known for his thorough examination of Western philosophical tradition, particularly from Kant onward. He was a leading member of the Frankfurt School.

American Israel Public Affairs Committee (AIPAC): AIPAC is a pro-Israel lobbying group designed to strengthen ties between the United States and Israel. It is a grassroots, domestic lobby described by the *New York Times* as "the most important organization affecting America's relationship with Israel." Its policy is to support the views of the Israeli government within the United States.

Almond, J. Lindsay (1898–1986): During his time as governor, Almond is best known for closing public schools across Virginia to prevent integration in 1958. His name has become synonymous with the Massive Resistance movement.

AME Church: Reverend Richard Allen founded the church out of the antislavery movement in 1816. It is a predominately African American Methodist denomination and was the first major religious denomination of its kind in the Western World. The church was born in protest of racial discrimination and slavery and has maintained a strong commitment to serve the needy and to speak out against injustice.

American Negro Historical Society: Robert Adger, W. M. Dorsey, and Jacob C. White, Jr., among others, founded the Society in Philadelphia in 1897. They collected and preserved materials that reflect the black experience in the nineteenth and twentieth centuries. These records are held at the Historical Society of Pennsylvania.

Angelou, Maya (1928–2014): Dr. Angelou was an acclaimed American poet, novelist, memoirist, dramatist, actress, and civil rights activist. One of her best known works is *I Know Why the Caged Bird Sings* (1969). She spoke at President Bill Clinton's inauguration, worked with Martin Luther King Jr. and Malcolm X, and has received numerous awards and recognitions. She was professor of American Studies at Wake Forest University.

Aptheker, Herbert (1915–2003): A political activist, ardent civil rights supporter, and Marxist, Aptheker wrote more than 50 books. He is best known for his three-volume *Documentary History of the Negro People in the United States.* He was a major voice for the American left in the 1950s and 1960s.

Association for the Study of African American Life and History (ASALH): Carter G. Woodson and Jesse E. Moorland founded the association in 1915 in order to foster the study and appreciation of African American history. The association has been credited with founding Black History Month and publishing *The Journal of African American History.*

Baker, Ella (1903–1986): Baker worked with such organizations as NAACP, SCLC, and SNCC helping organize grass roots activism during the civil rights movement. For over 50 years, she worked behind the scenes with such leaders as W. E. B. Du Bois and Martin Luther King Jr.

Baldwin, James (1924–1987): Baldwin was a writer and social activist whose works focused on race, sexuality, and class. His most well-known works are *Go Tell It on the Mountain* (1953) and *Giovanni's Room* (1956). *Notes of a Native Son* (1955) is a well-known collection of essays. He called attention to the difficult obstacles faced by black, gay, and bisexual men in American society.

Bender, Rita (Schwerner): Bender is an attorney who focuses her interests on family law, assisted reproduction, and mental health issues. Bender's first husband, Michael Schwerner, was one of three civil rights workers killed by a Klansman in 1964 in Philadelphia, Mississippi. Ray Killen was finally convicted of manslaughter in 2005.

Bennett, William (1943–): Bennett was secretary of education from 1985 to 1988 under the Republican administration of President Ronald Reagan. He later served as Director of the Office of National Drug Control Policy under George H. W. Bush, among other titles. During the Reagan administration, he recommended major cuts to education and he has been an outspoken critic of affirmative action, and a conservative voice for school vouchers, curriculum reform, and religion in education. In 2000 he created an online, publically traded education corporation called K12.

Berrigan brothers (Phillip 1923–2002; Daniel 1921–): Brothers Phillip and Daniel Berrigan were peace, civil rights, and antipoverty activists during the Vietnam War, even serving prison terms for their activism.

Bethune, Mary McLeod (1875–1955): Bethune was an African American educator and activist who founded a school for black students in Daytona Beach, Florida, which later became the Bethune-Cookman School. She was president of the college for a total of 20 years, making her one of the only black or female college presidents at the time. She was a national leader on civil rights and education and a close personal friend and associate of Eleanor Roosevelt. Bethune was president of the National Association of Colored Women's Clubs and founded the National Council of Negro Women.

Bevel, James (1936–2008): Bevel was a close advisor to Martin Luther King Jr. He strongly influenced King's vocal opposition to the Vietnam War. In 1963, Bevel was critical in convincing King to engage children in the movement. The "children's crusade" in Birmingham, Alabama helped turn the tide of public opinion against segregationists. In later years, his reputation became marred by the fringe associations he supported and by an incest charge that led to imprisonment.

Big Bethel AME Church: Founded in 1847 by Richard Allen, Henry M. Turner, and Joseph Flipper, the church is now the oldest African American congregation in its section of Atlanta. The church has attracted speakers such as Nelson Mandela and President Taft, making it a historic landmark.

Birmingham Children's March: In May 1963, hundreds of children left school to be arrested, set free, and then arrested again for attempting to march nonviolently to see the mayor of Birmingham and talk about city-wide segregation. Also known as the Children's Crusade, the march was organized by James Bevel and had the blessing of Martin Luther King Jr. Birmingham police chief Bull Connor unleashed fire hoses and police dogs on the children, bringing a world spotlight and national outrage at Birmingham officials and at the conditions in the American South. Many claim that President John F. Kennedy's endorsement of racial equality and the passage of the Civil Rights Act of 1964 was a direct result of the reaction.

Black Enterprise Magazine: The magazine, published monthly, provides 3.7 million African American professionals with essential business information, advice, investing, and wealth-building counseling. It was founded by Earl Graves Sr. in 1970 and was the first of its kind.

Black Leadership Forum: Joseph Lowery founded the organization in 1977 to coordinate black leadership efforts and empower African Americans politically and socially. Today, the forum works to promote the legislative and policy interests of African Americans and to make sure the needs of the black community are met through public policy and legislation.

Black Panthers: The Black Panthers were founded by Huey Newton and Bobby Seale to protect blacks from police brutality in 1966. Over time, the organization became more radical, supporting black nationalism. It was called "the greatest threat to internal security in the country" by FBI director J. Edgar Hoover.

Black Power: Black Power was a slogan associated with a movement primarily in the late 1960s and early 1970s. At the height of the civil rights movement, Black Power adherents promoted black interests and values, inspired racial pride, and created black political and cultural institutions. Black Power advocates strongly endorsed black self-determination.

Bond, Horace Mann (1904–1972): Bond was an academic, earning a doctorate from the University of Chicago at a time when few African Americans were able to go to college. He then served as president of Fort Valley State College and Lincoln University, his alma mater, becoming Lincoln's first African American university president. He eventually returned to the South and became dean of the School of Education at Atlanta University. He participated in research for the NAACP that led to the *Brown v. Board of Education* decision.

Bright Hope Baptist Church: Founded in 1911 from the expansion of a small prayer group, Bright Hope has become a beacon in the North Philadelphia community. Its fourth pastor, Reverend William H. Gray III, became a congressman and ultimately the majority whip in 1989.

Brooke, Edward (1919–): Brooke was the first African American elected to the Senate by popular vote in 1967 and served until 1979 as a Republican. He was also attorney general of Massachusetts from 1962 until 1967, with the distinction of being the first elected African American attorney general of any state. He is the only African American to have served multiple terms in the U.S. Senate. Brooke was awarded the Congressional Gold Medal in 2008 for service to the United States.

Brooks, Gwendolyn (1917–2000): Brooks was the first African American to win a Pulitzer Prize in 1950 for her book of poetry, *Annie Allen*. She was also the poet laureate of Illinois, poet laureate consultant in poetry to the Library of Congress, and taught at some of the top universities in America. As she matured, her work became more political and critical of American society.

Brotherhood of Sleeping Car Porters: In 1925, it became the first black labor organization to be chartered by the American Federation of Labor. Its leaders included A. Philip Randolph, C. L. Dellums, and E. D. Nixon, all of whom played significant roles in the civil rights movement. See also Randolph, A. Philip.

Brown v. Board of Education of Topeka, Kansas: The Warren Court ruled in 1954 that separate but equal schools for black and white students were unconstitutional. It overturned *Plessy v. Ferguson*, which ruled in favor of separate but equal schooling and was a huge step forward for integration and for the civil rights movement.

Brown, Robert J. (Bob) (1935–): Chairman and CEO of B&C Associates, the oldest public relations firm in NC and the oldest African American owned public relations firm in the US. Brown is a strong supporter of community and education programs and founded the International BookSmart Foundation, distributing millions of books to disadvantaged parts of Africa. He is the only U.S. businessman who met with Nelson Mandela during his imprisonment at Pollsmoor prison in South Africa.

Brown, Sterling (1901–1989): Brown was born in Washington, D.C., and educated at Dunbar High School, Williams College, and Harvard. He was a distinguished academic and writer whose poetry was influenced by black music such as jazz, spirituals, and the blues. He taught at Howard University, Lincoln University, and Fisk University. He is also known for his literary and poetic works, which include *Southern Road* (1932) and *No Hiding Place* (1980). In 1984, The District of Columbia named him its first poet laureate.

Brown, William Wells (1814–1884): Brown was a well-known abolitionist and writer, who is said to have written the first novel by a black man, titled *Clotel* (1853). He is also considered to be the first black playwright and gave antislavery lectures in New York and Massachusetts.

Bryant, C. C. (1917–2007): An active civil-rights worker, Bryant became president of the Mississippi Pike County branch of the NAACP in 1954; eventually he served as vice-president of the Mississippi State branch under Medgar Evers. With Bob Moses, he organized a voter registration drive in 1961 in McComb, MS. He endured bombings of his barbershop and home and became well-known for his tireless grassroots work for equality.

Burnham, Margaret (1944–): A civil rights attorney, Burnham worked for the NAACP Legal Defense Fund for two years before moving on to various law firms. She was part of the team of lawyers that defended her childhood friend, Angela Davis. In 1977, she was appointed Associate Justice of Boston Municipal Court, and was the first African American woman to serve in the Massachusetts judiciary. In 1993, President Nelson Mandela appointed her to an international human rights commission—a precursor to the Truth and Reconciliation Commission. She primarily works on civil rights and employment cases. In 2002, she joined the faculty of the Northeastern University School of Law, where she founded and directs the Civil Rights and Restorative Justice Project.

Byrd, Harry F. (1887–1966): Byrd was the 50th governor of Virginia beginning in 1925, dominated Virginia politics for much of the first part of the twentieth century with his political machine, and is known for modernizing Virginia's government. He is also known for his opposition to integration of Virginia's public schools, advocating for the massive resistance movement, and his pay-as-you-go fiscal policy.

Carmichael, Stokely (1941–1998). Carmichael is best known for being a prominent leader of the Student Nonviolent Coordinating Committee and for rising to power through the Black Power movement. He also was an active participant in the 1961 Freedom Rides. In 1966, he became chairman of SNCC and in 1967, honorary prime minister of the Black Panther Party. In 1969, he moved to West Africa, adopting the name of Kwame Ture.

Carnegie Foundation: The foundation was begun by Andrew Carnegie in 1905 to report on the state of education in the United States. It has produced the Teachers Insurance and Annuity Association, the Educational Testing Service, and worked to provide federal aid for higher education. The organization also provided major support for improving the state of southern education in the early twentieth century.

Carter, Robert (Bob) (1912–2012): Carter worked closely with Thurgood Marshall and came to succeed him within the NAACP as general counsel. Throughout his career with the NAACP he argued 22 cases before the Supreme Court, 21 of which he won. His research and study of the law often encouraged him to push legal and constitutional positions to their limits, which resulted in the overturning of *Plesy v. Ferguson* in the *Brown* decision. In later years, he became a federal judge in New York and helped to open the police force to larger number of minorities.

Chaney, James (1943–1964): Chaney was one of three civil rights activists who were murdered by Ku Klux Klansmen in 1964, following his work registering black voters in Philadelphia, Mississippi.

Chenault, Kenneth (1951–): Chenault became the CEO and chairman of American Express in 2001, making him the third black CEO of a Fortune 500 company.

Chisholm, Shirley (1924–2005): Chisholm was the first black woman elected to Congress, serving as congresswoman of New York's 12th district for seven terms between 1969 to 1983. She promoted such issues as childcare, education, the repeal of the draft, and improvement of the quality of life for inner city residents. In 1972 she became the first woman to run for the Democratic presidential nomination.

Clark, Kenneth (1914–2005): Clark was a black psychologist whose research on race relations and the attitudes of children toward race were highly influential. He worked alongside his wife, Mamie Phipps Clark. The "doll test" influenced the justices of the Supreme Court in the *Brown v. Board* decision. In the 1940s, he established a center for child development in Harlem to offer psychological services to poor, black children. He was the first black professor to get tenure at City College of New York. He later became the first black president of the American Psychological Association.

Clark, Septima (1898–1987): Known as the "Grandmother of the American Civil Rights Movement," she was the vice president of the Charleston chapter of the NAACP and a strong civic activist. Barred from teaching in Charleston, she developed the Citizenship Schools, teaching basic literacy skills so that people would be able to register to vote. She worked closely with W. E. B. Du Bois and the SCLC that adopted the program in 1961. Clark was active within the YWCA and taught in public schools for most of her life.

Cleaver, Eldridge (1953–1998): Cleaver joined the Black Panthers in 1966, after two stints in prison during which he wrote his influential memoir *Soul on Ice*. In 1968, he was involved in a shoot out between several Black Panthers and Oakland police, which resulted in Cleaver fleeing the country to Cuba and Argentina until 1975. After he returned to the United States, he became involved in various disparate movements.

Cleaver, Kathleen (1945–): Cleaver was a notable female member of the Black Panther Party, even running for state office in California. She married Eldridge Cleaver in 1967 and worked as communications secretary for the Black Panther Party. After Eldridge Cleaver's escape, she joined him in Algeria. She returned to the United States to create a defense fund for her husband, whose case was not fully resolved until 1980. They divorced in 1987. In 1989, she received a J.D. degree from Yale, and joined Emory University's law faculty in 1992.

Clinton, Hillary (1947–): Clinton served as secretary of state from 2009 to 2013, senator from New York from 2001 to 2009, was a candidate for the Democratic presidential nomination in 2008, and first lady during Bill Clinton's presidency. Aside from her career in politics, she has been named one of the top 100 most influential lawyers in America twice and has always been an advocate for children's issues.

Committee on Government Contracts Compliance: In 1951, President Truman created the committee to oversee compliance with legislation passed by Roosevelt in 1941. Roosevelt's legislation made discrimination with the federal government or defense industries based on race, color, creed, or origin illegal.

***Communist Manifesto*:** Written by Karl Marx and Friedrich Engels in 1848, the *Communist Manifesto* lays out the basic principles of the communist philosophy based on theories on the nature of society and politics. The *Manifesto* describes the inevitable class struggle that ensues from capitalism, eventually leading to the rise of the working classes.

Congress of Racial Equality: CORE was founded in 1942 by a group of civil rights activists, only two of whom were black (James Farmer and George Houser). Very active in the Freedom Rides of 1961, the desegregation of Chicago schools, the organization of the Freedom Summer campaign, and the 1963 March on Washington, CORE members were strongly committed to the principles of nonviolence. By 1951, there were 53 chapters. In June 1964, three CORE activists were murdered by the Klan in Mississippi.

Since 1968, CORE has been led by Roy Innis, and the organization has become more conservative with time. During the civil rights movement, it was considered one of the "Big Four" leadership organizations (along with SCLC, SNCC, and NAACP).

Connor, Eugene (Bull) (1897–1973): Connor was the Birmingham commissioner of public safety for 22 years, during which time he was known for his brutality toward civil rights protesters and activists. He was an ardent segregationist. The Birmingham Children's March was a protest against his segregationist policies.

Cowan, Polly (1913–1976): Cowan was a Jewish American woman who worked with Dorothy Height to empower African American women fighting for civil rights. Together, they founded Wednesdays in Mississippi and worked to assist impoverished women of the South.

Crummell, Alexander (1819–1898): Crummell was a black priest who developed ideals of Pan Africanism, spending nearly 20 years in Africa doing missions work and attempting to persuade American blacks to colonize Africa. Upon his return to the United States, he and his congregation founded the first independent black Episcopal church in Washington, D.C., of which he was rector for nearly 20 years.

Current, Gloster (1913–1997): Current was the NAACP director of Branch and Field Services and deputy executive director for more than 30 years. He played a strong role in growing the NAACP from 500 to 1,700 branches during his tenure. An ordained Methodist minister, he was also an accomplished jazz musician.

Curry, Constance (Connie) (1933–): Curry is a fellow at the Institute for Women's Studies at Emory University. She is a writer and activist who is best known for her award winning book *Silver Rights* (1995), which discusses the plight of a black family trying to obtain the best education possible for their children in newly integrated schools. She is a veteran of the civil rights movement, and became the first white female on the executive committee of SNCC. A native of Greensboro, North Carolina, she is a graduate of Agnes Scott College and the Woodrow Wilson College of Law.

Daley Machine: Richard J. Daley served as chairman of the Cook County Democratic Central Committee from 1953 and as mayor of Chicago from 1955. Until his death in 1976, he dominated party and civic affairs. The Democratic political machine was often perceived as corrupt, and while many of Daley's subordinates went to jail, Daley was never accused of wrongdoing. Richard Michael Daley, Daley's son, became mayor in 1989 and served 22 years. Thus the family influence on Chicago continued.

Dellums, Ronald (Ron) (1935–): Dellums was elected to the House of Representatives in 1970, serving for nearly 30 years. He was the first African American elected to Congress from northern California. He embraced socialism, strongly opposed the Vietnam War, fought against Reagan's missile and stealth bomber programs, and was deeply involved in antiapartheid activities relating to South Africa. In 2006, he won a contested election for mayor of Oakland, California.

Delta Sigma Theta: Delta Sigma Theta is a sorority of black women founded in 1913 at Howard University. The sisterhood has more than 200,000 members and over 900 chapters throughout the world. The service sorority focuses on economic and educational development, political and international awareness and involvement, and physical and mental health of its members. It is an important networking organization for black women.

Dixon, Marcus (1984–): Dixon was accused of raping an underage classmate in Georgia in 2004. Some believed the charges were racially motivated, and the case raised questions of "legal lynchings." The jury found him guilty of statutory rape and aggravated child molestation and sentenced him to ten years in prison. On appeal, the Georgia Supreme Court overturned his conviction of aggravated child molestation, and he was released the same year.

Double V: In 1941, James G. Thompson, a cafeteria worker in Kansas, wrote a letter to the *Pittsburgh Courier* (the most widely read black newspaper in America at the time), urging a double victory campaign—victory over fascism abroad and discrimination at home. Much of the effort was directed toward jobs at home. The goals of the campaign were never fully realized, leading to further efforts at equal rights once the war ended.

Douglass, Fredrick (1818–1895): An incredible orator and former slave, Douglass became a leading abolitionist, writer, and statesman. He wrote several autobiographies, which became very influential; and he later was the first African American to run for the vice presidency, running on the small Equal Rights Party ticket.

Du Bois, W. E. B. (1868–1963): Born in Massachusetts, Du Bois was an educator, civil rights activist, and journalist. After graduating from Fisk University, he became the first African American to earn a doctorate from Harvard in 1895 and went on to teach at Atlanta University. *The Souls of Black Folk,* published in 1903, offered an alternative perspective to Booker T. Washington. He demanded the same opportunities for blacks as whites had in America, also arguing that African Americans had a responsibility to uplift those with fewer opportunities. As a political activist, Du Bois was a cofounder of the NAACP and Niagara Movement and helped organize several Pan-African conferences, His magnum opus, *Black Reconstruction in America,* was published in 1935. He became a communist in 1961 and moved to Ghana. See also Niagara Movement.

Edward Waters College: Edward Waters College is a historically black college in Jacksonville, Florida. It was founded in 1866 by the AME pastor William G. Steward with a mission to educate freed slaves.

Einstein, Albert (1879–1955): Einstein was a German-born physicist, best known for his theory of relativity, which is one of the two pillars of modern physics. After completing his education in Switzerland, he produced much of his work while at the Patent Office. Returning to Germany in 1914, he won the Nobel Prize in Physics in 1921. In 1933, he renounced his German citizenship (after Hitler came to power) and emigrated to the United States. He was appointed professor of theoretical physics at Princeton, retiring in 1945. He has been called one of the greatest physicists of all time.

Ellington, Duke (1899–1974): Ellington was an African American musician who led his orchestra for over 50 years. He composed over 1,000 works, helping to develop modern jazz and big band music. He is considered one of the greatest composers in American history.

Eyes on the Prize: This 14-part documentary television series chronicles various aspects of the civil rights movement, from the Montgomery bus boycott to the Voting Rights Act of 1965. It went on to win six Emmys, among other awards. It is a major account of America's most significant social justice movement.

Farmer, James (1920–1999): Farmer is best known for conceiving and organizing the 1961 Freedom Ride that called attention to the inequities of segregation in the South. He cofounded the organization that later became CORE. At the age of 21, Farmer was invited to meet President Roosevelt and was later considered to be one of the Big Four leaders of the civil rights movement. In 1966, he left the movement, disillusioned with its acceptance of race separation and black nationalism as a strategy. Ultimately, he served in the Nixon administration. In 1998, Clinton awarded him the Presidential Medal of Freedom. See also Congress of Racial Equality.

Farr, Sam (1941–): Sam Farr served for 12 years in the California State Assembly and six years as Monterey County Supervisor; he has been the representative for California's 17th District in the U.S. House of Representatives since 1993.

Faubus, Orval (1910–1994): In 1955 he became the 36th governor of Arkansas, serving six consecutive terms until 1967. He ran as a progressive candidate and was a relatively liberal figure who did not use race as an issue until school desegregation forced him to take a position. In 1957, he tried to block the federally mandated desegregation of Little Rock's Central High School, bringing in the Arkansas National Guard to prevent African American students from entering. The nine students, known as the Little Rock Nine, had to endure enraged mobs. President Eisenhower called in National Guard and Army troops to restore order. Ultimately schools were opened, but Faubus became a hero to white supremacists, ensuring his continued reelection.

Fellowship of Reconciliation (FOR): The fellowship was founded in 1915 by a large group of pacifists. The American Civil Liberties Union came out of FOR in 1920 and FOR worked very closely with CORE to sponsor the first Freedom Ride in 1947.

Fisk Jubilee Singers: Founded in 1871 to raise funds for the college, Fisk Jubilee Singers are an all black a cappella group at Fisk University. The group is credited with bringing slave songs to the world stage and has been honored by the Library of Congress for their 1909 recording of "Swing Low, Sweet Chariot."

Fisk University: Founded in 1866 in Nashville, TN, Fisk has had a major role in shaping black learning and culture in America. Among its distinguished alumni, faculty and board members are W.E.B. Du Bois, Booker T. Washington, Ida B. Wells-Barnett, Sterling Brown, James Weldon Johnson, John Lewis, and Nikki Giovanni.

Frazier, E. Franklin (1894–1962): Frazier was an African American teacher and sociologist who specialized in analyzing black family structures and race relations in the United States. He earned his Ph.D. at the University of Chicago. His most famous book, *The Negro Family in the United States* (1939) was an early effort to explore the historical forces affecting the black family. Frazier taught at Morehouse, Fisk, and Howard and influenced generations of black students. Before his death, he published 8 books and myriad articles. He has been criticized by some for claiming that black families were dysfunctional because of absent fathers, a fact that he tied to the heritage of slavery.

Free African Societies: Free blacks Richard Allen and Absalom Jones founded the Free African Societies during the Revolutionary War as the first black mutual aid society in Philadelphia.

Freedom Rides: The Freedom Rides, sponsored by CORE, began in 1961 when seven blacks and six whites set out on public buses to test the ruling in *Boynton v. Virginia* declaring segregation of public transportation illegal. The riders were met with extreme violence, which brought attention to the deep racial hatreds and fear of integration. The people on the rides adopted nonviolence, but understood the possibility that they would be met with violence. The goal was to directly challenge segregation policies. President Kennedy was forced to take action against the violence across the South.

Freedom's Journal: Founded by free blacks in New York City, John Russwurm and Samuel Cornish ran what was the first newspaper in American to be owned and operated by African Americans. It denounced those who attacked African Americans and those who supported slavery. The paper closed in 1829, replaced by *The Rights of All*.

Friedan, Betty (1921–2006): Author of the 1963 book *The Feminine Mystique*, Friedan was a key feminist activist for most of her life. She organized the Women's Strike for Equality and the National Organization for Women and was a strong supporter of the Equal Rights Amendment of 1972.

Garnet, Henry Highland (1815–1882): Garnet was an abolitionist, educator, minister, and brilliant orator. He supported a more militant approach, calling for emigration of American blacks to Mexico, West Indies, or Liberia. He founded the African Civilization Society. Once the Civil War ended, he became president of Avery College in Pittsburgh, Pennsylvania, in 1868.

In 1881, he became the US minister to Liberia and died there two months later.

Garvey, Marcus (1887–1940): Garvey's intense support of black nationalism and the Pan-Africanism movement sparked a philosophy known as Garveyism. This philosophy promotes the repatriation of American blacks to Africa and the redemption of African nations from colonial powers. Garvey founded UNIA-ACL (Universal Negro Improvement Association and African Communities League), and the Black Star Line, a shipping line that would facilitate his goals.

Gavin, James Raphael III (1945–): Dr. Gavin is a black physician, known for his work with diabetes, and is a former president of the American Diabetes Association. In addition, he has served as the CEO and chief medical officer of Healing Our Village, specializing in advocacy and training for health care professionals and minority communities. He has received numerous awards, and taught at many esteemed universities, including Indiana and Emory University.

Goodlett, Carlton (1915–1997): An African American family physician, Goodlett turned a San Francisco weekly tabloid, the *Sun-Reporter*, into an influential chain of eight newspapers. He was a tireless advocate for civil rights, and was the first African American since Reconstruction to mount a serious candidate for the governorship of California in 1966. He fought strongly about such issues as improving public housing and desegregating San Francisco's labor unions.

Goodman, Andrew (1943–1964): Goodman was a young white college student who worked with other activists during Freedom Summer to register blacks to vote. After being arrested for speeding and being told to leave the county, he and his associates were shot and killed by members of the Ku Klux Klan in Philadelphia, Mississippi.

Gore, Albert (Al) (1948–): Gore is a former vice president, Democratic presidential candidate, US senator, and US congressman. He also won the Nobel Peace Prize (2007) for his work in making the public aware of the effects of climate change with his documentary *An Inconvenient Truth*.

Gray, Fred (1930–): Gray is a prominent black civil rights attorney from Alabama. His clients included Martin Luther King Jr., Rosa Parks, and the victims of the Tuskegee Syphillis study. He became a legal advisor to the Montgomery Improvement Association and in 1956 was the lead counsel in *Browder v. Gayle*, the Supreme Court case that upheld lower court decisions prohibiting segregation on city buses. He also represented the students attempting to desegregate K-12 and higher education institutions. He was president of the National Bar Association in 1985 and the first African American president of the Alabama State Bar.

Gray, Garland (1902–1977): Gray was a Virginia senator from Waverly who worked with the Massive Resistance movement to prevent integration of

Virginia public schools. He helped found Defenders of State Sovereignty and Individual Liberties, which formed 28 chapters with 12,000 members by 1955. Governor Stanley created the Gray commission, named for Garland Gray, to create a plan to keep Virginia segregated as long as possible.

Greenberg, Jack (1924–): Greenberg was the only white director-counsel of the NAACP Legal Defense Fund from 1961 to 1984, handpicked by Thurgood Marshall. He was involved with such influential cases as *Brown v. Board of Education, Alexander v. Holmes County Board of Education, Griggs v. Duke Power Company,* and *Furman v. Georgia,* all of which deal with racial equality. He argued over 40 cases before the Supreme Court and participated in human rights missions around the world. He has been on the law faculty at Columbia, Yale, and Harvard and was dean of Columbia College from 1989 to 1993. He teaches at Columbia Law School.

Habermas, Jurgen (1929–): Habermas is a German philosopher who focuses on the political domain and on issues of knowledge, communication, and rational behavior. He has influenced contemporary philosophy as well as political-legal thought, developmental psychology, theology, communication studies, and sociology. Habermas is viewed as one of the most influential philosophers in the world.

Hamer, Fannie Lou (1917–1977): A civil rights activist from Montgomery County, Mississippi, Hamer became famous for saying she was "sick and tired of being sick and tired." The daughter of sharecroppers, her family struggled to survive. In the 1950s, she attended a protest meeting and subsequently became very active in registering people to vote. She was a key organizer of the Mississippi Freedom Summer for the Student Nonviolent Coordinating Committee and became the vice-chair of the Mississippi Freedom Democratic Party.

Hamilton, Grace (1907–1992): In 1965, Hamilton became the first African American woman elected to the Georgia General Assembly, one of eight African Americans to go to the state legislature in the 1965 special election. She held office for 18 years. During the 1940s, she was the executive director of the Atlanta Urban League. She focused her greatest attention on schooling, voting rights, health care, and housing.

Harlem Youth Council, Inc.: Founded in 1987, the Harlem Youth Council is a nonprofit organization that provides social services to the youth of Harlem. The main focus is on job training, workshops, and employment assistance.

Hastie, William H. (1904–1976): Hastie attended Dunbar High School in Washington, D.C., Amherst College, and Harvard Law School where he was on the editorial board of *Harvard Law Review.* In the 1930s, he became a race relations advisor to President Franklin D. Roosevelt. In 1937, he became the first African American federal judge when he was appointed to US District Court of the Virgin Islands. During World War II, he served as civilian aide to Secretary of War Stimson until he stepped down to protest the unequal treatment of blacks, a cause he fought for throughout the war. He worked with Houston and Marshall on cases leading up to the 1954 *Brown v. Board* decision. In 1949, he was appointed to the Third U.S. Circuit Court of Appeals and served for 21 years, including several as chief judge.

Hedgeman, Anna (1899–1990): A mid-westerner, Hedgeman was inspired to become an educator after hearing W. E. B. Du Bois speak at Hamline University, where she was a student. Following college, she taught English and History at Rust College in Mississippi. Experiencing discrimination in the South, she became more actively engaged in the civil rights movement. In the 1920s, she began a career with the YWCA, and served as executive director of numerous branches in Ohio and the northeast. Between 1954 and 1958, Hedgeman served in the cabinet of New York City mayor Robert Wagner, Jr.—the first black woman to hold that position. She helped plan the 1963 March on Washington. In the 1960s and 1970s, she authored two books.

Herskovits, Melville J. (1895–1963): An American anthropologist, Herskovits studied at the University of Chicago and Columbia where he was influenced by Franz Boas. He taught at Columbia and Howard, before moving to Northwestern University and creating the first substantial program of African studies at an American university in 1948. He published several works regarding black culture, such as *The Myth of the Negro Past* and *Man and His Works*. He had an interest in economics, African folk art and music, and incorporated these into his anthropological studies.

Higginbotham, A. Leon (1928–1998): Educated at Purdue, Antioch, and Yale University Law School, Higginbotham held legal positions in public and private practice in Philadelphia. Between 1964 and 1993, he was a federal judge. In 1990, he became Chief Judge of the Federal appeals court in Philadelphia. Subsequently, he became a professor at Harvard's Kennedy School of Government. A Presidential Medal of Freedom recipient in 1995, Higginbotham was committed to social justice and is said to have been one of a handful of black jurists considered by President Lyndon Johnson for a Supreme Court appointment. He authored several books, and was a strong and outspoken advocate for racial justice.

Hope, John (1868–1936): Hope was an educator who taught at and was the first black president in 1906 of Morehouse College. In 1929, he became the first black president of Atlanta University. He is also known for his political activism, as a founding member of the Niagara Movement, the first president of the Commission on Interracial Cooperation, and an active member of the NAACP. He strongly supported opportunities for blacks in Atlanta in the areas of public education, recreational facilities, housing, health care, and jobs.

Houston, Charles Hamilton (1895–1950): Known as the "man who killed Jim Crow," Houston participated in nearly every civil rights case that went before the Supreme Court between 1930 and *Brown v. Board of Education*. A brilliant lawyer, he served as dean of Howard University Law School, NAACP litigation director, and is known for training Justice Thurgood Marshall.

Howard University: Founded in 1866, Howard is one of the predominant historically-black universities in America. Within two years of its founding, Howard quickly expanded from a theological seminary with the addition of a college of Liberal Arts and Medicine. Early support came from the Freedmen's Bureau, and from the US Congress. Howard's first black president, Mordecai Johnson, served from 1926–1960 and expanded the university to 10 fully accredited schools and 6,000 students. Located in Washington, DC, Howard University faculty and students have played a major role in the civil rights movement. Howard also boasts among its alumni and faculty some of the leading black intellectuals, scholars, activists, and artists in America. Its Law School became a major center for prosecuting civil rights cases, including *Brown v. Board of Education.*

Hughes, Langston (1902–1967): American poet, novelist, and playwright, Hughes was one of the first people to incorporate jazz rhythms and dialect to depict the life of urban blacks. He a central figure of the Harlem Renaissance and associated with all of the prominent figures of Harlem's golden era. He had a prolific literary career, beginning with his first book of poetry *The Weary Blues* (1926). He used his poetry and his reputation to depict African American culture and work for civil rights through an Afro-centric message.

Hurley, Ruby (1909–1980): Born in Virginia, Hurley became active in civil rights in the 1930s. In 1943, she became the national Youth Secretary for the NAACP and established the first permanent NAACP office in the Deep South. She served in several leadership positions within the NAACP and worked alongside Amzie Moore and Medgar Evers on civil rights issues in the Mississippi Delta, investigating the murder of Emmett Till, working on the case of Autherine Lucy, and engaging with Roy Wilkins and Thurgood Marshall. In the 1960s, she became nationally prominent on local and national television. She was one of the first women of color to be seen as a black feminist activist.

Hurston, Zora Neale (1891–1960): Hurston is an acclaimed writer and anthropologist who rose to popularity during the Harlem Renaissance. Her most popular work is *Their Eyes Were Watching God* and she collaborated with such writers as Langston Hughes. She wrote four novels and more than 50 short stories, plays, and essays.

Jackson, George (1941–1971): Jackson was a prominent Black Panther, a Marxist, and a cofounder of the Black Guerrilla Family. He is best known for being one of the Soledad Brothers, a group of inmates at the California's Soledad Prison who were charged with the murder of a white prison guard. Angela Davis's involvement with him and his brother brought greater prominence to his case.

Jackson, James (1914–2007): Jackson, a Virginian who helped start the Southern Negro Youth Congress, became a black official in the Communist Party in the 1940s and 1950s, leading to his indictment at the height of McCarthyism in 1951 for teaching about violent revolution. Afterward, he roamed the country in hiding for five years, until he surrendered and was convicted of conspiracy under the Smith Act, which was then overturned following *Yates v. United States* in 1957.

Jackson, Jesse (1941–): Jackson is an active civil rights figure and Baptist minister who ran for the Democratic presidential nomination in 1984 and 1988. He worked closely with Martin Luther King Jr. in SCLC during the 1960s, heading its economic program Operation Breadbasket in Chicago. His organizational involvements ultimately merged to form Rainbow/PUSH. He is a frequent voice of racial activism on major television and news networks and has travelled extensively internationally as America's envoy for specific causes.

Jackson, Juanita (1913–1992): Admitted to the bar in 1950, Jackson was the first black woman to practice law in Maryland. After *Brown v. Board of Education*, she filed the suits that made Maryland the first southern state to integrate its public schools. She also advocated cases that forced Baltimore city agencies to hire black public employees and that desegregated both state and municipal public facilities and parks. She worked on the White House Conference on Children in 1940 and the White House Conference to Fulfill These Rights in 1966. In 1987 she was inducted to the Maryland Woman's Hall of Fame.

Jeanes Fund, Anna T.: Quaker and philanthropist Anna Jeanes established the Jeanes Foundation with $1,000,000 inherited from her father in 1907. The purpose of the foundation was to train and employ African American teachers and supervisors dedicated to upgrading vocational training programs.

Johns, Vernon (1892–1965): An early activist in the civil rights movement, Johns was a farmer, a pastor, and a mentor to Martin Luther King Jr. Educated at the Virginia Theological Seminary and Oberlin College, he was known for his bold activism, controversial sermons, and challenging his congregations to do more. He preceded Martin Luther King Jr. as the pastor of Dexter Avenue Baptist Church from 1947 to 1952, and his ideas paved the way for MLK's socially active ministerial teachings.

Johnson, James Weldon (1871–1938): Johnson was a poet, teacher, diplomat, and civil rights activist known for his work as general secretary for the NAACP from 1920 to 1930 and as a literary mover of the Harlem Renaissance in New York. He published three important anthologies of black poetry, volumes of original work including *Fifty Years and Other Poems*, and three books on race issues in America. From 1930 until his death in 1938, he taught literature at Fisk and New York Universities.

Jones, J. Raymond (1900–1991): Known as the Harlem Fox, Jones was the first black leader of Tammany Hall and a force in New York City politics. He founded the Carver Democratic Club in the 1920s, ran Democratic political strategy during the civil rights era, and served on city council in the 1960s. His important political leadership and mentorship influenced the lives and careers of leaders from Mayors William O'Dwyer and Robert Wagner and Manhattan Borough President Percy Sutton to Reps. Adam Clayton Powell and Charles Rangel and Presidents Lyndon B. Johnson and Harry S. Truman.

King, Coretta Scott (1927–2006): The wife of Martin Luther King Jr., Coretta Scott King was herself a leading figure of the civil rights movement. In college she joined the NAACP, and eventually conceived, organized, and performed a series of Freedom Concerts that raised funds for the SCLC. She became the first woman to give the Class Day address at Harvard, served as a liaison for peace and justice organizations in the Vietnam War, and founded the Martin Luther King Jr. Center for Nonviolent Social Change after her husband's assassination.

Lafayette, Bernard (1940–): Rev. Dr. Lafayette started his long career in civil rights activism as a part of the Freedom Riders campaign in 1959 for which he was jailed in Birmingham. Subsequently, he helped form the Student Nonviolent Coordinating Committee in 1960. He worked through SNCC to direct the Alabama Voter Registration Project (1962). He also was appointed by Martin Luther King Jr. as the the national program administrator for SCLC and coordinated the 1968 Poor People's Campaign. In 2009, he accepted an appointment as Distinguished Senior Scholar in Residence at Emory's Candler School of Theology.

Lawson, James (1928–): Rev. Lawson met Dr. Martin Luther King Jr. at Oberlin, after which he left school to become a field secretary for the Fellowship of Reconciliation and an organizer for the Nashville student movement's 1960 sit-in campaign. His time in jail as a conscientious objector to the Korean War and as a Methodist missionary in India led to his famous work teaching non-violent resistance workshops for the Freedom Riders movement. He chaired a sanitation worker's strike in Memphis in 1968 before serving in Los Angeles as pastor of the Holman United Methodist Church. In 2009 he returned to teach at Vanderbilt University, from which he had been expelled in the 1960s as a result of his sit-in work.

Lawyer's Club of Atlanta: Founded in 1922 by 12 white men, the club originally convened to discuss unethical practices by bar members and flaws in the member standards of existing bar organizations. Incorporated in 1939, it grew into a strong collection of concerned lawyers that provided a place for discourse on ethical standards in the profession. Current membership is around 1700 lawyers.

Levison, Stanley (1912–1979): Levison was an attorney, supporter, and friend of Martin Luther King Jr. A Jewish lawyer from New York City, he met Dr. King while raising funds for the Montgomery bus boycott, and in 1956 helped conceive the organization that became the Southern Christian

Leadership Conference. He worked closely with Dr. King, drafting speeches, managing papers, and editing *Stride Toward Freedom*. Eventually, the FBI used Levison's suspected communism to justify surveillance on Dr. King himself.

Locke, Alain (1885–1954): From an early age as a Harvard grad and the first African American Rhodes scholar, Locke was an important author, teacher, and philosopher of pluralism, culture, and race. He chaired the Department of Philosophy at Howard University from 1918 to 1953, where he developed a notion of "ethnic race," emphasizing the social and cultural dimensions of race over the biological ones. He is ultimately known as the "Father" and philosophical architect of the Harlem Renaissance, particularly after publishing *The New Negro* anthology in 1925. See also New Negro.

Long, Carlton: A graduate of Columbia University, Long received a Rhodes Scholarship in 1984 and inspired many students to achieve the distinction as well. Among those he inspired was Benjamin Jealous, of whom Long was one of the first black male teachers, who later headed the NAACP. Long taught in the political science department at Columbia University from 1990 to 1996. He is the cofounder of an international education consulting firm, Lawrence-Long & Co.

Louis, Joe (1914–1981): The worldwide heavyweight champion from 1937 to 1949, Louis became an idol and hero in American culture, one of the first African Americans to achieve such a celebrity status. Known as the Brown Bomber, he won 26 championship fights. He immortalized himself by winning against Benito Mussolini's emissary, Primo Carnera, in 1935, and German boxer Max Schmeling in 1938, who Hitler claimed represented Ayran superiority. Louis served his country by enlisting in the US Army during World War II.

Lucy, Autherine (1929–): Lucy grew up in Alabama and earned a B.A. in English from Miles College, a black institution, in 1952. That year, Lucy was the first African American accepted to the University of Alabama. After discovering her race, the university moved to block her enrollment. Thurgood Marshall and other lawyers sued the university, winning in the US Supreme Court in 1955. In Feb. 1956, violent mobs that protested her presence gave university officials cause to expel her, which her attorneys unsuccessfully challenged. She received her degree in 1992.

Macmurray, John (1891–1976): Macmurray was a Scottish scholar and philosopher who focused mostly on religion and the self as an agent. He earned a degree in classics from the University of Glasglow and an M.A. from Balliol College, Oxford in 1919. He was head of the Department of Philosophy at University College, London, as the Grote Professor of Mind and Logic and served as professor and chair in moral philosophy at the University of Edinburgh. His publications include *Freedom in the Modern World* (1932), *The Self as Agent* (1957), and *Search for Reality in Religion* (1965).

Malcolm X (1925–1965): A prominent leader of the Black Power movement and civil rights activist, Malcolm X, nee Little, grew up in the foster system after his father's likely murder by white supremacists for his open support of Marcus Garvey. While serving a jail sentence for burglary, he began to study the Nation of Islam and its leader, Elijah Muhammad. After his parole, he changed last name to X to signify his lost tribal name and became a minister and national spokesperson for the Nation of Islam. He oversaw a membership increase from 500 to 30,000 members from 1952 to 1963 and is known for his strong Black Power philosophy. Malcolm X broke from the NOI in 1964 to found his own religious organization, the Muslim Mosque Inc. He was assassinated in 1965 and over 1,500 people attended his funeral.

Marcuse, Herbert (1898–1979): Renowned as one of the most important philosophers of the twentieth century and heavily influenced by his teacher, Martin Heidegger, Marcuse joined the Frankfurt Institute for Social Research with Theodor Adorno and Max Horkheimer, which relocated to New York from Germany during World War II. Marcuse focused on modern social theory, especially Marxism, earning him notoriety as the "Father of the New Left." His works include *The One-Dimensional Man* (1964), *Soviet Marxism* (1958), and *An Essay on Liberation* (1969).

Marshall, Thurgood (1908–1993): Marshall was the first black Supreme Court Justice in the United States, serving from 1967 until 1991. He attended Howard University Law School under Charles Hamilton Houston's tutelage, and became chief counsel for the NAACP. He amassed a highly successful record of winning civil rights cases, including, most notably *Brown v. Board of Education* (1954). President John F. Kennedy named him to the US Court of Appeals for the Second Circuit, after which he served as US solicitor general, winning 14 cases at the Supreme Court. In 1967, America's most successful Supreme Court lawyer became an Associate Justice of the Court, where he served until retirement.

Martin, Martin A.: Along with Spottswood Robinson, Martin was a law partner to Oliver Hill. During the 1940s, he worked with astute attention to the law to get Virginia to address educational inequalities under segregation. As Hill expanded his efforts, he called upon fellow Howard law school graduate Martin to operate an office in Danville. Martin died in the 1960s.

Mays, Benjamin (1894–1984): Mays influenced a generation of African American leaders and was himself an important scholar, educator, and civil rights activist. Educated at Bates College, he started as a pastor before joining Morehouse University as faculty. After receiving his Ph.D. from the University of Chicago, he became dean of the School of Religion at Howard University. In 1940, he was elected president of Morehouse College. Throughout, he remained a scholar of African American Christianity, publishing nine books, including *Seeking to Be Christian in Race Relations*, and nearly 2,000 articles. See also Morehouse College.

McCarthy, Joseph (1908–1957): Born in Wisconsin, McCarthy graduated from Marquette University with a law degree but was largely unsuccessful in law. He ran a dirty but successful campaign for a circuit court judgeship, before quitting to serve in the Marines in World War II. After the war, he beat Senator Robert La Follete of Wisconsin to become a Republican senator. Sensing that he might not win reelection, McCarthy seized upon the American public's fear of communism by announcing a list of 205 State Department members who were ostensibly American Communist Party members. Appointed chairman of the Government Committee on Operations of the Senate, he investigated public workers and private citizens for communist alignment for three years. The military and President Eisenhower began uncovering and revealing McCarthy's dishonesty and corruption to the press, which turned the tide against him. He was censured by the Senate in 1954 and stripped of his power.

McDew, Charles (1938–): McDew helped found the Student Non-Violent Coordinating Committee in 1960 and served as its chairman from 1961 to 1964. He started his activism in 8th grade protesting for the religious freedom of Amish students in Ohio, and in 1960 became involved in the Orangeburg, South Carolina lunch counter sit-ins. Joining SNCC, he organized for the Freedom Rides and the Mississippi Freedom Summer of 1964. He continued his activism after John Lewis took over in 1964, managing antipoverty programs in D.C., Boston, and San Francisco. He taught civil rights and African American history at Metropolitan State University in Minneapolis until his retirement.

Melish, Rev. W. Howard (1910–1986): Rev. Melish was famously ousted from his Brooklyn parish in 1957 for his chairmanship of the National Council of American–Soviet Friendship. He believed in peace between the Soviet Union and the United States, and firmly supported civil rights, spending 10 years raising money for the civil rights movement with the Southern Conference Education Fund. A graduate of Harvard and the Episcopal Theological School, Rev. Melish became a target of Joseph McCarthy. In 1982, he rejoined his Brooklyn church as an assisting priest, where he stayed until his death.

Meredith, James (1933–): Meredith was the first black student to attend the University of Mississippi. He applied to the segregated University of Mississippi in 1961 and was admitted, but the registrar denied him enrollment after discovering his race. He sued and won at the US Supreme Court. His arrival at Ole Miss sparked riots, quelled only by the National Guard presence. After graduating in 1963, he went on to receive economics and law degrees in Nigeria and New York. In 1966, he organized the March Against Fear from Memphis, Tennessee, to Jackson, Mississippi, and was shot by a sniper early on. He continued to be active in politics for the remainder of his career, joining the ranks of the Republican Party.

Mississippi Freedom Democratic Party (MFDP): Founded during the Freedom Summer of 1964, the MFDP challenged the Mississippi Democratic Party's denial of voting rights to African Americans by attempting to displace them as the Mississippi Delegation at the Democratic National Convention. The NAACP, CORE, SCLC, and SNCC aided their cause at the convention, and MFDP delegate Fannie Lou Hamer spoke on national television about the violence and intimidation experienced by Mississippi blacks registering to vote. They did not succeed in gaining seats, but they advocated strongly and helped pave the way for the Voting Rights Act of 1965.

Mitchell, Charlene (1930–): Mitchell joined the American Youth for Democracy at 13 in 1943, beginning a lifelong career of socialist activism. She led the effort to free Angela Davis, rejuvenated the Communist Party USA in the 1960s and ran as its candidate for president in 1968, the first black woman to do so. She advocated with the Committees of Correspondence for Democracy and Socialism, supported African liberation movements, and worked globally for civil rights. She ran unsuccessfully for Senate against Daniel Moynihan in 1988, and served as an official international observer in the 1994 postapartheid South African elections.

Mitchell, Clarence Jr. (1911–1984): Mitchell directed the NAACP Washington Bureau and served as its chief lobbyist from 1950 to 1979. Often called the "101st US Senator" in recognition of his importance and determination, he tirelessly worked to secure passage of key civil rights laws: the Civil Rights Acts of 1957, 1960, and 1964, the 1965 Voting Rights Act, and the 1968 Fair Housing Act. His family's papers, housed at the Library of Congress, are one of the nation's most important civil rights archives. In 1980 Carter awarded him the Presidential Medal of Freedom and the Baltimore City courthouse is named in his honor.

Moore, Amzie (1911–1982): An ardent civil-rights worker in the Mississippi Delta, Moore conceived of the voter registration campaign that became the central focus of Freedom Summer in 1964. He was employed by the U.S. Post Office from 1935 before serving in the U.S. Army in World War II. Following the war, he opened small businesses in Cleveland, MS that also became meeting places for civil rights efforts. From the 1950s, he helped build the Regional Council of Negro Leadership (RCNL). His house was often used by civil-rights workers in the area as a "safe house."

Morehouse College: Founded in 1867 by Rev. William Jefferson White as the Augusta Theological Institute, historically black Morehouse College has educated generations of African American men who include Martin Luther King Jr., Sanford D. Bishop, Julian Bond, Bakari Sellers, the actor Samuel L. Jackson, and myriad other successful men. Morehouse also boasts three Rhodes Scholars. Renamed in 1913, President John Hope expanded the Atlanta-based college's strengths in preparing African Americans for teaching and ministry to include all areas. Dr. Benjamin Mays, who took over in 1940, built Morehouse's international reputation for scholarship, grew the faculty and mentored a generation of leaders. Morehouse College houses the Martin Luther King Jr. Collection, and is an important source of scholarship in African American history and culture.

Moron, Alonzo (1909–1971): Born in the Virgin Islands, Moron enrolled at the Hampton Institute Trade School in Virginia at 14, working odd jobs to support himself. From 1928 to 1932, he studied sociology at Brown University, graduating cum laude and Phi Beta Kappa before receiving a Masters from the University of Pittsburgh in 1933. He served as commissioner of public welfare for the Virgin Islands, before returning to the United States and getting a law degree as a Rosenwald Fellow at Harvard in 1947. He returned to the historically black Hampton Institute as a general business manager, ultimately becoming the first black president of Hampton in 1949, taking it from a trade school to university during his tenure.

Muhammad, Elijah (1897–1975): Muhammad grew up Elijah Poole in Georgia and quit school after 4th grade to feed his family. Seeking economic opportunities, he moved his family to Detroit, Michigan, where in 1931 he met W. D. Fard, founder of the Nation of Islam. He changed his name and adopted Fard's ideas, leading the NOI to Chicago after Fard's disappearance. With his controversial preaching of racial separation over integration, and focus on economic support, Muhammad built the NOI into a national organization with the help of apostle Malcolm X. See also Nation of Islam.

Murphy, Tom (1952–2012): Murphy served as spokesman for the Connecticut Department of Education for nearly two decades. He discussed the challenging requirements of No Child Left Behind and watched Education Commissioner Ted Sergi build one of the nation's top-scoring school systems. He additionally observed the challenges of landmark civil rights education case *Sheff v. ONeill*, in which the Connecticut Supreme Court ruled that the state had an active obligation to provide an equal educational opportunity for every school child, and that school districting caused inequities due to racial and ethnic isolation.

Murray, Pauli (1910–1985): Murray was a civil rights activist and feminist who defied and broke racial and gender boundaries throughout her career. Arrested in 1940 for refusing to sit in the back of a bus, she joined CORE while attending Howard University and in 1943 published essays including *Negroes Are Fed Up* in *Common Sense* and her famous poem *Dark Testament*. Awarded a Rosenwald Fellowship at Harvard Law, she was denied admission because of her gender, and instead attained a J.D. from the University of California Berkeley in 1945. She developed legal techniques in *States' Laws on Race and Color* (1950) that guided the NAACP's 1954 *Brown* arguments. She cofounded the National Organization for Women in 1966 after receiving the first J.S.D. Yale Law gave to an African American. In 2012, she became an Episcopal Saint, 27 years after her death.

NAACP Legal Defense Fund (LDF): Founded in 1940 under the leadership of Thurgood Marshall, the Legal Defense Fund served as the legal force behind the civil rights movement and a constant advocate of human rights. After winning *Brown v. Board of Education* (1954), the LDF filed hundreds of cases against school districts throughout the period of "Massive Resistance." In 1957 the LDF became independent of the NAACP. Besides success in desegregation of schools, the LDF won voting rights in *Smith v. Allwright* (1943), ended antimiscegenation laws in *Loving v. Virginia* (1967), eradicated employment discrimination in *Griggs v. Duke Power Company* (1971), and challenged the death penalty in *Furman v. Georgia* (1972). Their ranks include figures such as Jack Greenberg, Julius Chambers, and Elaine Jones.

NAACP (National Association for the Advancement of Colored People): After the 1908 race riot in Springfield, Illinois, several white liberals called for a meeting on racial justice, which occurred in New York. An invitation to more than 60 people included Ida B. Wells-Barnett and W. E. B. Du Bois, and from that the organization was born in February 1909. The NAACP grew into the largest and oldest civil rights organization in America, building a national network of local offices to advocate for racial justice on economic, political, moral, and legal issues. During the Great Depression, the NAACP worked through ally Eleanor Roosevelt and the Congress of Industrial Organizations to secure jobs for African Americans, leading to the desegregation of the Armed Forces. The NAACP helped organize the 1963 March on Washington, advocated against lynching for 30 years, and created the Legal Defense Fund. It is renowned as a force for economic advancement, equal health care and education, voter empowerment, and criminal justice. See also Niagara Movement.

Nabrit, James (Jim) Jr. (1900–1997): Nabrit was a prominent civil rights attorney who argued several cases for the NAACP Legal Defense Fund, including *Bolling v. Sharpe*, a *Brown* companion case. He graduated from Morehouse College in 1923 and Northwestern University Law School in 1927. He became dean of Howard University School of Law in 1958 and served as the University's second black president from 1960 to 1969. He also served as deputy ambassador to the United Nations. He is known as a leading civil rights advocate and scholar in constitutional law.

Nation of Islam (NOI): Founded in the 1930s by Wallace D. Fard, eventually Fard Muhammad, the Nation of Islam started as a collection of beliefs founded in Islam and black nationalism and grew into one of the most powerful organizations in African American history. Elijah Muhammad joined W. D. Fard, a direct representative of Allah, in developing the central philosophies of the organization, including the inherent superiority and originality of blacks over whites, leading to support for strict racial separation. Malcolm X and Muhammad Ali increased its notoriety and grew membership from 400 to 100,000–300,000 from 1952 to 1964. Often controversial, the NOI was isolated from other civil rights groups by its rejection of nonviolence. Louis Farrakhan took over after Malcolm X split with NOI, and eventually led the organization himself.

National Council of Negro Women (NCNW): Founded by Dr. Mary McLeod Bethune in 1935, the organization worked to represent African American women throughout the civil rights movement. Dr. Bethune built a national network of African American women's organizations and published a magazine *African Woman's Journal* that encouraged political activism and community organizing. Joining with other civil rights organizations, the NCNW worked to address New Deal discrimination, establish the Fair Employment Practices Committee, and attain a national voice for women and family concerns. Dr. Bethune helped draft the UN Charter as a delegate to the conference, and by 1960 under Dr. Dorothy Height, the NCNW worked for equal housing, voter registration, education, and economic services and opportunities.

National Science Foundation: Created by Congress in 1950, the National Science Foundation provides funding to support largely nonmedical but fundamental research and education in science and engineering. The organization funds approximately 20 percent of federally supported research, making more than 10,000 awards each year, and focuses on fields such as mathematics, computer science, physics, and social sciences.

National Urban League (NUL): Formed from the merger of several committees focused on improving the urban and industrial conditions of male and female African Americans in New York in 1911, the NUL became a crucial advocate for the economic, political, and social rights of African Americans. Ruth Standish Baldwin and Dr. George Edmund Hayes were early figures, the latter serving as the first executive secretary. The NUL focused on breaking down barriers to economic opportunity for blacks, advocating and supporting the civil rights movement, and continuing the fight for equal economic and political rights.

New Negro: Famously found in Howard University philosopher Alain LeRoy Locke's 1925 essay "The New Negro," the term described the African American prepared to undo the racial, social, political, legal, and economic barriers that had constrained black opportunities and advancement for generations. Locke advocated for a new generation of African Americans who would oppose Jim Crow and advocate for civil rights.

New York African Free School: Founded by the New York Manumission Society in 1787, the school started as a single-room schoolhouse with 40 students. Their goal was to educate black children, many of whom were the children of slaves. When it became a part of the New York City public school system in 1935, the school had taught thousands of children.

Newark Eagles: Part of the Negro National Baseball League, the Newark Eagles formed from the Brooklyn Eagles and Newark Dodgers under Abe and Effa Manley in 1936. Under their leadership, the team fostered the Negro League's biggest talents, including Willie Wells, Leon Day, and Monte Irvin. The team won the Negro World Series in 1946, but disbanded in 1948 after Jackie Robinson broke racial barriers and entered the Major League.

Newton, Huey (1942–1989): In 1966, Newton cofounded the Black Panther Party for Self Defense with Bobby Seale and helped lead the Black Power movement of the 1960s. The Panthers were known for militancy and believed that violence had to be met with force for change to occur. Newton had run-ins with the law throughout his life, the most serious of which was his conviction of voluntary manslaughter in a 1967 killing of a police officer in Oakland. Newton's case was dismissed after a "Free Huey" campaign brought public support to his cause. He went on to receive a Ph.D. from UC Santa Cruz in 1980. He died in 1989 after he was shot in Oakland.

Niagara Movement: Started by W. E. B. Du Bois in 1905, the Niagara Movement challenged the more accomodationist views of Booker T. Washington, seen by many as too conciliatory. The group wrote a manifesto that demanded the right to vote, elimination of segregation on public transit, and the guarantee of basic rights to African Americans. Several members of the movement, importantly including Du Bois, founded the NAACP in 1909, and disbanded the Niagara group in 1910. See also NAACP.

Niebuhr, Reinhold (1892–1971): Niebuhr was an influential American Protestant theologian and scholar, best known for his "Christian Realism." He focused on the persistent roots of evil in human life, calling attention to man's egotism, class interests, and nationalism. He was a radical critic of capitalism, and ran for office several times on a socialist ticket. He spoke out forcefully against the Ku Klux Klan during his years in Detroit. Among his best known works are the two-volume *The Nature and Destiny of Man* (1943) and *The Irony of American History* (1952). He served as a pastor of Bethel Evangelical Church in Detroit from 1915 to 1928 and then taught at Union Theological Seminary in New York City from 1928 to 1960, winning the 1964 Presidential Medal of Freedom. His writings influenced Martin Luther King Jr's posture on nonviolence.

Panetta, Leon (1938–): Secretary Panetta is most well known for his service in Obama's cabinet, first as director of the Central Intelligence Agency and then as secretary of defense, from which he retired in 2013. Long before his career in national security, Panetta served as the director for the US Office of Civil Rights under Nixon. During his tenure, he managed the integration of 500+ southern public school districts. He was elected to the US House of Representatives from California in 1976, and subsequently directed President Clinton's Office of Management and Budget in 1993. He advocated for civil rights right until his retirement, and during his tenure, dismantled barriers to women in combat in the US Armed Forces.

Parks, Rosa (1913–2005): Rosa Parks is known for her refusal to give up her seat on a Montgomery, Alabama, public bus to a white passenger. She joined the NAACP in 1943 after marrying Raymond Parks and served as secretary to NAACP president E. D. Nixon until 1957. She was arrested in 1955 after refusing to give up her seat, inciting a boycott that crippled the Montgomery public transit system. After a year of fighting, the city ended the law that segregated buses. She moved to Detroit, served on Planned Parenthood's board, and founded the Rosa and Raymond Parks Institute for Self-Development.

Patterson, Frederick D. (1901–1988): Named after Frederick Douglass, Patterson was raised by his sister in Texas and received his doctorate in veterinary medicine from Iowa State College in 1923. He started teaching at Tuskegee University in 1928. Over 25 years, he rose to head of the veterinary division, director of the School of Agriculture, and finally, the third president of the university. He founded the School of Veterinary Medicine during his tenure. In 1944, he founded the United Negro College Fund, a source of funds and support for historically black colleges and universities, as well as their students. President Ronald Reagan recognized him in 1985 for starting the College Endowment Funding Plan, and gave him the Presidential Medal of Freedom two years later.

Peabody Education Fund: The fund was created by George Peabody following the Civil War in 1867 to educate impoverished whites in the most destitute areas of the Deep South. Because there were no schools established for freedmen, it could not benefit them. In 1910, the Peabody College for Teachers was created in Nashville, Tennesse.

Phelps-Stokes Fund: The fund was established in 1911 to connect leaders in Africa and the Americas to improve quality of life. Endowed by Caroline Phelps Stokes in her will, it particularly focused on education of the underprivileged, including African Americans, Native Americans, and Africans. The fund's successes in Liberia are particularly well known, where it founded the Booker Washington Institute. It seeded a number of educational organizations, including the South African Institute of Race Relations and the United Negro College Fund, and supported US research on African American educational issues.

Ramses Club: Established by Dorothy Height and several fellow black students at New York University during the Harlem Renaissance, club members aimed to learn more and engage in African American culture. They attended events such as lectures and readings given by such figures as W. E. B. Du Bois, Langston Hughes, and Paul Robeson.

Randolph, A. Philip (1889–1979): Starting from the National Negro Congress in 1936, Randolph became a leader within the American labor party, socialist, and civil rights movements. He organized the Brotherhood of Sleeping Car Porters in 1925, which became the first predominantly black labor union and motivated President Franklin D. Roosevelt to end discrimination in defense jobs. He organized the prayer pilgrimage in 1957 for the civil rights bill, the March on Washington in 1963, and advocated the Freedom Budget in 1966 that would fight poverty.

Redding, Louis (1901–1998): The first black lawyer in Delaware, he was part of the NAACP legal team that brought *Brown v. Board of Education* before the Supreme Court. A graduate of Brown (1923) and Harvard Law School (1928), he compiled the 1950 case that desegregated the University of Delaware, which became the first institution with federal funds to integrate. He was a prominent civil rights lawyer in his career spanning 57 years, also arguing *Burton v. Wilmington Parking Authority* (1961) case, which outlawed segregation of public accommodations.

Rheedlen Centers for Children and Families in New York: Rheedlen was founded in Harlem in 1970 with the intention of reducing truancy. Geoffrey Canada became president in 1990 and used the annual $3 million budget to build and provide teen programs to reduce violence and provide safe after-school activities. The organization eventually became Canada's Harlem Children's Zone, which initially focused on a 24-block area to study and reduce the negative impacts of poverty on the safety and well-being of children. The HCZ continues to grow and constantly take on new issues of concern.

Richardson, Judy (1944–): Richardson worked with the SNCC for three years in the 1960s in Georgia, Alabama, and Mississippi. Richardson joined the Swarthmore Political Action Committee in college, and in 1963 spent her weekends assisting the Cambridge, MD community in desegregating public accommodations. Later in life, she produced documentaries and books about the civil rights movement, including *Eyes on the Prize, Malcolm X: Make It Plain,* and *Hands on the Freedom Plow: Personal Accounts by Women in SNCC,* which includes 52 memoirs of women bravely working for civil rights in the 1960s.

Ricks, Willie (a.k.a. Mukassa Dada) (1943–): Ricks was a community organizer and prominent civil rights activist who first gained recognition for his work as a field secretary for SNCC with John Lewis. He planned sit-ins, demonstrations, and marches throughout the South. Eventually, he split ideologically from the SNCC and joined the Black Panther Party with Stokely Carmichael, where he instigated and spread the term "Black Power."

Robeson, Paul (1898–1976): Born in New Jersey, Robeson attended Rutgers University on scholarship, the third African American to do so. He won 15 varsity sports letters and graduated Phi Beta Kappa. He earned a law degree from Columbia University, while also playing in the National Football League, but quit law in 1923 after facing discrimination, and turned to theater, film,

254 / Appendix B

and music. He became a famous and influential actor and an internationally known singer whose credits include the lead in *The Emperor Jones* by Eugene O'Neill, and films *Jericho*, *Show Boat* (1936) and *Tales of Manhattan* (1942). He vocally supported racial equality and Pan-Africanism, for which the government accused him of communism during the McCarthy-led Red Scare, and inhibited his work. He published his autobiography in 1958.

Robinson, Jackie (1972–1919): Born in Georgia, Robinson played football, basketball, track, and baseball throughout his childhood and won his region's baseball MVP award in 1938. He studied at UCLA, becoming the first student to win letters in four sports. He served in the US Army until 1944 when he was court-martialed for refusing to give up his seat on a segregated bus and honorably discharged. He started playing in the Negro Leagues of baseball until the Brooklyn Dodgers hired him to play, making him the first African American player in Major League baseball. He faced harassment and threats, but became a national hero as Rookie of the Year and the National League's MVP in 1949.

Robinson, James (1907–1972): A clergyman and founder of Operation Crossroads Africa, Robinson is known for his humanitarian work. A 1938 graduate of Union Theological Seminary and previously of Lincoln University, he pastored Harlem's Morningside Presbyterian Church, engaging in social justice projects. His travels in Africa in 1954 led him to found Operation Crossroads Africa, which coordinated volunteers to build infrastructure and improve education in African communities. The OCA preceded the Peace Corps, and was recognized by President Kennedy for its importance in the latter's conception.

Robinson, Spottswood III (1916–1998): A 1939 graduate of Howard Law School, Robinson was a prominent civil rights attorney in Virginia most known for arguing one of the five *Brown v. Board of Education* 1954 cases. Out of college he joined the Legal Defense and Educational Fund in Virginia and developed expertise in constitutional law and 14th amendment law. He was dean of Howard Law school from 1960 to 1963, when he was named a judge of the US District Court in D.C. In 1966, President Lyndon Johnson named him to the US Court of Appeals in D.C., of which he became chief judge in 1981, the first African American to hold the post.

Roosevelt, Eleanor (1884–1962): After marrying Franklin Delano Roosevelt in 1905, Eleanor involved herself in her husband's career. While he was president, she transformed the role of the First Lady by writing opinion columns, traveling across the country, and giving press conferences on important issues. Her tireless advocacy of human rights, including many minority and socioeconomic issues, made her an important humanitarian leader and a key ally of the civil rights movement. She served as the first chair of the UN Commission on Human Rights and later served on the Kennedy administration's Presidential Commission on the Status of Women.

Rosenberg Foundation: Established in 1935 by California businessman Max L. Rosenberg, the organization has provided thousands of grants. Grounded in the belief that every Californian should have equitable opportunities, the foundation works to help underprivileged children, involve immigrants and racial minorities into civic institutions, reform the criminal justice system, and strengthen the economic health of families.

Rosenwald, Julius (1862–1932): Known for his humility and hard work, Rosenwald owned Sears, Roebuck and Company and built its merchandise shipping business. A successful businessman and multimillionaire, Rosenwald focused on philanthropy and built a friendship with Booker T. Washington after reading his autobiography. On his 50th birthday in 1912, he gave $700,000 (currently $16 million), including $25,000 to the Tuskegee Institute, which Washington used in part to fund education for black children in the Deep South. Almost 5,000 Rosenwald-backed schools were built, which educated 35 percent of black children in the South.

Rustin, Bayard (1912–1987): An important organizer of the civil rights movement, he worked closely with Martin Luther King Jr., promoting a philosophy of nonviolence informed by the Quaker religion, Mahatma Gandhi, and A. Philip Randolph. An incredibly effective organizer, he started working for King in 1955, assisting with the Montgomery boycott in 1956, and coordinating the March on Washington in 1963. He cofounded the A. Philip Randolph Institute for African American trade union members. His work in civil rights and LGBT advocacy gained him much renown, recorded in his writings in *Down the Line* (1971) and *Strategies for Freedom* (1976).

Russell, Judith: Russell is a lecturer in political science at Columbia. Her area of specialty is American politics. She was vice president for research and policy at The New York City Partnership before returning to a teaching position.

Schwerner, Michael (Mickey) (1939–1964): A field organizer for the Congress of Racial Equality, he was killed by the Ku Klux Klan in Philadelphia, Mississippi, while promoting voter registration for African Americans. He graduated from Columbia's School of Social Work, and moved from New York to Mississippi to work for CORE with his wife, Rita. He saw Mississippi as a decisive battleground for racial equality in America, and persisted in his work despite death threats. After being arrested for a traffic violation, he and two fellow workers James Chaney and Andy Goodman were murdered by Ku Klux Klan members. See also Bender, Rita.

Scottsboro Nine: The Scottsboro Nine refers to nine African American boys who were accused of assault and the rape of two white women. They were arrested and charged in March 1931, and eight were sentenced to death. The NAACP and International Labor Defense battled to appeal their cases, reaching the US Supreme Court in November 1932. The Court reviewed the seven convictions upheld by the Alabama Supreme Court and reversed them on due process. Litigation continued for years, but ultimately Alabama released the four youngest defendants, and paroled all but one, who escaped. The widely publicized case revealed the discrimination and violence faced by blacks in the Jim Crow South.

Seale, Robert (Bobby) (1936–): Seale is an African American political activist who advocated militant black empowerment over the nonviolent rhetoric of the civil rights movement. He grew up in California and joined the US Air Force in 1955. He met Huey Newton while protesting the Cuba blockade and they quickly became friends. Seale and Newton formed the Black Panthers in 1966, which became the Black Panther Party. Focusing on community outreach, the Panthers spread across the nation. Seale spent four years in prison following charges that he conspired to start riots at the DNC in Chicago, and afterward began writing, publishing *A Lonely Rage* in 1978 and a cookbook in 1987.

Sellers, Cleveland (1944–): Sellers was a civil rights activist from the age of 15 onward, starting in North Carolina and moving south, becoming a founding member and program director of SNCC. He was injured and arrested during the Orangeburg Massacre, a protest that turned violent on South Carolina State University's campus. The only person imprisoned (unfairly), he spent his seven-month sentence writing his autobiography, *The River of No Return*. Once released, he completed his education and received degrees from Shaw University, Harvard, and UNC-Greensboro. He received a full pardon 25 years after his conviction. Ultimately, Sellers became president of Voorhees College.

Shaw University: Founded in 1865 and located in Raleigh, North Carolina, Shaw University is the oldest historically black university in the South. In 1873, it became the first US collegiate institution to build a female dormitory, and in 1881 Shaw founded Leonard Medical School, the first southern four-year program to train black doctors and pharmacists. By 1900, Shaw had educated more than 30,000 black teachers. In 1960, Ella Baker organized a conference at Shaw, her alma mater, that initiated the SNCC.

Shirek, Maudelle (1911–2013): Shirek grew up on a farm in Arkansas, before moving to Berkeley in the 1940s. She served on City Council in Berkeley, California from 1984 to 2004, becoming known as the "Conscience of the Council." She championed needle exchanges to prevent the spread of HIV/AIDS, extended domestic benefits to same-sex partners, and divested Berkeley from companies doing business in apartheid South Africa. Berkeley's City Hall is named in her honor.

Shuttlesworth, Fred (1922–2011): Born in Alabama, Shuttlesworth became pastor of the Bethel Baptist Church in 1953. He led the Alabama Christian Movement for Human Rights, which was the most important civil rights organization in Birmingham in the 1950s and 19560s, formed to continue the court-halted work of the NAACP in Alabama. A founding minister of the SCLC in 1957 with Dr. King, he organized two weeks of demonstrations in Birmingham in 1963 against segregation, which in part led to the Civil Rights Act of 1964 and the Voting Rights Act of 1965. Through personal injury, arrest, and tumult, he fought for the civil rights movement and became one of its most dedicated leaders.

Sinquefield, Richard Anderson (1825–1910): Rev. Richard Sinquefield published a record of his 42 years of work as an itinerant preacher in the AME Church of West Arkansas in 1909. He acquired his education while a slave, and served the abolition movement after his escape. He and his peers challenged societal notions that African Americans could not learn, working toward emancipation and education for all.

Slater Fund, John F.: The fund was established in 1882 to support the industrial and vocational higher education of newly freed African Americans in the South, with an early emphasis on training teachers. John F. Slater, a Connecticut textiles manufacturer, initiated the fund with a $1 million gift, and by 1931 it had contributed over $2.2 million to expand higher education for blacks in the South. In 1932, it merged with the Peabody Fund, the Jeanes Fund, and the Virginia Randolph Fund to form the Southern Education Foundation, Inc.

Smith, Bessie (1894–1937): Smith started singing professionally in 1912 and performed to success in vaudeville and black theatre throughout the 1920s. Clarence Williams brought her to New York to record her first album, *Down-Hearted Blues*, which was immensely popular and made her one of the most successful black artists of her time. She recorded blues with such jazz musicians as James P. Johnson and Louis Armstrong. In 1929, she made her film debut in *St. Louis Blues*. She continued to perform and record into the Great Depression after leaving Columbia Records, but struggled with alcoholism and died in a tragic car accident in 1937.

Smith, Kelly Miller (1920–1984): Born in Mississippi, Smith attended Morehouse College in Atlanta, Georgia, where he joined the campus chapter of the NAACP, beginning a long career of nonviolent civil rights advocacy. After receiving his divinity degree from Howard University, he moved to Nashville in 1951. There, he founded a group called the Nashville Christian Leadership Council in 1958, which helped organize lunch-counter student sit-ins. He pastored the First Baptist Church in Nashville, and eventually became president of the NAACP. He also served as assistant dean of Vanderbilt University's Divinity School.

Southern Christian Leadership Conference (SCLC): The SCLC was founded in 1957 to coordinate the actions of civil rights protest groups in the South. Under Martin Luther King Jr., the organization coordinated black churches to achieve rights for African Americans via nonviolent methods. Following the Montgomery bus boycott, which incited the SCLC's formation, Bayard Rustin wrote working papers to expand the tactics to other cities. The SCLC coordinated the actions of local committees throughout the South, and is known for the Crusade for Citizenship, its work in Birmingham and Selma, Alabama, and the March on Washington.

Southern Negro Youth Congress: Formed in 1937 by young leaders who met at the 1936 National Negro Congress in Chicago, the organization advocated civil rights issues in employment and voter discrimination, and made great progress educating African Americans in the rural South about their rights and strategies for protests. It met for the first time in Richmond, Virginia, in 1937, attended by 534 delegates. With a peak membership of 11,000 and the support of Mary McLeod Bethune, A. Philip Randolph and W. E. B. Du Bois, the organization helped build the civil rights movement in the 1950s in spite of intimidation by the Ku Klux Klan and opposition from the FBI.

Southern Poverty Law Center: Known for its successful legal victories against hate groups and focus on promoting tolerance, the SPLC began its work in 1971 under Morris Dees and Joseph Levin Jr. Julian Bond served as its first president from 1971 to 1979, at which time the organization brought its first cases against the Ku Klux Klan and other hate groups. A notable publication, *Teaching Tolerance,* influences generations of teachers and calls attention to ongoing problems of race in American society.

Southern Regional Council (SRC): The SRC formed as the Commission on Interracial Cooperation in 1919 to advocate and work against racial injustice in the South. It has conducted research on racial and economic conditions in the South and published background reports in its journal *New South* (now *Southern Changes*), compiling an invaluable record. Howard Odum, its civil rights era leader, focused on reform of economic, social, and political issues to achieve racial equality. The council's projects include the Voter Education Project (which became independent in 1971) and the Lillian Smith Book Award (est. 1968), which recognizes authors who advance racial and social equality in the American South. See also Voter Education Project.

Stanley, Thomas B. (1890–1970): Stanley was governor of Virginia in the years directly after *Brown v. Board of Education.* Originally moderate in his stance, Stanley caved to pressure from the Byrd Organization and others that strongly opposed desegregation, creating the committee that would draft Virginia's response to *Brown.* The Legislature approved the Stanley Plan in 1956, which allowed the governor to shut down any school that might desegregate. These massive resistance plans severely disrupted state-supported education. Stanley subsequently beame an executive of First National Bank.

Steinem, Gloria (1934–): Steinem grew to prominence as an outspoken social advocate in the 1960s, championing women's rights. She graduated from Smith College in 1956 and studied in India. In 1963 she published her famous exposé of New York's Playboy Club. She wrote political columns for *New York* magazine and joined prominent feminists to start the National Women's Caucus in

1971. She founded *Ms* magazine, a feminist publication that discussed crucial women's issues, including domestic violence. She published an essay collection in 1983 and wrote throughout the 1980s and 1990s as she defeated breast cancer, married, and continued to advocate for equality.

Steptoe, E. (Eldridge) W. (1936–2009): A black landowner and businessman in Amite County, Mississippi, Steptoe protected and guided the young civil-rights activists in SNCC and CORE. He was an important participant in the Mississippi Freedom Movement.

Student Nonviolent Coordinating Committee (SNCC): Founded in April 1960 at Shaw University, the committee led the sit-in student protest movements that occurred across the South during the civil rights movement. Ella Baker organized the conference, attendees of which conceived a community based student-run group to coordinate protests. Nonviolence was strongly stated in its guiding documents, and Marion Barry was the first elected chairman. SNCC students and leaders worked on the 1961 Freedom Rides, the 1964 Mississippi Freedom Summer, and the 1963 March on Washington. Notable members include Julian Bond, James Lawson, John Lewis, Bob Moses, Diane Nash, and Stokely Carmichael.

Sutton, Percy (1920–2009): Sutton began his long political career in the 1950s as a Democrat in Harlem, joining the ranks of the "Gang of Four" prominent black politicians in New York. He served in World War II as an intelligence officer for the Tuskegee Airmen and supported his law degree through the GI Bill. After serving in the Korean War, he started a law practice in 1953. His most well-known client was Malcolm X, who Sutton represented both before and after his death. In the 1960s he was arrested as a Freedom Rider in Mississippi and Alabama, and he served as Manhattan's borough president for more than 10 years, after which he invested in radio and theater and remained a leader until his death.

Tawney, Richard (R.H.) (1880–1962): Tawney grew up in Calcutta, India, and studied modern history at Balliol College, Oxford University. In 1917, he became a lecturer at the London School of Economics. He became a professor of economic history in 1931. His work in sociology heavily influenced education, including *Secondary Education for All* (1922) and *Education: the Socialist Policy* (1924). He was a strong proponent of adult education. He also published economic and political works, mostly on the flaws of capitalism, including *The Acquisitive Society* (1920) and *Equality* (1931). *Religion and the Rise of Capitalism* (1926) calls attention to the societal problems that accrue from a focus on the acquisition of wealth.

Terrell, Mary Church (1863–1954): Terrell was one of the first black women to earn a college degree, graduating in Classics from Oberlin College in 1884. She worked in education, rising from teacher to the D.C. Board of Education, the first black woman in the United States to do so. She was a founder of the NAACP and the first president of the National Association of Colored Women. She worked ardently for women's suffrage and the segregation of public facilities in DC ended in 1953 when she was 90 years old.

Thurman, Howard (1899–1981): Thurman became a Baptist minister in 1925 and pastored in Oberlin, Ohio. He joined the faculty of Morehouse and Spelman colleges in Atlanta as a religion professor, and in 1929 studied with Rufus Jones, a known Quaker pacifist, at Haverford. Thurman then began to focus and write about peaceful activism rooted in faith, in an essay called "Peace Tactics and a Racial Minority." He served as the dean of Howard University (1932–1944), leaving to help found the first racially integrated, intercultural church in the United States. In 1958, Thurman became the first black dean of Marsh Chapel at Boston University, making him the first tenured black dean of a majority white university.

Thurmond, Strom (1902–2003): Serving 48 years as a senator from South Carolina, Thurmond was a powerful and controversial politician throughout the twentieth century. He is known for conducting the longest filibuster on record against the passage of the 1957 Civil Rights Act. He switched parties in 1964 to the Republicans in opposition to civil rights legislation. He wrote the Southern Manifesto after *Brown v. Board of Education* (1954) that described southern resistance to desegregation. In his later years, he supported legislation to establish MLK Day, and served as president pro tempore of the Senate.

Tillich, Paul (1886–1965): Tillich was a renowned German philosopher and theologian, who moved to the United States after Hitler came to power in 1933. He taught at Union Theological Seminary and was considered one of the most prominent Protestant thinkers, and his work became a foundation of Martin Luther King Jr.'s philosophy. King wrote his dissertation on Tillich's work in 1953 and grappled with Tillich's Christian existentialism. Tillich ended his career at the University of Chicago, to which he had moved in 1962. His most famous works are *The Courage to Be* (1952), *Dynamics of Faith* (1957), and *Systemic Theology* Vols. 1–3 (1951–1963).

Tisdale, Charles (1927–2007): Tisdale bought *The Advocate*, a weekly newspaper in Jackson, Mississippi, in 1978. After the civil rights era, Tisdale realized that much remained to be done. He changed *The Advocate* to be a hard-hitting journalistic paper that exposed corruption in the Mississippi government and reported on the injustices and civil rights violations African Americans and impoverished whites experienced in the Deep South. Tisdale received death threats throughout the 1980s and 1990s for his work, and the paper's offices were frequently threatened by shootings and fire bombings.

Truth, Sojourner (1797–1883): Truth was born Isabella Baumfree into a slave family owned by Colonel Hardenbergh in New York and was subsequently sold to John Dumont. She had several children, and after New York emancipated all slaves in 1827, her son was illegally sold to a man in Alabama. She fought and won a case to free him, becoming the first black woman to win a challenge against a white man in a US court. In 1843 she changed her name and became a powerful abolitionist and advocate of women's rights. She met William Lloyd Garrison and Frederick Douglass, and famously gave her "Ain't I a Woman" speech at the Ohio Women's Rights Convention in 1851. She worked throughout the Civil War to secure freedom and rights for slaves and women in the South.

Tubman, Harriet (1820–1913): The most famous conductor on the Underground Railroad, Tubman took 19 trips to the South to rescue over 300 slaves and lead them to freedom in the North. In 1856, her capture was valued at $40,000. In New England, she attended antislavery meetings and during the Civil War, she served as a cook, nurse, and spy for the Union. She was the first woman to lead an armed expedition in the war, an expedition that freed 700 slaves. She lived in Auburn, New York, where she suffered increasing symptoms of a head injury from early in life. She is one of the most famous civilian figures of American antebellum history. See also Underground Railroad.

Tucker, Samuel W. (1913–1990): Tucker started his civil rights career in 1939, conducting the first nonviolent sit-in of the civil rights movement at a library in Alexandria. He attended Howard University as an undergraduate, and qualified for the Virginia Bar in 1933 on the basis of his independent study and work in a law office. A partner of Hill, Tucker and Marsh, he led NAACP's legal challenge of many post– *Brown v. Board of Education* cases, famously arguing *Green v. County School Board of New Kent County* (1968) before the Supreme Court, which ruled that schools had an "affirmative duty" to desegregate. He worked to end racial discrimination in jury selection and challenged racial bias in death penalty convictions, taking on 150 cases in 1967 alone.

Tuskegee Institute: The Tuskegee Institute, which became a university in 1985, is a historically black, private university founded in 1881. After Lewis Adams, a former slave, secured authorization for a black normal school in Tuskegee from the Alabama senate, former slaveowner George Campbell helped find its first principal, Booker T. Washington. Washington took the school to prominence, gaining the institution's independence. Robert Moton took over after his death, in 1915, and founded the first hospital, the Tuskegee V.A. Hospital in 1923, the first staffed by black professionals. Dr. Frederick Patterson took over in 1935, founded a veterinary school, and built the Tuskegee Airman flight-training program, famous for its World War II contributions. Several presidents have visited the university, George Washington Carver taught there, and it has been declared a National Historic Landmark. See also Washington, Booker T.

Underground Railroad: From 1810 to 1850, the Underground Railroad brought 100,000 slaves from southern plantations to freedom in the North. It consisted of a network of homes and safe locations ("stations") that sheltered runaway slaves as they travelled north. Along the way, many provided money and goods ("stockholders") and "conductors," including Harriet Tubman, led runaways from station to station.

United Christian Youth Movement of North America: Started in 1934, the movement represented 42 Protestant youth agencies. By 1945, over 10,000,000 people were served. Conferences were held beginning in 1936 to engage Christian youth in meaningful action. Dorothy Height was involved during her college years and the organization helped develop her leadership skills and devotion to civil rights.

United Youth Committee Against Lynching: Organized by Dorothy Height and Juanita Jackson, the committee worked to increase awareness of lynchings. They organized marches in New York City, networked over 100 New York-area youth groups, and fought for congressional antilynching legislation. The group organized an Anti-Lynching Day across the country that coordinated demonstrations from Houston to Harlem.

Universal Negro Improvement Association (UNIA): Marcus Garvey founded UNIA with Amy Ashwood on July 20, 1914, after he read Booker T. Washington's autobiography, *Up from Slavery*. He envisioned providing education and support for blacks, and by 1920 the organization had thousands of chapters from the United States to Africa. Garvey advocated black political and economic nationalism, developing philosophies that informed the Nation of Islam, and he supported the "Back to Africa" movement.

Upward Bound: Established in 1965 by the Higher Education Act, the program works to help underrepresented and low-income high school students to prepare for college. It provides instruction in key academic areas like math and composition through tutoring, work-study, and other, often specifically targeted programs. Notable alumni of the program include Oprah Winfrey, Viola Davis, and Angela Bassett.

Voter Education Project (VEP): The Kennedy administration started the VEP in 1962 to coordinate civil rights organizations under the Southern Regional Council on their voter registration and education initiatives. The nonpartisan project organized SCLC, SNCC, CORE, NAACP, and NUL in their voter registration efforts and brought it direct funding through private, tax-free contributions. The VEP was motivated in part by the goal of reducing confrontational action by civil rights groups, but the latter viewed the funding as important and helpful in doing their work. The VEP continued to work after the passage of the Voting Rights Act in 1965, until it closed in 1992. See also Southern Regional Council.

Walden, Austin Thomas (A. T.) (1885–1965): Walden was a prominent black lawyer in Georgia during the civil rights era. He received his J.D. from the University of Michigan Law School in 1911, and began practicing law in Macon, Georgia, in 1912. He worked for the Atlanta Urban League and was president of the NAACP Atlanta branch. He worked to equalize pay for black teachers and won a lawsuit that ultimately called for the desegregation of Georgia schools, including the University of Georgia. In 1964, he was appointed judge of the Atlanta Municipal court, the first black judge in Georgia since Reconstruction.

Wallace, George (1919–1998): Wallace served four terms as governor of Alabama, first elected in 1962. Stating that he would defend segregation and "stand in the school house door," he became known for his staunch opposition to the civil rights movement. This won him several primaries and he ran for president four times, on platforms that strongly opposed "forced busing" for integration, and an American Independent Party run that denounced blacks, students, and Vietnam pacifists. His 1972 campaign was cut short by an assassination attempt that left him in a wheelchair. In his 1982 campaign for governor, he changed his views and built a coalition of blacks, organized labor, and others to advance public education in the "New South."

Warren, Earl (1891–1974): President Eisenhower appointed Warren Chief Justice of the Supreme Court in 1953. Warren attended UC Berkeley, earning both his B.A. and J.D. degrees. He practiced briefly in San Francisco and became Alameda County district attorney in 1925, winning three subsequent elections. He served three terms as governor of California before becoming a justice. Among the most important rulings of the Warren Court were *Brown v. Board of Education,* the upholding of the Voting Rights Act of 1965, *Miranda v. Arizona,* and *Gideon v. Wainwright.* He retired in 1969.

Washington, Booker T. (1856–1915): Born a slave on a plantation in Virginia, Washington became a leading civil rights activist, creator of the Atlanta Compromise, founding member of the NAACP, and advisor to several presidents of the United States. His determination to educate himself took him to the Hampton Institute, after which he founded Tuskegee Normal and Industrial Institute, now Tuskegee University. He focused on economic empowerment, rather than political and social rights. He was not only an influential leader of early civil rights, but also the most well-known African American leader of his generation.

Watergate: The Watergate scandal began in 1972 when five burglars were caught attempting to bug the Democratic National Committee's offices at the Watergate Hotel in D.C. The FBI established within months that the incident was part of a larger effort by President Nixon's campaign to spy on and sabotage his opponents. After many senior-level resignations and Senate hearings, President Nixon himself resigned in 1974 and was pardoned by his successor, President Gerald Ford.

Watts Riots: The riots began on August 11, 1965, when a California patrolman arrested Marquette Frye, an African American man, for DUI. Tension between the officer and a crowd watching Frye's arrest turned violent, and incited a large-scale riot in the Watts neighborhood in South Central Los Angeles. Predominantly African American and very poor, Watts saw fires, looting, and gun fights over six days, resulting in 34 deaths, over 1,000 injuries, and $50–150 million in property damage. About 14,000 National Guard troops responded to restore order. A later investigation revealed that longstanding tensions, unemployment rates, dilapidated housing, and poor schools precipitated the events.

Watts, Robert B. (1922–1998): After service with the armed forces from 1943 to 1945, Watts got his J.D. from the University of Maryland and became a prominent civil rights attorney, working with the Baltimore NAACP to release civil rights activists from jail. He served as cocounsel for the NAACP with Thurgood Marshall and was the first African American appointed to the Municipal Court of Baltimore City in 1960. He won awards for outstanding legal service to the poor and for promoting racial equality.

Wednesdays in Mississippi: Dorothy Height and National Council of Negro women members travelled to Selma, Alabama in 1963 to witness the discrimination and abuse faced by African American women and children in the South, particularly by law enforcement. This led to Wednesdays in Mississippi in March of 1964, when Height and others held a conference in Atlanta to address the safety of female civil rights workers. With Polly Cowan, Height then worked to organize two teams of northern women to travel South to make and maintain relationships with women in southern civil rights activism. The program lasted two years, creating interracial networks of white and black church women to support SNCC workers in voter registration projects. See also Cowan, Polly.

Wells-Barnett, Ida B. (1862–1931): Wells-Barnett was a journalist, activist, and cofounder of the NAACP, who focused especially on lynching in the United States. She fought for civil rights her whole life, starting when she sued a railroad company (before *Plessy v. Ferguson*) after she was forcibly removed from the seat she refused to cede to a white passenger. She started writing, and in 1889 became a partner in the newspaper *Free Speech and Headlight*. She helped develop women's and reform organizations in Chicago, working tirelessly for women's suffrage. In 1906, she joined W. E. B. Du Bois's Niagara Movement. She published two influential pamphlets in the early 1890s titled *Southern Horrors: Lynch Law in All Its Phases* and *The Red Record*, examining lynching and racism in the southern United States.

West, Cornel (1953–): A provocative philosopher and public intellectual, West has taught at Yale, Harvard, University of Paris, Union Theological Seminary, and Princeton. West's influential thinking about race, gender, and socialism has shaped modern philosophy. He has written 20 books and is the recipient of the American Book Award. He served as an honorary chair of the Democratic Socialists of America. His most influential works include *Race Matters* (1994) and *Democracy Matters* (2004).

White, Walter (1893–1955): White was the head of the NAACP for nearly twenty-five years from 1931 to 1955. Born in Atlanta, he graduated from Atlanta University in 1916. When the Atlanta Board of Education decided to stop 7th grade for black students to fund a new high school for white students, he organized a protest, starting his long career in civil rights advocacy. He founded the Atlanta NAACP branch and started working nationally in 1918. As executive secretary of the NAACP from 1931 to 1955, he started the Legal Defense Fund, which made *Brown v. Board of Education* possible, convinced FDR to start the Fair Employment Practices Commission and end defense hiring discrimination, got Truman to desegregate the armed forces, and fought for antilynching legislation.

Wilberforce University: Founded in 1856, Wilberforce is the oldest private, historically black university, named after abolitionist William Wilberforce. Its location a historical stop on the Ohio Underground Railroad, Wilberforce early became a force in black education. During the Civil War, the university struggled with falling enrollment, until AME Bishop Daniel Payne purchased the property in 1862. He became its first president. The university educated generations of African American scholars, doctors, teachers, and politicians, and includes among its professors and students W. E. B. Du Bois, William S. Scarborough, and Floyd Flake.

Wilkins, Roy (1901–1981): Wilkins started his lifelong work in civil rights as a journalist from Missouri. He took over the NAACP *Crisis* magazine from W. E. B. Du Bois in the 1930s, and helped bring *Brown* to the Court. He joined A. Philip Randolph and Arnold Aronson in forming the Leadership Conference on Civil Rights in 1950 and became executive secretary of the NAACP in 1955. He worked on the March on Washington in 1963, the Selma-Montgomery marches in 1965, and advised Presidents from Kennedy to Carter on civil rights issues. He helped pass the Civil Rights Acts of the 1950s and 1960s and increased membership from 25,000 in 1930 to 400,000 when he stepped down in 1977.

Women's Political Council: Mary Fair Burks established the WPC in 1946 to improve the status of African Americans in Montgomery, Alabama. Its members, mostly middle class professionals, worked to civically engage and lobby on behalf of the black community. They helped initiate the Montgomery bus boycott in 1955, a precipitating event of the national civil rights movement, at which time they had over 200 members. Many members taught with Burks at Alabama State College, which investigated them for participating in the boycotts and eventually caused their resignation and the dispersal of the group.

Woodson, Carter G. (1875–1950): Born in Virginia, Woodson was one of the first African Americans to receive his Ph.D. from Harvard, which he did in 1912. He previously studied at Berea College and the University of Chicago, and worked as an education superintendent in the Philippines. In 1915, he cofounded the Association for the Study of Afro-American Life and History, and established the *Journal of Negro History*. This work earned him recognition as one of the first scholars of black history. Woodson was one of the first academics to study black history, and wrote books including *A Century of Negro Migration* (1918), *The Negro in Our History* (1922), and *Mis-Education of the*

Negro (1933). He lobbied to establish Negro History Week in February 1926, which evolved into Black History Month.

World Congress of Organizations of the Teaching Profession: Founded in 1951 from a merger of several international organizations of teachers, the WCOTP worked to advocate for teachers worldwide, merging in 1993 with its previous rival, the International Federation of Free Teachers' Unions, to form Education International. The organization advocates for fair teacher practices and equal pay, working to eliminate discrimination in educational professions.

Wright, Richard (1908–1960): Wright rose to fame as an African American poet and author who wrote about race relations throughout the United States. He grew up in Mississippi and only received a 9th grade education. He read American literature voraciously, ultimately joining the Federal Writers' Project. After moving to New York, he published *Uncle Tom's Children*, four stories that earned him a 1939 Guggenheim Fellowship. *Native Son* (1940) topped best-seller lists, and in 1945 published his most famous novel, *Black Boy*, an autobiographical work that detailed racial violence in the South. He moved to Paris in 1946 and continued to publish works on race and violence, including nonfiction *Black Power* (1954) and *The Long Dream* (1958).

Young, Whitney Jr. (1921–1971): Young started out as a teacher after attending Kentucky State Industrial College and then served in World War II. Earning his Masters in social work from the University of Minnesota, he joined the Urban League of St. Paul, which was working to find jobs for African Americans. He became the executive director of the National Urban League in 1961. He made the League a cosponsor of the March on Washington, prevented the League from going bankrupt and expanded its staff and mission. Young advised Presidents Kennedy, Nixon, and Johnson, to whom he presented the Domestic Marshall Plan, which shaped Johnson's policies and won Young the Presidential Medal of Freedom in 1968.

Zellner, Bob (1939–): Zellner grew up in southern Alabama amidst a family and culture of Ku Klux Klan members. While in college, his interest in the civil rights movement grew, and for his senior thesis he interviewed key leaders like Rosa Parks and Martin Luther King Jr. Graduating in 1961, he became the first white field secretary of SNCC, coordinating grassroots campaigns in Alabama, Georgia, and Virginia. He was jailed for his work over 18 times and was represented in court by black lawyers after white ones would refuse. He became a lecturer on social justice, race, and activism, and his own advocacy and civil disobedience continued. In 2000, he helped negotiate a land dispute for which he was arrested, and in 2013 he was arrested for protesting North Carolina's voter restrictions.

Notes

Foreword

1. Howard Gardner, *Leading Minds: An Anatomy of Leadership* (New York: Basic Books, 1995), 50.

Introduction
Black Leadership: A Collective Biography

1. Dorothy Height, *Explorations in Black Leadership*, Contemporary Lens on Black Leadership, Confronting Racism. For this and future references to the interviews in the Explorations in Black Leadership series, see www.blackleadership.virginia.edu
2. Gwen Moore, Ibid., Biographical Details of Leadership: Influence of Race and Gender on Leadership.
3. There is a rich social scientific literature on both leadership and race that focuses on the challenges faced by minorities. This literature addresses issues of trust, belief, legitimacy, and rapport and explores how race enters into hierarchical relationships. Sociologists analyze how cultural beliefs impact the potential for success, and examine how external characteristics such as gender, race, occupation, and educational attainment directly correlate with expectations for high status positions and the willingness to respect the authority of another. Women and minorities all too frequently face resistance that limits their ability to be recognized leaders and to maintain positions of authority. See, for example, Ronald A. Heifetz, *Leadership without Easy Answers* (Cambridge, MA: Belknap Press, 1994); Martin Chemers, "Leadership Effectiveness: Functional, Constructivist and Empirical Perspectives," in Dean van Knippenberg and Michael A. Hogg, eds., *Leadership and Power: Identity Processes in Groups and Organizations* (London: Sage Publications, 2003); Joseph Berger, Cecilia Ridgeway, M. Hamit Fisek and Robert Norman, "The Legitimation and Delegitimation of Power and Prestige Orders," *American Sociological Review*, Vol. 63 (June, 1998), 379–405.
4. Richard L. Zweigenhaft and G. William Domhoff, *Blacks in the White Establishment?: A Study of Race and Class in America* (New Haven, CT: Yale University Press, 1991), 175.
5. Berger et al., *American Sociological Review*, 397.
6. http://www.census.gov/newsroom/releases/archives/income_wealth/cb10-144.html.

7. http://www.census.gov/newsroom/releases/archives/income_wealth/cb12-172
.html

8. Mark Mather, "U.S. Children in Single-Mother Families," Population Reference
Bureau Data Brief, May 2010, 3. See also http://www.prb.org/pdf10/single
-motherfamilies.pdf

9. http://www.census.gov/prod/2012pubs/p20-566.pdf, p. 3. Asians experienced
the highest proportion of college graduates at 50 percent. In this category,
Hispanics remain at the lowest end at 13 percent, yet their income levels are
higher than those of black Americans by close to $6,000.

10. Solomon Moore, "Study Shows High Cost of Criminal Corrections" *The
New York Times,* March 2, 2009, A13; Ann E. Carson and William J. Sabol,
"Prisoners in 2011" (Washington, D.C.: US Dept. of Justice Bureau of Justice
Statistics, Dec. 2012), NCJ239808, p. 8. http://bjs.ojp.usdoj.gov/content/pub/
pdf/p11.pdf

11. Walter R. Allen, "African American Family Life in Societal Context: Crisis and
Hope," *Sociological Forum,* Vol. 10, No. 4, 591. For a further exploration of
these issues, see Eduardo Bonilla-Silva, *Racism Without Racists* (Lanham, MD:
Rowman and Littlefield, 2010); Joe Feagin and Karyn McKinney, *The Many
Costs of Racism.* (Lanham, MD: Rowman and Littlefield, 2003); Sharon Hays,
Flat Broke with Children (New York: Oxford University Press, 2003); Karen
Lacy, *Blue-Chip Black* (Berkeley, CA: University of California Press, 2007); Mary
Pattillo-McCoy, *Black Picket Fences* (Chicago, IL: Univerity of Chicago Press,
1999); Melvin Oliver and Thomas Shapiro, *Black Wealth/White Wealth: A New
Perspective on Racial Inequality* (New York: Routledge. 2006).

12. Cornel West, *Race Matters.* Boston, MA: Beacon Press, 2001.

13. Lynette Clementson and Allison Samuels, "We Have the Power," *Special Report:
Redefining Race in America. Newsweek* (September 18, 2000), 56–58.

14. Zweigenhaft and Domhoff, *Blacks in the White Establishment?: A Study of Race
and Class in America,* 145–152.

15. Elice E. Rogers, "Afritics from Margin to Center: Theorizing the Politics of
African American Women as Political Leaders," *Journal of Black Studies,* Vol. 35,
No. 6 (July 2005), 703.

16. Wade W. Nobles, "African Philosophy: Foundations for Black Psychology,"
in Reginald L. Jones, ed., *Black Psychology,* 3rd edition (Berkeley, CA: Cobb
and Henry Publishers, 1991), 47–63. See also Rogers, "Afritics from Margin
to Center: Theorizing the Politics of African American Women as Political
Leaders," *Journal of Black Studies,* 701–714.

17. The pronoun "we" is used here to denote the joint decisions of Julian Bond and me.
Together, we designed the nature and structure of the interviews in the *Explorations
in Black Leadership* project, and we came to a common understanding of the project's larger value and purpose. This book is the result of that strong collaboration.

18. We know that there are other African American leaders who actively pursue a nonpartisan approach to political leadership, rejecting the two-party system. Lenora
Fulani, for example, was the first African American and woman to appear on the
ballot in all 50 states, running for president in 1988. For an analysis of her role as a
political activist, see Omar H. Ali, "Lenora Branch Fulani: Challenging the Rules
of the Game," in Bruce A. Glasrud and Cary D. Wintz, *African Americans and the
Presidency: The Road to the White House* (New York: Routledge, 2010), 129–148.

19. Rita Dove, *Explorations in Black Leadership*, Biographical Details of Leadership, The Poet's Bond to Humanity.
20. Pero Gaglo Dagbovie, *African American History Reconsidered* (Urbana, Chicago: University of Illinois Press, 2010), 45–47. Dagbovie represents the views of Manning Marable in advocating for more "living histories" of African Americans centered on their personal life experiences.
21. Henry Louis Gates, Jr., ed., *Bearing Witness: Selections from African-American Autobiography in the Twentieth Century* (New York: Pantheon Books, 1991), 4.
22. Aaron S. Williams, *Explorations in Black Leadership*, Contemporary Lens on Black Leadership, What Leaders Do.
23. Stephen R. Covey, *The Seven Habits of Highly Effective People* (New York: Simon & Schuster, 1989); Stephen R. Covey, *The 8th Habit: From Effectiveness to Greatness* (Philadelphia, PA: The Running Press, 2006); Sheryl Sandberg, *Lean In: Women, Work, and the Will to Lead* (New York: Alfred A. Knopf, 2013). Although Covey and Sandberg are among the best known authors, many others have produced well known works. Among them are Jim Kouzes and Barry Posner, Bruce Avolio, John Maxwell, Warren Bennis, and Howard Gardner.
24. Warren Bennis, *Managing the Dream: Reflections on Leadership and Change* (Cambridge, MA: Perseus Publishing, 2000), 5–6; Bennis has published over a 40 year period and has produced close to 40 books. For a recent book of interest, see Warren Bennis and Burt Nanus, *Leaders: Strategies for Taking Charge* (New York: Harper Business Essentials, 2004).
25. Bennis, *Managing the Dream*, 281, 282.
26. Howard Gardner, *Leading Minds: An Anatomy of Leadership* (New York: Basic Books, 1995), 42–43.
27. Ibid., 8–9 (quote); see also 50.
28. Ibid., 13.
29. For an annotated bibliography, see Ronald W. Walters and Cedric Johnson, *Bibliography of African American Leadership: an Annotated Guide*. Westport, CT: Greenwood Press, 2000.
30. W. E. B. Du Bois, *The Souls of Black Folk* (Boston: Bedford/St. Martin's, 1997), 38.
31. Ernest Allen, Jr. "Du Boisian Double Consciousness: The Unsustainable Argument," *The Massachusetts Review*, Vol. 43, No. 2 (2002), 217–253.
32. Henry Louis Gates, Jr. and Cornel West, *The Future of the Race* (New York: Alfred A. Knopf, 1996), 3.
33. Ronald W. Walters and Robert C. Smith, *African American Leadership* (Albany, NY: State University of Press, 1999), 33.
34. Ibid., 74ff.
35. Ibid., 75. Representative books which deal with this topic include Walters and Smith, *African American Leadership*; Jacob Gordon, *Black Leadership for Social Change* (Westport, CT: Greenwood Press, 2000); Lea Esther Williams, *Servants of the People* (New York: St. Martins Press, 1966); Zweigenhaft and Domhoff, *Blacks in the White Establishment?*; West, *Race Matters*; Robert Smith, *We Have No Leaders: African Americans in the Post-Civil Rights Era* (Albany, NY: State University of New York Press, 1996); Ronald Walters and Cedric Johnson, *Bibliography of African American Leadership: An Annotated Guide* (Westport, CT: Greenwood Press, 2000).

36. Gordon, *Black Leadership for Social Change*, 41–56, 101–132. Gordon makes a useful distinction between ideological/intellectual and social movements. See also Williams, *Servants of the People*, xii–xiv, 1–9. For compilations on black leadership, see Henry Louis Gates, Jr. and Cornel West, *The African American Century: How Blacks Have Shaped Our Country* (New York: The Free Press, 2000) and David DeLeon, *Leaders from the 1960s: A Biographical Sourcebook of American Activism* (Westport, CT: Greenwood Press, 1994).

37. Ronald Walters and Robert Smith contend that at least until the 1980s, "...nearly all the students who sought to explain Black leadership theoretically did so in terms of the subordinate power position of Blacks relative to Whites." See Walters and Smith, *African American Leadership*, 64.

38. Gordon, *Black Leadership for Social Change*, 5.

39. Ibid., 35.

40. See, for example, M. Elaine Burgess, *Negro Leadership in a Southern City* (Chapel Hill: University of North Carolina Press, 1962); Daniel C. Thompson, *The Negro Leadership Class* (Englewood Cliffs, NJ: Prentice Hall, 1963); Everett C. Ladd, Jr., *Negro Political Leadership in the South* (New York: Atheneum, 1966); Jacob U. Gordon, *Black Leadership for Social Change*; Robert Smith, *We Have No Leaders: African Americans in the Post-Civil Rights Era*; Robert C. Smith, "System Values and African American Leadership," in Manning Marable and Kristin Clarke, eds., *Barack Obama and African American Empowerment: The Rise of Black America's New Leadership* (New York: Palgrave Macmillan, 2009); Manning Marable, *Black Leadership* (New York: Columbia University Press, 1998); Walters and Smith, *African American Leadership*, 17–21; Lenora Fulani, "Race, Identity, and Epistemology," in Lois Holzman and John Morss, eds., *Postmodern Psychologies, Societal Practice, and Political Life* (New York: Routledge, 2000), 151–164.

41. Williams, *Servants of the People*, 13–14.

42. Nathan I. Huggins, "Afro-Americans," in John Higham, ed., *Ethnic Leadership in America.* (Baltimore, MD: Johns Hopkins University Press, 1978), 107–108.

43. Bruce J. Avolio, *Full Leadership Development: Building the Vital Forces in Organizations.* (London: Sage Publications, 1999), xi–xii.

44. Anne Maydan Nicotera and Mircia J. Clinkscales with Felicia Walker, *Understanding Organizations through Culture and Structure: Relational and Other Lessons From the African American Organization.* (Mahwah, NJ: Lawrence Erlbaum Associates Publishers, 2003), 12, 68.

45. Marable, *Black Leadership*, 12–13.

46. Mary Frances Berry, *Explorations in Black Leadership*, Contemporary Lens on Black Leadership, Black Leadership: Engaging Issues of Race.

47. Johnnetta Cole, *Conversations: Straight Talk with America's Sister President* (New York: Doubleday, 1993), 1.

1 Defining Self: Oral history, Storytelling, and Leadership

1. Robert Franklin, *Explorations in Black Leadership*, Biographical Details of Leadership, Leadership: Potential. For url for QR code, see https://blackleader ship.virginia.edu/01QR

2. Katherine Nelson, "Self and Social Functions: Individual Autobiographical Memory and Collective Narrative," *Memory*, Vo. 11, No. 2 (Mar. 2003), 125; Sally Chandler, "Oral History across Generations: Age, Generational Identity and Oral Testimony," *Oral History*, Vol. 33, No. 2 (Autumn 2005), 50; William Cronon, "A Place for Stories: Nature, History, and Narrative," *The Journal of American History*, Vol. 78, No. 4 (Mar. 1992), 1347–1376.

3. Kathryn Nasstrom, "Between Memory and History: Autobiographies of the Civil Rights Movement and the Writing of Civil Rights History," *The Journal of Southern History*, Vol. LXXIV, No. 2 (May 2008), 347.

4. George W. Noblit and Van O. Dempsey, *The Social Construction of Virtue: The Moral Life of Schools* (Albany, NY: State University of New York Press, 1996), 207.

5. Adetayo Alabi, *Telling Our Stories: Continuities and Divergences in Black Autobiographies* (New York: Palgrave Macmillan, 2005), 5–7. Alabi analyzes such forms as folktales, epics, praise poems, religious testimonies, and witches' and wizards' confessions as examples of oral autobiographical approaches.

6. Joseph L. White, "Toward a Black Psychology," in Reginald L. Jones, ed., *Black Psychology*, 3rd edition (Berkeley, CA: Cobb and Henry Publishers, 1991), 10–11.

7. Adetayo Alabi, *Telling Our Stories*, 7, 12.

8. Ibid.

9. Joanne M. Braxton, *Black Women Writing Autobiography: A Tradition within a Tradition* (Philadelphia, PA: Temple University Press, 1989), 5. Braxton gratefully acknowledges the work of James Cone on the spirituals and the blues as foundational to her analysis of the role of the black autobiographer.

10. Ibid., 2, 30, 144.

11. Richard W. Leeman, ed., *African-America Orators: A Bio-Critical Sourcebook.* (Westport, CT: Greenwood Publishing Group, Inc., 1996), xiv–xx.

12. Stephen Butterfield, *Black Autobiography in America* (Amherst, MA: The University of Massachusetts Press, 1974), 284; Pero Gaglo Dagbovie, *African American History Reconsidered* (Urbana,,IL: University of Illinois Press, 2010), 46–47; Johnnetta Cole, *Conversations: Straight Talk with America's Sister President* (New York: Doubleday, 1993), 3; Van Dempsey and George Noblit, "Cultural Ignorance and School Desegregation: A Community Narrative," in Mwalimu J. Shujaa, *Beyond Desegregation: The Politics of Quality in African American Schooling* (Thousand Oaks, CA: Corwin Press, 1996), 117–118.

13. Henry Louis Gates, Jr., ed., *Bearing Witness: Selections from African-American Autobiography in the Twentieth Century* (New York: Pantheon Books, 1991), 4.

14. Vincent P. Franklin, *Living Our Stories, Telling Our Truths: Autobiography and the Making of the African-American Intellectual Tradition* (New York: Scribner and Sons, 1995), 13.

15. Gates, *Bearing Witness* 3, 6.

16. Butterfield, *Black Autobiography in America*,1, 6.

17. Ibid., 2–3.

18. For a starting point on the extensive literature on how personal memory relates to historical fact, see Valerie Raleigh Yow, *Recording Oral History: A Guide for the Humanities and Social Sciences*, 2nd edition (New York: Altamira Press, 2005), 58–62.

19. Barre Toelken, *The Dynamics of Folklore* (New York: Houghton Mifflin Company, 1979), 344–345.

20. Gates, *Bearing Witness*, 3, 7.

21. Codirector Julian Bond has known many of these leaders for years. Dialogue between him and interviewees often begin off camera with banter over shared events and shared interests. In many cases, memories go back to formative periods in youthful days, amid active engagement in the early stages of the civil rights movement. In some cases, lifelong friendships were created through those experiences. In other cases, paths crossed in legislative, policymaking circles, or nonprofit communities. People seem more willing to share stories and insights about themselves when there is established trust. Implicitly, the contexts of one another's lives resonate.

22. Mary Futrell, *Explorations in Black Leadership*, Biographical Details of Leadership, Education: Secondary.

23. Ibid.

24. Vernon Jordan, ibid., Contemporary Lens on Black Leadership, Influential People: Black Role Models.

25. Ibid.

26. Nikki Giovanni, ibid., Contemporary Lens on Black Leadership, A Poet's Constituency.

27. Ibid., Biographical Details of Leadership, How to Become a Poet.

28. Ibid., Early Childhood Influences.

29. Ibid., How to Become a Poet.

30. Ibid., Knoxville Segregation.

31. David J. Garrow, *Bearing the Cross: Martin Luther King, Jr., and the Southern Christian Leadership Conference* (Norwalk, CT: The Easton Press, 1986), 56.

32. Henry Marsh, *Explorations in Black Leadership*, Historical Focus on Race, Reflections on *Brown*.

33. Bill Gray, ibid., Historical Focus on Race, Reflections on *Brown*.

34. Carol Moseley Braun, ibid., Biographical Details of Leadership, Learning About Political Activism. For url for QR code, see https://blackleadership.virginia.edu/02QR

35. John Lewis, ibid., Contemporary Lens on Black Leadership, Ending Acts of Violence.

36. Elaine Jones, ibid., Biographical Details of Leadership, Education: Law School.

37. Bobby Lee Rush, ibid., Historical Focus on Race, The Killing of Fred Hampton.

38. Charles Ogletree, ibid., Contemporary Lens on Black Leadership, Leadership: Vision, Philosophy, and Style.

39. Ibid., Historical Focus on Race, Influence of *Brown*.

40. It is worth noting here Angela Davis's discussion in *Blues Legacies and Black Feminism* on the particular capacity of oral culture as a space for maintaining a discourse that cannot be maintained in other ways, as in the case, for instance, of women's blues as a space in which a discourse on domestic abuse, a taboo subject, could be opened (25). She discusses also the capacity of the African American oral tradition to preserve valuable aspects of culture from the time of slavery while simultaneously registering protest (xix); see Angela Davis, *Blues Legacies and Black Feminism* (New York: Pantheon Books, 1988).

41. Carol Moseley Braun, *Explorations in Black Leadership*, Contemporary Lens on Black Leadership, How are Leaders Created?
42. Bobby Rush, ibid., Inspired By History: Abraham Lincoln and Kit Carson.
43. Amiri Baraka, ibid., Biographical Details of Leadership, Influential Literature.
44. Robert Franklin, ibid., Biographical Details of Leadership, Influential Literature.
45. Benjamin Jealous, ibid., Biographical Details of Leadership, Leadership Development: Choosing a Career in Social Justice.
46. Nikki Giovanni, ibid., Historical Focus on Race, Answering to Ancestors.
47. Ibid., Contemporary Lens on Black Leadership, Generational Issues.
48. Amiri Baraka similarly notes individuals in the world of music who influenced his understanding of rhythm and verse and explicitly references these figures as part of a "historical continuum" that can be a source of pride and inspiration. See Baraka, *Explorations in Black Leadership*, Historical Focus on Race, Jazz and the Blues.
49. Vernon Jordan, ibid., Biographical Details of Leadership, Influential People: Ruby Hurley.
50. Nikki Giovanni, ibid., Biographical Details of Leadership, Early Childhood Influences.
51. Elaine Jones, ibid., Biographical Details of Leadership, Leadership: Risk-Taking.
52. Johnnetta Cole, ibid., Biographical Details of Leadership, Graduate School Experiences.
53. Ibid., Historical Focus on Race, Environment in Massachusetts.
54. Robert Franklin, ibid., Contemporary Lens on Black Leadership, Leadership: Developing Future Leadership.
55. Eleanor Holmes Norton, ibid., Contemporary Lens on Black Leadership, Leadership: Philosophy.
56. Ibid., Biographical Details of Leadership, Social Consciousness: Race and Gender.
57. Ibid., Leadership: Philosophy.
58. Elaine Jones, ibid., Contemporary Lens on Leadership, Leadership Styles. For url for QR code, see https://blackleadership.virginia.edu/03QR
59. Jacquelyn Dowd Hall, "'You Must Remember This'": Autobiography as Social Critique," *The Journal of American History* Vol. 85, No. 2 (Sept. 1998), 440, n.2. For the important connections between memory and history in the creation of civil rights autobiography, see Nasstrom, "Between Memory and History: Autobiographies of the Civil Rights Movement and the Writing of Civil Rights History," *The Journal of Southern History*, 325–364.
60. Hall, " 'You Must Remember This'", *Journal of American History*, 465.
61. Johnnetta B. Cole, *Conversations*, 3.

2 Families: Extended and Fictive Kin, Racial Socialization, Diligence

1. Eleanor Holmes Norton, *Explorations in Black Leadership*, Biographical Details of Leadership, Influential People: Family.

2. Ibid. For url for QR code, see https://blackleadership.virginia.edu/04QR
3. Andrew Billingsley, *Black Families in White America* (New Jersey: Prentice Hall, Inc., 1968), 21.
4. David Popenoe, "American Family Decline, 1960–1990: A Review and Appraisal," *Journal of Marriage and Family*, Vol. 55, No. 3 (Aug.1993), 527–542; Frances Goldscheider and Linda Waite, *New Families, No Families?: The Transformation of the American Home* (Berkeley, CA: University of California Press, 1991); Jay MacLeod, *Ain't No Makin' It*. (Boulder, CO: Westview Press, Inc, 1987), 50–60; William J. Wilson, *The Truly Disadvantaged* (Chicago, IL: University of Chicago Press, 1987). For further discussion on this issue see, Maxine Baca Zinn, "Feminism and Family Studies for a New Century," *Annals of the American Academy of Political and Social Science*, Vol. 571 (2000), 42–56; Stephanie Coontz, *The Way We Never Were: American Families and the Nostalgia Trap* (New York: Basic Books, 1992).
5. These include William Gray, Calvin Butts, Eleanor Holmes Norton, Nikki Giovanni, Vivian Pinn, Charles Rangel, William Raspberry, Diane Watson, Oliver Hill, Lucius Theus, Douglas Wilder, Armstrong Williams, Earl Graves, Gwen Ifill, Gwen Moore, James Clyburn, Barbara Lee, Geoffrey Canada, and Roger Wilkins.
6. For further discussion of these themes, see Linda Chatters, Robert Joseph Taylor, and Rukmalie Jayakody, "Fictive Kinship Relations in Black Extended Families," *Journal of Comparative Family Studies*, Vol. 25, No. 3 (Autumn 1994), 297–312; Shirley A. Hill and Joey Sprague, "Parenting in Black and White Families: The Interaction of Gender with Race and Class," *Gender and Society*, Vol. 13, No. 4 (Aug.1999), 480–502; Elmer P. Martin and Joanne Mitchell Martin, *The Black Extended Family* (Chicago, IL: The University of Chicago Press, 1978); Wade Nobles, "African American Family Life: An Instrument of Culture," in Harriette Pipes McAdoo, ed., *Black Families* (Thousand Oaks, CA: Sage Publications, Inc., 2007), 69–78.
7. Nobles, "African American Family Life: An Instrument of Culture," in *Black Families*; Niara Sudarkasa, "An Exposition of the Value Premises underlying Black Family Studies," *Journal of the National Medical Association*. Vol. 19 (May 1975), 235–239; Niara Sudarkasa, "Interpreting the African Heritage in Afro-American Family Organization," in *Black Families*, 29–47. White families honor blood (or consanguineal) ties but also place primary emphasis on relational ties via marriage, while black families tend to reinforce the centrality of the family based on multigenerational blood ties.
8. Herbert Gutman, *The Black Family in Slavery and Freedom: 1750–1925* (New York: Random House, 1976), *201–204*; Frank Furstenberg, "The Making of the Black Family: Race and Class in Qualitative Studies in the Twentieth Century," *Annual Review of Sociology*, Vol. 33 (2007), 432; Leanor Boulin Johnson and Robert Staples, *Black Families at the Crossroads: Challenges and Prospects* (San Francisco, CA: Jossey-Bass, 2005), 251.
9. Johnson and Staples, ibid.; Karen Hansen, *Not-So-Nuclear Families: Class, Gender and Networks of Care* (New Brunswick, NJ: Rutgers University Press, 2005); Carol Stack, *All Our Kin* (New York: Basic Books, 1974).

10. Robert Joseph Taylor, Linda M. Chatters, M. Belinda Tucker, and Edith Lewis, "Developments in Research on Black Families: A Decade Review," *Journal of Marriage and the Family*, Vol. 52, No. 4, (Nov., 1990), 997.
11. Amiri Baraka, *The Autobiography of LeRoi Jones* (Chicago, IL: Lawrence Hill Books, 1984), 11–22 passim.
12. Ibid., 18–19.
13. Amiri Baraka, *Explorations in Black Leadership*, Biographical Details of Leadership, Influential People: Parents.
14. Elmer Martin and Joanne Martin conducted a thorough study of black families in the 1970s. They found that black families of that era had a deep respect for elders because of the wisdom they held from surviving racism and difficult times: "Elderly members of black extended families have knowledge of survival techniques which they learned through their own life experiences or which were passed on to them by earlier generations of black people." See *The Black Extended Family*, 35–36.
15. Keisha Saul, "Black History Month Profile: Poet Amiri Baraka," *The African*, June 1, 2013, http://www.africanmag.com/ARTICLE-626-design001.
16. Baraka, *Autobiography of LeRoi Jones*, 17.
17. Ibid., 22.
18. Ibid., 42.
19. Baraka, *Explorations in Black Leadership*, Biographical Details of Leadership, Influential People: Parents.
20. Ibid., Great Grandmother.
21. Rev. Calvin Butts, ibid., Biographical Details of Leadership, Early Mentors: Extended Kin; Early Mentors: Uncle Leon and Uncle James.
22. John Lewis, ibid., Biographical Details of Leadership, Influential People: Family.
23. Diane Watson, ibid., Biographical Details of Leadership, Early Teachers and Community.
24. Charles Rangel, ibid., Biographical Details of Leadership, Influential People: Family.
25. Nikki Giovanni, ibid., Biographical Details of Leadership, Early Childhood Influences.
26. Clarence Thomas, *My Grandfather's Son: A Memoir* (New York: HarperCollins, 2007), 3–12.
27. Clarence Thomas, *Explorations in Black Leadership*, Historical Focus on Race, Reflections on Brown, Personal Experiences and Race Consciousness; Biographical Details of Leadership, Grandfather's Influence; Contemporary Lens on Black Leadership, Learning and Teaching Leadership: The Right and the Just. See also, Thomas, *My Grandfather's Son*, 12.
28. Thomas, *My Grandfather's Son*, 10–21.
29. Ibid., 7, x[quote].
30. bell hooks, "Revolutionary Parenting," in Karen Hansen and Anita Garey, eds., *Families in the U.S.: Kinship and Domestic Policies* (Philadelphia, PA: Temple University Press, 1998), 587–596.
31. Clarence Thomas, *Explorations in Black Leadership*, Biographical Details of Leadership, Influential People: Neighbors and Sister Mary Virgilius. For url for QR code, see https://blackleadership.virginia.edu/05QR

32. Linda Chatters, Robert Joseph, and Rukmalie Jayakody, "Fictive Kinship Relations in Black Extended Families," *Journal of Comparative Family Studies*, Vol. 25, No. 3 (Autumn1994), 301–303.

33. Yvonne Scruggs-Leftwich, *Explorations in Black Leadership*, Biographical Details of Leadership, Influential People: Parents; Social Consciousness: Gender.

34. Ibid., Influential People: Parents.

35. Ibid.

36. For further documentation of these ideas, see Andrew Billingley, *Climbing Jacob's Ladder* (New York: Simon & Schuster, 1992), 30–35; Johnson and Staples, *Black Families at the Crossroads*, 245–246; Taylor et al., "Developments in Research on Black Families," *Journal of Marriage and Family* (1990), 1000.

37. Carol Moseley Braun, *Explorations in Black Leadership*, Historical Focus on Race: Memories of *Brown v. Board of Education*.

38. Oliver Hill, ibid., Biographical Details of Leadership, Influential People.

39. Lucius Theus, ibid., Biographical Details of Leadership, The Community.

40. Douglas Wilder, ibid., Biographical Details of Leadership, Influential People and Community.

41. Patricia Reid-Merritt, *Sister Power: How Phenomenal Black Women Are Rising to the Top* (New York: John Wiley & Sons, 1996), 39–42.

42. Johnnetta Cole, *Conversations: Straight Talk with America's Sister President* (New York: Doubleday, 1993), 9–10.

43. Mary Futrell, *Explorations in Black Leadership*, Biographical Details of Leadership, Influential People: Community Members. For more information on Futrell's background and family context, see chapter 3.

44. Taylor et al., "Developments in Research on Black Families," *Journal of Marriage and the Family*, 994 ff.

45. Pamela P. Martin and Harriette Pipes McAdoo, "Sources of Racial Socialization: Theological Orientation of African American Churches and Parents," in *Black Families*, 4th edition. (Thousand Oaks, CA: Sage Publications, Inc., 2007), 126ff.

46. For additional examples, see Vernon Jordan, *Explorations in Black Leadership*, Historical Focus on Race, Social Consciousness: Segregation; William Raspberry, Biographical Details of Leadership, Parental Teachings and Community Values; Robert Franklin, Biographical Details of Leadership, Influential People: Parents.

47. See interviews of Roger Wilkins, Eleanor Holmes Norton, Johnnetta Cole, Diane Watson, Gwen Ifill, and Gwen Moore for examples of racial pride messages.

48. Billingsley, *Climbing Jacob's Ladder*, 223–227; Nobles, "African American Family Life," in *Black Families*, 74–76; Stephanie I. Coard and Robert M. Sellers, "African American Families as a Context for Racial Socialization," in Vonnie C. McLoyd, Nancy E. Hill, and Kenneth A. Dodge, eds., *African American Family Life: Ecological and Cultural Diversity* (New York: Guilford Press, 2005), 264–267; Martin and McAdoo, "Sources of Racial Socialization," *Black Families*, 132–133.

49. Amiri Baraka, *Explorations in Black Leadership*, Historical Focus on Race: Responses to Racism. For url for QR code, see https://blackleadership.virginia.edu/06QR

50. Nobles, "African American Family Life," in *Black Families*, 74.

51. Amiri Baraka, *Explorations in Black Leadership,* Historical Focus on Race: Reflections on *Brown.*

52. Lionel D. Scott, Jr., "The Relation of Racial Identity and Racial Socialization to Coping with Discrimination among African American Adolescents," *Journal of Black Studies,* Vol. 33, No. 4 (Mar. 2003), 520–538.

53. Aldon Morris and Naomi Braine, "Social Movements and Oppositional Consciousness," in *Oppositional Consciousness: The Subjective Roots of Social Protest* (Chicago, IL: The University of Chicago, Press, 2001), 22; Cedric Johnson, *Revolutionaries to Race Leaders: Black Power and the Making of African American Politics* (Minneapolis, MN: University of Minnesota Press, 2007), 42–43, 53–54, 71.

54. Earl Graves, *Explorations in Black Leadership,* Biographical Details of Leadership, Influential People: Parents.

55. Earl Graves, ibid., Historical Focus on Race, Social Consciousness: Race and Society.

56. Clarence Thomas, ibid., Biographical Details of Leadership, Grandfather's Influence.

57. For more information on the personal background of Franklin, see chapter 4.

58. Robert Franklin, *Explorations in Black Leadership,* Biographical Details of Leadership, Influential People: Parents.

59. William H. Gray, ibid., Biographical Details of Leadership, Leadership—Foundational Experiences.

60. Vernon Jordan, ibid., Historical Focus on Race, Social Consciousness: Segregation.

61. Yvonne Scruggs-Leftwich, ibid., Biographical Details of Leadership, Influential People: Parents; Social Consciousness: Gender. For url for QR code, see https://blackleadership.virginia.edu/07QR

62. Carol Moseley Braun, ibid., Biographical Details of Leadership, Influential People: Parents, Grandparents, and Artists.

63. Barbara Lee, ibid., Biographical Details of Leadership, Gender Consciousness: Mother.

64. Billingley, *Climbing Jacob's Ladder,* 223.

65. W. E. B. Du Bois, *The Souls of Black Folk* (Boston: Beford/St. Martin's, 1997), 38.

66. Clarence Thomas, *My Grandfather's Son,* 21–26.

67. Clarence Thomas, *Explorations in Black Leadership,* Historical Focus on Race: Reflections on *Brown.*

68. Ibid., Historical Focus on Race, Personal Experiences and Race Consciousness.

69. Geoffrey Canada, ibid., Biographical Details of Leadership, Work Ethic from Grandfather.

70. Carol Moseley Braun, ibid., Contemporary Lens on Black Leadership, Doing the "Best Job" as a Leadership Philosophy.

71. Lois Benjamin, *Three Black Generations at the Crossroads* (Lanham, MD: Rowman & Littlefield, 2007); Hill and Sprague, "Parenting in Black and White Families," *Gender and Society* (1999), 480–502; Billingsley, *Climbing Jacob's Ladder.*

72. Carter Savage, "'Because We Did More with Less': The Agency of African American Teachers in Franklin, Tennessee: 1890–1967," *Peabody Journal of*

Education, Vol. 76, No. 2 (Jan. 2001), 170–203; Michael Herndon and Joan Hirt, "Black Students and Their Families: What Leads to Success in College," *Journal of Black Studies*, Vol. 34, No. 4 (Mar. 2004), 489–513.

73. Vernon Jordan, *Explorations in Black Leadership*, Biographical Details of Leadership, Education: Undergraduate. For url for QR code, see https://black leadership.virginia.edu/08QR

74. Yvonne Scruggs-Leftwich, ibid., Biographical Details of Leadership, Social Consciousness—Gender.

75. Calvin Butts, ibid., Biographical Details of Leadership, Family Influences.

76. For more information on the personal background of Henry Marsh, see chapter 5.

77. Henry Marsh, *Explorations in Black Leadership*, Biographical Details of Leadership, Influential People—Parents.

78. Ibid.

79. Robert Bernard Hill, *The Strengths of African American Families* (Lanham, MD: University Press of America, Inc, 1999); Hill and Sprague, "Parenting in Black and White Families," *Gender and Society*, (1999), 480–502; Johnson and Staples, *Black Families at the Crossroads*, 262–264.

80. Paula Giddings, *When and Where I Enter: the Impact of Black Women on Race and Sex in America* (New York: Amistad, 2006), 101; Savage, "Because We Did More with Less," *Peabody Journal of Education* (2001), 170–203.

81. Amiri Baraka, *Explorations in Black Leadership*, Biographical Details of Leadership, Influential People: Parents.

82. E. Franklin Frazier, *The Negro Family in the United States* (Chicago, IL: The University of Chicago Press, 1939). See also Norman R. Yetman, "Patterns of Ethnic Integration in America," in Norman Yetman, ed., *Majority and Minority: The Dynamics of Race and Ethnicity in American Life*, (Boston, MA: Allyn and Bacon, 1999), 227–271.

83. Anthony M. Platt, "Introduction," in E. Franklin Frazier, *The Negro Family in the United States* (Notre Dame, IN: University of Notre Dame Press, 2001), xxv. Platt's introduction offers a thoughtful overview of Frazier's work, placing it in historiographical context with other works and trends.

84. Gunnar Myrdal, *An American Dilemma: The Negro Problem and Modern Democracy* (New York: Harper & Brothers Publishers, 1944), Vol. II, 930–931.

85. Daniel P. Moynihan, *The Negro Family: The Case for National Action* (Washington, D.C.: Office of Policy Planning and Research, 1965).

86. http://www.dol.gov/oasam/programs/history/moynchapter4.htm. Moynihan's view was supported and reinforced by Jessie Bernard, widely cited as one of the founders of family sociology. He argued that black female-headed families reflected a distinctly black adherence to hedonistic lifestyles. See Bernard, *Marriage and Family among Negroes* (Englewood Cliffs, NJ: Prentice-Hall, 1966).

87. Critics claimed that Moynihan used simplistic logic, inadequate empirical evidence, and based his report on inaccurate premises. He was criticized for attacking the morality of the black family and was viewed as something of a racist. Both black and white religious leaders gathered to demand that "family stability" not be the focus of the White House Conference on Civil Rights.

Throughout the country, black leaders like Floyd McKissick, Martin Luther King, Jr., John Lewis, and Bayard Rustin reacted angrily. Floyd McKissick of the Congress of Racial Equality (CORE) asserted that Moynihan's fallacy was that he assumed that everyone's family structure should look like that of middle-class America. It was, in fact, the "damn system that needs changing and Moynihan was essentially 'blaming the victim.'" George Wiley, founder of the National Welfare Rights Organization, critiqued Moynihan for focusing on problems within the black family when racism was still such a destructive and prevalent force.

Scholars also responded to Moynihan's thesis, giving rise to a "revisionist" scholarship. This research sought to reframe black families as similar to white families in their structure and norms and to further identify the unique strengths of black families. Some scholars focused on the adaptive abilities of black families and their resiliency despite oppressive conditions and racism. Their work cited cultural strengths of black families including a strong work ethic, a focus on children, an incorporation of extended kin in daily life, a respect for elders, and a tradition of help and assistance that oriented family members around the functional necessity to aid one another. See Billingsley, *Climbing Jacob's Ladder*; Hill and Sprague, "Parenting in Black and White Families," *Gender and Society;* Martin and Martin, *The Black Extended Family.* For further discussion, see Kay S. Hymowitz, "The Black Family: 40 Years of Lies," *City Journal* (Summer 2005); Thomas Meehan, "Moynihan of the Moynihan Report," *The New York Times Magazine* (July 31, 1966). Among revisionist work, probably the most well known was the historical analysis in *The Black Family in Slavery and Freedom: 1750–1925.* Gutman used plantation records to prove that black enslaved families were not pathologically dysfunctional. Gutman pointed to significant numbers of relationships that were consecrated through marriage, had a patriarchal structure, and were governed by two parents. For additional relevant materials critical of Moynihan's approach, see Giddings, *When and Where I Enter,* 325 ff..

88. William J. Wilson, *The Declining Significance of Race* (Chicago, IL: University of Chicago Press, 1978); William J. Wilson, *The Truly Disadvantaged: the Innter City, the Underclass, and Public Policy* (Chicago, IL: University of Chicago Press, 1987).

89. See, for example, Kathryn Edin and Maria Kefalas, *Promises I Can Keep: Why Poor Women Put Motherhood Before Marriage* (Berkeley, CA: University of California Press, 2005); Sharon Hays, *Flat Broke with Children* (New York: Oxford University Press, 2003); Karyn Lacy, *Blue-Chip Black: Race, Class, and Status in the New Black Middle Class* (Berkeley, CA: University of California Press, 2007); Annette Lareau, *Unequal Childhoods: Class, Race and Family Life* (Berkeley, CA: University of California Press, 2003); Mary Pattillo-McCoy, *Black Picket Fences* (Chicago, IL: University of Chicago Press, 1999); Debra Van Ausdale and Joe Feagin, *The First R: How Children Learn Race and Racism* (Lanham, MD: Rowman and Littlefield Publishers, 2001).

90. For a good general overview, see Walter R. Allen, "African American Family Life in Societal Context: Crisis and Hope," *Sociological Forum,* Vol. 10, No. 4, Special Issue: African Americans and Sociology: A Critical Analysis (Dec., 1995), 569–592.

91. Eleanor Holmes Norton, *Explorations in Black Leadership*, Contemporary Lens on Black Leadership: Social Consciousness: Race, Class and Society.

92. Jason DeParle and Sabrina Tavernise, "For Women Under 30, Most Births Occur Outside Marriage," *The New York Times*, February 18, 2012. [http://www.nytimes.com/2012/02/18/us/for-women-under-30-most-births-occur-outside-marriage.html?pagewanted=all&_r=0]

93. http://www.cdc.gov/nchs/data/nvsr/nvsr48/nvs48_16.pdf

94. John Lewis, *Explorations in Black Leadership*, Contemporary Lens on Black Leadership, The American House and MLK's Dream.

3 Education: Caring Communities

1. Carol Moseley Braun, *Explorations in Black Leadership*, Contemporary Lens on Black Leadership, Nurturing Future Leaders.

2. Others who comment on the relative value of segregated and integrated education include Carol Moseley Braun, Elaine Jones, Eleanor Holmes Norton, Angela Davis, Julian Bond, Henry Marsh, and Diane Watson.

3. Dennis Hevesi, "William Raspberry, Prizewinning Columnist, Dies at 76," *The New York Times*, Jul. 18, 2012, A20.

4. William Raspberry, *Explorations in Black Leadership*, Biographical Details of Leadership, Parental Teachings and Community Values.

5. Chuck Conconi, "Making a Difference," *Washingtonian* (Dec. 2003), 43–46.

6. William Raspberry, *Explorations in Black Leadership*, Biographical Details of Leadership, Discovering a Personal Career Path; "William Raspberry," in *Contemporary Authors Online* (Farmington Mills, MI: The Gale Group, 2002).

7. "Raspberry Gets Company, at Last," Capital Comment, *Washingtonian* (Dec. 1993).

8. Johnnetta B. Cole, *Conversations: Straight Talk with America's Sister President* (New York: Doubleday, 1993), 6–7, 10.

9. Cole, *Conversations*, 5.

10. Johnnetta Cole, *Explorations in Black Leadership*, Historical Focus on Race, Race Consciousness.

11. Mary Catherine Bateson, *Composing a Life* (New York: The Atlantic Monthly Press, 1989), 43–44; Cole, *Conversations*, 12.

12. Mary Hatwood Futrell, "Mama and Miss Jordan," *Reader's Digest* 135 (Jul. 1989), 75.

13. Jean Hunter, "For the VEA President Opportunity Comes Wearing Overalls," *Virginia Journal of Education*, Vol. 70, No. 1 (Sept. 1976), 14.

14. "7000 Teachers Rally for Kids," *VEA News* (Feb. 1977), 1.

15. Eve Zibart, "Educator From Alexandria Elected President of NEA, *The Washington Post*, Jul. 3, 1983, B1.

16. For biographical details, see *Explorations in Black Leadership* interview. Also see http://www.thehistorymakers.com/biography/freeman-hrabowski-39

17. Geoffrey Canada, *Fist Stick Knife Gun: A Personal History of Violence in America* (Boston, MA: Beacon Press, 1995) is Canada's first-hand account of his early life experiences in the South Bronx.

18. For biographical details, see *Explorations in Black Leadership* interview; also see http://www.biography.com/people/geoffrey-canada-537578

19. Felicia R. Lee, "Coping: For Harlem's Children, a Catcher in the Rye," *The New York Times*, January 9, 2000. See also Paul Tough, "The Harlem Project," *New York Times Magazine* (June 20, 2004), 1–14 [http://www.most.ie/webreports /HarlemChildrenszonenytimes_062004.pdf]

20. Rita Dove, *Explorations in Black Leadership*, Biographical Details of Leadership, Father's Racial Socialization Messages.

21. Ibid., Influential People: Parents.

22. Ibid., Integrated Schools.

23. Ibid., Black Literary Role Models.

24. For a full biography, see http://people.virginia.edu/~rfd4b/compbio.html

25. Charles Ogletree, *Explorations in Black Leadership*, Historical Focus on Race, Reflections on *Brown*.

26. Henry Allen Bullock, *A History of Negro Education in the South from 1619 to the Present* (New York: Praeger, 1967), 3.

27. Gunnar Myrdal, *An American Dilmma: The Negro Problem and Modern Democracy*, Vol. II (New York: Harper Brothers, 1944), 887; Bullock, *Negro Education in the South*, 11–12. See also http://www.pbs.org/wnet/slavery/expe rience/education/history.html

28. Bullock, *Negro Education in the South*, 10, 14–15.

29. V. P. Franklin, *Black Self-Determination: A Cultural History of African-American Resistance* (New York: Lawrence Hill Books, 1992), 164.

30. Ibid.,165.

31. Adam Fairclough, "'Being in the Field of Education and also Being a Negro... Seems...Tragic': Black Education in the Jim Crow South," *The Journal of American History*, Vol. 87, No. 1 (June 2000), 67. See also V. P. Franklin, *Black Self-Determination*, 147–185.

32. Adam Fairclough, *Teaching Equality: Black Schools in the Age of Jim Crow* (Athens, GA: University of Georgia Press, 2001), 3. The famous educational philosopher Paulo Freire argued that educational pedagogies in the United States and elsewhere around the globe, structured around capitalist values, continue to treat the underclasses as disposable and expendable, thereby perpetuating inequality. See Paulo Freire, *Pedagogy of the Oppressed*, trans. Myra B. Ramos (New York: Herder and Herder, 1970).

33. Fairclough, *Teaching Equality*, 9.

34. Illiteracy rates for whites in 1870 were reported at 8.5 percent. See http://site-maker.umich.edu/educationalequity/african_american_timeline

35. Fairclough, "Being in the Field of Education,"*Journal of American History*, 65–66.

36. V. P. Franklin, "Introduction," in V. P. Franklin and Carter Julian Savage, eds., *Cultural Capital and Black Education* (Greenwich, CT: Information Age Publishing, 2004), xii.

37. Carter Julian Savage, "Cultural Capital and African-American Agency: The Economic Struggle for Effective Education for African Americans in Franklin, Tennessee, 1890–1967," *The Journal of African American History*, Vol. 88 (Spring 2002), 208. See also Paul David Phillips, "Education of Blacks in Tennessee

during Reconstruction, 1865–1870" and Dorothy Granberry, "Origins of an African American School in Haywood County," in Carroll Van West, ed., *Trial and Triumph: Essays in Tennessee's African American History* (Knoxville, TN: University of Tennessee Press, 2002), 145–183; Franklin, *Black Self-Determination*, 147–185; Franklin, "Introduction," *Cultural Capital and Black Education*, xiv.

38. John S. Butler, "The Return of Open Debate," *Society* (March–April 1996), 14–15. See also V. P. Franklin, "Cultural Capital and Black Higher Education: The AME Colleges and Universities as Collective Economic Enterprises, 1865–1910," *Cultural Capital and Black Education*, 35–47. Lincoln University, in Pennsylvania, was founded by a Presbyterian minister and his wife in 1854 and has the distinction of being the first degree-awarding HBCU in the United States.

39. Myrdal, *American Dilemma II*, 890–891.

40. Horace Mann Bond, "The Negro Elementary School and the Cultural Pattern," *Journal of Educational Sociology*, Vol. 13, No. 8 (Apr. 1940), 480; Adam Fairclough, *A Class of Their Own: Black Teachers in the Segregated South* (Cambridge, MA: Harvard University Press, 2007), 14.

41. For further discussion of this issue, see Michael Fultz, "Black Public Libraries in the South in the Era of De Jure Segregation," *Libraries and the Cultural Record*, Vol. 41, No. 3 (Summer 2006), 338–359 and Michael Fultz, Teacher Training and African American Education in the South, 1900–1940," *The Journal of Negro Education*, Vol. 64, No. 2 (Spring 1995), 196–210.

42. William H. Watkins, "Reclaiming Historical Visions of Quality Schooling: The Legacy of Early 20th-Century Black Intellectuals," in Mwalimu Shujaa, ed., *Beyond Desegregation: The Politics of Quality in African American Schooling* (Thousand Oaks, CA: Corwin Press, Inc., 1996), 6–26. In 1895, Mary Church Terrell became the first African American and one of two women to serve on the Board of Education in the District of Columbia. See Beverly Washington Jones, *Quest for Equality: The Life and Writings of Mary Eliza Church Terrell, 1864–1954* (New York: Carlson Publishing Inc., 1990), 48.

43. In his famous 1895 Atlanta speech, Washington said: "To those of my race...who underestimate the importance of cultivating friendly relations with the Southern white man.... I would say: 'Cast down your bucket where you are,—cast it down in making friends in every manly way of the people of all races by whom we are surrounded. Cast it down in agriculture, mechanics, in commerce, in domestic service, and in the professions.... Our greatest danger is that in the great leap from slavery to freedom we may overlook the fact that the masses of us are to live by the productions of our hands.... No race can prosper till it learns that there is as much dignity in tilling a field as in writing a poem. It is at the bottom of life we must begin, and not at the top." See Booker T. Washington, *Up From Slavery: An Autobiography* (New York: Dodd, Mead & Company, 1965), 98; 139–40 [quote]; Myrdal, *American Dilemma*, II, 889.

44. W. E. B. Du Bois argued for this most persuasively in "The Talented Tenth":"If we make money the object of man-training, we shall develop money-makers but not necessarily men; if we make technical skill the object of education, we may possess artisans, but not in nature, men. Men we shall have only as we make

manhood the object of the schools—intelligence, broad sympathy, knowledge of the world that was and is, and of the relation of men to it—this is the curriculum of that Higher Education that must underlie true life." See "TheTalented Tenth," in August Meier, Elliott Rudwick and Francis Broderick, eds., *Black Protest Thought in the Twentieth Century* (New York: Macmillan, 1985), 48. To support his agenda, DuBois spearheaded the Niagara Movement and issued a call for full civil rights for African Americans. By 1911, the Niagara Movement evolved into the NAACP.

45. *Explorations in Black Leadership,* Historical Focus on Race, Private Education.
46. Ibid., Biographical Details of Leadership, Parental Teachings and Community Values.
47. Adam Fairclough, "'Being in the Field of Education,'" *The Journal of American History,* 68. For details on disparities between black and white education, see Bullock, *Negro Education in the South,* Chapter 7, 167ff; Fultz, "Teacher Training and African-American Education;" and Vanessa Siddle Walker, "African American Teaching in the South: 1940–1960," *American Educational Research Journal,* Vol. 38, No. 4 (Winter 2001), 755ff.
48. Bullock, ibid., 147.
49. Fultz, "Teacher Training and African American Education," 197–201.
50. Fairclough, *Teaching Equality,* 11–12.
51. Fairclough, ibid., 14; Fairclough, *A Class of Their Own,* 15.
52. Fairclough, "Being in the Field of Education," *The Journal of American History,* 88; Fairclough, *Teaching Equality,* 57–58.
53. Fairclough, ibid., 16; see also Fairclough, *A Class of Their Own,* 4–5.
54. Vanessa Siddle-Walker, "Valued Segregated Schools for African-American Children in the South, 1935–1969: A Review of Common Themes and Characteristics," *Review of Educational Research,* Vol. 73, No. 3 (Autumn 2000), 259.
55. For a fuller description of these conditions, see Bullock, *History of Negro Education in the South,* Chapter 7.
56. Fairclough, *A Class of Their Own,* 267–306.
57. See, for example, Vivian Gunn Morris and Curtis L. Morris, *The Price They Paid: Desegregation in an African American Community* (New York: Teachers College Press, 2002); Vivian Gunn Morris and Curtis L. Morris, *Creating Caring and Nurturing Educational Environments for African American Children* (Westport, CT: Bergin and Garvey, 2000); David S. Cecelski, *Along Freedom Road: Hyde County, North Carolina, and the Fate of Black Schools in the South* (Chapel Hill, NC: University of North Carolina Press, 1994); Siddle Walker, "Valued Segregated Schools for African American Children in the South, 1935–1969," *Review of Educational Research,* Vol. 70, No. 3 (Autumn, 2000), 253–285; Lauri Johnson, "A Generation of Women Activists: African American Female Educators in Harlem, 1930–1950," *The Journal of African American History,* Vol. 89, No. 3 (Summer 2004), 223–240.
58. Fairclough, *Teaching Equality,* 43.
59. Siddle-Walker, "Valued Segregated Schools," *Review of Educational Research,* 267–270.
60. Ibid., 272.

61. Ibid., 271–274. See also Van Dempsey and George Noblit, "Cultural Ignorance and School Desegregation, A Community Narrative," in Mwalimu J. Shujaa, ed., *Beyond Desegregation: The Politics of Quality in African American Schooling* (Thousand Oaks, CA: Corwin Press, 1996), 115 ff; Morris, *The Price They Paid,* 94–109; Morris, *Creating Caring and Nurturing Cultural Environments.*

62. Ibid.

63. Asa Hilliard, "Foreward," in Morris, *Price They Paid,* xi. See also Morris and Morris, *Creating Caring and Nurturing Educational Environments for African American Children,* 174ff. The work of the Morris's centers on Trenholm High School in Tuscumbia, Alabama, but their findings are consistent with those of other scholars. See ibid., 1–3 and fn 67 below.

64. Fairclough, *A Class of Their Own,* 4.

65. Fairclough, *A Class of Their Own,* 311 ff.

66. Siddle-Walker, "Valued Segregated Education," *Review of Educational Research,* 265 ff.

67. Emilie V. Siddle Walker, "Can Institutions Care? Evidence from the Segregated School of African American Children," in Shujaa, *Beyond Desegregation: The Politics of Quality in African American Schooling,* 215–216.

68. Paulo Freire, the Brazilian Marxist philosopher, argued for a "pedagogy of love" as a means to overcome capitalist oppressive systems of education. Such a pedagogy could lead to liberation and societal transformation if networks of parents, teachers, and community members came together to reinforce a set of common values. The human values he stressed for effective learning included humility, courage, self-confidence, self-respect, and respect for others. In effect, he was describing what occurred in many of these segregated communities. See Antonia Darder, *Reinventing Paulo Freire: A Pedagogy of Love* (Boulder, CO: Westview Press, 2002), 45–49.

69. Steven F. Lawson and Charles Payne, *Debating the Civil Rights Movement, 1945–1968* (New York: Rowman and Littlefield, 2006), 117–119.

70. Fairclough, *A Class of Their Own,* 309–353. Fairclough contends that some of the teachers were bullied into silence, as the NAACP launched their judicial strategies. See Adam Fairclough, "The Costs of *Brown*: Black Teachers and School Integration," *Journal of American History,* Vol. 91, No. 1 (June 2004), 51 ff.

71. Aldon Morris and Naomi Braine, "Social Movements and Consciousness," in Jane Mansbridge and Aldon Morris, eds., *Oppositional Consciousness: The Subjective Roots of Social Protest* (Chicago, IL: The University of Chicago Press, 2001), 25.

72. bell hooks, *Teaching to Transgress: Education as the Practice of Freedom* (New York: Routledge, 1994), 2.

73. Sabrina Hope King, "The Limited Presence of African-American Teachers," *Review of Educational Research,* Vol. 63, No. 2 (Summer 1993), 119.

74. For discussions of resistance practices, see Myrdal, *American Dilemma,* II, 750ff; Johnson, "A Generation of Women Activists: African American Female Educators in Harlem, 1930–1950," *The Journal of African American History,* 223–240; Vanessa Siddle Walker, "Organized Resistance and Black Educators' Quest for School Equality, 1878–1938," *Teachers College Record,* Vol. 107, No. 3 (Mar. 2005), 355–388; Fairclough, *Teaching Equality,* 46 ff.

75. Fairclough, *A Class of Their Own*, 10, 19–22.
76. Cole, *Conversations*, 13.
77. Johnnetta Cole, *Explorations in Black Leadership*, Biographical Details of Leadership, Grandmother's Influence; Education Experiences; Cole, *Conversations*, 15.
78. Julian Bond, ibid., Historical Focus on Race, Private Education.
79. Freeman Hrabowski III, ibid., Biographical Details of Leadership, Educational Experience in North.
80. Hrabowski, ibid., Setting Educational Goals.
81. Freeman Hrabowski, Interview by Kids of America, St. Veronica's Academy, March 31, 2005. See http://my.schooljournalism.org/?p=48328
82. Johnnetta B. Cole, *Conversations*, 164.
83. Freeman A. Hrabowski, III, "Reflections on America's Academic Achievement Gap: A 50-Year Perspective," W. Augustus Low Lecture, University of Maryland Baltimore County, May 5, 2004.
84. Mary Futrell, *Explorations in Black Leadership*, Historical Focus on Race, Social Consciousness: Segregation.
85. Geoffrey Canada, ibid., Biographical Details of Leadership, Role of Chance in Educational Path.
86. Interview with Johnnetta Cole, Sun Valley, Idaho, (June 28, 1996) [http://www.achievement.org/ autodoc/printmember/col0int-1]; *Conversations*, 10.
87. Johnnetta Cole, *Explorations in Black Leadership*, Biographical Details of Leadership, Education Experiences.
88. Geoffrey Canada, ibid., Biographical Details of Leadership, Learning to Read.
89. William Raspberry, ibid., Biographical Details of Leadership, Parental Teachings and Community Values.
90. Ibid., Influential Teachers.
91. Mary Futrell, ibid., Biographical Details of Leadership, Influential People: Mother.
92. Ibid., Influential People: Community Members; See also "A Historic Chapter in American Education Comes to a Close: An Exclusive Interview with Mary Hatwood Futrell, *Black Issues in Higher Education*, Vol. 6, No. 9 (July 6, 1989), 7–8, 11.
93. Mary Futrell, *Explorations in Black Leadership*, Biographical Details of Leadership, Education: Secondary.
94. Futrell, *Reader's Digest*, 75. See also Mary Hatwood Futrell, "Remembering That Very Special Schoolteacher," *Christian Science Monitor*, Apr. 3, 1984, 24–25.
95. Mary Futrell, *Explorations in Black Leadership*, Historical Focus on Race, Social Consciousness: Segregation. See also Darrell Laurant, *A City Unto Itself: Lynchburg, Virginia in the 20th Century* (Lynchburg, VA: Laurant and the News and Advance, 1977), 91–92.
96. *Explorations in Black Leadership*, Biographical Details of Leadership, Leadership: Foundational Experiences.
97. For a fuller treatment of culturally relevant teaching, see Gloria Ladson-Billings, *The Dreamkeepers: Successful Teachers of African American Children* (San Francisco, CA: Jossey-Bass, 1994).

98. Freeman Hrabowski, *Explorations in Black Leadership*, Biographical Details of Leadership, Influences: Parents as Teachers.

99. Ibid., Foundational Experiences: Teaching and Leading.

100. Ibid., Contemporary Lens on Black Leadership, Vision for Math Education in America.

101. Mary Futrell, ibid., Biographical Details of Leadership, Education: Secondary. For url for QR code, see https://blackleadership.virginia.edu/09QR

102. Geoffrey Canada, ibid., Biographical Details of Leadership, Early Influences in Bronx.

103. *Black Issues in Higher Education* (July 6, 1989), 8–9. See also Mary Hatwood Futrell and Walter A. Brown, "The School Reform Movement and the Education of African American Youth: A Retrospective Update," Vol. 69, No. 4 (Autumn 2000), *The Journal of Negro Education*, 288–304.

104. The term "ethic of caring" can be found in Morris and Morris, *Price They Paid*, 75. Much of the literature on best practices in education calls attention to the critical value of this environmental attitude.

105. Geoffrey Canada, *Explorations in Black Leadership*, Historical Focus on Race, Defining Success.

106. Rita Dove, ibid., Biographical Details of Leadership, Integrated Schools.

107. Ibid., High School Community; Influential People—Teachers and Poets.

108. Ibid., Black Literary Role Models.

109. Geoffrey Canada, ibid., Biographical Details of Leadership, Undergraduate Education: Bowdoin College.

110. Ibid.

111. William Raspberry, ibid., Biographical Details of Leadership, From Okolona to Indianapolis: Life Experiences.

112. Ibid., Personal Career Path Discovery.

113. Cole, *Conversations*, 17.

114. Johnnetta Cole, *Explorations in Black Leadership*, Biographical Details of Leadership, Education Experiences.

115. Ibid., Black Community.

116. Ibid., Career Vision; Graduate School Experiences; Cole, *Conversations*, 20.

117. Freeman Hrabowski, *Explorations in Black Leadership*, Biographical Details of Leadership, Influences: Parents as Teachers; Mentors: Teachers and Ministers; Community in Birmingham; Parents' Assistance with Education; Setting Educational Goals; Foundational Experiences: Teaching and Leading; Leaders from Birmingham: Angela Davis and Condoleeza Rice. See also Susan Kinzie, "A Magnetic Force: Dynamic Chief Has Driven Boom at UMBC," *Washington Post*, May 30, 2007, B01; Interview with Freeman Hrabowski, Kids of America, St. Veronica's Academy (March 31, 2005).

118. Johnnetta Cole, *Explorations in Black Leadership*, Contemporary Lens on Black Leadership, Evaluation of Spelman Experiences.

119. Hrabowski, ibid., Biographical Details of Leadership, Education: Graduate School.

120. Ibid., Historical Focus on Race, Impact of *Brown*.

121. See Chapter 5, "Law and Social Change: Catalyst for Leadership," pp. 137–166.

122. Fairclough, *A Class of Their Own*, 4–5.

123. Eleanor Holmes Norton, *Explorations in Black Leadership*, Historical Focus on Race, Reflections on *Brown*.

124. Ibid., Hrabowski, *Reflections on Brown*. (He was in the 10th grade, and his parents refused to expose him personally to this abuse.)

125. An excellent discussion of the meaning of the Brown decision can be found in "Round Table: Brown v. Board of Education, Fifty Years After," in *The Journal of American History*, Vol. 91, No. 1 (June 2004), 19–118.

126. King, "Limited Presence of African-American Teachers," *Review of Educational Research* (Summer 1993), 135.

127. See, especially, Adam Fairclough, "The Costs of *Brown:* Black Teachers and School Integration," *Journal of American History*, Vol. 91, No. 1, (June 2004), 43–55 and Kevin Gaines, "Whose Integration Was It? An Introduction," Round Table: Brown v. Board of Education, Fifty Years After, in ibid., 19–25.

128. King, "Limited Presence of African American Teachers," *Review of Educational Research* (Summer 1993), 120 ff. In November 2010, Secretary of Education Arne Duncan reported the above data on African American teachers: http://www.ed.gov/news/speeches/secretary-arne-duncans-remarks-national-council-accreditation-teacher-edu; http://www.americanprogress.org/issues/race/report/2014/05/04/88962/teacher-diversity-revisited/.

129. King, "Limited Presence of African American Teachers," *Review of Educational Research* (Summer 1993), 122.

130. Dempsey and Noblit, "Cultural Ignorance and School Desegregation," in Shujaa, *Beyond Desegregation,* 115–116; Lawson and Payne, *Debating the Civil Rights Movement*, 145.

131. Patricia A. Edwards, "Before and after School Desegregation: African American Parents' Involvement in Schools," in Shujaa, *Beyond Desegregation,* 145; see also Michelle Foster, "Education and Socialization: A Review of the Literature," in William Watkins, James Lewis, and Victoria Chou, *Race and Education: The Roles of History and Society in Educating African American Students* (Boston, MA: Allyn and Bacon, 2001), 200–224; A. Wade Boykin, "Comment: The Challenges of Cultural Socialization in the Schooling of African American Elementary School Children: Exposing the Hidden Curriculum," in ibid., 190–199; Fairclough, *A Class of Their Own*, 12.

132. Edwards, "Before and after School Desegregation, " in Shujaa, ed., *Beyond Desegregation,* 142. Kathy Ann Jordan, "Discourses of Difference and the Overrepresentation of Black Students in Special Education," *The Journal of African American History*, Vol. 90, No. 1/2 (Winter/Spring 2005), 128 ff. As late as 2005, African American children continue to be overrepresented in all 13 legally sanctioned disability categories. Teacher referrals account for more than 80 percent of such placements, leading Jordan to believe that "historical constructions of racial inferiority still seem to prevail." (p. 131)

133. Morris and Morris, *Price They Paid*, 88.

134. Harvey Kantor and Barbara Brenzel, "Urban Education and the 'Truly Disadvantaged': The Historical Roots of the Contemporary Crisis, 1945–1990," *Teachers College Record*, Vol. 94, No. 2 (Winter 1992), 281–284.

135. Sheryll Cashin, *The Failures of Integration: How Race and Class Are Undermining the American Dream* (New York: Public Affairs Press, 2004), 96.

136. Kantor and Brenzel, "Urban Education and the 'Truly Disadvantaged,'" *Teachers College Record*, 287–292.

137. Cathy Cohen and Claire Nee, "Educational Attainment and Sex Differentials in African American Communities," *American Behavioral Scientist*, Vol. 43, No. 7 (Apr. 2000), 1196.

138. Rita Dove, *Explorations in Black Leadership*, Biographical Details of Leadership: Integrated schools.

139. Geoffrey Canada, ibid., Biographical Details of Leadership, Choosing Career: Helping Children Succeed.

140. Ibid., Historical Focus on Race, Segregated Education in North.

141. Poverty rates in the United States differ dramatically by race. In 2011, the US Department of Health and Human Services reported that 37.4 percent of black children under eighteen lived in poverty. For whites, the comparable figure is 12.5 percent. See http://aspe.hhs.gov/hsp/12/povertyandincomeest /ib.shtml

142. Charles Payne, "'The Whole United States is Southern!' *Brown v. Board* and the Mystification of Race," *Journal of American History*, Vol. 91, No. 1 (June 2004), 83–84.

143. Hrabowski, W. Augustus Low Lecture, May 5, 2004. This data was compiled through the National Assessment of Educational Progress.

144. Elizabeth Gehrman, "Baby College and Beyond: Canada Talks about How to Address the Problems in Public Education Today," *Harvard Undergraduate Gazette* (March 20, 2008), http://news.harvard.edu/gazette/story/2008/03 /%E2%80%98baby-college%E2%80%99-and-beyond/; *Atlanta Black Star* (March 29, 2013), http://atlantablackstar.com/2013/03/29/more-than-half-of -black-male-high-school-dropouts-are-unemployed-study-says/

145. "High School Dropout Rates," in Child Trends Data Bank, http://www .childtrends.org/?indicators=high-school-dropout-rates, 2013; The Sentencing Project, http://www.sentencingproject.org/template/page.cfm?id=122

146. Gehrman, "Baby College and Beyond," *Harvard Undergraduate Gazette,* March 20, 2008. For differences between 1950 and today, see Cohen and Nee, "Educational Attainment and Sex Differentials," *American Behavioral Scientist,* 1192.

147. Hrabowski, W. Augustus Low Lecture, May 5, 2004, citing study by R. Roach, "Remediation Reform," *Black Issues in Higher Education*, Vol. 17, No. 12 (August 3, 2000), 16–23.

148. Kelsey Sheehy, "High School Students Not Prepared for College, Career," *U.S. News and World Report Blog*, August 22, 2012, http://www.usnews.com /education/blogs/high-school-notes/2012/08/22/high-school-students-not -prepared-for-college-career

149. "Educational Attainment in the United States: 2009," Population Characteristics, *United States Census Bureau*, issued February 2012, http://www.census.gov /prod/2012pubs/p20-566.pdf, p. 7.

150. Mary Futrell, *Explorations in Black Leadership*, Historical Focus on Race, Influence of *Brown*.

151. Katori Hall, ibid., Biographical Details of Leadership, The Impact of Neighborhoods and Schools.

152. http://www.census.gov/newsroom/releases/archives/facts_for_features_special _editions/cb10-ff14.html

153. Nancy Feyl Chavkin, "Introduction: Families and the Schools," in *Families and Schools in a Pluralistic Society*, ed. Nancy F. Chavkin (Albany, NY: State University of New York Press, 1993), 2.

154. Horace Mann Bond, "The Present Status of Racial Integration in the United States, with Especial Reference to Education," *The Journal of Negro Education*, Vol. 21, No. 3 (Summer 1952), 246, 249.

155. Ibid., 241–242.

156. William F. Tate, Gloria Ladson-Billings, and Carl A. Grant, "The *Brown* Decision Revisited: Mathematizing a Social Problem," in Shujaa, *Beyond Desegregation*, 34–35.

157. There are multiple studies of school system success. See, for example, Tabbye M. Chavous et al., "Racial Identity and Academic Attainment among African American Adolescents," *Child Development*, Vol. 74, No. 4 (Jul.–Aug. 2003), 1076–1090; Christine J. Faltz and Donald O. Leake, "The All-Black School: Inherently Unequal or a Culture-Based Alternative?," in Shujaa, *Beyond Desegregation,*, 227–252; Nancy Feyl Chavkin, "Introduction: Families and the Schools," in Chavkin, ed., *Families and Schools in a Pluralistic Society*, 1–17; Dorothy Rich, "Building the Bridge to Reach Minority Parents: Education Infrastructure Supporting Success for All Children," in Chavkin, ed., *Families and Schools in a Pluralistic Society*, 235–244.

158. http://www.city-data.com/city/Okolona-Mississippi.html

159. http://www.takebabysteps.com/

160. Tina Rosenberg, "The Power of Talking to Your Baby," *The New York Times*, The Opinion Pages, April 10, 2013 [http://opinionator.blogs.nytimes.com /2013/04/10/the-power-of-talking-to-your-baby/]

161. William Raspberry, *Explorations in Black Leadership*, Biographical Details of Leadership, Baby Steps: Giving Back to Community. For url for QR code, see https://blackleadership.virginia.edu/10QR

162. http://www.hcz.org/about-us/history

163. Geoffrey Canada, *Explorations in Black Leadership*, Biographical Details of Leadership, Goals for Harlem's Children Zone. For url for QR code, see https:// blackleadership.virginia.edu/11QR

164. Paul Tough, "The Harlem Project," *New York Times Magazine*, 1–14; Interview with Charlie Rose, June 22, 2004; Geoffrey Canada, "Improving Outcomes for Children and Youth Through a Place-Based Strategy," PNC Newsmakers, February 2, 2006, http://fdncenter.org/pnd/newsmakers

165. Geoffrey Canada, *Reaching Up for Manhood: Transforming the Lives of Boys in America* (Boston, MA: Beacon Press, 1998), ix–xii.

166. Paul Tough, *Whatever It Takes: Geoffrey Canada's Quest to Change Harlem and America* (New York: Houghton Mifflin Company, 2008), 19.

167. http://www.hcz.org/home

168. Tough, *Whatever It Takes: Geoffrey Canada's Quest to Change Harlem and America*, 264.

169. http://www.hcz.org/our-results

170. Geoffrey Canada, *Explorations in Black Leadership*, Contemporary Lens on Black Leadership, Greatest Conbtribution: Helping the Disadvantaged.

171. Christie Kelley, "Titusville Native Hrabowski Honored for Education Work," *Birmingham News*, February 6, 2002.

172. http://www.umbc.edu/meyerhoff/program_history.html; http://www.umbc.edu/meyerhoff/program_results.html
173. http://www.umbc.edu/meyerhoff/the_meyerhoff_model.html; Freeman Hrabowski, III, "The Access Imperative," Robert H. Atwell Lecture, 89th Annual Meeting of the American Council on Education, February 11, 2007.
174. Freeman Hrabowski, *Explorations in Black Leadership*, Contemporary Lens on Black Leadership, Vision for Math Education in America.
175. Ibid., Vision, Philosophy and Style.
176. Ibid., Reaching Different Groups: Authenticity; Hrabowski, "The Access Imperative," Atwell lecture.
177. Fairclough, *A Class of Their Own*, 314–317.
178. Michael J. Weiss, "Who's to Blame for the Nation's Poor Schools? Teacher Union Boss Mary Futrell says Reagan's the One," *People* (July 25, 1983), 57; "National Rise Reported in Teacher Pay," *The New York Times*, February 26, 1988, D19; James Marnell, "Newsmakers: Ex-Education Chief Needed a Lesson in Cooperation," *The Times Mirror Company*, June 25, 1989, Part 1, p. 2.
179. Mary Futrell, *Explorations in Black Leadership*, Biographical Details of Leadership, Leadership: Foundational Experiences.
180. Mary Hatwood Futrell, "Missing, Presumed Lost: The Exodus of Black Teachers," *The Black Collegian*, Vol. 19, No. 4 (Mar.-Apr. 1989), 77.
181. Carol Innerst, "Multiculturalism Boosters Discuss Making It Palatable," *The Washington Times*, March 11, 1992, Nation, A4; http://www.gwo.edu/~edpol/ccst.html
182. See above, pp. 67–68.
183. Johnnetta B. Cole, Interview, Sun Valley, Idaho (June 28, 1996), in *Academy of Achievement*, http://www.achievement.org/autodoc/printmember/col0int-1
184. Cole, *Conversations*, 56–58.
185. Ibid., 159.
186. Johnnetta Cole, *Explorations in Black Leadership*, Contemporary Lens on Black Leadership, Evaluation of Spelman Experiences.
187. *Conversations*, 171.
188. Johnnetta Cole, *Explorations in Black Leadership*, Historical Focus on Race, Reflections on the Legacy of Brown. For url for QR code, see https://blackleadership.virginia.edu/12QR
189. Rita Dove, ibid., Biographical Details of Leadership, The Poet's Bond to Humanity.
190. Ibid., Leadership: Vision, Philosophy, Style.
191. Ibid., Race Consciousness, Race Transcendence. For url for QR code, see https://blackleadership.virginia.edu/13QR
192. Carol Moseley Braun, ibid., Contemporary Lens on Black Leadership, Nurturing Future Leaders.
193. Elaine Jones, ibid., Contemporary Lens on Black Leadership, Influence of Public Education in America.
194. George W. Noblit and Van O. Dempsey, *The Social Construction of virtue: The Moral Life of Schools* (Albany, NY: State University of New York Press, 1996), 14, 73–75; Lani Guinier, "From Racial Liberalism to Racial Literacy," *Journal of American History*, Vol. 91, No. 1 (June 2004), 114.

4 Networks: Role Models, Mentors, Organizations

1. The authenticity of the proverb has been the subject of some controversy. There is no single source. However, the sentiment has been expressed in numerous African societies in slightly different form. These include the Banyoro kingdom (western Uganda), the Bahaya (Tanzania), the Igbo (Nigeria), and Wajita (Tanzania). In Kenya, a proverb in Kiswahili translates to approximately the same as the stated proverb. Whatever the derivation, the proverb reflects a social reality that relates the well-being of the child to the larger community. See Editor's note, H-Africa: http://www.h-net.org/~africa/threads/village.html. See also http://www.afriprov.org/index.php/african-proverb-of-the-month/23-1998proverbs/137-november-1998-proverb.html

2. Vernon Jordan, *Explorations in Black Leadership,* Influential People: Black Role Models.

3. Yvonne Scruggs Leftwich, ibid., Biographical Details of Leadership, Influence of Community.

4. Others who remember the centrality of networks and connections in their lives mentioned in this chapter are William Gray, Benjamin Hooks, Carol Moseley Braun, Mary Futrell, Sanford Bishop, Lucius Theus, Earl Graves, Nikki Giovanni, and Mary Frances Berry.

5. Hillary Rodham Clinton, *It Takes a Village* (New York: Simon & Schuster, 1996).

6. Robert Franklin, *Crisis in the Village: Restoring Hope in African-Amerian Communities* (Minneapolis, MN: Fortress Press, 2007), 13.

7. Franklin, ibid., 3.

8. Ibid., 3–5.

9. Melissa Harris-Lacewell, *Barbershops, Bibles and BET: Everyday Talk and Black Political Thought* (Princeton, NJ: Princeton University Press, 2004), xxiii.

10. Ibid., 4–5.

11. A useful research study exploring this adaptation is that of Frank F. Furstenberg, Jr., with assistance of Alisa Belzer, Colleen Davis, Judith A. Levine, Kristine Morrow, and Mary Washington. "How Families Manage Risk and Opportunity in Dangerous Neighborhoods," in William Julius Wilson, ed. *Sociology and the Public Agenda* (London: Sage Publications, 1993), 231–258.

12. Dorothy Height, *Open Wide the Freedom Gates: A Memoir* (New York: Perseus Books, 2003), 3.

13. Ibid., 6–7, 13; Dorothy Height, *Explorations in Black Leadership,* Historical Focus on Race, Influence of Women's Clubs.

14. Height, *Open Wide the Freedom Gates,* 3.

15. Mary Church Terrell, "What Role Is the Educated Negro Woman to Play in the Uplifting of Her Race?" in Beverly Washington Jones, ed., *Quest for Equality: The Life and Writings of Mary Eliza Church Terrell, 1863–1954* (New York: Carlson Publishing Inc., 1990), 154–156.

16. Jones, *Quest for Equality,* 17–24; see also V. P. Franklin and Bettye Collier-Thomas, "For the Race in General and Black Women in Particular: The Civil Rights Activities of African American Women's Organizations, 1915–1950," in Bettye Collier-Thomas and V.P. Franklin, eds., *Sisters in the Struggle: African American Women in the Civil Rights-Black Power Movement* (New York: New

York University Press, 2001), 21–41; Bettye Collier-Thomas, *Jesus, Jobs, and Justice: African American Women and Religion* (New York: Alfred A. Knopf, 2010), Chapters 7–8; Karen A. Johnson, *Uplifting the Women and the Race: The Educational Philosophies and Social Activism of Anna Julia Cooper and Nannie Helen Burroughs* (London, Garland Publishing, Inc., 2000), 131 ff.

17. Dorothy Height, *Explorations in Black Leadership*, Historical Focus on Race, Influence of Women's Clubs. For url for QR code, see https://blackleadership .virginia.edu/14QR

18. Ibid., Biographical Details of Leadership, Influential People: Mother.

19. Ibid., Leadership: Activism.

20. Collier-Thomas, *Jesus, Jobs, Justice*, 382, 452.

21. Franklin, *Crisis in the Village*, 6.

22. Robert M. Franklin, *Another Day's Journey: Black Churches Confronting the American Crisis* (Minneapolis, MN: Augsburg Fortress Publishers, 1997), 3.

23. Ibid., 5.

24. Franklin, *Crisis in the Village*, 7.

25. Robert Franklin, *Explorations in Black Leadership*, Biographical Details of Leadership, Influential People: Parents.

26. Ibid., Influential People: Grandmother.

27. Elaine Jones, ibid., Historical Focus on Race, Social Consciousness: Segregation.

28. Ibid., Biographical Details of Leadership, Influential People; Social Consciousness: Gender.

29. Ibid., Influential People.

30. Vernon E. Jordan, Jr. and Annette Gordon-Reed, *Vernon Can Read* (New York: Perseus Books, 2001), 13.

31. Ibid., 20.

32. Vernon Jordan, *Explorations in Black Leadership*, Biographical Details of Leadership, Career: Early Development.

33. Ibid., Influential People: Parents.

34. Bobby Lee Rush, ibid., Biographical Details of Leadership, Familial Influences: Being an Example.

35. Wynetta Y. Lee, "Striving Toward Effective Retention: The Effect of Race on Mentoring African American Students," *Peabody Journal of Education*, Vol. 74, No. 2 (Jan. 1999), 32. Lee carefully distinguishes between mentors and role models, citing Vander Putten: "'role-modeling is more general, more pervasive and thus a more frequently-occurring activity than mentoring.' Role modeling is much less formal in structure, and the role model could be completely unaware that someone is modeling his or her behavior."

36. Ibid., 31.

37. Psychologists and sociologists make a distinction between natural and planned mentoring. For further discussion of this, see Lynn A. Thompson and Lisa Kelly-Vance, "The Impact of Mentoring on Academic Achievement of At-risk Youth," *Children and Youth Services Review*, Vol. 23, No. 3 (Mar. 2001), 229. See also Jean Rhodes et. al., "Youth Mentoring in Perspective: Introduction to the Special Issue," *American Journal of Community Psychology*, Vol. 30, No. 2 (Apr. 2002),150; Jean Rhodes, Jean Grossman and Nancy Resch, "Agents of Change: Pathways through Which Mentoring Relationships Influence Adolescents'

Academic Adjustment," *Child Development*, Vol. 71, No. 6 (Nov.–Dec. 2000), 1663.

38. Rhodes et al., "Youth Mentoring In Perspective: Introduction to the Special Issue," *American* Journal *of Community Psychology*, 151.

39. Jean Grossman and Jean Rhodes, "The Test of Time: Predictors and Effects of Duration in Youth Mentoring Relationships, " *American Journal of Community Psychology*, Vol. 30, No. 2 (Ap. 2002), 213 ff.

40. Nikki Giovanni, *Explorations in Black Leadership*, Biographical Details of Leadership, Early Childhood Influences.

41. Mary Frances Berry, ibid., Biographical Details of Leadership, Innate Leadership Tendency: Reacting to Injuustice; Reflections on *Brown v. Board of Education*.

42. Bobby Rush, ibid., Biographical Details of Leadership, Mentors: Franklin Elementary School.

43. Vernon Jordan, ibid., Historical Focus on Race, Influence of Community.

44. Jordan and Gordon-Reed, *Vernon Can Read*, 29.

45. Ibid., 30.

46. Gary Pomerantz, "Jordan 'Shaped by Atlanta' Transition Chief Credits Family, Black Community for Inspiring His Success," *The Atlanta Constitution and Journal*, November 29, 1992, Section A, page 1.

47. Vernon Jordan, *Explorations in Black Leadership*, Contemporary Lens on Black Leadership, Influential People: Black Role Models.

48. Zina Rodriguez, "Legends: NAACP Women who Have Made a Difference," *The New Crisis* (March/April 2000), 24.

49. Belinda Robnett, *How Long? How Long? African-American Women in the Struggle for Civil Rights* (New York: Oxford University Press, 1997), 72.

50. Vernon Jordan, *Explorations in Black Leadership*, Biographical Details of Leadership, Influential People: Ruby Hurley.

51. Height, *Open Wide the Freedom Gates*, 71; Dorothy Height, *Explorations in Black Leadership*, Biographical Details of Leadership, Influence of Travel.

52. Height, *Open Wide the Freedom Gates*, 78–79.

53. Ibid., 83.

54. Ibid.

55. Ibid., 85.

56. Ibid., 87.

57. http://www.ncnw.org/about/height.htm

58. Height, *Open Wide the Freedom Gates*, 94.

59. Jane Mansbridge, "The Making of Oppositional Consciousness," in Jane Mansbridge and Aldon Morris, eds., *Oppositional Consciousness: The Subjective Roots of Social Protest* (Chicago, IL: The University of Chicago Press, 2001), 4–5.

60. Vernon Jordan, *Explorations in Black Leadership*, Historical Focus on Race, Influence of Black Business. For url for QR code, see https://blackleadership .virginia.edu/15QR

61. Jordan and Gordon-Reed, *Vernon Can Read*, 17.

62. Vernon Jordan, Jr. with Lee A. Daniels, *Make It Plain: Standing Up and Speaking Out* (New York: Public Affairs, 2008), xiii.

63. Ibid., xi.

64. C. Eric Lincoln and Lawrence Mamiya, *The Black Church in the African American Experience* (Durham, NC: Duke University Press, 1990), 8.
65. Ibid., 3.
66. Ibid., 3–6.
67. Ibid., 8.
68. William Lockhart, "Building Bridges and Bonds: Generating Social Capital in Secular and Faith-Based Poverty-to-Work Programs," *Sociology of Religion*, Vol. 66, No. 1 (Spring 2005), 47. Current studies of black religion suggest that those involved in Church-based religious activities are less likely to be involved in aberrant behaviors. See Byron Johnson, Sung Joon Jang, Spencer De Li, and David Larson, "The 'Invisible Institution' and Black Youth Crime: The Church as an Agency of Local Social Control," *Journal of Youth and Adolescence*, Vol. 29, No. 4 (Aug. 2000), 492.
69. Lincoln and Mamiya, *Black Church*, 8.
70. Johnny Williams, "Linking Beliefs to Collective Action: Politicized Religious Beliefs and the Civil Rights Movement," *Sociological Forum*, Vol. 17, No. 2 (June 2002), 204 ff.
71. Gloria Ladson-Billings, *Beyond the Big House: African American Educators on Teacher Education* (New York: Teachers College Press, 2005), 137.
72. Franklin, *Crisis in the Village*, 112ff.
73. Ibid., 114.
74. Robert Franklin, *Explorations in Black Leadership*, Biographical Details of Leadership, Influential People: Pastor.
75. Interview with Robert Franklin at The Roundtable on Religion and Social Welfare Policy, Nelson Rockefeller Institute of Government, Albany, NY (September 6, 2004), http://lists101.his.com/pipermail/smartmarriages/2004-September/002536.html
76. Robert Franklin, *Explorations in Black Leadership*, Biographical Details of Leadership, Influential People: Pastor. For url for QR code, see https://black leadership.virginia.edu/16QR
77. Ibid., Leadership: Early Development.
78. Ladson-Billings, *Beyond the Big House*, 137.
79. William H. Gray, *Explorations in Black Leadership*, Biographical Details of Leadership, Influence of Racial Discrimination.
80. Ibid., Influential People: Black Ministers.
81. Ibid., Influence of Racial Discrimination. For url for QR code, see https://black leadership.virginia.edu/17QR
82. Lincoln and Mamiya, *Black Church*, 12.
83. Ibid., 231.
84. Ibid., 218–219.
85. Ibid., 219.
86. James Traub, "Hopefuls, Street Toughs; Power Brokers; Networkers; Strivers; Grande Dames; Musclemen; Exiles; Reformers; Purists; Clones; Big Mouths; Outsiders; Air Kissers; Fanatics; Gossips; Nightclubbers; Floyd Flake's Middle America," *The New York Times*, October 19, 1997.
87. http://abyssinian.org/about-us/reverend-dr-calvin-o-butts-iii/
88. Calvin Butts, *Explorations in Black Leadership*, Contemporary Lens on Black Leadership, Being "Faithful to the Task."

89. Ibid., Pan-African Vision.
90. Frederick C. Harris, "Religious Resources in an Oppositional Civic Culture," in Mansbridge and Morris, eds., *Oppositional Consciousness: The Subjective Roots of Social Protest*, 38ff.
91. Marybeth Gasman, Patricia Louison, and Mark Barnes, "Giving and Getting: Philanthropic Activity among Black Greet-Letter Organizations," in Gregory Parks, ed., *Black Greek-Letter Organizations in the Twenty-First Century: Our Fight Has Just Begun* (Lexington, KY: The University Press of Kentucky, 2008), 189.
92. Theda Skocpol, Ariane Liazos, and Marshall Ganz, *What a Mighty Power We Can Be: African American Fraternal Groups and the Struggle for Racial Equality* (Princeton: Princeton University Press, 2006), 13–14, 19.
93. Jessica Harris and Vernon C. Mitchell Jr., "A Narrative Critique of Black Greek-Letter Organizations and Social Action," in Parks, ed., *Black Greek Letter Organizations in the Twenty-First Century*, 143 ff..
94. Dorothy J. Height, "'We Wanted the Voice of a Woman to the Heard'—Black Women and the 1963 March on Washington," in Collier-Thomas and Franklin, eds., *Sisters in the Struggle: African American Women in the Civil Rights—Black Power Movement*, 83–91. Dorothy Height writes poignantly about the insensitivity to women's public participation in the 1963 March on Washington. She refers to other black women, like Pauli Murray, who spoke out about gender discrimination, and thereby "galvanized the women" (p. 90). She calls this "blatantly insensitive treatment of black women…a new awakening." This march, she writes, "…brought into bold relief the different perspectives of men and women on the whole issue of gender" (p. 91). See also Harris and Mitchell, "A Narrative Critique of Black Greek-Letter Organizations and Social Action," in Parks, ed., *Black Greek Letter Organizations*, 154–156.
95. Mary Futrell refers to the various educational associations on both the local, state, and national levels that she headed. For more specifics, see Chapter 3, Education, p. 68 for more details. For quote, see Patricia Reid-Merritt, *Sister Power: How Phenomenal Black Women are Rising to the Top* (New York: John Wiley & Sons, 1996), 176.
96. Fraternal organizations and churches actively interacted with national organizations (discussed in Chapter 5) to build the networks that would fight for full inclusion of African Americans into civic democracy (Skocpol, *What a Mighty Power We Can Be*, 20). Among those discussed later are the National Urban League, the NAACP, the United Negro College Fund, the Association for the Study of Negro Life and History. Later, there was the Southern Christian Leadership Conference and the Student Nonviolent Coordinating Committee.
97. Sanford Bishop, *Explorations in Black Leadership*, Contemporary Lens on Black Leadership, Impact of Black Social Organizations.
98. Ibid., Biographical Details of Leadership, Early Influences: Family, Church, and the Boy Scouts.
99. Bobby Rush, ibid., Biographical Details of Leadership, Boy Scouts and the Military: Positive and Negative Role Models.
100. Calvin Butts, ibid., Biographical Details of Leadership, Scouts and Scoutmasters.
101. Ibid., Historical Focus on Race, Black Panthers in Chicago; Biographical Details of Leadership, Choosing Political Pathways.

102. Ibid., Biographical Details of Leadership, Choosing Political Pathways; Political Mentor: Harold Washington.

103. Elaine Jones, ibid., Biographical Details of Leadership, Leadership: Risk-Taking.

104. Bobby Rush, ibid., Biographical Details of Leadership, Boy Scouts and the Military: Positive and Negative Role Models.

105. Lucius Theus, ibid., Contemporary Lens on Black Leadership, Military Ethic. For biographical information, see http://www.arlingtoncemetery.net/lucius-theus.htm

106. Ibid., Historical Focus on Race, Military and Culture.

107. Earl Graves, ibid., Biographical Details of Leadership, Influence of Armed Service.

108. Ibid.

109. Elaine Jones, ibid., Biographical Details of Leadership, Leadership: Risk Taking. For url for QR code, see https://blackleadership.virginia.edu/18QR

110. Ibid., Peace Corps Experiences.

111. Ibid., Historical Focus on Race, Education: Discrimination at Law School.

112. Ibid., Contemporary Lens on Black Leadership, Social Consciousness: Race and Society.

113. Robert Franklin, ibid., Biographical Details of Leadership, Career: Early Development.

114. Ibid.

115. For biographical information, see Gayle J. Hardy, *American Women Civil Rights Activists: Bibliographies of 68 Leaders, 1825–1992* (London: McFarland & Company, Inc., 1993), 182–185; Jonathan Tilove, "Height Still on Top of Civil Rights," *The Times-Picayune*, June 22, 2003; http://www.biography.com/people/dorothy-height-40743

116. Fahizah Alim, "Civil Rights, Equality Fuel Activist's Life," *The Sacramento Bee*, July 26. 2003.

117. http://naacplegaldefensefund.org/

118. For biographical information, see http://www.americanbar.org/content/dam/aba/migrated/women/margaretbrent/07/JonesBio_TownHall.authcheckdam.pdf.

119. Caroline V. Clarke and Jonathan Sapers, "Jones for the defense," *Black Enterprise*, Vol. 24, No. 1 (Aug. 1993), 64 ff.

120. Vernon E. Jordan, Jr., Biography Resource Center, The Gale Group, 2000.

121. Marjorie Williams, "Clinton's Mr. Inside," *Vanity Fair*, Vol. 56 (Mar. 1993), 172–175, 207–213.

122. Robert M. Franklin, Jr., "An Ethic of Hope: The Moral Thought of Martin Luther King, Jr.," *Union Seminary Quarterly Review*, Vol. XL, No. 4 (1986), 41–52.

123. See http://www.itc.edu/

124. http://www.itc.edu/about/missionvision/

125. Gayle White, "Theology Center's Next Leader is Preacher, Teacher and More; Man wih a Plan: Franklin Hopes to Get Churches More Involved in Helping Neighborhoods," *The Atlanta Journal and Constitution*, October 13, 1996, 8G.

126. http://rush.house.gov/about-me/biography
127. National Public Radio Interviews: "Voting Rights Act" (April 18, 2005); Tavis Smiley Show, "Death Penalty" (February 4, 2003).
128. Mary Ann French, "The Radical Departure of Bobby Rush," *The Washington Post,* May 3, 1993, C1.
129. Don Wycliff, "Soul Survivor: Bobby Rush Narrowly Escaped a Deadline Police Raid and Later Won a Long-Shot Bid for Congress," *Chicago Tribune Magazine* (November 16, 2003), 15, 26.
130. Howard Gardner, *Leading Minds: An Anatomy of Leadership* (New York: Basic Books, 1995), 14, 50.
131. Wade W. Nobles, "African Philosophy: Foundations of Black Psychology," in Reginald L. Jones, ed., *Black Psychology,* 3rd ed. (Berkeley, CA: Cobb & Henry Publishers, 1991), 48 ff.
132. Franklin, *Crisis in the Village,* 4.

5 Law and Social Change: Catalyst for Leadership

1. Mary Frances Berry, *Explorations in Black Leadership,* Historical Focus on Race, Reflections on *Brown v. Board of Education.*
2. Douglas Wilder, ibid., Historical Focus on Race, Impact of *Brown.*
3. Other important black leaders represented in this chapter are Roger Wilkins, Sanford Bishop, William Gray, Johnnetta Cole, Vernon Jordan, Elaine Jones, Eleanor Holmes Norton, and Dorothy Height.
4. Roger Wilkins, *Explorations in Black Leadership,* Historical Focus on Race, Reflections on *Brown.*
5. Michael Klarman, in *From Jim Crow to Civil Rights: The Supreme Court and the Struggle for Racial Equality* (New York: Oxford University Press, 2004), traces the political, economic, social, demographic, ideological, and international factors that caused changes in race attitudes and practices and effected changes in the law. See pp. 443 ff.
6. Sanford Bishop, *Explorations in Black Leadership,* Historical Focus on Race, *Brown:* A Lifetime of Impact.
7. William Gray, ibid., Historical Focus on Race, Reflections on *Brown.* For a longer quote, see Chapter 1, p. 27.
8. Johnnetta Cole, ibid., Historical Focus on Race, Reflections on *Brown.*
9. Vernon Jordan, ibid., Historical Focus on Race, Reflections on *Brown.*
10. John Conyers, ibid., Historical Focus on Race, Memories of *Brown v. Board of Education.*
11. Roger Wilkins, ibid., Biographical Details of Leadership, Influential Events.
12. Elaine Jones, ibid., Historical Focus on Race, Race Consciousness.
13. Eleanor Holmes Norton, ibid., Historical Focus on Race, Personal Connection to *Brown;* Biographical Details of Leadership, Influence of the Civil Rights Movement.
14. Ibid., Influence of the Civil Rights Movement.
15. Roger Wilkins, ibid., Historical Focus on Race, Reflections on *Brown.*
16. Dorothy Height, ibid., Reflections on *Brown;* Leadership, Philosophy.

17. Oliver Hill, ibid., Contemporary Lens on Black Leadership, Leadership: Development.
18. Oliver W. Hill, Sr., *The Big Bang: Brown vs Board of Education, and Beyond: The Autobiography of Oliver W. Hill, Sr.* (Winter Park, Florida: FOUR-G Publishers, 2000), 71.
19. Oliver Hill, *Explorations in Black Leadership*, Biographical Details of Leadership, Education: Law School
20. Hill, *The Big Bang*, 72.
21. Richard Kluger, *Simple Justice: The History of Brown v. Board of Education and Black America's Struggle for Equality* (New York: Alfred A. Knopf, 1976), 126; Genna Rae McNeil, *Groundwork: Charles Hamilton Houston and the Struggle for Civil Rights* (Philadelphia, PA: University of Pennsylvania Press, 1983), 65–75.
22. Oliver Hill, *Explorations in Black Leadership*, Biographical Details of Leadership, Education: Law School.
23. Quoted in Kluger, *Simple Justice*, 128.
24. Kluger, ibid.
25. Oliver Hill, *Explorations in Black Leadership*, Contemporary Lens on Black Leadership, Leadership: Development.
26. Hill was in the US Army, serving in the European theater, from 1943 to 1945; during the Kennedy administration, he was assistant to the Federal Housing Commissioner at HUD.
27. See http://www.olddominionbarassociation.com/
28. For more detailed discussion of Oliver Hill's career development, see Kluger, *Simple Justice*, 471–477, 485–508 passim.
29. Oliver Hill, *Explorations in Black Leadership*, Historical Focus on Race, Influence of Civil Disobedience.
30. Ibid., Leadership: Vision, Philosophy, and Style.
31. Hill, *The Big Bang*, 148–149; *Explorations in Black Leadership*, Historical Focus on Race, Personal Connection to *Brown*; Kluger, *Simple Justice*, 455.
32. Sylvia Charmaine, "Attorney Oliver W. Hill, Sr.: Challenging Tradition," *About Time Magazine* (February 1993), 11; Hill, *The Big Bang*, 148–151; *Explorations in Black Leadership*, Historical Focus on Race, Filing Suit in Prince Edward County.
33. *Beyond Brown: Pursuing the Promise, Cases and Lawyers*, http://www.pbs.org/beyondbrown/history/oliverhill.html.
34. Robert Pratt, *The Color of Their Skin: Education and Race in Richmond, Virginia, 1954–1989* (Charlottesville, VA: University Press of Virginia, 1992), 1 ff. See also Sara K. Eskridge, "Virginia's Pupil Placement Board and the Practical Applications of Massive Resistance, 1956–1966," *Virginia Magazine of History and Biography*, Vol. 118, No. 3 (Jan. 2010), 246–276.
35. Oliver Hill, *Explorations in Black Leadership*, Historical Focus on Race, Legacy of *Brown*. For url for QR code, see https://blackleadership.virginia.edu/19QR
36. Interview of Henry Marsh III by Akida T. Mensah (October 1, 1982), Church Hill Oral History Project, Virginia Commonwealth University Special Collections Library.
37. Henry Marsh, *Explorations in Black Leadership*, Historical Focus on Race, Social Consciousness: Segregation.

38. Ibid., Biographical Details of Leadership, Career: Vision.
39. Ibid., Historical Focus on Race, Social Consciousness: Segregation.
40. Ibid., Biographical Details of Leadership, Career: Vision. For url for QR code, see https://blackleadership.virginia.edu/20QR
41. Ibid., Historical Focus on Race, Influence of the Civil Rights Movement.
42. Ibid., Biographical Details of Leadership, Career: Early Development.
43. Ibid., Historical Focus on Race, Influence of the Civil Rights Movement.
44. Rick Sauder, "Key player in city politics soon to act in state arena," *The Richmond News Leader*, January 4, 19921.
45. Sauder, ibid.
46. For details of this case, see Chapter 6, pp. 194–195.
47. Sara Lawrence-Lightfoot, *I've Known Rivers: Lives of Loss and Liberation* (Reading, MA: Addison-Wesley Publishing Company, 1994), 114–115, 147–148.
48. Charles Ogletree, *Explorations in Black Leadership*, Biographical Details of Leadership, Influential People: Black Lawyers. For url for QR code, see https://blackleadership.virginia.edu/21QR
49. Charles J. Ogletree, Jr., *All Deliberate Speed: Reflections on the First Half Century of Brown v. Board of Education* (New York: W. W. Norton & Company, 2004), 25.
50. Lawrence-Lightfoot, *I've Known Rivers*, 169–176.
51. Ogletree, *All Deliberate Speed*, 26.
52. Ibid., 23.
53. Lawrence-Lightfoot, *I've Known Rivers*, 173–175.
54. Ogletree, *All Deliberate Speed*, 34–35.
55. *Explorations in Black Leadership*, Biographical Details of Leadership, Influential People: Teacher.
56. Ogletree, *All Deliberate Speed*, 36–39.
57. Charles Ogletree, *Explorations in Black Leadership*, Biographical Details of Leadership, Education: Shifts.
58. Ibid., Historical Focus on Race, Influence of *Brown*.
59. Ibid.
60. Ogletree, *All Deliberate Speed*, 61–78 passim.
61. Ibid., 94.
62. Meryl Rothstein, "Ogletree: 50 Years after Brown, Segregation Persists," *The Brown Daily Herald*, Vol. CXXXIX, No. 124, December 4, 2003.
63. Lawrence-Lightfoot, *I've Seen Rivers*, 149.
64. Charles Ogletree, *Explorations in Black Leadership*, Contemporary Lens on Black Leadership, Career: Education.
65. http://www.law.harvard.edu/news/2001/08/29_ogletree.html
66. Marisol Bello, "New Leader Tried to Boost NAACP," *USA Today*, May 21, 2008, 3A; Amy Perkel Madsen, "Benjamin Jealous '94: A Force for Change," *Columbia College Today Magazine* (March/April 2009), http://www.college.columbia.edu/cct/mar_apr09/features2.
67. Ellis Cose, "Facing Facts," *Newsweek*, March 2, 2009, http://www.newsweek.com/id/185805
68. Benjamin Jealous, "Commentary: NAACP Agenda Still 'Radical' after 100 Years," June 25, 2009, http://www.cnn.com/2009/LIVING/06/22/jealous.naacp/

69. Benjamin Jealous, *Explorations in Black Leadership*, Biographical Details of Leadership, Leadership Development: Choosing a Career in Social Justice. For url for QR code, see https://blackleadership.virginia.edu/22QR

70. Ibid., Biographical Details of Leadership, Influential Figures: Family Members and Mentors.

71. Kelly Brewington, "Hopeful Note Sounded for NAACP Chief; Delegates Hope Can End Organization's Time of Troubles," *The Baltimore Sun*, July 18, 2008

72. "Benjamin Jealous," *Contemporary Black Biography*, Vol. 70 (Farmington Hill, MI: Gale, 2009), http://galenet.galegroup.com/servlet/BioRC

73. *Explorations in Black Leadership*, Biographical Details of Leadership, Early Influences: Teachers.

74. Madsen, "Benjamin Jealous '94: A Force for Change," *Columbia College Today Magazine*, (March/April 2009).

75. Ibid.

76. *Explorations in Black Leadership*, Biographical Details of Leadership, Influences on Leadership Development: Columbia College.

77. Cose, "Facing Facts," *Newsweek*, http://www.newsweek.com/id/185805

78. For more information on Charles Tisdale, see Jocelyn Y. Stewart, "Charles Tisdale, 80; Used Mississippi Newspaper to Fight Bias," *Los Angeles Times*, July 14, 2007, http://articles.latimes.com/2007/jul/14/local/me-tisdale14

79. Adam Serwer, "The Other Black President: The NAACP Confronts a New Political—and Racial—Era," February 16, 2009, http://prospect.org/article/other-black-president

80. Cecilia Gutierrez Venable, "Benjamin Todd Jealous," BlackPast.org, http://www.blackpast.org/aah/jealous-benjamin-todd-1973

81. Madsen, "Benjamin Jealous '94: A Force for Change," *Columbia College Today* http://www.college.columbia.edu/cct/mar_apr09/features2

82. *Explorations in Black Leadership*, Biographical Details of Leadership, Leadership Development: Choosing a Career in Social Justice.

83. *Explorations in Black Leadership*, Biographical Details of Leadership, Leadership in Legal Defense Projects: Troy Davis Case.

84. Ibid., Contemporary Lens on Black leadership, Leadership: Philosophy, Vision, and Style.

85. Ibid., Leaders' Obligations to the Black Community.

86. Ibid., Biographical Details of Leadership, Reflections on *Brown v the Board*.

87. Madsen, Benjamin Jealous '94," *Columbia College Today*, http://www.college.columbia.edu/cct/mar_apr09/features2

88. *Explorations in Black Leadership*, Contemporary Lens on Black Leadership, Greatest Contributions.

89. Farai Chideya, Interview with Benjamin Jealous, July 15, 2009, www.takeaway.org

90. Wayne Washington, "Sellers Tries to Make a Name of His Own," *The State*, June 5, 2006, http://web.ebscohost.com

91. Jack Bass and Jack Nelson, *The Orangeburg Massacre* (Mercer, SC: Mercer University Press, 1996), 7–8.

92. Ibid., 76.

93. Ibid., 126.

94. Washington, "Sellers Tries to Make a Name of His Own," *The State*, June 5, 2006.
95. Ibid..
96. Bakari Sellers, *Explorations in Black Leadership*, Biographical Details of Leadership, Legacy of Orangeburg Massacre.
97. Michel Martin, "What Would Martin Do? South Carolina Community Leaders Debate Civil Rights," *Tell Me More (NPR)*, January 21, 2008, http://www.npr.org/templates/story/story.php?storyId=18282841
98. *Explorations in Black Leadership*, Biographical Details of Leadership: Formative Childhood Experiences: Denmark Recreation Center.
99. Edward Michell and Atu Koffie-Lart, "21 Year-Old Morehouse Grad Runs for Congress," *The Maroon Tiger* (Morehouse College), October 29, 2006.
100. Eric Fingerhut, "How AIPAC Makes Friends on College Campuses," *Jewish News*, Vol. 63, Issue 4 (January 22, 2009), 28.
101. *Explorations in Black Leadership*, Biographical Details of Leadership, Reflections on *Brown v the Board*.
102. Martin, "What Would Martin Do?," *Tell Me More (NPR)*, January 21, 2008.
103. *Explorations in Black Leadership*, Biographical Details of Leadership, Legacy of Orangeburg Massacre.
104. Ibid., Leadership Development: Choosing Law as Career.
105. Washington, "Sellers tries to make a name of his own," *The State*, June 5, 2006.
106. Patrick Caddell and Bakari Sellers, "SC New Democrats: Our Time Has Come," *The Times and Democrat*, April 23, 2009, http://thetandd.com/news/opinion/s-c-new-democrats-time-has-come/article_49226143-2ed5-5708-81b6-7ed79247e021.html
107. Gwen Ifill, *The Breakthrough: Politics and Race in the Age of Obama* (New York: Doubleday, 2009), 218.
108. Bakari Sellers, *Explorations in Black Leadership*, Contemporary Lens on Black Leadership, Goals for New African American Leaders. For url for QR code, see https://blackleadership.virginia.edu/23QR
109. Ibid., Biographical Details of Leadership, Influential Experiences: Orangeburg Massacre and Morehouse College.
110. Ibid., Influence of Civil Rights Community on Goals.
111. Ifill, *The Breakthrough*, 217.
112. Washington, "Sellers Tried to Make a Name of His Own," *The State*, June 5, 2006.
113. For specific statements about the value of the *Brown* decision from interviewees, see Mary Frances Berry, Historical Focus on Race, Reflections on *Brown v. Board of Education*; Freeman Hrabowski, Historical Focus on Race, Personal Impact of *Brown*; Sanford Bishop, Jr., Historical Focus on Race, *Brown*: A Lifetime of Impact; and John Conyers, Jr., Historical Focus on Race, Memories of *Brown v. Board of Education*.
114. Risa Goluboff, *The Lost Promise of Civil Rights* (Cambridge, MA: Harvard University Press, 2007), 5–6.
115. Kluger, *Simple Justice*, 3–25.
116. Steven F. Lawson and Charles Payne, *Debating the Civil Rights Movement, 1945–1968* (New York: Roman and Littlefield, 2006), 116ff.

117. Benjamin Hooks, *Explorations in Black Leadership*, Historical Focus on Race, Legacy of *Brown*. For url for QR code, see https://blackleadership.virginia.edu/24QR

6 The Civil Rights Movement: Grassroots Leadership—Living "in struggle"

1. Dick Gregory, *Explorations in Black Leadership*, Historical Focus on *Brown*, Social Consciousness: Race and Society.
2. Freeman Hrabowski, ibid., Biographical Details of Leadership, Foundational Experiences: Birmingham Children's Crusade. For url for QR code, see https://blackleadership.virginia.edu/25QR
3. Robert Moses, *Explorations in Black Leadership*, Biographical Details of Leadership, Philosophy of Struggle—Albert Camus and civil rights movement. For url for QR code, see https://blackleadership.virginia.edu/26QR
4. Howard Zinn, *SNCC: The New Abolitionists* (Boston, MA: Beacon Press, 1964), 216.
5. John Lewis, *Explorations in Black Leadership*, Contemporary Lens on Black Leadership, Ending Acts of Violence.
6. Cynthia G.Fleming, *Yes We Did? From King's Dream to Obama's Promise* (Lexington, KY: The University Press of Kentucky, 2009), 40.
7. John Lewis with Michael D'Orso, *Walking with the Wind: A Memoir of the Movement* (New York: Simon & Schuster, 1998), 36–39, 61.
8. See Chapter 4, pp. 118–119, for more information.
9. E. Franklin Frazier, *The Negro Church in America* (New York: Schocken Books, 1964), 29, 30. See also E. Eric Lincoln and Lawrence H. Mamiya, *The Black Church in the African American Experience* (Durham, North Carolina, Duke University Press, 1990), 8.
10. Lincoln and Mamiya, *Black Church in the African American Experience*, 4–5.
11. Aldon Morris, *The Origins of the Civil Rights Movement: Black Communities Organizing for Change* (New York: The Free Press, 1984), 96–99..
12. Lewis, *Walking with the Wind*, 12, 15, 55.
13. Lincoln and Mamiya, *Black Church in the African American Experience*, 12.
14. Ibid., 15; Donald T. Phillips, *Martin Luther King, Jr., On Leadership* (New York: Warner Books, 1999), 58; see also Steven F. Lawson, *Running for Freedom: Civil Rights and Black Politics in America Since 1941* (Philadelphia, PA: Temple University Press, 1991), 66–67.
15. John Lewis, *Explorations in Black Leadership*, Biographical Details of Leadership, Meeting Dr. Martin Luther King, Jr.
16. Lewis, *Walking With the Wind*, 56.
17. Ibid. 70–71, 87–88.
18. John Lewis, *Explorations in Black Leadership*, Biographical Details of Leadership, Meetingwith Dr. Martin Luther King, Jr.
19. Lewis, *Walking With the Wind*, 75–78.
20. Ibid.

21. John Lewis, *Explorations in Black Leadership*, Biographical Details of Leadership, Learning to Disturb Things.
22. Lewis, *Walking With the Wind*, 81.
23. John Lewis, *Explorations in Black Leadership*, Biographical Details of Leadership: Influential People-Pastors; Learning to Disturb Things.
24. Ibid., Historical Focus on Race, Jim Lawson, and the Nashville Sit-Ins.
25. Lewis, *Walking With the Wind*, 82–83.
26. John Lewis, *Explorations in Black Leadership*, Historical Focus on Race, Jim Lawson, and the Nashville Sit-Ins.
27. Kim Lawton, with Bob Abernathy. Report on Congressman John Lewis and his role in civil rights movement. WNET-TV, Religion and Ethics Newsweekly, January 14, 2005.
28. John Lewis, *Explorations in Black Leadership*, Biographical Details of Leadership, Civil Rights as an Extension of Faith. For url for QR code, see https://blacklead ership.virginia.edu/27QR
29. Ibid., Contemporary Lens on Black Leadership, Ending Acts of Violence.
30. Ibid., A Call to Disturb the Order.
31. Ibid., Contemporary Lens on Black Leadership: You Must Have a Vision; The American House and MLK's Dream; The Vision's Relation to Faith.
32. Alan Johnson, "Self-emancipation and Leadership: The Case of Martin Luther King," in Colin Barker, Alan Johnson, and Michael Lavalette, eds., *Leadership and Social Movements* (Manchester, England: Manchester University Press, 2001), 99 ff.
33. "John Robert Lewis," in Jessie Carney Smith, ed., *Notable Black American Men* (Detroit: Gale Research, 1998), 719; Danny Lyon, "The Nashville Sit-Ins: Nonviolence Emerges, *Southern Exposure* 9 (Spring 1981), 30–32.
34. Manning Marable, *Black Leadership* (New York: Columbia University Press, 1998), xiii.
35. John Lewis, *Explorations in Black Leadership*, Contemporary Lens on Black Leadership, Ending Acts of Violence.
36. Ibid., Biographical Details of Leadership, The March on Washington Speech.
37. Ibid., Contemporary Lens on Black Leadership, Ending Acts of Violence.
38. http://www.house.gov/johnlewis/bio.html
39. Other black political leaders also look back to the religious underpinnings of the civil rights movement for the spiritual grounding for public service. Sanford D. Bishop, congressional representative for Georgia's Second District, credits religious leaders Martin Luther King, Jr., Malcolm X, and Louis Farrakhan for inspiring him to a "ministry of public service." See Sanford Bishop, *Explorations in Black Leadership*, Biographical Details of Leadership, Morehouse and Beyond: MLK and Others; Spiritual Influences: Malcolm X and the Nation of Islam; Contemporary Lens on Black Leadership, Ministry of Public Service.
40. Remarks by Representative John Lewis, Democratic National Convention, July 16, 1992, in *Federal News Service*.
41. David Grann, "Saint Lewis," *The New Republic*, Vol. 219, No. 14 (October 5, 1998), 12.
42. John Lewis, "At a Crossroads on Gay Unions," *The Boston Globe*, October 25, 2003, A15.

43. John Lewis, "'Equal Justice' Only an Illusion," *The Atlanta Journal-Constitution*, January 26, 2004. Cited in http://www.house.gov/johnlewis/pro040126.html

44. http://johnlewis.house.gov/press-release/rep-john-lewis-calls-court-decision-%E2%80%9C-dagger%E2%80%9D-heart-voting-access

45. John Lewis, Testimony for the US Senate Judiciary Committee Hearing on from Selma to Shelby County: Working Together to Restore the Protections of the Voting Rights Act (July 17, 2013), http://www.judiciary.senate.gov/pdf/7-17-13LewisTestimony.pdf

46. John Lewis, *Explorations in Black Leadership*, Biographical Details of Leadership, Greatest Contribution: The Civil Rights Movement.

47. Julian Bond, Ibid., Contemporary Lens on Black Leadership, Influence of SNCC Years.

48. Ibid., Historical Focus on Race, Civil Rights Leadership.

49. Juan Williams, "What Next?," *Washington Post Magazine*, June 21, 1987; accessed from http://web.lexis-nexis.com/universe/printdoc

50. Steven A. Holmes, "N.A.A.C.P. Post gives Julian Bond New Start," *The New York Times*, February 28, 1998, 6; Julian Bond, *Explorations in Black Leadership*, Biographical Details of Leadership, Experiences of Community.

51. Julian Bond, Ibid., Biographical Details of Leadership, Private Education.

52. *Speak Truth to Power: A Quaker Search for an Alternative to Violence*, American Friends Service Committee, 1955, https://afsc.org/sites/afsc.civicactions.net/files/documents/Speak_Truth_to_Power.pdf, p. 68.

53. Julian Bond, *Explorations in Black Leadership*, Biographical Details of Leadership, Ethos of Quakerism.

54. The derivation of the concept goes back to the mid-seventeenth century, when Children of the Light or Friends of the Truth, as they originally called themselves, felt called to direct the light of divine wisdom into dark areas of human existence and witness to the truth that they knew best from experience. (Larry Ingle, "Living the Truth, Speaking to Power," http://www2.gol.com/users/quakers/living_the_truth.htm. Thus, the Quaker adage had a religious basis, but it could also be applied without that understanding. Julian Bond, when interviewed in 1962, acknowledged that he simply did not think about religion. See Rose and Greenya, *Black Leaders Then and Now*, 33.

55. Julian Bond, *Explorations in Black Leadership*, Biographical Details of Leadership, Ethos of Quakerism.

56. Julian Bond, ibid., Consensual Leadership.

57. Joanne Grant, *Ella Baker: Freedom Bound*. Foreward by Julian Bond. (New York: John Wiley & Sons, 1998), 100 ff.; Andrew B. Lewis, *The Shadows of Youth: The Remarkable Journey of the Civil Rights Generation* (New York: Hill and Wang, 2009), 9–10.

58. Grant, *Ella Baker*, 136–37; Lewis, *Shadows of Youth*, 10.

59. Barbara Ransby, "Behind-the-Scenes View of a Behind-the-Scenes Organizer: The Roots of Ella Baker's Political Passions," in Bettye Collier-Thomas and V. P. Franklin,eds., *Sisters in the Struggle: African American Women in the Civil Rights-Black Power Movement* (New York: New York University Press, 2001), 44–46; see also Bettye Collier-Thomas, *Jesus, Jobs, and Justice: African American Women and Religion* (New York: Alfred A. Knopf, 2010), 366–475, esp. 424; Karen A.

Johnson, *Uplifting the Women and the Race: The Educational Philosophies and Social Activism of Anna Julia Cooper and Nannie Helen Burroughs* (London: Garland Publishing, Inc., 2000), 131 ff. See also Charles Payne, "Ella Baker and Models of Social Change," *Signs*, Vol. 13, No. 4 (Summer 1989), 885–899.

60. Grant, *Ella Baker*, 25 ff.
61. Barbara Ransby, "Behind-the-Scenes View of a Behind-the-Scenes Organizer," *Sisters in the Struggle*, 43.
62. Grant, *Ella Baker*, 132, 136–137.
63. Lewis, *Shadows of Youth*, 285; Grant, *Ella Baker*,143, 211. *Fundi* is a Swahili word that relates to the ability of a person within community to pass on the wisdom, craft, and knowledge of elders.
64. Ransby, "Behind the Scenes View," *Sisters in the Struggle*, 42.
65. Payne, "Ella Baker and Models of Social Change," *Signs*, 890.
66. Marable, *Black Leadership*, xiv–xv.
67. Robert Moses, *Explorations in Black Leadership*, Biographical Details of Leadership, Experiencing Mississippi and Amzie Moore.
68. Julian Bond, Ibid., Contemporary Lens on Black Leadership, Consensual Leadership. For url for QR code, see https://blackleadership.virginia.edu/28QR
69. Rose and Greenya, *Black Leaders Then and Now*, 34–35. In 1962, Bond was disappointed in King. He believed that King could catalyze action while jailed (and an object of sympathy), but that he was a less effective organizer in other contexts. For an excellent analysis of King's leadership style, see Johnson,"Self-emancipation and Leadership: The Case of Martin Luther King," in Barker et.al., eds., *Leadership and Social Movements*, 96–115.
70. Julian Bond, *Explorations in Black Leadership*, Contemporary Lens on Black Leadership, Influence of SNCC Years.
71. Ibid., Consensual Leadership.
72. http://atlinq.com/about%20us.html
73. DeLeon, ed., *Leaders from the 1960s*, 45–46.
74. Vanessa Murphree, *The Selling of Civil Rights: The Student Nonviolent Coordinating Committee and the Use of Public Relations* (London: Routledge, 2006), 27–28.
75. Ibid., 44–46.
76. Clayborne Carson, *In Struggle: SNCC and the Black Awakening of the 1960s* (Boston: Harvard University Press, 1981), 71. Murphree claims the core staff field secretaries and workers numbered 96, and also lists projects in North Carolina. See Murphree, *Selling of Civil Rights*, 5.
77. Murphree, *Selling of Civil Rights*, 55–56.
78. Ibid., 70–72..
79. Ibid., 65.
80. Thomas Rose and John Greenya, *Black Leaders: Then and Now* (Garrett Park, MD: Garrett Park Press, 1984), 14.
81. Julian Bond, *Explorations in Black Leadership*, Historical Focus on Race, Martin Luther King, Jr.
82. John Neary, *Julian Bond, Black Rebel* (New York: William Morrow and Company, 1971), 69–74.
83. Ibid., 75–79.
84. Cited in James Forman, *The Making of Black Revolutionaries* (New York: Macmillan, 1972), 445–446.

85. *Time*, January 21, 1966.
86. See *Meet the Press* transcript, January 30, 1966 (Washington, DC: Merkle Press, 1966), 1–11.
87. David Treadwell, "Why Julian Bond's Political Star Has Fallen," *Los Angeles Times*, February 23, 1987, 2A.
88. Julian Bond, *Explorations in Black Leadership*, Contemporary Lens on Black Leadership, Georgia Legislature.
89. David Treadwell, "A Paradoxical Parable; Julian Bond: High Hopes Turn Sour," *Los Angeles Times*, February 22, 1987, 1.
90. Julian Bond, *Explorations in Black Leadership*, Contemporary Lens on Black Leadership, Georgia Legislature.
91. Ibid., Congressional Race.
92. During this period, he and wife, Alice, to whom he had been married for over 25 years, divorced. In addition, he responded to a federal drug investigation charging cocaine possession, and had to figure out his next steps. While the divorce moved forward, he was acquitted of the charges a few months later.
93. Julian Bond, *Explorations in Black Leadership*, Contemporary Lens on Black Leadership, NAACP Leadership.
94. Ibid., Leadership Vision, Philosophy, and Style.
95. Julian Bond, "Uniting the Races," *Playboy* (January 1970), 128, 154.
96. Julian Bond, 92nd Annual NAACP Convention Address, New Orleans, Louisiana, July 8, 2001, quoting from Pierre Pradervand, *The Gentle Art of Blessing*, http://www.hartford-hwp.com/archives/45a/535.html
97. Julian Bond, *Explorations in Black Leadership*, Contemporary Lens on Black Leadership,Influence of SNCC Years.
98. Ibid., Historical Focus on Race, SNCC. James Clyburn was another person who was motivated for a lifetime of political leadership as a result of his experiences in the earliest days of student activism. He clearly remembers the power of meeting with Martin Luther King, meetings at Shaw University and at Morehouse College, his participation in mock debates, and his realization that he "had a role to play in all of this." James E. Clyburn, *Explorations in Black Leadership*, Historical Focus on Race, *Brown* Changed the World; Biographical Details of Leadership, A Baseball Coach and MLK, Jr.
99. In an interview in 1980, Bond indicated that in his speeches, he uses the civil rights movement as an inspirational message for political activism. "The typical speech for me . . . is to say to this audience of college students . . . that you are the descendants of a generation that once made a tremendous difference in the United States on the question of war and the question of race, and there's no reason at all in the world why your generation can't make the same difference." Rose and Greenya, *Black Leaders Then and Now*, 40.
100. *Explorations in Black Leadership*, Contemporary Lens on Black Leadership, Vision, Philosophy, and Style.
101. Angela Davis, *An Autobiography* (New York: International Publishers, 1974), 78, 89.
102. Ibid., 79.
103. Ibid., 82–83.

104. Erik S. McDuffie, *Sojourning for Freedom: Black Women, American Communism, and the Making of Black Left Feminism* (Durham, NC: Duke University Press, 2011), 141–146.
105. Angela Davis, *Explorations in Black Leadership*, Biographical Details of Leadership, Mother's Activism.
106. Davis, *An Autobiography*, 84.
107. Davis, ibid., 88–91; Angela Davis, *Explorations in Black Leadership*, Biographical Details of Leadership, Early Education in Birmingham.
108. *Explorations in Black Leadership*, ibid.
109. Davis, *An Autobiography*, 94–95, 101.
110. Ibid., 109.
111. McDuffie, *Sojourning for Freedom*, 197.
112. Angela Davis, *Explorations in Black Leadership*, Biographical Details of Leadership, Friends: Bettina Aptheker.
113. Ibid., Mother's Activism.
114. Davis, *An Autobiography*, 129–131.
115. Angela Davis, *Explorations in Black Leadership*, Biographical Details of Leadership, Historic Events: Birmingham Church Bombing. For url for QR code, see https://blackleadership.virginia.edu/29QR
116. Davis, *An Autobiography*, 133–136.
117. Ibid., 142.
118. On the East coast, SNCC was turning toward black militancy. Cleveland Sellers, for example, had been elected program secretary of SNCC in 1965. By 1966, he helped popularize the cry of "Black Power," and by 1968, he was arrested and imprisoned (unfairly) for his alleged role in the Orangeburg Massacre. For further discussion of the influence these events had, see Chapter 5. For discussion of Sellers and SNCC, see Jack Bass and Jack Nelson. *The Orangeburg Massacre* (Mercer, SC: Mercer University Press, 1996).
119. Stephen Tuck, *We Ain't What We Ought to Be: The Black Freedom Struggle from Emancipation to Obama* (Cambridge, MA: Harvard University Press, 2010), 329, 335.
120. Lewis, *Shadows of Youth*, 214–221.
121. Angela Davis, *Explorations in Black Leadership*, Biographical Details of Leadership, Activism Within Academic Career.
122. Davis, *An Autobiography*, 152 ff.
123. Ibid., 156, 180.
124. Angela Davis, *Explorations in Black Leadership*, Contemporary Lens on Black Leadership, Leaders as Teachers.
125. DeLeon, *Leaders from the 1960s*, 494.
126. Davis, *An Autobiography*, 189; McDuffie, *Sojourning for Freedom*, 197–198.
127. Ibid., 161, 164; Angela Davis, Lecture at Harvard University Conference, March 1987, published in *Contemporary Literary Criticism*, Vol. 77, 125.
128. Angela Davis, *Explorations in Black Leadership*, Contemporary Lens on Black Teachers, Leaders as Teachers.
129. De Leon, *Leaders from the 1960s*, 495.
130. Davis, *An Autobiography*, 250 ff.

131. Ibid., 277–279; De Leon, *Leaders from the 1960s,* 491.
132. Nikki Giovanni, *Explorations in Black Leadership,* Contemporary Lens on Black Leadership, Being an Artist.
133. Freeman Hrabowski, ibid., Biographical Details of Leadership, Leaders from Birmingham: Angela Davis and Condoleezza Rice.
134. Angela Y. Davis, *If They Come in the Morning: Voices of Resistance* (New York: The Third Press, 1971), 13–19, 254 ff.
135. Angela Davis, *Explorations in Black Leadership,* Contemporary Lens on Black Leadership, Experience in Prison.
136. Nikhil Singh, *Black Is a Country: Race and the Unfinished Struggle for Democracy* (Cambridge, MA: Harvard University Press, 2004), 214, 114; Jacquelyn Dowd Hall, "The Long Civil Rights Movement and the Political Uses of the Past," *The Journal of American History,* Vol. 91, No. 4 (Mar. 2005), 1246–1247; Kevin K. Gaines, *Uplifting the Race: Black Leadership, Politics, and Culture in the Twentieth Century* (Chapel Hill, NC: The University of North Carolina Press, 1996), xi–xiv.
137. Julian Bond, *A Time to Speak, A Time to Act: The Movement in Politics* (New York: Simon & Schuster, 1972) 102–103.
138. Angela Davis, *Explorations in Black Leadership,* Contemporary Lens on Black Leadership, Experience in Prison.
139. De Leon, *Leaders from the 1960s,* 497.
140. Angela Davis, *Explorations in Black Leadership,* Contemporary Lens on Black Leadership, Leaders as Teachers.
141. Gary Younge, "'We Used to Think There Was a Black Community,'" *The Guardian,* November 8, 2007, 10.
142. Angela Davis, *Explorations in Black Leadership,* Contemporary Lens on Black Leadership, Leaders as Teachers.
143. Ibid., Reaching Different Groups.
144. Hall, "The Long Civil Rights Movement and the Political Uses of the Past," *The Journal of American History,* 1233–1264.
145. The term "imagined community" is borrowed from Benedict Anderson, *Imagined Communities* (London: Verso, 2006). Anderson speaks of nations formed of citizens who have no direct knowledge of one another, but who nonetheless come together through shared culture and purpose.
146. The famous anthropologist Melville Herskovits claimed that many of these communal groups were survivals from African experiences. See *The Myth of the Negro Past* (Boston, MA: Beacon Press, 1941), Chapters VI and VII, 143–260.
147. Fleming, *Yes We Did? From King's Dream to Obama's Promise,* 36.
148. Peniel E. Joseph, *Dark Days, Bright Nights* (New York: Basic Civitas Books, 2010), 1.
149. For a full explication of this struggle from emancipation to the present, see Tuck, *We Ain't What We Ought to Be: The Black Freedom Struggle from Emancipation to Obama.*
150. Leon F Litwack, "'Fight the Power!' The Legacy of the Civil Rights Movement," *Journal of Southern History,* Vol. 75, No. 1 (Feb. 2009), 4.
151. Julian Bond's father had spent considerable time in Africa by the time the civil rights movement erupted in the United States.

152. Litwack, "Fight the Power," *Journal of Southern History,* 6; Singh, *Black Is a Country: Race and the Unfinished Struggle for Democracy,* 214.
153. Julian Bond, "The Media and the Movement: Looking Back from the Southern Front," in Brian Ward, ed., *Media, Culture, and the Modern African American Freedom Struggle* (Gainesville, FL: University Press of Florida, 2001), 17, 25.
154. Angela Davis, *Explorations in Black Leadership,* Historical Focus on Race, Reflections on *Brown.*
155. Julian Bond, ibid., Historical Focus on Race, Reflections on *Brown.*
156. John Lewis, ibid., Historical Focus on Race, Reflections on *Brown.*
157. Lewis, *Walking With the Wind,* 54–55.
158. Ibid., 57.
159. Bond, "The Media and the Movement," in Ward, ed., *Media, Culture and the Modern African American Freedom Struggle,* 27.
160. Ibid., 26.
161. Lewis, *Shadows of Youth,* 25–29.
162. For the impact of Birmingham events on individuals who participated in them and on the nation, see Horace Huntley and John W. McKerley, *Foot Soldiers for Democracy: The Men, Women, and Children of the Birmingham Civil Rights Movement* (Chicago, IL: University of Illinois Press, 2009).
163. Lewis, *Shadows of Youth,* 29.
164. Lewis, *Walking With the Wind,* 56; Rose and Greenya, *Black Leaders: Then and Now,* 14.
165. Tuck, *Ain't What we Ought to Be,* 268 ff.
166. Lewis, *Shadows of Youth,* 30–34.
167. Bond, "The Media and the Movement," in Ward, ed., *Media, Culture, and the African American Freedom Struggle,* 27–28. See also Lewis, *Shadows of Youth,* 35.
168. Lewis, ibid., 72.
169. Rose and Greenya, *Black Leaders Then and Now,* 15. John Lewis claimed that the people he met became as close as "any brother or sister...because they were people you could share your dreams, your hopes, and your aspirations with."
170. Morris, *Origins of the Civil Rights Movement,* 285.
171. Fleming, *Yes We Did?,* 172.
172. For detailed descriptions of these involvements see, for example, Tom Dent, *Southern Journey: A Return to the Civil Rights Movement* (New York: William Morrow and Company, 1997), and John Dittmer, *Local People: The Struggle for Civil Rights in Mississippi* (Chicago, IL: University of Illinois Press, 1994).
173. Zinn, *SNCC: The New Abolitionists,* 216.
174. Bobby Rush, *Explorations in Black Leadership,* Biographical Details of Leadership,Mentors: SNCC.
175. Barbara Lee, ibid., Contemporary Lens on Black Leadership, Leadership Development.
176. Ibid., For url for QR code, see https://blackleadership.virginia.edu/30QR
177. Freeman Hrabowski, ibid., Biographical Details of Leadership, Foundational Experiences: Birmingham Children's Crusade.
178. Ibid., Contemporary Lens on Black Leadership, Personal Impact of Social Movements.

179. Gwendolyn Moore, ibid., Biographical Details of Leadership, Product of the times: A 60's Person. For url for QR code, see https://blackleadership.virginia.edu/31QR

180. Bill T. Jones, ibid., Contemporary Lens on Black Leadership, Reflections on Gay Rights and Civil Rights.

181. Zinn, SNCC: The New Abolitionists, 2.

182. Leigh Raiford and Renee C. Romano, "Introduction: The Struggle Over Memory," in Renne C. Romano and Leigh Raiford, eds., The Civil Rights Movement in American Memory (Athens, GA: The University of Georgia Press, 2006), xi-xxiv.

183. W. Fitzhugh Brundage, ed., Where These Memories Grow: History, Memory and Southern Identity (Chapel Hill, NC: The University of North Carolina Press, 2000), 6–10; Lawson, Running for Freedom: Civil Rights and Black Politics in America Since 1941, xi.

184. Maurice Hawlbachs (1877–1945), a French sociologist, developed the concept of collective memory. He argued that memory is an essential aspect of social identity for both individuals and groups. Since so much of our lives take place in social contexts, private memory incorporates those group experiences. Memory is selective and collective memories are not always objective. Nonetheless, they feed into group consciousness and group identity. See Brundage, ed., Where These Memories Grow, 4; Maurice Hawlbachs, On Collective Memory (Chicago, IL: The University of Chicago Press, 1992). Another French thinker, Pierre Nora, explores the "lieux de memoires," which create a national consciousness. Their work is critical to those who argue that the memory of the civil rights movement had a transformative national impact.

185. For details of the Selma march, see Taylor Branch, At Canaan's Edge: America in the King Years 1965–1968 (New York: Simon & Schuster, 2006), 18ff.; for the Lewis quote, see David Remnick, The Bridge: The Life and Rise of Barack Obama (New York: Alfred A. Knopf, 2010), frontispiece.

186. Fleming, Yes, We Did?, 113–114.

187. Charles Rangel, Explorations in Black Leadership, Biographical Details of Leadership, Influential People: Family; Contemporary Lens on Black Leadership, How Leaders are Made.

7 Leadership Lessons

1. Oliver Hill, Explorations in Black Leadership, Contemporary Lens on Leadership, Leadership: Vision.

2. Vivian Pinn, ibid., Biographical Details of Leadership, Early Interest in Medicine; Leadership Development: Speaking Up.

3. Earl Graves, ibid., Biographical Details of Leadership, Influential People: Parents.

4. Yvonne Scruggs Leftwich, ibid., Influential People: Mother; Influential People: Parents.

5. Yvonne Scruggs-Leftwich was the deputy mayor of Philadelphia, Pennsylvania; New York State's housing commissioner in Governor Mario Cuomo's Cabinet;

HUD's deputy assistant secretary and simultaneously, the executive director of President Carter's Urban and Regional Policy Group; and director of the Urban Policy and National Policy Institutes, at the Joint Center for Political and Economic Studies, in Washington, D.C. For ten years, she served as the executive director and COO of the Black Leadership Forum. She is also a professor at the National Labor College. John Conyers, US representative from Michigan tells a similar story about watching his father, who was a union organizer in Detroit. See John Conyers, *Explorations in Black Leadership*, Biographical Details of Leadership, Parents Set Examples with Union Activism.

6. Sanford Bishop, *Explorations in Black Leadership*, Biographical Details of Leadership, Extracurricular Activities as Leadership practice.

7. Sanford Bishop, ibid., Morehouse and Beyond: MLK and Others; Spiritual Influences: Malcolm X and the Nation of Islam.

8. Sanford Bishop, ibid., Contemporary Lens on Black Leadership, Ministry of Public Service.

9. Sanford Bishop, ibid., Biographical Details of Leadership, NAACP Legal Defense Fund.

10. Others who tell similar stories about community members are Gwen Moore (Biographical Details of Leadership, Influential People: Family and Other Figures), James Clyburn (Biographical Details of Leadership: A Baseball Coach and MLK), Floyd Flake (Contemporary Lens on Black Leadership, Race and Society). For other examples, see chapter 4.

11. Floyd Flake, *Explorations in Black Leadership*, Historical Focus on Race, Race Consciousness.

12. Barbara Lee, ibid., Biographical Details of Leadership, Mills College: Shirley Chisholm.

13. Barbara Lee, ibid., Oakland Mentor: Ron Dellums; Berkeley Mentors: Carlton Goodlet and Maudelle Shirek.

14. Armstrong Williams, ibid., Biographical Details of Leadership, Influential People: Strom Thurmond and Mr. Williams, Sr.; Career Path Toward Public Relations: Influential People; Eleanor Holmes Norton, ibid., Biographical Details of Leadership, Influential People: Black Role Models; Charles Rangel, ibid., Biographical Details of Leadership, Raymond Jones and Political Beginnings.

15. Nikki Giovanni, ibid., Historical Focus on Race, Knoxville Segregation; Biographical Details of Leadership: Early Childhood Influences.

16. Nikki Giovanni, ibid., Biographical Details of Leadership, How to Become a Poet.

17. Aldon Morris and Naomi Braine, "Social Movements and Oppositional Consciousness," in Aldon Morris and Jane Mansbridge, eds., *Oppositional Consciousness: The Subjective Roots of Social Protest* (Chicago, IL: University of Chicago Press, 2001), 20–37.

18. Henry Louis Gates, Jr., and Cornel West, *The African American Century: How Black Americans Have Shaped Our Country* (New York: The Free Press, 2000), xiii, xv.

19. Morris and Braine, "Social Movements and Oppositional Consciousness," *Oppositional Consciousness*, 22–23.

20. Eleanor Holmes Norton, *Explorations in Black Leadership*, Biographical Details of Leadership, Social Consciousness: Race and Segregation.

21. Johnnetta Cole, ibid., Biographical Details of Leadership, Black Community.
22. Charles J. Ogletree, Jr., *All Deliberate Speed: Reflections on the first half century of Brown v. Board of Education* (New York: W.W. Norton & Company, 2004), 26, 28.
23. Charles Ogletree, *Explorations in Black Leadership*, Biographical Details of Leadership, Influential People: Family.
24. Ibid.
25. Floyd Flake, ibid., Historical Focus on Race, Race Consciousness. For url for QR code, see https://blackleadership.virginia.edu/32QR
26. Carol Moseley Braun, ibid., Biographical Details of Leadership, Living in the Bucket of Blood.
27. Amiri Baraka, ibid., Contemporary Lens on Black Leadership, Resistance.
28. Elaine Jones, ibid., Biographical Details of Leadership, Career: Early Development.
29. Ibid., Historical Focus on Race, Influence of Racial Discrimination.
30. Ibid., Contemporary Lens on Black Leadership, Leadership: Development.
31. Barbara Lee, ibid., Contemporary Lens on Black Leadership, Faith and Leadership. Lee also insists that she holds firm to a strict separation of Church and State. Her commitment to her faith tradition is strictly personal.
32. Floyd Flake, ibid., Contemporary Lens on Black Leadership, Leadership: Philosophy.
33. Gwen Moore, ibid., Contemporary Lens on Black Leadership, Leadership: Vision, Philosophy, Style.
34. William Raspberry, ibid., Historical Focus on Race, Past vs. present barriers to racial equality.
35. Vivian Pinn, ibid., Biographical Details of Leadership, Overcoming Gender and Racial Resistance.
36. Mary Frances Berry, ibid., Contemporary Lens on Black Leadership, Black Leadership: Engaging Issues of Race.
37. Charles Rangel, ibid., Contemporary Lens on Black Leadership: Fostering Future Leadership.
38. Benjamin Hooks, ibid., Contemporary Lens on Black Leadership, Social Consciousness: Race and Gender.
39. Barbara Lee, ibid., Historical Focus on Race, Racial and Social Consciousness.
40. Gwen Moore, ibid., Contemporary Lens on Black Leadership, Race-Transcending Leader.
41. Bakari Sellers, ibid., Biographical Details of Leadership, Influential People: Parents, Teachers, Mentors; Contemporary Lens on Black Leadership, Vision for Leadership: Transcending Race.
42. Benjamin Jealous, ibid., Contemporary Lens on Black Leadership, Race Consciousness in Contemporary America.
43. Ibid., Biographical Details of Leadership, Impact of Historical Events on Leadership Goals; Contemporary Lens on Black Leadership, Race Consciousness in Contemporary America. Such optimism that race transcendence is possible is not reserved for the very young. Unusual among our interviewees, Armstrong Williams claimed that he never experienced any racially based prejudice or slights from whites. "My father says the greatest weapon to breaking down any

barrier is the human heart, how you feel about yourself. And my father taught us to have a lot of pride and a lot of self-confidence." Racism, he pointed out, could come from both black and white sources, and he recalls a time at his black college when he was perceived as "too black" in skin tone to be able to succeed in a school election. Mentored and supported by Strom Thurmond, Williams became a third-generation Republican. He argued that it is possible to be a race-transcending leader, and to focus on larger societal issues. While he notices the race of individuals, he makes no assumptions based on race. He insisted that he does not perceive himself as vulnerable because of the experiences of other blacks. "Race is just a label that we put on things to understand it." See Armstrong Williams, *Explorations in Black Leadership*, Biographical Details of Leadership, Educational Experiences and Race; Contemporary Lens on Black Leadership, Race-Transcending Leadership.

44. John Clyburn, ibid., Biographical Details of Leadership, More Influential Figures.
45. Douglas Wilder, ibid., Contemporary Lens on Black Leadership, Leadership: Vision, Philosophy and Style.
46. Earl Graves, ibid., Historical Focus on Race, Leadership: Development.
47. John Conyers, ibid., Biographical Details of Leadership, Parents Weigh In Differently about Political Changes.
48. Barbara Lee, ibid., Contemporary Lens on Black Leadership, Leadership Philosophy: Having Faith and Taking Care.
49. Douglas Wilder, ibid., Contemporary Lens on Black Leadership, Leadership: Vision, Philosophy and Style. For url for QR code, see https://blackleadership.virginia.edu/33QR
50. Geoffrey Canada, ibid., Contemporary Lens on Black Leadership, Staying True to the Mission; Greatest Contribution: Helping the Disadvantaged.
51. James Clyburn, ibid., Contemporary Lens on Black Leadership, Be the Good Samaritan.
52. Sanford Bishop, ibid., Contemporary Lens on Black Leadership, Vision, Philosophy, Style.
53. Mary Frances Berry, ibid., Biographical Details of Leadership, Innate Leadership Tendency: Reaction to Injustice; Leadership: Personal Vision.
54. Ibid., World Vision and Worldly Priorities.
55. Freeman A. Hrabowski, III, "The Access Imperative," The Robert H. Atwell Lecture, 89th Annual Meeting of the American Council on Education, Washington, D.C., February 11, 2007.
56. Johnnetta B. Cole, *Conversations* (New York: Doubleday, 1993), 7.
57. Johnnetta Cole, *Explorations in Black Leadership,* Historical Focus on Race, Race Consciousness.
58. Bill Gray, ibid., Contemporary Lens on Black Leadership, Leadership: Vision.
59. Benjamin Hooks, ibid., Contemporary Lens on Black Leadership, Social Consciousness: Racial Uplift.
60. Ibid., Historical Focus on Race, Social Consciousness: Race.
61. Ibid.
62. Barbara Lee, ibid., Historical Focus on Race, Racial and Social Consciousness.
63. Ibid., Biographical Details of Leadership, Student Leadership and Achievement.

64. Mary Frances Berry, ibid., Biographical Details of Leadership, Innate Leadership Tendency: Reacting to Injustice.
65. Ibid., Formative Childhood Experiences.
66. Rose and Greenya, *Black Leaders Then and Now*, 45.
67. William Raspberry, *Explorations in Black Leadership*, Biographical Details of Leadership, Parental Teachings and Communal Values.
68. http://www.takebabysteps.com/
69. William Raspberry, *Explorations in Black Leadership*, Biographical Details of Leadership. Parental Teachings and Communal Values.
70. Vivian Pinn, ibid., Biographical Details of Leadership, Greatest Contribution: Mentoring Others.
71. Armstrong Williams, ibid., Contemporary Lens on Black Leadership, Contemporary Issues: Crisis of the Family, Materialism.
72. Gwen Moore, ibid., Biographical Details of Leadership, Product of the Times: A '60s Person.
73. Gwen Moore, ibid., Contemporary Lens on Black Leadership, Vision: Helping the Disadvantaged.
74. Gwen Moore, ibid., Obligation to Lift Up Others.
75. Roger Wilkins, ibid., Contemporary Lens on Black Leadership, Divisions in the Black Community.
76. Ibid., Black Underclass. For url for QR code, see https://blackleadership.virginia.edu/34QR
77. Others who make this claim about the power of the civil rights movement include Mary Frances Berry, Carol Moseley Braun, and the many people discussed in chapter 6.
78. Patricia Reid-Merritt, *Sister Power: How Phenomenal Black Women Are Rising to the Top* (New York: John Wiley & Sons, 1996), 93–94.

Bibliography

NOTE: All endnote references to interviews with black leaders can be found at www.blackleadership.virginia.edu

"7000 teachers rally for kids," *VEA News*. February 1977.

"A Historic Chapter in American Education Comes to a Close: An Exclusive Interview with Mary Hatwood Futrell. *Black Issues in Higher Education*, Vol. 6, No. 9 (July 6, 1989), 6–11.

Alabi, Adetayo. *Telling Our Stories: Continuities and Divergences in Black Autobiographies.* New York: Palgrave, 2005.

Ali, Omar H. "Lenora Branch Fulani: Challenging the Rules of the Game." In Bruce A. Glasrud and Cary D. Wintz, eds., *African Americans and the Presidency: The Road to the White House*. New York: Routledge, 2010.

Allen, Ernest, Jr. "Du Boisian Double Consciousness: The Unsustainable Argument." *The Massachusetts Review*, Vol. 43, No. 2 (Summer 2002), 217–253.

Allen, Walter R. "African American Family Life in Societal Context: Crisis and Hope." *Sociological Forum*, Vol. 10, No. 4, Special Issue: African Americans and Sociology: A Critical Analysis (Dec., 1995), 569–592.

Alim, Fahizah. "Civil Rights, Equality Fuel Activist's Life," *The Sacramento Bee,* July 26, 2003.

Anderson, Benedict. *Imagined Communities.* London: Verso, 2006.

Avolio, Bruce J. *Full Leadership Development: Building the Vital Forces in Organizations.* London: Sage Publications, 1999.

Avolio, Bruce J. and Bernard M. Bass, eds. *Developing Potential Across a Full Range of Leadership: Cases on Transactional and Transformational Leadership.* New Jersey: Lawrence Erlbaum Associates, 2002.

Baraka, Amiri. *The Autobiography of Leroi Jones.* Chicago, IL: Lawrence Hill Books, 1984.

Barnett, Bernice McNair. " Invisible Black Women Leaders in the Civil Rights Movement: The Triple Constraints of Gender, Race, and Class." *Gender and Society,* Vol. 7, No. 2 (June, 1993), 165–182.

Bartley, Numan V. *The Rise of Massive Resistance: Race and Politics in the South During the 1950's.* Baton Rouge, LA: Louisiana State University Press, 1997.

Bass, Jack and Jack Nelson. *The Orangeburg Massacre.* Mercer, SC: Mercer University Press, 1996.

Bateson, Mary Catherine. *Composing a Life.* New York: The Atlantic Monthly Press, 1989.

Bello, Marisol. "New leader tried to boost NAACP," *USA Today*, May 21, 2008, 3A.

Benjamin, Lois. *Three Black Generations At the Crossroads: Community, Culture, and Consciousness*. 2nd ed. Lanham, MD: Rowman and Littlefield, 2007.

Bennis, Warren. *Managing the Dream: Reflections on Leadership and Change*. Cambridge, MA: Perseus Publishing, 2000.

Berger, Joseph, Cecilia Ridgeway, M. Hamit Fisek, and Robert Norman. "The Legitimation and Delegitimation of Power and Prestige of Orders." *American Sociological Review*, Vol. 63 (June 1998), 379–405.

Bernard, Jessie. *Marriage and Family Among Negroes*. Englewood Cliffs, NJ: Prentice-Hall, Inc., 1966.

Beyond Brown: Pursuing the Promise, Cases and Lawyers. [http://www.pbs.org/beyond brown/history/oliverhill.html]

Billingsley, Andrew. *Black Families in White America*. New Jersey: Prentice-Hall, Inc., 1968.

Billingsley, Andrew. *Climbing Jacob's Ladder: The Enduring Legacy of African-American Families*. New York: Simon & Schuster, 1992.

Bond, Horace Mann. "The Negro Elementary School and the Cultural Pattern." *Journal of Educational Sociology*, Vol. 13, No. 8 (Apr., 1940), 479–489.

Bond, Horace Mann. "The Present Status of Racial Integration in the United States, with Especial Reference to Education." *The Journal of Negro Education*, Vol. 21, No. 3 (Summer 1952), 241–250.

Bond, Julian. 92nd Annual NAACP Convention Address, New Orleans, LA (July 8, 2001). [http://www.hartford-hwp.com/archives/45a/535.html]

Bond, Julian. *A Time to Speak, A Time to Act*. New York: Simon & Schuster, 1972.

Bond, Julian. "The Media and the Movement: Looking Back from the Southern Front." In Brian Ward, ed., *Media, Culture, and the Modern African American Freedom Struggle*. Gainesville, FL: University Press of Florida, 2001.

Bond, Julian. "Uniting the Races." *Playboy* (January 1970), 128, 154.

Bonilla-Silva, Eduardo. *Racism Without Racists*. Lanham, MD: Rowman and Littlefield, 2010.

Boykin, A. Wade. "Comment: The Challenges of Cultural Socialization in the Schooling of African American Elementary School Children: Exposing the Hidden Curriculum." In William Watkins, ed., *Race and Education: The Roles of History and Society in Educating African American Students*. Boston, MA: Allyn and Bacon, 2001.

Branch, Taylor. *At Canaan's Edge: America in the King Years 1965–1968*. New York: Simon & Schuster, 2006.

Braxton, Joanne M. *Black Women Writing Autobiography: A Tradition within a Tradition*. Philadelphia, PA: Temple University Press, 1989.

Brewington, Kelly. "Hopeful note sounded for NAACP chief: Delegates Hope Jealous Can End Organization's Time of Troubles," *The Baltimore Sun*, July 18, 2008.

Brundage, W. Fitzhugh, ed. *Where These Memories Grow: History, Memory and Southern Identity*. Chapel Hill, NC: The University of North Carolina Press, 2000.

Bullock, Henry Allen. *A History of Negro Education in the South from 1619 to the Present*. New York: Praeger Publishers, 1970.

Burgess, M. Elaine. *Negro Leadership in a Southern City*. Chapel Hill, NC: University of North Carolina Press, 1962.

Butler, John S. "The Return of Open Debate." *Society* (March/April, 1996), 11–18.

Butterfield, Stephen. *Black Autobiography in America*. Amherst, MA: The University of Massachusetts Press, 1974.

Caddell, Patrick and Bakari Sellers. "South Carolina New Democrats: Our Time Has Come," *The Times and Democrat*, April 23, 2009. [http://thetandd.com/news/opinion/s-c-new-democrats-time-has-come/article_49226143-2ed5-5708-81b6-7ed79247e021.html]

Canada, Geoffrey. *Fist Stick Knife Gun: A Personal History of Violence in America*. Boston, MA: Beacon Press, 1995.

Canada, Geoffrey. "Improving Outcomes for Children and Youth Through a Place-Based Strategy," PNC Newsmakers, February 2, 2006. [http://fdncenter.org/pnd/newsmakers]

Canada, Geoffrey. *Reaching Up for Manhood: Transforming the Lives of Boys in America*. Boston, MA: Beacon Press, 1998.

Carson, Ann E. and William J. Sabol. "Prison Spending Outpaces All But Medicaid," *The New York Times*, March 2, 2009.

Carson, Ann E. and William J. Sabol. "Prisoners in 2011," Bulletin, U.S. Department of Justice, December 2012. [http://www.bjs.gov/content/pub/pdf/p11.pdf]

Carson, Clayborne. *In Struggle: SNCC and the Black Awakening of the 1960s*. Cambridge, MA: Harvard University Press, 1981.

Carson, Clayborne. "Two Cheers for *Brown v. Board of Education*." *Journal of American History*, Vol. 91, No. 1 (June 2004), 26–31.

Cashin, Sheryll. *The Failures of Integration: How Race and Class Are Undermining the American Dream*. New York: Public Affairs Press, 2004.

Cecelski, David S. *Along Freedom Road: Hyde County, North Carolina, and the Fate of Black Schools in the South*. Chapel Hill, NC: University of North Carolina Press, 1994.

Chandler, Sally. "Oral History across Generations: Age, Generational Identity and Oral Testimony." *Oral History*, Vol. 33, No. 2 (Autumn 2005), 48–56.

Chappell, David L. *A Stone of Hope: Prophetic Religion and the Death of Jim Crow*. Chapel Hill, NC: University of North Carolina Press, 2004.

Charmaine, Sylvia. "Attorney Oliver W. Hill, Sr.: Challenging Tradition." *About Time Magazine*, (February 1993), 10–13.

Chatters, Linda, Robert Joseph Taylor, and Rukmalie Jayakody. "Fictive Kin Relations in Black Extended Families." *Journal of Comparative Family Studies*, Vol. 25, No. 3 (Autumn 1994), 297–312.

Chavkin, Nancy Feyl. "Introduction: Families and the Schools." In Nancy F. Chavkin, ed., *Families and Schools in a Pluralistic Society*. Albany, NY: State University of New York Press, 1993.

Chavous, Tabbye M. et al. "Racial Identity and Academic Attainment among African American Adolescents." *Child Development*, Vol. 74, No. 4 (Jul.–Aug., 2003), 1076–1090.

Chemers, Martin. "Leadership Effectiveness: Functional, Constructive and Empirical Perspectives." In *Leadership and Power: Identity Processes in Groups and Organizations*. Thousand Oaks, CA: Sage Publications, 2003.

Chideya, Farai. Interview with Benjamin Jealous, July 15, 2009 [www.takeaway.org]

Clarke, Caroline V. and Jonathan Sapers. "Jones for the Defense." *Black Enterprise*, Vol. 24, No. 1, (August 1993), 64–68.

Clementson, Lynette and Allison Samuels. "We Have the Power." Special Report: Redefining Race in America. *Newsweek* (September 18, 2000), 56–58.

Clinton, Hillary Rodham. *It Takes a Village*. New York: Simon & Schuster, 1996.

Coard, Stephanie I and Robert M. Sellers. "African American Families as a Context for Racial Socialization." In Vonnie C. McLoyd, Nancy E. Hill, and Kenneth A. Dodge, eds., *African American Family Life: Ecological and Cultural Diversity*. New York: Guilford Press, 2005.

Cohen, Cathy and Claire Nee. "Educational Attainment and Sex Differentials in African American Communities." *American Behavioral Scientist*, Vol. 43, No. 7 (April 2000), 1159–1206.

Cole, Elizabeth and Safiya Omari. "Race, Class and the Dilemmas of Upward Mobility for African Americans." *Journal of Social Issues*, Vol. 59, No. 4 (2003), 785–802.

Cole, Johnnetta B. *Conversations: Straight Talk with America's Sister President*. New York: Doubleday, 1993.

Cole, Johnnetta B. *Dream the Boldest Dreams*. Atlanta, GA: Longstreet Press, 1997.

Cole, Johnnetta B. Interview, *Academy of Achievement*, June 28, 1996. [http://www .achievement.org/autodoc/printmember/col0int-1]

Collier-Thomas, Bettye. *Jesus, Jobs, and Justice: African American Women and Religion*. New York: Alfred A. Knopf, 2010.

Collier-Thomas, Bettye and V. P. Franklin, eds. *Sisters in the Struggle: African American Women in the Civil Rights-Black Power Movement*. New York: New York University Press, 2001.

Conconi, Chuck. "Making a Difference." *Washingtonian*, December 2003.

Contemporary Authors Online, Gale 2006. Reproduced in Biography Resource Center. Farmington Hill, MI: Thomson Gale. 2006. [http://galenet.galegroup.com/servlet /BioRC]

Conyers, James L. Jr., ed. *Engines of the Black Power Movement: Essays on the Influence of Civil Rights Actions, Arts, and Islam*. London: McFarland & Company, Inc., 2007.

Coontz, Stephanie. *The Way We Never Were: American Families and the Nostalgia Trap*. New York: Basic Books, 1992.

Cose, Ellis. "Facing Facts," *Newsweek*, March 2, 2009 [http://www.newsweek.com/id /185805]

Cronon, William. "A Place for Stories: Nature, History, and Narrative." *The Journal of American History*, Vol. 78, No. 4 (March 1992), 1347–1376.

Cross, Jr., William E., Thomas A. Parham, and Janet E. Helms. "The Stages of Black Identity Development: Nigrescence Models." In Reginald L. Jones, ed., *Black Psychology*, 3rd ed. Berkely, CA: Cobb & Henry Publishers, 1991.

Dagbovie, Pero Gaglo. *African American History Reconsidered*. Urbana, IL: University of Illinois Press, 2010.

Daniel, Philip T. K. "Accountability and Desegregation: Brown and Its Legacy." *The Journal of Negro Education*, Vol. 73, No.3, Special Issue: *Brown v. Board of Education* at 50 (Summer 2004), 255–267.

Darder, Antonia. *Reinventing Paulo Freire: A Pedagogy of Love*. Boulder, CO: Westview Press, 2002.

Davis, Angela. *An Autobiography*. New York: International Publishers, 1974.

Davis, Angela. *Blues Legacies and Black Feminism*. New York: Pantheon Books, 1988.

Davis, Angela Y. *If They Come in the Morning: Voices of Resistance*. New York: The Third Press, 1971.

Davis, Angela Y. Lecture, Harvard University Conference (March 1987), published in *Contemporary Literary Criticism*, Vol. 77, 124–127.

Davis, Donn G. "Learning for Leaders: Notes on a Pedagogy for the Praxis of Black Political Leadership." In John Davis, ed., *Perspectives in Black Politics and Black Leadership*. New York: University Press of America, 2007.

Davis, John, ed. *Perspectives in Black Politics and Black Leadership*. New York: University Press of America, 2007.

DeLeon, David. *Leaders from the 1960s: A Biographical Sourcebook of American Activism*. Westport, CT: Greenwood Press, 1994.

Dempsey, Van and George Noblit. "Cultural Ignorance and School Desegregation: A Community Narrative." In Mwalimu J. Shujaa, ed., *Beyond Desegregation: The Politics of Quality in African American Schooling*. Thousand Oaks, CA: Corwin Press, 1996.

Dent, Tom. *Southern Journey: A Return to the Civil Rights Movement*. New York: William Morrow and Company, 1997.

DeParle, Jason and Sabrina Tavernise. "For Women Under 30, Most Births Occur Outside Marriage." *The New York Times*, February 18, 2012.

Dittmer, John. *Local People: The Struggle for Civil Rights in Mississippi*. Chicago, IL: University of Illinois Press, 1994.

Doughtery, Jack. "From Anecdote to Analysis: Oral Interviews and New Scholarship in Educational History." *The Journal of American History*, Vol. 86, No. 2 (Sept. 1999), 712–723.

Du Bois, W. E. B. " Does the Negro Need Separate Schools,?" *Journal of Negro Education*, Vol. IV (Jul. 1935), 328–335.

Du Bois, W. E. B. *The Souls of Black Folk*. Edited with introduction by David W. Blight and Robert Gooding-Williams. Boston, MA: Bedford/St. Martin's, 1997.

Du Bois, W. E. B. "The Talented Tenth." In August Meier, Elliott Rudwick and Francis Broderick, eds., *Black Protest Thought in the Twentieth Century*. New York: Macmillan, 1985.

Dudziak, Mary. "*Brown* as a Cold War Case." *Journal of American History*, Vol. 91, No. 1 (June 2004), 32–42.

Dwyer, Owen J. "Interpreting the Civil Rights Movement: Contradiction, Confirmation, and the Cultural Landscape." In Rennee C. Romano and Leigh Raiford, eds., *The Civil Rights Movement in American Memory*. Athens, GA: University of Georgia Press, 2006.

Edin, Kathryn and Maria Kefalas. *Promises I Can Keep: Why Poor Women Put Motherhood before Marriage*. Berkeley, CA: University of California Press, 2005.

Edwards, Patricia A. "Before and After School Desegregation: African American Parents' Involvement in Schools." In Mwalimu J. Shujaa, ed., *Beyond Desegregation: The Politics of Quality in African American Schooling*. Thousand Oaks, CA: Corwin Press, 1996.

Eskridge, Sara K. "Virginia's Pupil Placement Board and the Practical Applications of Massive Resistance, 1956–1966." *Virginia Magazine of History and Biography*, Vol. 118, No. 3 (Jan. 2010), 246–276.

Evans, William McKee. *Open Wound: The Long View of Race in America*. Chicago, IL: University of Illinois Press, 2009.

Fairclough, Adam. *A Class of Their Own: Black Teachers in the Segregated South*. Cambridge, MA: Harvard University Press, 2007.

Fairclough, Adam. "'Being in the Field of Education and also Being a Negro...Se ems...Tragic': Black Teachers in the Jim Crow South." *The Journal of American History*. Vol. 87, No. 1 (June 2000), 65–91.

Fairclough, Adam. *Teaching Equality: Black Schools in the Age of Jim Crow.* Athens, GA: University of Georgia Press, 2001.

Fairclough, Adam. "The Costs of *Brown:* Black Teachers and School Integration." *Journal of American History* Vol. 91, No. 1 (June 2004), 43–55.

Faltz, Christine J. and Donald O. Leake. "The All-Black School: Inherently Unequal or a Culture-Based Alternative?" In Mwalimu J. Shujaa, ed., *Beyond Desegregation: The Politics of Quality in African American Schooling.* Thousand Oaks, CA: Corwin Press, 1996.

Feagin, Joe and Karyn McKinney. *The Many Costs of Racism.* Lanham, MD: Rowman and Littlefield, 2003.

Feldstein, Ruth. "'I Don't Trust You Anymore': Nina Simone, Culture, and Black Activism in the 1960s." *The Journal of American History,* Vol. 91, No. 4 (March 2005), 1349–1379.

Fingerhut, Eric. "How AIPAC Makes Friends on College Campuses." *Jewish News.* Vol. 63, Issue 4 (January 22, 2009), 28.

Fleming, Cynthia Griggs. *Yes We Did? From King's Dream to Obama's Promise.* Lexington, KY: The University Press of Kentucky, 2009.

Forman, James. *The Making of Black Revolutionaries.* New York: Macmillan, 1972.

Foster, Michelle. "Education and Socialization: A Review of the Literature." In William Watkins, James Lewis, and Victoria Chou, eds., *Race and Education: The Roles of History and Society in Educating African American Students.* Boston, MA: Allyn and Bacon, 2001.

Franklin, Robert M., Jr. "An Ethic of Hope: The Moral Thought of Martin Luther King, Jr." *Union Seminary Quarterly Review,* Vol. 40, No. 4 (1986), 41–52.

Franklin, Robert M., Jr. *Another Day's Journey: Black Churches Confronting the American Crisis.* Minneapolis, MN: Augsburg Fortress Press, 1997.

Franklin, Robert M., Jr. *Crisis in the Village: Restoring Hope in African-American Communities.* Minneapolis, MN: Augsburg Fortress Press, 2007.

Franklin, Vincent P., and Bettye Collier-Thomas. "For the Race in General and Black Women in Particular: The Civil Rights Activities of African American Women's Organizations, 1915–1950." In Bettye Collier-Thomas and V.P. Franklin, eds., *Sisters in the Struggle: African American Women in the Civil Rights-Black Power Movement.* New York: New York University Press, 2001.

Franklin, Vincent P., and Carter Julian Savage, eds. *Cultural Capital and Black Education: African American Communities and the Funding of Black Schooling, 1865 to the Present.* Greenwich, CT: Information Age Publishing, Inc., 2004.

Franklin, Vincent P. *Living Our Stories, Telling our Truths: Autobiography and the Making of the African-American Intellectual Tradition.* New York: Scribner and Sons, 1995.

Franklin, Vincent P. *Black Self-Determination: A Cultural History of African-American Resistance.* New York: Lawrence Hill Books, 1992.

Frazier, E. Franklin. *The Negro Church in America.* New York: Schocken Books, 1964.

Frazier, E. Franklin. *The Negro Family in the United States.* Chicago, IL: The University of Chicago Press, 1939.

French, Mary Ann. "The Radical Departure of Bobby Rush." *The Washington Post,* May 3, 1993, C1.

Freire, Paulo. *Pedagogy of the Heart.* Trans. Donaldo Macedo and Alexandre Oliveira. New York: Continuum, 1997.

Freire, Paulo. *Pedagogy of the Oppressed.* Trans. Myra Bergman Ramos. New York: Continuum, 2000.

Fulani, Lenora. "Race, Identity, and Epistemology." In Lois Holzman and John Morss, eds., *Postmodern Psychologies, Societal Practice, and Political Life*. New York: Routledge, 2000.

Fultz, Michael. "African American Teachers in the South, 1890–1940: Growth, Feminization, and Salary Discrimination." *Teachers College Record*, Vol. 96, No. 3 (Spring 1995), 544–568.

Fultz, Michael. "Black Public Libraries in the South in the Era of De Jure Segregation." *Libraries and the Cultural Record*, Vol. 41, No. 3 (Summer 2006), 338–359.

Fultz, Michael. "Teacher Training and African American Education in the South, 1900–1940." *The Journal of Negro Education*, Vol. 64, No. 2 (Spring 1995), 196–210.

Furstenberg, Frank, Jr. "The Making of the Black Family: Race and Class in Qualitative Studies in the Twentieth Century." *Annual Review of Sociology*, Vol. 33 (2007), 432.

Furstenberg, Frank Jr. "How Families Manage Risk and Opportunity in Dangerous Neighborhoods." In William Julius Wilson, ed., *Sociology and the Public Agenda*. London: Sage Publications, 1993.

Futrell, Mary Hatwood. "Mama and Miss Jordan." *Reader's Digest* 135 (July 1989), 75–76.

Futrell, Mary Hatwood. "Missing, Presumed Lost: The Exodus of Black Teachers." *The Black Collegian*, Vol. 19, No. 4 (March–April 1989), 77.

Futrell, Mary Hatwood. "Remembering that Very Special Schoolteacher." *Christian Science Monitor*, April 3, 1984, 24–25.

Futrell, Mary Hatwood and Walter A. Brown. "The School Reform Movement and the Education of African American Youth: A Retrospective Update." *The Journal of Negro Education*, Vol. 69, No. 4 (Autumn 2000), 288–304.

Gaines, Kevin. *Uplifting the Race: Black Leadership, Politics, and Culture in the Twentieth Century.* Chapel Hill, NC: The University of North Carolina Press, 1996.

Gaines, Kevin. "Whose Integration Was It? An Introduction," Round Table: *Brown v. Board* of Education, Fifty Years After." *The Journal of American History,* Vol. 91, No. 1 (June 2004), 19–25.

Gardner, Howard. *Leading Minds: An Anatomy of Leadership.* New York: Basic Books, 1995.

Garrow, David J. *Bearing the Cross: Martin Luther King, Jr., and the Southern Christian Leadership Conference.* Norwalk, CT: The Easton Press, 1986.

Gates, Bill. "Smarter School Reform: How to Spend Less and Boost Student Achievement." *The Washington Post*, February 28, 2011, A15.

Gates, Henry Louis Jr. and Cornel West. *The African-American Century: How Blacks Have Shaped Our Country.* New York: The Free Press, 2000.

Gates, Henry Louis Jr., ed. *Bearing Witness: Selections from African-American Autobiography in the Twentieth Century.* New York: Pantheon Books, 1991.

Gates, Henry Louis Jr. and Cornel West. *The Future of the Race.* New York: Alfred A. Knopf, 1996.

Gasman, Marybeth. "Giving and Getting: Philanthropic Activity among Black Greek-Letter Organizations." In Gregory Parks, ed., *Black Greek-Letter Organizations in the Twenty-First Century.* Lexington, KY: The University Press of Kentucky, 2008.

Gehrman, Elizabeth. "Baby College and Beyond: Canada Talks about How to Address the Problems in Public Education Today." *Harvard Undergraduate Gazette*, March 20, 2008.

Giddings, Paula. *When and Where I Enter: the Impact of Black Women On Race and Sex In America.* New York: W. Morrow, 1984.

Gilmore, Glenda. *Defying Dixie: The Radical Roots of Civil Rights, 1919–1950*. New York: W.W.Norton, 2008.

Goldscheider, Frances and Linda Waite. *New Families, No Families? The Transformation of the American Home*. Berkeley, CA: University of California Press, 1991.

Goluboff, Risa. *The Lost Promise of Civil Rights*. Cambridge, MA: Harvard University Press, 2007.

Gordon, Jacob U. *Black Leadership for Social Change*. Westport, CT: Greenwood Press, 2000.

Graham, Sandra. "Motivation in African Americans." *Review of Educational Research*, Vol. 64, No. 1 (Spring 1994), 55–117.

Granberry, Dorothy. "Origins of an African American School in Haywood County." In Carol Van West, ed., *Trial and Triumph: Essays in Tennessee's African American History*. Knoxville, TN: University of Tennessee Press, 2002.

Grann, David. "Saint Lewis." *The New Republic*, Vol. 219, No. 14 (October 5, 1998), 12 ff.

Grant, Joanne. *Ella Baker: Freedom Bound*. New York: John Wiley & Sons, 1998.

Grossman, Jean and Jean Rhodes. "The Test of Time: Predictors and Effects of Duration in Youth Mentoring Relationships." *Journal of Community Psychology*, Vol. 39, No. 2 (April 2002), 199–219.

Guinier, Lani. "From Racial Liberalism to Racial Literacy." *Journal of American History*. Vol. 91, No. 1 (June 2004), 92–118.

Gutman, Herbert. *The Black Family in Slavery and Freedom: 1750–1925*. New York: Random House, 1976.

Hacker, Andrew. *Two Nations: Black and White, Separate, Hostile, Unequal*. New York: Charles Scribner's Sons, 1992.

Hansen, Karen. *Not-so-Nuclear Families: Class, Gender and Networks of Care*. New Brunswick, NJ: Rutgers University Press, 2005.

Hall, Jacquelyn Dowd. "The Long Civil Rights Movement and the Political Uses of the Past." *The Journal of American History*, Vol. 91, No. 4 (March 2005), 1233–1264.

Hall, Jacquelyn Dowd. "'You Must Remember This': Autobiography as Social Critique." *The Journal of American History*, Vol. 85, No. 2 (September 1998), 439–465.

Hardy, Gayle, J. *American Women Civil Rights Activists: Bibliographies of 68 Leaders, 1825–1992*. London: McFarland & Company, Inc., 1993.

Harris, Fredrick C. "Religious Resources in an Oppositional Civic Culture." In Jane Mansbridge and Aldon Morris, eds., *Oppositional Consciousness: the Subjective Roots of Social Protest*. Chicago, IL: University of Chicago Press, 2001.

Harris, Jessica and Vernon C. Mitchell Jr. "A Narrative Critique of Black Greek-Letter Organizations and Social Action." In Gregory Parks, ed., *Black Greek Letter Organizations in the 21st Century*. Lexington, KY: The University Press of Kentucky, 2008.

Harris-Lacewell, Melissa. *Barbershops, Bibles, and BET: Everyday Talk and Black Political Thought*. Princeton, NJ: Princeton University Press, 2004.

"Hatwood Wins top HR award." *VEA News*, April 1976.

Hawlbachs, Maurice. *On Collective Memory*. Ed. and trans. Lewis A. Coser. Chicago, IL: University of Chicago Press, 1992.

Hays, Sharon. *Flat Broke with Children: Women In the Age of Welfare Reform*. New York: Oxford University Press, 2003.

Heifetz, Ronald A. *Leadership Without Easy Answers*. Cambridge, MA: Belknap Press, 1994.

Height, Dorothy. *Open Wide the Freedom Gates: A Memoir.* New York: Perseus Books, 2003.

Height, Dorothy. "'We Wanted the Voice of a Woman to the Heard'—Black Women and the 1963 March on Washington." In Bettye Collier-Thomas and V.P. Franklin, eds., *Sisters in the Struggle: African American Women in the Civil Rights–Black Power Movement.* New York: New York University Press, 2001.

Herndon, Michael and Joan Hirt. "Black Students and Their Families: What Leads to Success in College." *Journal of Black Studies,* Vol. 34, No. 4 (March 2004), 489–513.

Herskovits, Melville. *The American Negro: A Study in Racial Crossing.* Westport, CT: Greenwood Press, 1985.

Herskovits, Melville. *The Myth of the Negro Past.* Boston, MA: Beacon Press, 1941.

Hevesi, Dennis. "William Raspberry, Prizewinning Columnist, Dies at 76." *The New York Times,* July 18, 2012, A20.

Hill, Robert Bernard. *The Strengths of African American Families: Twenty-five Years Later.* Lanham, MD: University Press of America, 1999.

Hill, Shirley A. and Joey Sprague. "Parenting in Black and White Families: The Interaction of Gender with Race and Class." *Gender and Society,* Vol. 13, No. 4 (Aug. 1999), 480–502.

Hill, Oliver W., Sr. *The Big Bang: Brown v Board of Education, and Beyond; The Autobiography of Oliver W. Hill, Sr.* Winter Park, FL: FOUR-G Publishers, 2000.

Hine, Darlene Clark, Wilma King, and Linda Reed. '*We Specialize in the Wholly Impossible': A Reader in Black Women's History.* New York: Carlson Publishing, Inc., 1995.

Holmes, Steven A. "NAACP Post gives Julian Bond New Start." *The New York Times,* February 28, 1998, 6.

hooks, bell. "Revolutionary Parenting." In Karen Hansen and Anita Garey, eds. *Families in the US: Kinship and Domestic Policies.* Philadelphia, PA: Temple University Press, 1998.

hooks, bell. *Teaching to Transgress: Education as the Practice of Freedom.* New York: Routledge, 1994.

Hrabowski, Freeman A. III, Diane M. Lee, and John S. Martello. "Educating Teachers for the 21st Century: Lessons Learned." *The Journal of Negro Education,* Vol. 68, No. 3 (July. 1999), 293–305

Hrabowski, Freeman A. III. Interview with Kids of America, St. Veronica's Academy, March 31, 2005. [http://my.schooljournalism.org/?p=48328]

Hrabowski, Freeman A. III. "Reflections on America's Academic Achievement Gap: A 50-Year Perspective," W. Augustus Low Lecture, University of Maryland Baltimore County, May 5, 2004.

Hrabowski, Freeman A. III. "The Access Imperative," The Robert H. Atwell Lecture, 89th Annual Meeting of the American Council on Education, Washington, D.C., February 11, 2007.

Huggins, Nathan Irvin. "Afro-Americans." In John Higham, ed., *Ethnic Leadership in America.* Baltimore, MD: Johns Hopkins University Press, 1978.

Hunter, Jean. "For the VEA President, Opportunity comes wearing overalls." *Virginia Journal of Education,* Vol. 70, No. 1 (September 1976), 14–17.

Huntley, Horace and John W. McKerley. *Foot Soldiers for Democracy: The Men, Women, and Children of the Birmingham Civil Rights Movement.* Chicago, IL: University of Illinois Press, 2009.

Hymowitz, Kay S. "The Black Family: 40 Years of Lies." *City Journal* (Summer, 2005). [http://www.city-journal.org/html/15_3_black_family.html]

Ifill, Gwen. *The Breakthrough: Politics and Race in the Age of Obama*. New York: Doubleday, 2009.

Innerst, Carol. "Multiculturalism Boosters Discuss Making It Palatable." *The Washington Times*, March 11, 1992, Nation A4.

Jealous, Benjamin. "Commentary: NAACP Agenda Still 'Radical' after 100 Years" (June 25, 2009) [http://www.cnn.com/2009/LIVING/06/22/jealous.naacp/]

"Jealous, Benjamin." In *Contemporary Black Biography*, Vol. 70, Farmington Hill, MI: Gale, 2009. [http://galenet.galegroup.com/servlet/BioRC]

Johnson, Alan. "Self-emancipation and Leadership: The Case of Martin Luther King." In Colin Barker, Alan Johnson, and Michael Lavalette, eds., *Leadership and Social Movements*. Manchester, England: Manchester University Press, 2001.

Johnson, Byron, Sung Joon Jang, Spencer De Li, and David Larson. "The 'Invisible Institution' and Black Youth Crime: The Church as an Agency of Local Social Control." *Journal of Youth and Adolescence*, Vol. 29, No. 4 (Aug. 2000), 479–498.

Johnson, Cedric. *Revolutionaries to Race Leaders: Black Power and the Making of African American Politics*. Minneapolis, MN: University of Minnesota Press, 2007.

Johnson, Karen A. *Uplifting the Women and the Race: The Educational Philosophies and Social Activism of Anna Julia Cooper and Nannie Helen Burroughs*. London: Garland Publishing, Inc., 2000.

Johnson, Lauri. "A Generation of Women Activists: African American Female Educators in Harlem, 1930–1950." *The Journal of African American History*, Vol. 89, No. 3 (Summer 2004), 223–240.

Johnson, Leanor Boulin and Robert Staples. *Black Families at the Crossroads: Challenges and Prospects*. San Francisco, CA: Jossey-Bass,, 2005.

Jones, Beverly Washington. *Quest for Equality: the Life and Writings of Mary Eliza Church Terrell, 1863–1954*. New York: Carlson Publishing, Inc., 1990.

Jordan, Kathy Ann. "Discourses of Difference and the Overrepresentation of Black Students in Special Education." *The Journal of African American History*, Vol. 90, No. 1/2 (Winter/Spring 2005), 128–149.

"Jordan, Vernon E., Jr." In *Biography Resource Center*, The Gale Group, 2000.

Jordan, Vernon E. and Annette Gordon Reed. *Vernon Can Read*. New York: Perseus Books, 2001.

Jordan, Vernon E., Jr. with Lee A. Daniels. *Make It Plain: Standing Up and Speaking Out*. New York: Public Affairs, 2008.

Joseph, Peniel E. *Dark Days, Bright Nights*. New York: Basic Civitas Books, 2010.

Kantor, Harvey and Barbara Brenzel. "Urban Education and the 'Truly Disadvantaged': The Historical Roots of the Contemporary Crisis, 1945–1990." *Teachers College Record*. Vol. 94, No. 2 (Winter 1992), 278–314.

Kelley, Christie. "Titusville Native Hrabowski Honored for Education Work." *Birmingham News*, February 6, 2002.

King, Sabrina Hope. "The Limited Presence of African-American Teachers." *Review of Educational Research*, Vol. 63, No. 2 (Summer 1993), 115–149.

Kinzie, Susan. "A Magnetic Force: Dynamic Chief Has Driven Boom at UMBC." *Washington Post*, May 30, 2007, B01.

Klarman, Michael. *From Jim Crow to Civil Rights: The Supreme Court and the Struggle for Racial Equality*. New York: Oxford University Press, 2004.

Kluger, Richard. *Simple Justice: The History of Brown v. Board of Education and Black America's Struggle for Equality*. New York: Alfred A. Knopf, 1976.

Kouzes, James and Barry Posner. *The Leadership Challenge: How to Get Extraordinary Things Done in Organizations.* San Francisco, CA: Jossey-Bass, 1987.

Lacy, Karyn. *Blue-Chip Black: Race, Class, and Status in the New Black Middle Class.* Berkeley, CA: University of California Press, 2007.

Ladd, Everett C., Jr. *Negro Poltiical Leadership in the South.* New York: Atheneum, 1966.

Ladson-Billings, Gloria. *Beyond the Big House: African American Educators on Teacher Education.* New York: Teachers College Press, 2005.

Ladson-Billings, Gloria. *The Dreamkeepers: Successful Teachers of African American Children.* San Francisco, CA: Jossey-Bass, 1994.

Lareau, Annette. *Unequal Childhoods: Class, Race and Family Life.* Berkeley, CA: University of California Press, 2003.

Laurant, Darrell. *A City Unto Itself: Lynchburg, Virginia in the 20th Century.* Lynchburg, VA: Laurant and the News and Advance, 1977.

Lawrence-Lightfoot, Sara. *I've Known Rivers: Lives of Loss and Liberation.* Reading, MA: Addison-Wesley Publishing Company, 1994.

Lawson, Steven F. and Charles Payne. *Debating the Civil Rights Movement, 1945–1968.* New York: Rowman and Littlefield, 2006.

Lawson, Steven F. "Freedom Then, Freedom Now: The Historiography of the Civil Rights Movement." *The American Historical Review,* Vol. 96, No. 2 (Apr., 1991), 456–471.

Lawson, Steven F. *Running for Freedom: Civil Rights and Black Politics in America since 1941.* Philadelphia, PA: Temple University Press, 1991.

Lawton, Kim with Bob Abernathy. Report on Congressman John Lewis and his role in civil rights movement. WNET-TV, *Religion and Ethics Newsweekly,* January 14, 2005.

Lee, Felicia. "Coping: For Harlem's Children, a Catcher in the Rye." *The New York Times,* January 9, 2000.

Lee, Wynetta Y. "Striving Toward Effective Retention: The Effect of Race on Mentoring African American Students." *Peabody Journal of Education,* Vol. 74, No. 2 (Jan.1999), 27–44.

Lewis, Andrew B. *The Shadows of Youth: The Remarkable Journey of the Civil Rights Generation.* New York: Hill and Wang, 2009.

Lewis, Jesse L. and John Hayman. *Empowerment of a Race: The Revitalization of Black Institutions.* Montgomery, AL: Black Belt Press, 1999.

Lewis, John. "At a Crossroads on Gay Unions." *The Boston Globe,* October 25, 2003.

Lewis, John. "'Equal Justice' Only an Illusion." *The Atlanta Journal-Constitution,* January 26, 2004.

Lewis, John. Testimony before U.S. Senate Judiciary Committee Hearing, From Selma to Shelby County: Working Together to Restore the Protections of the Voting Rights Act, July 17, 2013. [http://www.judiciary.senate.gov/pdf/7-17-13LewisTestimony.pdf]

Lewis, John with Michael D'Orso. *Walking with the Wind: A Memoir of the Movement.* New York: Simon & Schuster, 1998.

Leeman, Richard W. *African-America Orators: A Bio-Critical Sourcebook.* Westport, CT: Greenwood Publishing Group, Inc., 1996.

Lincoln, E. Eric and Lawrence H. Mamiya. *The Black Church in the African American Experience.* Durham, NC:, Duke University Press, 1990.

Ling, Peter T. "A Question of Leadership"—Review of Belinda Robnett, *How Long? How Long? African-American Women in the Struggle for Civil Rights." Reviews in American History,* Vol. 27, No. 2 (June 1999), 289–297.

Litwack, Leon F. "'Fight the Power!' The Legacy of the Civil Rights Movement." *Journal of Southern History*, Vol. 75, No. 1 (February 2009), 3–28.

Lockhart, William. "Building Bridges and Bonds: Generating Social Capital in Secular and Faith-Based Poverty-to-Work Programs." *Sociology of Religion*, Vol. 66, No. 1 (Spring 2005), 45–60.

Lyon, Danny. "The Nashville Sir-Ins; Nonviolence Emerges, *Southern Exposure 9* (Spring 1981), 30–32.

MacLeod, Jay. *Ain't No Makin' It*. Boulder, CO: Westview Press, 2004.

Madsen, Amy Perkel. "Benjamin Jealous '94: A Force for Change." *Columbia College Today Magazine* (March/April 2009).

Mansbridge, Jane. "Complicating Oppositional Consciousness." In Jane Mansbridge and Aldon Morris, eds., *Oppositional Consciousness: The Subjective Roots of Social Protest*. Chicago, IL: University of Chicago Press, 2001.

Mansbridge, Jane. "The Making of Oppositional Consciousness." In Jane Mansbridge and Aldon Morris, eds., *Oppositional Consciousness: The Subjective Roots of Social Protest*. Chicago, IL: The University of Chicago Press, 2001.

Mansbridge and Aldon Morris, eds. *Oppositional Consciousness: The Subjective Roots of Social Protest*. Chicago, IL: University of Chicago Press, 2001.

Marable, Manning. *Black Leadership*. New York: Columbia University Press, 1998.

Marnell, James. "Newsmakers: Ex-Education Chief Needed a Lesson in Cooperation." *The Times Mirror Company* (June 25, 1989), Part 1, p. 2.

Martin, Elmer P. and Joanne Mitchell Martin. *The Black Extended Family*. Chicago, IL: The University of Chicago Press, 1978.

Martin, Michel. "What Would Martin Do? South Carolina Community Leaders Debate Civil Rights." *Tell Me More (NPR)*, January 21, 2008 [http://web.ebscohost.com]

Martin, Pamela P. and Harriette Pipes McAdoo. "Sources of Racial Socialization: Theological Orientation of African American Churches and Parents." In *Black Families*, 4th edition. Thousand Oaks, CA: Sage Publications, 2007.

Massey, Douglas S. and Nancy A. Denton. *American Apartheid: Segregation and the Making of the Underclass*. Cambridge, MA: Harvard University Press, 1993.

Mather, Mark. "U.S. Children in Single-Mother Families," Population Reference Bureau Data Brief, May 2010. [http://www.prb.org/pdf10/single-motherfamilies.pdf]

McDuffie, Erik S. *Sojourning for Freedom: Black Women, American Communism, and the Making of Black Left Feminism*. Durham, NC: Duke University Press, 2011.

McNeil, Genna Rae. *Groundwork: Charles Hamilton Houston and the Struggle for Civil Rights*. Philadelphia, PA: University of Pennsylvania Press, 1983.

Meehan, Thomas. "Moynihan of the Moynihan Report." *The New York Times Magazine*, July 31, 1966.

Mensah, Akida T. Interview with Henry L. Marsh III, Church Hill Oral History Project, October 1, 1982. [www.library.vcu.edu/jbc/speccoll/vbha/church/marsh.html]

Michell, Edward and Atu Koffie-Lart. "21 Year-Old Morehouse Grad Runs for Congress, *The Maroon Tiger*, October 29, 2006.

Moore, Solomon. "Study Shows High Cost of Criminal Corrections." *The New York Times Magazine*, March 2, 2009.

Morris, Aldon. *The Origins of the Civil Rights Movement: Black Communities Organizing for Change*. New York: The Free Press, 1984.

Morris, Aldon and Naomi Braine. "Social Movements and Oppositional Consciousness." In Jane Mansbridge and Aldon Morris, eds., *Oppositional Consciousness: The Subjective Roots of Social Protest.* Chicago, IL: The University of Chicago, Press, 2001.

Morris, Vivian Gunn and Curtis L. Morris. *Creating Caring and Nurturing Educational Environments for African American Children.* Westport, CT: Bergin and Garvey, 2000.

Morris, Vivian Gunn and Curtis L. Morris. *The Price They Paid: Desegregation in an African American Community.* New York: Teachers College Press, 2002.

Moynihan, Daniel P. *The Negro Family: the Case for National Action.* Washington, D.C., U.S. Government Printing Office, 1965.

Murphree, Vanessa. *The Selling of Civil Rights: The Student Nonviolent Coordinating Committee and the Use of Public Relations.* London: Routledge, 2006.

Myrdal, Gunnar. *An American Dilemma: The Negro Problem and Modern Democracy.* 2 vols. New York: Harper & Brothers, 1944.

Nasstrom, Kathryn N. "Between Memory and History: Autobiographies of the Civil Rights Movement and the Writing of Civil Rights History." *The Journal of Southern History,* Vol. LXXIV, No. 2 (May 2008), 325–364.

Nasstrom, Kathryn D. "Down to Now: Memory, Narrative, and Women's Leadership in the Civil Rights Movement in Atlanta, Georgia." In Renee C. Romano and Leigh Raiford, eds., *The Civil Rights Movement in American Memory.* Athens, GA: The University of Georgia Press, 2006.

National Center for Education Statistics, U.S. Department of Education. Institute of Education Sciences: Fast Facts. [http://nces.ed.gov/fastfacts/display.asp?id=16]

"National Rise Reported in Teacher Pay." *The New York Times,* February 26, 1988, D19. http:///www.childrensdatabank.org/pdf/1_PDF.pd

Nelson, Katherine. "Self and Social Functions: Individual Autobiographical Memory and Collective Narrative." *Memory,* Vo. 11, No. 2 (March 2003), 125–136.

Newman, M. W. "The War Is Over in Richmond: Peace Pact Brings Business Surge." *Chicago Sun Times,* December 5, 1985.

Nicotera, Anne Maydan and Marcia J. Clinkscales with Felicia Walker. *Understanding Organizations through Culture and Structure: Relational and Other Lessons From the African-American Organization.* Mahwah, NJ: Lawrence Erlbaum Associates Publishers, 2003.

Nobles, Wade. "African American Family Life: An Instrument of Culture." In Harriette Pipes McAdoo, ed., *Black Families.* Thousand Oaks, CA: Sage Publications, 2007.

Nobles, Wade W. "African Philosophy: Foundations of Black Psychology." In Reginald L. Jones, ed., *Black Psychology,* 3rd ed. Berkeley, CA: Cobb & Henry Publishers, 1991.

Noblit, George W. and Van O. Dempsey. *The Social Construction of virtue: The Moral Life of Schools.* Albany, NY: State University of New York Press, 1996.

Ogbu, John U. "From Cultural Differences to Differences in Cultural Frame of Reference." In Patricia M. Greenfield and Rodney R. Cocking, eds., *Cross-Cultural Roots of Minority Child Development.* New Jersey: Lawrence Erlbaum Associates, 1994.

Ogletree, Charles J., Jr. *All Deliberate Speed: Reflections on the First Half Century of Brown v. Board of Education.* New York: W. W Norton & Company, 2004.

Oliver, Melvin L. and Thomas M Shapiro. *Black Wealth/White Wealth: a New Perspective On Racial Inequality.* New York: Routledge, 1995.

Olson, Lynn. "Losing 'The Most Effective Spokesman Ever." *Education Week,* June 14, 1989, 1, 24 ff.

Pattillo-McCoy, Mary. *Black Picket Fences*. Chicago, IL: University of Chicago Press, 1999.

Payne, Charles. "Ella Baker and Models of Social Change." *Signs*, Vol. 13, No. 4 (Summer 1989), 885–899.

Payne, Charles. "'The Whole United States is Southern!' *Brown v. Board* and the Mystification of Race." *Journal of American History*, Vol. 91, No. 1 (June 2004), 83–91.

Phillips, Donald T. *Martin Luther King, Jr., On Leadership*. New York: Warner Books, 1999.

Phillips, Paul David. "Education of Blacks in Tennessee during Reconstruction, 1865–1870." In Carol Van West, ed., *Trial and Triumph: Essays in Tennessee's African American History*. Knoxville, TN: University of Tennessee Press, 2002.

Popenoe, David. "American Family Decline, 1960–1990: A Review and Appraisal." *Journal of Marriage and the Family*, Vol. 55, No. 3 (August 1993), 527–542.

Poussaint, Renee. "Mary Hatwood Futrell—Women of the Year." *Ms. Magazine*, January 1985.

"Poverty in the United States: Frequently Asked Questions," National Poverty Center, Gerald R. Ford School of Public Policy, University of Michigan. [http://npc.umich.edu/poverty/#4]

Rich, Dorothy. "Building the Bridge to Reach Minority Parents: Education Infrastructure Supporting Success for All Children." In Nancy Feyl Chavkin, ed., *Families and Schools in a Pluralistic Society*. Albany, NY: State University of New York Press, 1993.

Platt, Anthony M. "Introduction." In E. Franklin Frazier, *The Negro Family in the United States*. Notre Dame, IN: University of Notre Dame Press, 2001.

Pomerantz, Gary. "Jordan 'shaped by Atlanta' Transition Chief Credits Family, Black Community for Inspiring His Success." *The Atlanta Constitution and Journal*, November 29, 1992.

Pradervand, Pierre. *The Gentle Art of Blessing*. New York: Atria Paperback, 1999.

Pratt, Robert. *The Color of Their Skin: Education and Race in Richmond, Virginia, 1954–1989*. Charlottesville, VA: University Press of Virginia, 1992.

Raiford, Leigh and Renee C. Romano. "Introduction: The Struggle Over Memory." In Renne C. Romano, ed., *The Civil Rights Movement in American Memory*. Athens, GA: The University of Georgia Press, 2006.

Ransby, Barbara. "Behind-the-Scenes View of a Behind-the-Scenes Organizer: The Roots of Ella Baker's Political Passions." In Betty Collier-Thomas, ed., *Sisters in the Struggle: African American Women in the Civil Rights- Black Power Movement*. New York: New York University Press, 2001.

"Raspberry Gets Company, at Last," *Washingtonian*, December 1993.

Reid-Merritt, Patricia. *Sister Power: How Phenomenal Black Women Are Rising to the Top*. New York: John Wiley & Sons, 1996.

Remnick, David. *The Bridge: The Life and Rise of Barack Obama*. New York: Alfred A. Knopf, 2010.

Reynolds, Barbara. *And Still We Rise: Interviews with 50 Black Role Models*. Washington, D.C.: USA Today Books, 1988.

Rhodes, Jean, Jean Grossman, and Nancy Resch. "Agents of Change: Pathways through Which Mentoring Relationships Influence Adolescents' Academic Adjustment." *Child Development*, Vol. 71, No. 6 (Nov.–Dec. 2000), 1663.

Rhodes, Jean, G. Anne Bogat, Jennifer Roffman, Peter Edelman, and Lisa Galasso. "Youth Mentoring in Perspective: Introduction to the Special Issue." *American Journal of Community Psychology,* Vol. 30, No. 2 (April 2002), 149–155.

Rich, Dorothy. "Building the Bridge to Reach Minority Parents: Education Infrastructure Supporting Success for All Children." In Nancy Feyl Chavkin, ed., *Families and Schools in a Pluralistic Society.* Albany, NY: State University of New York Press, 1993.

Robnett, Belinda. *How Long? How Long? African-American Women in the Struggle for Civil Rights.* New York: Oxford University Press, 1997.

Rodriguez, Zina. "Legends: NAACP Women Who Have Made a Difference." *The New Crisis* (March/April 2000), 23–24.

Rogers, Elice E. "Afritics from Margin to Center: Theorizing the Politics of African American Women as Political Leaders." *Journal of Black Studies,* Vol. 35, No. 6 (July 2005), 701–714.

Rose, Charlie. Interview with Geoffrey Canada. *PBS: The Charlie Rose Show,* June 22, 2004.

Rose, Thomas and John Greenya. *Black Leaders: Then and Now.* Garrett Park, MD: Garrett Park Press, 1984.

Rosenberg, Tina. "The Power of Talking to Your Baby." *The New York Times,* April 10, 2013.

Rothstein, Meryl. "Ogletree: 50 Years after Brown, Segregation Persists." *The Brown Daily Herald,* Vol. CXXXIX, No. 124, December 4, 2003.

Rush, Bobby Lee. Interviews with Tavis Smiley. "Voting Rights Act" (April 18, 2005) and "Death Penalty" (February 4, 2003). National Public Radio Interviews.

Sargent, Frederic O. *The Civil Rights Revolution: Events and Leaders, 1955–1968.* Jefferson, NC: McFarland & Company, 2004.

Sambol-Tosco, Kimberly. "Education, Arts & Culture." *Slavery and the Making of America.* [http://www.pbs.org/wnet/slavery/experience/education/history.html]

Sauder, Rick. "Key Player in City Politics Soon to Act in State Arena." *The Richmond News Leader,* January 4, 1992, 1.

Saul, Keisha. "Black History Month Profile: Poet Amiri Baraka." *The African,* June 1, 2013. [http://www.africanmag.com/ARTICLE-626-design001]

Savage, Carter. "'Because We Did More with Less': The Agency of African American Teachers in Franklin, Tennessee: 1890–1967." *Peabody Journal of Education,* Vol. 76, No. 2 (Jan. 2001), 170–203.

Savage, Carter Julian. "Cultural Capital and African American Agency: The Economic Struggle for Effective Education for African Americans in Franklin, Tennessee, 1890–1967." *The Journal of African American History,* Vol. 87 (Spring 2002), 206–235.

Scott, Lionel D., Jr. "The Relation of Racial Identity and Racial Socialization to Coping with Discrimination among African American Adolescents." *Journal of Black Studies,* Vol. 33, No. 4 (March 2003), 520–538.

Serwer, Adam. "The Other Black President: The NAACP Confronts a New Political—and Racial—Era," February 23, 2009. [www.prospect.org]

Shujaa, Mwalimu, ed. *Beyond Desegregation: The Politics of Quality in African American Schooling.* Thousand Oaks, CA: Corwin Press, Inc., 1996.

Siddle Walker, Vanessa. "African American Teaching in the South: 1940–1960." *American Educational Research Journal,* Vol. 38, No. 4 (Winter, 2001), 751–779.

Siddle Walker, Emilie V. "Can Institutions Care? Segregated Schooling of African American Children as a Context for Reform." In Mwalimu J. Shujaa, ed., *Beyond*

Desegregation: The Politics of Quality in African American Schooling. Thousand Oaks, CA: Corwin Press, 1996.

Siddle Walker, Vanessa. "Organized Resistance and Black Educators' Quest for School Equality, 1878–1938." *Teachers College Record,* Vol. 107, No. 3 (March 2005), 355–388.

Siddle Walker, Vanessa. "Valued Segregated Schools for African American Children in the South, 1935–1969: A Review of Common Themes and Characteristics." *Review of Educational Research,* Vol. 70, No. 3 (Autumn 2000), 253–285.

Singh, Nikhil. *Black Is a Country: Race and the Unfinished Struggle for Democracy.* Cambridge, MA: Harvard University Press, 2004.

Singh, Nikhil, ed. and intro. *Climbin' Jacob's Ladder: The Black Freedom Movement Writings of Jack O' Dell.* Berkeley, CA: University of California Press, 2010.

Skocpol, Theda, Ariane Liazos, and Marshall Ganz. *What a Mighty Power We Can Be: African American Fraternal Groups and the Struggle for Racial Equality.* Princeton, NJ: Princeton University Press, 2006.

Smith, Robert. "From Incorporation Toward Irrelevance: The Afro-American Freedom Struggle in the 21st Century." In John Davis, ed. *Perspectives in Black Politics and Black Leadership.* New York: University Press of America, 2007.

Smith, Robert C. "System Values and African American Leadership." In Manning Marable and Kristin Clarke, eds., *Barack Obama and African American Empowerment: The Rise of Black America's New Leadership.* New York: Palgrave Macmillan, 2009.

Smith, Robert. *We Have No Leaders: African-Americans in the Post-Civil Rights Era.* Albany, NY: State University of New York Press, 1996.

Stack, Carol. *All Our Kin.* New York: Basic Books, 1974.

Stewart, Jocelyn Y. "Charles Tisdale, 80; Used Mississippi Newspaper to Fight Bias." *Los Angeles Times,* July 14, 2007 [http://articles.latimes.com/2007/jul/14/local/me-tisdale14]

Sudarkasa, Niara. "An Exposition of the Value Premises Underlying Black Family Studies." *Journal of the National Medical Association,* Vol. 19 (1975), 235–239.

Sudarkasa, Niara. "Interpreting the African Heritage in Afro-American Family Organization." In H. P. McAdoo, ed., *Black Families.* Thousand Oaks, CA: Sage Publications, 1988.

"Survivor." *Chicago Tribune Magazine,* November 16, 2003, 14–17, 26.

Tate, William F., Gloria Ladson-Billings, and Carl A. Grant. "The *Brown* Decision Revisited: Mathematizing a Social Problem." In Mwalimu J. Shujaa, ed., *Beyond Desegregation: The Politics of Quality in African American Schooling.* Thousand Oaks, CA: Corwin Press, 1996.

Taylor, Robert Joseph, Linda M. Chatters, M. Belinda Tucker, and Edith Lewis. " Developments in Research on Black Families: A Decade Review." *Journal of Marriage and the Family,* Vol. 52, No. 4 (Nov.,1990), 993–1014.

Terrell, Mary Church. "What Role Is the Educated Negro Woman to Play in the Uplifting of Her Race?" In Beverly Washington Jones, ed., *Quest for Equality: The Life and Writings of Mary Eliza Church Terrell, 1863–1954.* New York: Carlson Publishing Inc., 1990.

Thomas, Clarence. *My Grandfather's Son: A Memoir.* New York: Harper Collins, 2007.

Thompson, Daniel C. *The Negro Leadership Class.* Engelwood Cliffs, NJ: Prentice Hall, 1963.

Thompson, Lynn A. and Lisa Kelly-Vance. "The Impact of Mentoring on Academic Achievement of At-risk Youth." *Children and Youth Services Review*, Vol. 23, No. 3 (March 2001), 227–242.

Tiloye, Jonathan. "Height Still on Top of Civil Rights." *The Times-Picayune*, June 22, 2003.

Toelken, Barre. *The Dynamics of Folklore*. New York: Houghton Mifflin Company, 1979.

Tough, Paul. "The Harlem Project." *New York Times Magazine*, June 20, 2004.

Tough, Paul. *Whatever It Takes: Geoffrey Canada's Quest to Change Harlem and America*. New York: Houghton Mifflin Company, 2008.

Traub, James. "Hopefuls; Street Toughs; Power Brokers; Networkers; Strivers; Grande Dames; Musclemen; Exiles; Reformers; Purists; Clones; Big Mouths; Outsiders; Air Kissers; Fanatics; Gossips; Nightclubbers; Floyd Flake's Middle America." *The New York Times Magazine*, October 19, 1997.

Treadwell, David. "A Paradoxical Parable; Julian Bond: High Hopes Turn Sour." *Los Angeles Times*, February 22, 1987, 1.

Treadwell, David. "Why Julian Bond's Political Star Has Fallen." *Los Angeles Times*, February 23, 1987, 2A.

Tuck, Stephen. *We Ain't What We Ought to Be: The Black Freedom Struggle from Emancipation to Obama*. Cambridge, MA: Harvard University Press, 2010.

Turque, Bill. "A New Page for a Strapped Library: Educator Helps Turn 'Hot Mess' into Oasis at D.C.'s Ballou High." *The Washington Post*, January 24, 2011, B1–B2.

Van Ausdale, Debra and Joe Feagin. *The First R: How Children Learn Race and Racism*. Lanham, MD: Rowman and Littlefield Publishers, Inc., 2001.

Van Delinder, Jean. *Struggles Before Brown: Early Civil Rights Protests and Their Significance Today*. Boulder, CO: Paradigm Publishers, 2008.

Van Knippenberg, Dean and Michael A. Hogg. *Leadership and Power: Identity Processes in Groups and Organizations*. London: Sage Publications, 2003.

Van West, Carroll. *Trial and Triumph*. Knoxville, TN: University of Tennessee Press, 2002.

Venable, Cecilia Gutierrez. "Benjamin Todd Jealous." *BlackPast.org*, [http://www.black past.org/aah/jealous-benjamin-todd-1973]

Walters, Ronald and Robert Smith. "Black Leadership: Toward a Twenty-First Century Perspective." In John Davis ed., *Perspectives in Black Politics and Black Leadership*. New York: University Press of America, 2007.

Walters, Ronald and Robert C. Smith. *African American Leadership*. Albany, NY: State University of New York Press, 1999.

Walters, Ronald and Cedric Johnson, *Bibliography of African American Leadership, an Annotated Guide*. Westport, CT: Greenwood Press, 2000.

Ward, Brian. "Forgotten Wails and Master Narratives." In Brian Ward, ed., *Media, Culture, and Memories of the Modern African American Freedom Struggle*. Gainesville, FL: University Press of Florida, 2001.

Washington, Booker T. *Up From Slavery: An Autobiography*. New York: Dodd, Mead & Company, 1965.

Washington, Wayne. "Sellers Tries to Make a Name of His Own." *The State*, June 5, 2006 [http://web.ebscohost.com]

Watkins, William H., James H. Lewis, and Victoria Chou. *Race and Education: The Roles of History and Society in Educating African American Students*. Boston, MA: Allyn and Bacon, 2001.

Watkins, William H. "Reclaiming Historical Visions of Quality Schooling: The Legacy of Early 20th-Century Black Intellectuals." In Shujaa, Mwalimu, ed., *Beyond Desegregation: The Politics of Quality in African American Schooling*. Thousand Oaks, CA: Corwin Press, Inc., 1996.

Watkins, William H. *The White Architects of Black Education*. New York: Teachers College Press of Columbia University, 2001.

Weiss, Michael J. "Who's to Blame for the Nation's Poor Schools? Teacher Union Boss Mary Futrell says Reagan's the One." *People*, July 25, 1983.

West, Cornel. *Race Matters*. Boston, MA: Beacon Press, 2001.

White, Gayle. "Theology Center's Next Leader Is Preacher, Teacher, and More; Man with a Plan: Franklin Hopes to Get Churches More Involved in Helping Neighborhoods." *The Atlanta Journal and Constitution*, October 13, 1996, 8G.

White, Joseph L. "Toward a Black Psychology." In Reginald L. Jones, ed., *Black Psychology*, 3rd edition. Berkeley, CA: Cobb and Henry Publishers, 1991.

Williams, Johnny E. "Linking Beliefs to Collective Action: Politicized Religious Beliefs and the Civil Rights Movement." *Sociological Forum*, Vol. 17, No. 2 (June 2002), 203–222.

Williams, Juan. "What Next?" *Washington Post Magazine*, June 21, 1987.

Williams, Lea Esther. *Servants of the People: the 1960s Legacy of African American Leadership*. New York: St. Martin's Press, 1996.

Williams, Marjorie. "Clinton's Mr. Inside." *Vanity Fair*, Vol. 56 (March 1993), 172–175, 207–213.

Wilson, William J. *The Declining Significance of Race*. Chicago, IL: University of Chicago Press, 1978.

Wilson, William J. *The Truly Disadvantaged*. Chicago, IL: University of Chicago Press, 1987.

Wycliff, Don. "Soul Survivor: Bobby Rush Narrowly escaped a Deadline Police Raid and Later Won a long-Shot Bid for Congress." *Chicago Tribune Magazine*, November 16, 2003, 14–17, 26.

Yetman, Norman R. "Patterns of Ethnic Integration in America." In Norman Yetman, ed., *Majority and Minority: The Dynamics of Race and Ethnicity in American Life*. Needham Heights, MA: Allyn and Bacon, 1999.

Younge, Gary. "'We Used To Think There was a Black Communiy.'" *The Guardian*, November 8, 2007, 10.

Yow, Valerie Raleigh. *Recording Oral History: A Guide for the Humanities and Social Sciences*, 2nd edition. New York: Altamira Press, 2005.

Zibart, Eve. "Educator From Alexandria Elected President of NEA." *The Washington Post*, July 3, 1983, B1.

Zinn, Howard. *SNCC: The New Abolitionists*. Boston, MA: Beacon Press, 1964.

Zinn, Maxine Baca. "Feminism and Family Studies for a New Century." *Annals of the American Academy of Political and Social Science*, Vol. 571 (Sept. 2000), 42–56.

Zweigenhaft, Richard L. and G. William Domhoff, *Blacks in the White Establishment?* New Haven, CT: Yale University Press, 1991.

Zweigenhaft, Richard L. and G. William Domhff, *Diversity in the Power Elite: How It Happened, Why It Matters*. New York: Rowman and Littlefield, 2006.

Index

NOTE: Dr. Martin Luther King Jr. is sometimes abbreviated as "MLK" in this index. Page numbers in **bold** indicate a glossary entry. Page numbers in *italics* indicate an illustration.

median income, 2, 93, 268n9
poverty rate, 2
resegregation of schools and, 90
unemployment, 90, 91
See also black middle class; poverty
Soledad Brothers, 151, 194, 195
sororities, 117, *123*, 124, **235**
Southern Christian Leadership Conference
    (SCLC), 12, 143, **257-8**
Ella Baker and, 180, 228
formation of, 180
Freeman Hrabowski and, 202
James Lawson and, 172
John Lewis and, 174
MLK and, 143, 257-8
and nonviolent protest, 143
and prophetic leadership, 143, 168
See also Abernathy, Ralph; Jackson,
    Jesse; King, Coretta Scott;
    Lafayette, Bernard; Levison,
    Stanley; Shuttlesworth,
    Fred
Southern Negro Youth Congress (SNYC),
    190, 191, **258**
Southern Poverty Law Center (SPLC),
    186, **258**
Southern Regional Council (SRC), 23,
    132, 150, **258**
Stanley, Thomas B., 147, **258**
Starr, Bill, 32, 156, 157
Steinem, Gloria, 128, **258-9**
Steptoe, E. W., 168, **259**
storytelling. *See* oral tradition
Student Nonviolent Coordinating
    Committee (SNCC), 12, 143, **259**
egalitarian/consensual structure in early
    years, 174-5, 186, 201
Ella Baker and, 143, 178, 180-1
as incubator, 201
John Lewis and, 143, 174, 175, 182, 184,
    186, 192-3, 201
Julian Bond and, 143, 177, 182-5, 186,
    201
and move toward black nationalism, 184,
    192-3, 307n118
Stokely Carmichael and, 160, 175, 184,
    192-3
and Vietnam War, 184-5
Sutton, Percy, 209, **259**

"talented tenth," 109
Tawney, Richard (R.H.), 116, **259**
Terrell, Mary Church, 74, 109, **259-60**,
    282n42
Theus, Lucius, 6, 47-8, 126
Thomas, Clarence
background, 39, 40, 43-5
and definition of black leadership, 12
and diligence, 58
and extended kin, 43-4, 53
and family, 43-5, 53, 58, 58-9
as mentor, 209
and neighbors and fictive kin, 44-5
and race pride, 59
Thoreau, Henry David, 173
Thurman, Howard, 127, **260**
Thurmond, Strom, 209, **260**, 312-13n43
Till, Emmett, murder of, 49, 53, 116,
    198-9
Tillich, Paul, 116, **260**
Tisdale, Charles, 157, **260**
tradition and change, relationship of,
    21-2, 31-5
travel, international, 126-9, 192, 217
Truth, Sojourner, 13, 73, 197, 222, **260-1**
Tubman, Harriet, 73, **261**
Tucker, Samuel W., 145, 146, *150*, **261**
Tuskegee Airmen, 126, 259, 261
Tuskegee Institute, 63, 69, 252, 255,
    261, 263
twice as good, need to be. *See* diligence

Underground Railroad, 12, **261-2**
unemployment, resegregation of schools
    and increase in, 90, 91
unions
black workers, 197, 253
teachers, 68-9, 266
United Christian Youth Movement of
    North America, 110, **262**
United Negro College Fund, 132
United Youth Committee Against
    Lynching, 110, **262**
Universal Negro Improvement Association
    (UNIA), 12, **262**
Upward Bound, 70, **262**

Vietnam War and anti-war movement,
    184-5, 186, 229

Yvonne Scruggs-Leftwich and, 207
Women's Political Council, 12, **265**
Woodson, Carter G., 13, 74, **265–6**
work ethic (diligence), 58–62, 77,
82–3, 84
See also collective responsibility
World Congress of Organizations of the
Teaching Profession (WCOTP),
69, **266**

World War II, and alienation of returning
veterans, 198
Wright, Richard, 153, **266**

YMCA/YWCA, 52–3, 115, 128
Young, Whitney Jr., 13, 129, **266**
Youth Negroes' Cooperative League, 181

Zellner, Bob, 164, **266**

CPSIA information can be obtained
at www.ICGtesting.com
Printed in the USA
LVOW04s2033020316

477498LV00012B/152/P

APR - - 2016